Mike Meyers' Certification
Passport ✷

CompTIA

A+®

Certification
Third Edition

Mike Meyers
Scott Jernigan

Mc
Graw
Hill

New York • Chicago • San Francisco
Lisbon • London • Madrid • Mexico City
Milan • New Delhi • San Juan
Seoul • Singapore • Sydney • Toronto

The *McGraw·Hill* Companies

Cataloging-in-Publication Data is on file with the Library of Congress

McGraw-Hill books are available at special quantity discounts to use as premiums and sales promotions, or for use in corporate training programs. For more information, please write to the Director of Special Sales, Professional Publishing, McGraw-Hill, Two Penn Plaza, New York, NY 10121-2298. Or contact your local bookstore.

Mike Meyers' CompTIA A+® Certification Passport, Third Edition

Copyright © 2007 by The McGraw-Hill Companies. All rights reserved. Printed in the United States of America. Except as permitted under the Copyright Act of 1976, no part of this publication may be reproduced or distributed in any form or by any means, or stored in a database or retrieval system, without the prior written permission of publisher, with the exception that the program listings may be entered, stored, and executed in a computer system, but they may not be reproduced for publication.

234567890 FGR FGR 0198

ISBN-13: Book P/N 978-0-07-226309-1 and CD P/N 978-0-07-226310-7
of set 978-0-07-226308-4

ISBN-10: Book P/N 0-07-226309-1 and CD P/N 0-07-226310-5
of set 0-07-226308-3

Sponsoring Editor Timothy Green	**Proofreader** Paul Tyler
Project Editor Jody McKenzie	**Indexer** Jack Lewis
Acquisitions Coordinator Jennifer Housh	**Production Supervisor** Jim Kussow
Technical Editors Dan LaChance Daniel Richardson	**Composition** Lucie Ericksen
	Illustration Lyssa Wald
Copy Editor Lisa Theobald	**Art Director, Cover** Jeff Weeks

Information has been obtained by McGraw-Hill from sources believed to be reliable. However, because of the possibility of human or mechanical error by our sources, McGraw-Hill, or others, McGraw-Hill does not guarantee the accuracy, adequacy, or completeness of any information and is not responsible for any errors or omissions or the results obtained from the use of such information.

Dedication

We dedicate this book to our students, past, present, and future. Thanks for making this job so fun!

Acknowledgments

As with every book, a lot of work from a lot of people went into making this happen.

Tim Green provided great support as our managing editor. Thanks for the encouragement and kindness when we ran well past our deadline.

Jody McKenzie was simply wonderful as our project editor, keeping us on track and focused. It was fun to work with you again!

Our acquisitions coordinator, Jenni Housh, did a marvelous job acquiring and coordinating, as she's wont to do.

Michael Smyer provided excellent photographs and line drawings for the book, bringing the quality up dramatically from previous editions. Plus he kept us on our toes with tech talk and challenges.

Cindy Clayton came in at the eleventh hour to add finishing touches on several chapters. Thanks for the edits, Cindy!

Lisa Theobald did amazing work as our copy editor, turning awkward phrases into eloquent prose. Excellent to work with you again, Lisa.

Our technical editors, Dan LaChance and Daniel Richardson, caught a few technical slips (and a couple of doozies!) and helped make this book a lot better than it would have been without them. Thanks!

Finally, thanks to proofreader Paul Tyler for catching some amazingly funny typos and some technical glitches that we all missed the first time through. Great work!

Contents

8 Hard Drives 159

11 Printers .. 263

13 Networks: Wired Networking . 329

Check-In

May I See Your Passport?

What do you mean you don't have a passport? Why, it's sitting right in your hands, even as you read! This book is your passport to a very special place. You're about to begin a journey, my friend, a journey toward that magical place called *certification*! You don't need a ticket, you don't need a suitcase—just snuggle up and read this passport, because it's all you need to get there. Are you ready? Let's go!

Your Travel Agent: Mike Meyers

Hello! I'm Mike Meyers, president of Total Seminars and author of a number of popular certification books. On any given day, you'll find me replacing a hard drive, setting up a Web site, or writing code. I love every aspect of this book you hold in your hands. It's part of a powerful book series called the Mike Meyers' Certification Passports. Every book in this series combines easy readability with a condensed format—in other words, it's the kind of book I always wanted when I went for my certifications. Putting a huge amount of information in an accessible format is an enormous challenge, but I think we have achieved our goal and I am confident you'll agree.

I designed this series to do one thing and only one thing—to get you the information you need to achieve your certification. You won't find any fluff in here. Scott and I packed every page with nothing but the real nitty gritty of the CompTIA A+ certification exams. Every page has 100 percent pure concentrate of certification knowledge! But we didn't forget to make the book readable, so I hope you enjoy the casual, friendly style.

My personal e-mail address is mikem@totalsem.com; Scott's e-mail is scottj@totalsem.com. Please feel free to contact either of us directly if you have any questions, complaints, or compliments.

Your Destination: CompTIA A+ Certification

This book is your passport to CompTIA A+ certification, the vendor-neutral industry standard certification for PC hardware technicians, the folks who build

and fix PCs. To get CompTIA A+ certified, you need to pass two exams. CompTIA offers three tracks to CompTIA A+ certification: a primary (referred to as the IT Technician track) and two secondary (Help Desk and Depot Technician tracks). All three tracks require you to take two exams, the first of which is called the *CompTIA A+ Essentials.*

The Essentials exam concentrates on your understanding of terminology and technology, your ability to perform fundamental tasks such as upgrading RAM, and your ability to provide basic Windows operating system support.

To follow the primary track, you would also take the *CompTIA A+ 220-602* exam, called the "602" or "IT Technician exam." The IT Technician exam builds on the Essentials exam, concentrating on advanced configuration and troubleshooting, including using the command line to accomplish tech tasks. This exam also includes network and Internet configuration questions.

To attain CompTIA A+ certification on one of the two secondary tracks, you would take Essentials and follow with either the *CompTIA A+ 220-603* exam (Help Desk Technician) or the *CompTIA A+ 220-604* exam (Depot Technician). Both exams test on a subset of the information covered in the IT Technician exam, but they go more in-depth on some subjects and have less coverage on other subjects. Nearly a third of all questions on the Help Desk Technician exam ask about managing, configuring, and troubleshooting operating systems, for example, whereas only one in five questions on the IT Technician exam hits that subject.

All of the exams are extremely practical, with little or no interest in theory. All questions are multiple choice or "click on the right part of the picture" questions. The following is an example of the type of question you will see on the exams:

> A dot-matrix printer is printing blank pages. Which item should you check first?
>
> **A.** Printer drivers
> **B.** Platen
> **C.** Print head
> **D.** Ribbon

The correct answer is D, the ribbon. You can make an argument for any of the others, but common sense (and skill as a PC technician) tells you to check the simplest possibility first.

CompTIA A+ certification can be your ticket to a career in IT or simply an excellent step in your certification pathway. This book is your passport to success on the CompTIA A+ certification exams.

Your Guides: Mike Meyers and Scott Jernigan

You get a pair of tour guides for this book, both me and Scott Jernigan. I've written numerous computer certification books—including the best-selling *All-in-One A+ Certification Exam Guide*—and written significant parts of others, such as the first edition of the *All-in-One Network+ Certification Exam Guide*. More to the point, I've been working on PCs and teaching others how to make and fix them for a *very* long time, and I love it! When I'm not lecturing or writing about PCs, I'm working on PCs or spanking Scott in Counter-Strike: Source—on the PC, naturally!

Scott has been playing with and working on PCs since before the Web went graphical (that's the mid-1990s for you youngsters) and teaching CompTIA A+ certification classes for nearly as long. When not doing the tech thing, you'll find him building Web sites, making videos, or manipulating digital photographs in Adobe Photoshop…and whiling away the hours with any number of computer games. This is the fifth book we have co-authored, plus Scott has been deeply involved in nearly every book I've written that *doesn't* have his name on the cover.

Why the Travel Theme?

The steps to gaining a certification parallel closely the steps to planning and taking a trip. All of the elements are the same: preparation, an itinerary, a route; even mishaps along the way. Let me show you how it all works.

This book is divided into 20 chapters. Each chapter begins with an *Itinerary* that provides objectives covered in each chapter, and an *ETA* to give you an idea of the time involved learning the skills in that chapter. Each chapter is broken down by objectives, either those officially stated by the certifying body or our expert take on the best way to approach the topics. Portable PCs appear in several CompTIA A+ competencies, for example, but the topic works best in book form when covered in a single chapter. Also, each chapter contains a number of helpful items to call out points of interest:

Exam Tip
Points out critical topics you're likely to see on the actual exam.

Travel Assistance
Shows you additional sources, such as books and Web sites, to give you more information.

Local Lingo

Describes special terms, in detail and in a way you can easily understand.

Travel Advisory

Warns you of common pitfalls, misconceptions, and downright physical peril!

The end of the chapter gives you two handy tools. The *Checkpoint* reviews each objective covered in the chapter with a handy synopsis—a great way to review quickly. Plus, you'll find end-of-chapter questions to test your newly acquired skills.

CHECKPOINT

But the fun doesn't stop there! After you've read the book, pull out the CD and take advantage of the free practice questions! Use the full practice exam to hone your skills and keep the book handy to check answers.

If you want even more practice, log on to http://www.osborne.com/passport, and for a nominal fee you'll get additional high-quality practice questions.

When you're acing the practice questions, you're ready to take the exam. *Go get certified*!

The End of the Trail

The IT industry changes and grows constantly, *and so should you*. Finishing one certification is just a step in an ongoing process of gaining more and more certifications to match your constantly changing and growing skills. Read the Career Flight Path at the end of the book to see where this certification fits into your personal certification goals. Remember, in the IT business, if you're not moving forward, you are way behind!

Good luck on your certification! Stay in touch.

Mike Meyers

Seriers Editor, *Mike Meyers' Certification Passport*

The Art
of the Tech

	NEWBIE	SOME EXPERIENCE	EXPERT
ETA	2 hours	1.5 hours	1 hour

When a mission-critical computer goes down, regardless of the industry, people get upset. Workers can't work, so they feel guilty. Employers can't get product out on time, so they feel anxious. Supervisors blame employees for fouling things up, or at least the employees fear such blame, even if they did not break the machine.

Into this charged atmosphere comes the tech, ready to fix the computer and move on to the next challenge. To accomplish this task, the tech requires three things. First, a good tech must know the broken machine inside and out, how it's *supposed* to work when it's working properly. Second, the tech has to calm the workers and supervisors and get answers to questions to gain relevant information about the problem. Finally, the tech must troubleshoot the problem and fix the machine.

This chapter starts with an overview of how computers work, and then dives into a section on dealing with customers, including how to get them to tell you what you need to know and smile about it. The chapter wraps up with a proven troubleshooting methodology to help you figure out the source of problems and point you to the quickest fixes.

 Objective 1.01 # How Computers Work

Computers work through a three-stage process: input, processing, and output (Figure 1.1). Input requires specific devices, such as the keyboard and mouse, that enable you to tell the computer to do something, such as open a program or display a word that you just typed. The operating system (OS) provides the interface and the tools so that the microprocessor and other chips can process

Output Processing

Input

FIGURE 1.1 Input, processing, and output

your request. The image on the monitor or sound from the speakers effectively tells you that the computer interpreted your command and has spit out the result.

Making this process work, however, requires the complex interaction of many components, including multiple pieces of hardware and layers of software. As a tech, you need to understand all the components and how they work together so that when something doesn't work properly, you can track down the source and fix it. A look at a modern program reveals that even a relatively simple-seeming action or change on the screen requires many things to happen within the computer.

Games such as Second Life (Figure 1.2) are huge, taking up multiple gigabytes of space on a hard drive. They simply won't fit into the random access memory (RAM) in most computers, so developers have figured out ways to minimize RAM usage.

In Second Life, for example, you move through the online world in a series of more or less seamlessly connected areas. Crossing a bridge from one island to another triggers the game to update the information you're about to see on the new island quickly, so you won't be out of the action and the illusion of being in the game world remains intact. Here's what happens when you press the W key on your keyboard and your character steps across the invisible zone line.

FIGURE 1.2 Second Life

The keyboard controller reads the grid of your keyboard and, on discovering your input, sends the information to the CPU through the wires of the motherboard (Figure 1.3). The CPU understands the keyboard controller because of a small program it loaded into RAM from the system BIOS stored on the system ROM chip on the motherboard when you first booted the computer.

Local Lingo

MMORPG Second Life is a *massively multiplayer online role-playing game (MMORPG)* that offers a unique twist on the genre. You can create just about anything you can imagine, as far as your time and talent can take you. Second Life has a functioning economy that spills out into the real world, meaning you can buy and sell things within the game and turn that into real US dollars, although the more common scenario is to spend real money to get virtual possessions.

The CPU and the application determine what should happen in the game, and on discovering that your character is about to cross the zone line, they trigger a whole series of actions. The application sends the signal to the OS that it needs a specific area loaded into RAM. The OS sends a signal to the

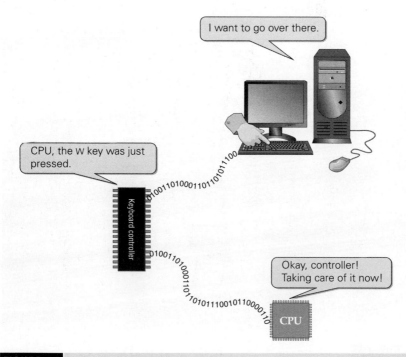

FIGURE 1.3 Keyboard to CPU

CPU that it needs data stored on the hard drive plus information stored on the Second Life servers. The CPU then sends the commands to the hard drive controller for it to grab the desired stored data and send it to RAM, while at the same time sending a command to the NIC to download the updated information (Figure 1.4).

The hard drive controller tells the hard drive to cough up the data—megabytes worth—and then sends that data through the motherboard to the memory controller, which puts it into RAM and communicates with the CPU when it's finished. The network card and network operating system communicate with the Second Life servers and download the necessary updated information. The CPU then uses the application and OS to process the new data, sending video data to the video card and sound data to the sound card, again through the wires on the motherboard (Figure 1.5).

The video card processor puts the incoming data into its RAM, processes the data, and then sends out commands to the monitor to update the screen. The sound card processor likewise processes the data and sends out commands to the speakers to play a new sound (Figure 1.6).

FIGURE 1.4 CPU to hard drive and NIC

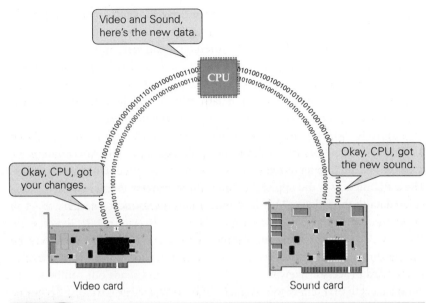

FIGURE 1.5 CPU to video card and sound card

FIGURE 1.6 Updating the screen and speakers

For all of this to work, the PC has to have electricity, so the direct current (DC) provided by the power supply and the alternating current (AC) provided to the power supply must both be the proper voltage and amperage.

Finally, because Second Life is a network application, the OS has to send information through the NIC and onto the Internet to update everyone else's computer. That way, the other characters in the game world see you move forward a step (Figure 1.7).

What do you see or hear with all these electrons zipping all over the place? Out of a seemingly blank vista (Figure 1.8), a castle begins to appear, building itself piece by piece as your computer processes the new information and updates the video screen. You hear music begin to play from your speakers. Within a few seconds, with the data describing the new island fully downloaded and processed, the world on your monitor looks very different (Figure 1.9). That's when all goes well. Many megabytes of data flowed from your hard drive and across the Internet, were processed by multiple processors, and were sent to the monitor and the speakers.

Good techs understand the components involved in inputting, processing, and outputting data, including devices that store data, such as hard drives. That's because if something doesn't work properly, a good tech can start answering the ultimate troubleshooting question—what can it be?—accurately. If your screen freezes or the sound goes "wonky," where in the process could the problem be?

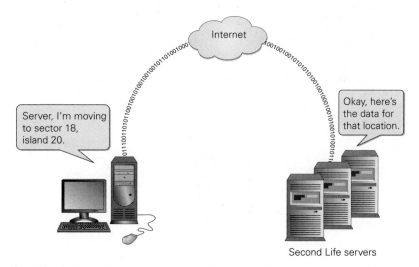

FIGURE 1.7 PC to Second Life servers

FIGURE 1.8 New area loading

FIGURE 1.9 Castle completed

As you go into any troubleshooting scenario, always keep the computing process in mind. This helps you sort through possibilities quickly and accurately. If you know all the stages, you won't miss a simple step, such as figuring out that a user can't print because the cleaning service accidentally turned off the print server the night before; and you won't waste time reinstalling printer drivers when the real issue was a stalled print job in the print queue.

Travel Assistance

This book outlines the processes involved with each facet of computing in the appropriate chapter. Chapter 11, for example, details the printing process. Chapter 13 covers the essentials of the networking process.

 Objective 1.02 Dealing with Customers

When you work with users, managers, and owners who are frustrated and upset because a computer or network is down and they can't work, your job takes on the role of detective and psychologist rolled into one. It takes skill to talk with fraught people and get answers to questions about how the PC got into the state it's in. Plus, you need to follow the rules of "tech-person decorum," with personal integrity and respect for the customer as well. Finally, use assertive communication to empathize with and educate the user. Great techs spend the time to develop these essential skills.

Eliciting Answers

Although each person is different, most users with a malfunctioning computer or peripheral will be afraid and automatically defensive about the problem. To help users overcome this initial attitude, you need to ask the right questions *and* listen to the customer's answers. Then ask the proper follow-up questions.

Always avoid accusatory questions, because they won't help you in the least. "What did you do?" generally gets a surly "Nothing" in reply and doesn't help you get closer to solving the problem. Better to ask oblique questions: "When did it last work?" "Has it ever worked in this way?" "Has any software changed recently?" "Any new hardware?"

By taking the user explicitly out of the questions initially, you show the person that you won't accuse him or her or judge his or her actions. You show that you're offering to help. After the initial tension eases, you'll often get more information, like a recitation of something the user might have tried or changed. These clues can help lead to a quick resolution of the problem.

You know the technology, but most users do not. This means that you'll often hear jargon used incorrectly and the wrong words used to describe a particular computer component or function. Don't bother to correct the user. Definitely don't add any jargon, acronyms, or abbreviations specific to computers. They simply confuse the user and make most people think you're talking down to them. Just ask direct questions in simple, non-jargon language to zero in on what precisely the user is trying to explain. Point at the machine or go to a working PC to have the user show what went wrong or what he or she was trying to accomplish.

Integrity

A computer tech must bring integrity to the job, just as with any other service professional. Treat anything said to you as a personal confidence, not to be repeated to coworkers or bosses. Respect the privacy and property of the user.

You have a lot of power when you sit in front of someone's computer. You can readily read private e-mail, discover surfed Web sites, and more. With a click of the Start button, you can know the last five programs the user ran, including Word and Solitaire, and the last few documents he or she worked on. Don't do this. You really don't want to know! Plus, if you get caught, your credibility will go through the floor and you might as well hand in your letter of resignation.

It's funny, but people assume ownership of things they use at work. John in accounting doesn't call the computer he uses anything but "my PC." The phone on Susie's desk isn't the company phone, it's "Susie's phone." Regardless of the logic or illogic involved with this sense of ownership, a tech needs to respect that feeling. Just as you would have other people behave with your things, treat their things the same way. Don't use or touch anything—keyboard, printer, laptop, monitor, mouse, phone, pen, paper, cube toy—without asking permission. Follow this rule even when the customer isn't looking!

Respect

The final key in communicating with the user revolves around respect. You don't do his or her job, but you should respect that job and person as an essential cog in your organization. Communicate with the user the way you would like him or her to communicate with you were the roles reversed.

Engage the user with the standard rules of civil conversation. Take the time to listen. Don't interrupt a story, but rather let it play out. You might hear something that leads to problem resolution. Use a level, non-accusatory tone, and never argue with the user. Remain positive in the face of adversity. Don't get defensive if you can't figure something out quickly and the user starts complaining. Take it in stride; smile and assure him or her that computer troubleshooting sometimes takes a while.

Avoid letting outside interruptions take your focus away from the user's computer problem or from the user. Things that break your concentration slow down the troubleshooting process immensely. And customers will feel insulted if you start chatting with your significant other about a movie date later that night when you're supposed to be fixing their computers. So set your cell phones and pagers to vibrate. Remember you do have voicemail.

If you discover that the user caused the problem, either through ignorance or accident, don't be judgmental or insulting. Don't minimize the importance of the problem. *You get paid because people make mistakes and machines break.* Chances are, you'll be back at that workstation six months or a year later, fixing something else. By becoming the user's advocate and go-to person, you create a better work environment. If a user's action caused the problem, explain how to do the task the user wanted to accomplish properly, and then have the user go through the process to reinforce what you said.

Assertiveness

In many cases, a PC problem is due to user error or neglect. As a technician, you must show users the error of their ways without creating anger or conflict. You do this by using assertive communication. *Assertive communication* is a technique that isn't pushy or bossy, but it's also not the language of a pushover. Assertive communication first requires you show the other person that you understand and appreciate the importance of his or her feelings. Use statements such as, "I know how frustrating it feels to lose data," or "I understand how infuriating it is when the network goes out and you can't get your job done." Statements like these cool off the situation and let the customer know you are on his or her side.

The second part of assertive communication is making sure the problem is clearly stated—without accusing the user directly: "Not keeping up with defragmenting your hard drive slows it down," or "Help me understand how the network cable keeps getting unplugged during your lunch hour." Lastly, tell the user what you need from them to prevent this error in the future. "Please call me whenever you hear that buzzing sound," or "Please check the company's

approved software list before installing anything." Always use "I" and "me," and never make judgments. "I can't promise the keyboard will work well if it's always getting dirty" is much better than "Stop eating cookies over the keyboard, you slob!"

Objective 1.03 Troubleshooting Methodology

Following a sound troubleshooting methodology helps you figure out and fix problems quickly. But because troubleshooting is as much art as science, no detailed step-by-step list of things to try in a particular order will suffice. You've got to be flexible. But here are the general steps.

First, you need to secure the proper tools for the job. Second, you should back up everything important before you start doing repair work. And third, analyze, test, and complete your troubleshooting.

Tech Toolkit

A tech toolkit should include a few basic tools and some spare parts for testing. The basic technician toolkit consists of a Phillips-head screwdriver and not much else—seriously—but a half-dozen tools round out a fully functional toolkit. Most kits have a star-headed Torx wrench, a nut driver or two, a pair of tweezers, a little grabber tool, and a hemostat to go along with Phillips-head and straight-slot screwdrivers (Figure 1.10). Additionally, you might want to carry a

FIGURE 1.10 Typical technician toolkit

flashlight, a magnifying glass, and an antistatic wrist strap for highly charged environments.

Always carry several *field replaceable units* (FRUs)—a fancy way to say *spare parts*—when going to a job site or workstation. Having several known-good components on hand lets you swap out a potentially bad piece of hardware to test whether that's the problem. I generally carry a couple of RAM sticks (DDR and DDR2), a PCI video card, a NIC, and a 300-watt power supply.

Backup

In many troubleshooting situations, you should back up critical files before making changes to a system. This is partly a maintenance issue. If you're in charge of a set of machines for your company, for example, make sure they're set up to back up critical files automatically on a regular basis.

Travel Assistance

Chapter 19 goes into detail on the tools in Windows 2000 and Windows XP used for backup, including System Restore, Backup (2000), the Backup and Restore Wizard (XP Pro), Automated System Recovery, the Emergency Repair Disk, and the Recovery Console.

If you run into a partially functional system, where you might have to reinstall the OS but can access the hard drive, you should definitely back up essential data. Back up e-mail, favorites, personal documents, and any data not stored on a regularly backed up server. Because you can always boot to a copy of Windows and go to the Recovery Console, you should never lose essential data barring anything short of a full-blown hard drive death.

Travel Advisory

Dead hard drives retain their data, so you can recover it—if you're willing to pay a lot of money. Having a good backup in place makes a lot more economic sense!

Exam Tip

The CompTIA A+ certification exams assume that all techs should back up systems *every time* before working on them, even though that's not how it works in the real world.

Steps

Troubleshooting a computer problem can create a great day for a computer tech—if he or she goes about solving the problem systematically and logically. Too many techs get into a rut, thinking that when symptom A occurs, the problem must be caused by problem A and must require solution A. This assumption might even be right nine times out of ten, but if you think this way, and the problem is really problem Z and requires a completely different solution, you're in trouble. What do you do when the fix doesn't work and you're sure it's got to be problem A? Your customer won't be happy, you'll end up frustrated or embarrassed, and you still won't have the problem fixed. Follow the right methodology and analyze, test, and complete your task.

Analyze

Everything starts with analyzing the problem. Because you know how everything *should* work, when you run into a computer problem the first question you should ask is, "What can it be?" Don't limit yourself in the initial analysis, but examine all possibilities.

Make sure you understand the nature of the problem first. A big portion of the initial fact-finding involves talking to the user with your newly honed customer communication skills. Practice those oblique questions to get the results you want.

When you run into big problems, like a completely dead PC or some weird issue that involves networking as well as a local machine, break them down into smaller parts. For a dead PC, for example, organize your inquiry into categories, like this:

- **Power** Check the AC connections and power switches on the power supply and UPS or surge suppressor.
- **Connectivity** Check inside the box to make sure nothing was unplugged.
- **CMOS** If you've got power (you see an LED lit up, for example), check CMOS to see if the hard drive shows up.
- **Operating system** If you see some life in the PC, but you get no boot option, try booting to the CD and running the Recovery Console. Check to see whether you can access the hard drive. If you have a boot option, try booting to Safe Mode or Last Known Good Configuration.

By breaking the problem into discrete chunks, you make a big problem more manageable. You can determine whether the problem lies in hardware failure or disconnection or in an OS or other software error.

Test

Once you determine what might have caused the problem, test your theories. The testing procedure follows a simple set of rules:

First, check the easy stuff. Is the failed device plugged in? Is it turned on? Does the printer have paper?

Second, use a process of elimination to narrow in on the problem. Use a notepad to write down what you've tried and what effect that effort had. Do one thing at a time. If you go into CMOS and make a whole series of changes to various settings, for example, and the computer suddenly works, what was wrong? You can't know when you make multiple changes. What if you've made other things break while fixing the first problem.

Third, swap out parts with known good parts from your stash of FRUs. With a dead or dying piece of hardware, you can generally get almost immediate results. A fried stick of RAM, for example, can create a dead PC. Pop in a good stick and you'll have a functional machine.

The power supply provides the only exception to the instant gratification of part-swapping. If you have a wonky computer that has intermittent problems, swap out the power supply and leave your FRU in the computer for a half day or longer. You need the user to road test the PC and report if he or she has the same problems.

Complete

Once you finish the testing phase, you can complete the troubleshooting process with three more steps:

First, evaluate the results of your actions. Run the system through its paces; don't just get it working and walk away. Make certain that the user can accomplish his or her primary tasks before you consider a job complete.

If you can't get the computer or peripheral working in a fairly short period of time, take the second step and call for help. Because you've taken notes on the symptoms and each troubleshooting step you've tried, you can quickly get a more senior tech up to speed on the problem and get suggestions for where you might go next.

Finally, document your results. Many companies have set forms for you to use to describe the problem and resolution of the problem. If not, then make some for yourself and other techs in your workplace. Documenting problems helps keep track of machines over time so you can make longer term determinations about retiring a machine or changing out more parts. If you and fellow techs fix a specific problem with Mary's machine several times, for example, you might decide to swap out her whole system rather than fix it a fourth time.

Documenting also helps fellow techs if they have to follow up on a task you didn't finish or work with a machine that you've worked on previously. The reverse is also true. If you get a call about Frank's computer, for example, and check the records to find other service calls on his computer, you might find that the fix for a particular problem is already documented. This is especially true if the problem is user-generated.

CHECKPOINT

✔**Objective 1.01: How Computers Work** Computers work in a three-stage process: input, processing, and output. Almost every process requires the complex interaction of many devices, including multiple pieces of hardware and layers of software. Good techs understand each process to facilitate their troubleshooting.

✔**Objective 1.02: Dealing with Customers** A tech's job takes on the role of psychologist as well as detective when users get into the mix. Asking the right questions—and avoiding the wrong ones—helps elicit answers for your troubleshooting. Avoid accusatory questions and focus on oblique ones. Treat customers properly, respecting their privacy and the sanctity of their possessions. Use a level, non-accusatory tone when conversing with customers and practice assertive communication.

✔**Objective 1.03: Troubleshooting Methodology** You need to have the right tools to accomplish your job. At the least, carry a Phillips-head screwdriver; also carry some FRUs for part swapping. Back up critical files before making changes to a computer. Analyze, test, and complete your troubleshooting. Start with the easy stuff, and then use the process of elimination to get to the bottom of the problem. Always document your work so you know what you've tried and can communicate this to your boss or to the customer.

REVIEW QUESTIONS

 1. While troubleshooting a fairly routine printing problem, the customer explains in great detail precisely what he was trying to do, what happened

when he tried to print, and what he had attempted as a fix for the problem. At what point should you interrupt him?

A. After he describes the first problem

B. As soon as you understand the problem

C. As soon as you have a solution

D. Never

2. While manning the help desk, you get a call from a distraught user who says her computer has a blank screen. What would be a useful follow-up question? (Select two.)

A. Is the computer turned on?

B. Is the monitor turned on?

C. Did you reboot?

D. What did you do?

3. While manning the help desk, you get a call from Sharon in accounting. She's lost a file that she knows she saved to her hard drive. Which of the following statements would direct Sharon to open her My Documents folder in the most efficient and professional manner?

A. Sharon, check My Documents.

B. Sharon, a lot of programs save files to a default folder, often to a folder called My Documents. Let's look there first. Click the Start button and move the mouse until the cursor hovers over My Documents. Click the left mouse button and tell me what you see when My Documents opens.

C. Probably just defaulted to My Docs. Why don't you open Excel or whatever program you used to make the file, then open a document, and point it to My Documents.

D. Look Sharon, I know you're a clueless noob when it comes to computers, but how could somebody lose a file? Just open up My Documents and look there for the file.

4. What tool should be in every technician's toolkit?

A. Pliers

B. Hammer

C. Straight-slot screwdriver

D. Phillips-head screwdriver

5. When is it appropriate to yell at a user?

 A. When he screws up the second time

 B. When he interrupts your troubleshooting

 C. When he screws up the fifth time

 D. Never

6. Al in marketing calls in for tech support, complaining that he has a dead PC. What is a good first question or questions to begin troubleshooting the problem?

 A. Did the computer ever work?

 B. When did the computer last work?

 C. When you say "dead," what do you mean? What happens when you press the power button?

 D. What did you do?

7. While manning the help desk, you get a call from Bryce in Sales complaining that he can't print and every time he clicks the network shared drive, his computer stops. He says he thinks it's his "hard driver." What would be a good follow-up question or statement?

 A. Bryce, you're an idiot. Don't touch anything. I'll be there in 5 minutes.

 B. OK, let's take this one step at a time. You seem to have two problems, one with printing and the second with the network shared drive, right?

 C. First, it's not a hard *driver*, but a hard *drive*. It doesn't have anything to do with the network share or printing, so that's just not right.

 D. When could you last print?

8. When troubleshooting a software problem on Phoebe's computer and listening to her describe the problem, your beeper goes off. It's your boss. What would be an acceptable action for you to make?

 A. Excuse yourself, walk out of the cube, and use a cell phone to call your boss.

 B. Pick up Phoebe's phone and dial your boss's number.

 C. Wait until Phoebe finishes her description and then ask to use her phone to call your boss.

 D. Wait until Phoebe finishes her description and run through any simple fixes; then explain that you need to call your boss on your cell phone.

9. You've just installed new printer drivers into Roland's computer for the big networked laser printer. What should you do to complete the assignment?

 A. Document that you installed new printer drivers.

 B. Tell Roland to print a test page.

 C. Print a test page and go to the printer to verify the results. Assuming everything works, you're done.

 D. Print a test page and go to the printer to verify the results. Document that you installed new printer drivers successfully.

10. What's an FRU?

 A. Foreign replacement unit, a cheaper part to replace an expensive, American-made part

 B. Field replacement unit, a known-good computer part to swap in or out in the troubleshooting process

 C. Free repair unit, a gimmick used by some companies to provide free tech support for the first-time customer

 D. Short for FRU Linux, a Linux distribution

REVIEW ANSWERS

1. **D** Don't interrupt the customer when he or she is telling you the problem!

2. **A B** Good follow-up questions would ask if the computer or monitor is turned on.

3. **B** The better explanation tells about the probable location of the file—in this case in My Documents—and does so without slang or jargon. It also doesn't assume knowledge on the part of the user. Finally, never call a user a "clueless noob"!

4. **D** The minimum tool every computer tech needs is a Phillips-head screwdriver.

5. **D** Don't yell at users.

6. **C** It's always a good idea to ask follow-up questions that clarify the situation. Both A and B are questions that you'll ask during the questioning of the user, but C is the better first question.

7. **B** Taking a non-accusatory approach with a question or questions that help clarify the problems is a good initial follow-up. Answer D would come up probably as a second or third question.

8. **D** This is a tough one, but because the user is in the midst of explanation, you shouldn't interrupt her. Also, use your own cell phone, not the user's equipment if at all possible.

9. **D** Always verify and document fixes.

10. **B** An FRU is a field replacement unit.

Ports and Connectors

	NEWBIE	SOME EXPERIENCE	EXPERT
ETA	2.5 hours	1.5 hours	1 hour

Mastering the craft of the PC technician requires that you learn a lot of details about what sometimes seems to be thousands of individual parts, connections, and settings. Even the most basic PC contains many hardware components, each with its own set of characteristics, shapes, sizes, and colors. Fortunately, it's much simpler than it seems! Computer makers use only a few types of connectors for most devices, so once you learn one type of connector, you'll know how to use it on any type of PC.

This chapter describes *integrated I/O devices*—the major connectors, plugs, and sockets that you'll find on a typical PC—and spells out many of the amazing array of acronyms and abbreviations used by techs. The CompTIA A+ certification exams expect you to recognize a particular part simply by seeing what type of connector attaches to that part, so pay attention, folks!

Objective 2.01 Legacy Multifunction Ports

Good techs don't go around saying, "Just plug that *doohickey* into the *whatchamacallit* on the back of the PC," and you shouldn't either. These things have names, after all, so you should get into the habit of using them. Every cable has a *connector* at the end that plugs into a corresponding *port* on a PC. Connectors carry data and sometimes power between devices attached to the PC. Ports are the *interfaces*, the "doorways" used to connect devices to the PC. Connectors and ports can be either male or female, defined as having pins or sockets, respectively.

Let's start with the two ancient multifunction ports that linger on most modern PCs: serial ports and parallel ports. Serial and parallel ports have a slight *D* shape, which allows only one proper way to insert a plug into the socket and makes it easier to remember what they're called. Technically, they're known as *D-sub* or *D-subminiature* connectors, but most techs call them *DB*.

Serial Ports

Serial ports come in 9-pin and 25-pin varieties (Figure 2-1). Of the two, the 9-pin (five pins on the top row, four on the bottom) variety is much more common, although even those are rapidly disappearing from modern PCs.

Serial ports transfer data 1 *bit* (the smallest unit of data in the PC world) at a time, with a maximum throughput speed of 115 *kilobits per second* (Kbps).

FIGURE 2.1 A 25-pin serial port and a 9-pin serial port

Devices that connected to the PC via the serial port included mice, external modems, label printers, personal digital assistants (PDAs), and digital cameras.

Exam Tip
Make sure you know that serial ports transfer data 1 bit at a time.

All devices in a PC get assigned certain *system resources,* and serial ports are no exception. The CPU uses input/output (I/O) addresses to give commands to devices; some devices use an interrupt request (IRQ) to contact the CPU.

Most motherboards have at least one serial port—appropriately called Serial Port 1. By default, this port gets assigned the I/O address 3F8 and IRQ 4 (COM1). The rare Serial Port 2 on a PC gets I/O address 2F8 and IRQ 3 (COM2) by default.

You can use the CMOS setup utility to change the resources assigned to devices built into the motherboard—such as serial ports. Further, you can enable or disable the serial port(s) in the CMOS setup utility to free up resources, although you'd need to do this only on old computers. Chapter 7 covers the CMOS setup utility in great detail.

Local Lingo
System setup utility Many techs refer to the CMOS program as the *system setup utility.* The latter term happens to be more accurate as no modern PC uses a *complementary metal-oxide semiconductor* chip to store CMOS information, but the older term has stuck. As one old tech said, looking me straight in the eye, "CMOS is CMOS, son."

Parallel Ports

Parallel ports are the 25-pin (13 on the top row, 12 on the bottom) female ports on the back of older PCs, as shown in Figure 2-2. Folks often incorrectly refer to

FIGURE 2.2 A 25-pin parallel port

parallel ports simply as "printer ports," but many other devices have used parallel ports, such as external CD-ROM drives, Zip drives, and scanners.

Exam Tip	
Parallel communications transfer data 8 bits, or 1 byte, at a time.	

Printers that connect to parallel ports on the PC have a *centronics* port rather than a parallel port. Centronics connectors have a central tongue with contacts rather than pins (Figure 2-3), and come in two varieties. The more common is the 36-pin IEEE 1284B connector; the rarely used variety is the mini centronics IEEE 1284C connector (Figure 2-4).

FIGURE 2.3 IEEE 1284B centronics connector and port

FIGURE 2.4 IEEE 1284C mini centronics connector

Local Lingo

IEEE IEEE stands for the Institute of Electrical and Electronics Engineers, the international organization that creates standards for electrical things, such as ports, cables, and connectors. You'll see them again later in this chapter.

Parallel ports traditionally get I/O address 378 and IRQ 7 (LPT1), but as with the serial port assignments, modern motherboards give you the option of changing this setting. Technological advances, such as the Extended Capability Port (ECP) and the Enhanced Parallel Port (EPP), offer improved throughput, to about 10 times faster than a standard parallel port.

Objective 2.02 # Standard Single-Function Ports

Every PC sports several single-function ports for connecting peripherals such as keyboards, monitors, and the like. With only a couple of exceptions, these standard ports support only a single type of device.

The Keyboard Port

Keyboards come in a variety of styles, from the plain-Jane, rectangular typewriter substitute to the exotically curved, multifunction gadget that's bristling

with special function *hotkeys* and equipped with ports of its own. Regardless of their appearance, however, all keyboards enable you to do one thing—enter commands into your PC.

Modern PCs have a purple 6-pin mini-DIN (commonly called a *PS/2 connector*) port (Figure 2-5). The mini-DIN port is keyed so you can insert the keyboard connector only one way.

The Mouse Port

Like keyboards, mice come in an array of sizes and shapes, and they use a variety of connectors to attach to the PC (see Figure 2-6). All mice enable you to manipulate the operating system (OS) and applications.

Traditionally, mice plugged into one of the serial ports on the back of the PC, but most motherboards today have a dedicated mini-DIN mouse port. Aside from color, the green mouse port appears identical to the purple PS/2 keyboard port, but they're not interchangeable.

FIGURE 2.5 A 6-pin mini-DIN connector

FIGURE 2.6 A serial mouse connector (left) and a PS/2 mouse connector

You can plug a PS/2 mouse connector into a PS/2 keyboard port, and vice versa, but they won't work. Mice go into mouse ports—keyboards go into keyboard ports. Some portable computers have a single black or gray mini-DIN port that can handle both a mouse and a keyboard (though obviously not at the same time!).

Video Ports

Standard cathode ray tube (CRT) monitors and many projectors connect to your PC using a 15-pin D-subminiature connector arranged in three rows of five pins each. The corresponding video port on the PC, as shown in Figure 2-7, accommodates only that connector. No other port on your PC looks like this one.

Many flat-panel liquid crystal display (LCD) monitors and some projectors use a specially keyed, 24-pin Digital Visual Interface (DVI) connector that plugs into a DVI port on the back of your video adapter card, as shown in Figure 2-8. DVI comes in several varieties, such as analog, *DVI-A,* and digital, *DVI-D.* Chapter 10 covers monitors and projectors in more detail.

FIGURE 2.7 A female 15-pin DB connector

| FIGURE 2.8 | DVI connector for a flat-panel monitor |

Local Lingo

Thin-film transistor The most common LCD monitors use a technology called *thin-film transistor (TFT)*. Many techs erroneously refer to all LCD monitors as TFTs.

Some video cards connect to display devices using three RCA connectors or five BNC connectors, called *component* and *RGB video*, respectively. Figure 2-9 shows both types of ports on monitors.

Components

FIGURE 2.9 RGB and component connectors

Audio Ports

At one time, audio was considered an extra add-on, but sound is standard issue on modern PCs. Most audio ports take the form of the popular 1/8" mini-audio connectors commonly seen on the Sony Walkman or other similar gadgets. A PC typically has at least three color-coded sound ports: a green speaker output port, a pink microphone input port, and a blue auxiliary input port, as shown in Figure 2-10. Better audio systems offer more jacks for rear speakers, center speaker, and subwoofer.

Travel Advisory

Some sound cards have audio ports that are all one color. If you run into one of those, you can try to figure out what the obscure symbols mean or get the information from a user manual or the manufacturer's Web site.

FIGURE 2.10 Sound card 1/8" mini-audio connectors

You will occasionally see variations, particularly on systems with high-performance sound cards. Some have separate outputs for each audio channel, or they may incorporate one or two special connectors called *Sony/Philips Digital Interface (S/PDIF)* ports, as shown in Figure 2-11. S/PDIF ports come in two flavors, electrical and optical. The electrical port uses an RCA connector on a coaxial cable; the optical uses a fiber connector. Some sound cards from Creative Labs use a 1/8" mini-audio jack for electrical S/PDIF.

Multimedia Ports

The convergence of television, music, and the computer has many newer PCs sporting various multimedia connectors. Some of these connectors, such as the *RG-6 coaxial* connector, have been around for a long time. The RG-6 connector sits on the video card or a dedicated TV tuner card and enables your PC to receive video and audio signals from a cable company or video cassette player. Other older connectors include *S-Video*—for sending video content from the PC to the TV—and *composite* connectors—for connecting left- and right-channel audio and a single video source into or out from the PC. Figure 2-12 shows an ATI All-in-Wonder card with the many multimedia connectors it offers.

The latest media center PCs designed to fit into your living room décor rather than on your desk come with *High Definition Multimedia Interface*

FIGURE 2.11 S/PDIF connectors, electrical (left) and optical (right)

FIGURE 2.12 Multimedia card

(HDMI) ports (Figure 2-13) for connecting the PC to a high-definition television (HDTV). The HDMI interface handles both the high-definition video signal and multichannel digital audio streams.

FIGURE 2.13 HDMI connector

MIDI/Joystick Ports

Older PCs have an integrated female DB-15 port for connecting joysticks or other game controllers. These ports also support MIDI devices, such as a music synthesizer keyboard, although you need a special breakout box to make the MIDI connection. Unlike DB-15 video connectors, MIDI/Joystick connectors have pins arrayed in two rows, with eight on the top and seven on the bottom, as shown in Figure 2-14.

Exam Tip

Make sure you know that the two-row, 15-pin DB connector can be used for both MIDI devices and joysticks.

Modem Ports

PC modem ports look identical to female telephone jacks and use standard, two-wire RJ-11 telephone cables and connectors (Figure 2-15). The locking clips on the male RJ-11 connectors secure the cable into the port. Most modems also have an output port for a telephone.

FIGURE 2.14 MIDI/Joystick port

FIGURE 2.15 RJ-11 ports on a modem

Network Interface Ports

Network interfaces come in two main varieties. Most network interface cards (NICs) and motherboards have an eight-wire RJ-45 port (Figure 2-16). RJ-45 connectors look like wider-than-normal RJ-11 telephone connectors and plug into the female RJ-45 ports in the same manner that RJ-11 telephone cables plug into a modem. High-end NICs have two fiber connections (in/out) of one variety or another. The most common fiber connectors are the SC-ST and the LC-LC (Figure 2-17).

> ## Local Lingo
> **NIC** Network interface cards (NICs) enable PCs to connect to a network. Techs call them NICs even when the network adapter is built into a motherboard and thus distinctly lacking in "card-ness."

FIGURE 2.16 An RJ-45 connector and port

FIGURE 2.17 SC-ST and LC-LC fiber connectors

Exam Tip

Make sure you know the difference between RJ-11 connectors and RJ-45 connectors, and that you can easily tell the difference between the two at a glance.

 Objective 2.03

Modern Multifunction Ports

Modern PCs use one or more multifunction ports to supplement or replace the aged serial and parallel ports. All newer machines have *universal serial bus (USB)* ports; many have *IEEE 1394 (FireWire)* ports; and a few have a *small computer systems interface (SCSI)* port. All three come in at least two varieties and can be used to connect everything from printers to digital cameras.

USB

USB comes in two flavors, USB and Hi-Speed USB. Regular USB—often mistakenly called USB 1.1—devices transfer data at speeds of 1.5 or 12 megabits per second (Mbps), making them much faster than parallel or serial communications. Hi-Speed USB is faster still, capable of bursts up to 480 Mbps. Note that despite the huge difference in speeds, Hi-Speed USB technology is fully backward-compatible with regular USB devices. You can plug a regular USB device into a Hi-Speed port, in other words, and it will work.

Local Lingo

USB 1.1 All current USB devices fall into the USB 2.0 specification. The initial specification that came to market was called *USB 1.1* and matched the data throughput and connections of the current USB 2.0 (not Hi-Speed) devices. Many techs and consumers continue to use the term USB 1.1 to describe the lower speed USB 2.0 devices. Some marketing materials distinguish between 1.5 and 12 Mbps USB devices as USB and Full-Speed USB, although the latter term is not used in the specification at all.

Exam Tip

The CompTIA A+ certification exams use the term USB 1.1 to describe the low-speed USB 2.0 devices.

USB ports come in three varieties, A, B, and mini. All are female and rectangular-shaped. The four contact pins are mounted on a plastic protrusion that keeps you from inserting the USB cable improperly. You plug the flat USB A connector into the corresponding port on a PC or USB hub—a generic term for a device with multiple USB ports (Figure 2-18). Most bigger peripherals, such as printers and scanners, have a B port into which you'd plug a B connector (Figure 2-19). Small USB devices, such as digital cameras and music players, use the mini port. Figure 2-20 shows a mini USB port and connector.

FIGURE 2.18 USB A-type port and connector

FIGURE 2.19 USB B-type port and connector

You can also find USB extenders. These have a USB A port on one end and a USB A connector on the other. You can use these for extending a mouse or keyboard cable and for connecting wide USB devices—such as thumb drives—to portable computers.

Many current devices, such as keyboards, mice, joysticks, microphones, scanners, printers, modems, PDAs, digital cameras, lap warmers, cup heaters, personal fans, lamps, and more, connect to the PC via USB.

FIGURE 2.20 Mini USB port and connector

Travel Assistance

For more information about USB, visit http://www.usb.org/.

USB devices are *hot-swappable*, which means that you can connect or disconnect them at any time without powering down your PC. USB technology enables you to connect up to 127 devices together in a series called a *daisy chain!*

Exam Tip

Remember that you can hot-swap USB devices and daisy-chain up to 127 USB devices together.

Travel Advisory

For the purposes of the CompTIA A+ Certification exams, you need to know that you can connect 127 devices together—but for real-life, on-the-job situations, it's a bad idea to hit this maximum. Some applications reserve bandwidth, and you could wind up with quite a mess. Too much of a good thing isn't good!

IEEE 1394

IEEE 1394 is an exciting communications technology created in a joint effort by Apple Computers, Texas Instruments, and the IEEE organization. The IEEE 1394 standard has been widely adopted not only by computer and peripheral makers, but also by manufacturers of home electronics such as digital video recorders.

Different manufacturers market IEEE 1394 technology under different trade names, such as *FireWire* (Apple), *iLink* (Sony), or *Lynx* (Texas Instruments), but they all refer to the same thing. Of these terms, FireWire is the most popular term among techs.

Local Lingo

FireWire, iLink, and Lynx The terms FireWire, iLink, and Lynx all refer to the IEEE 1394 interface.

The original specification for FireWire—*1394a*—calls for data transfers of up to 400 Mbps. The current generation of FireWire—*1394b*—is capable of speeds up to a blinding 800 Mbps. What's even more impressive is that the design spec for FireWire states that speeds of up to 1600 Mbps are possible. FireWire technology is a very good match for video, external hard drives, backup storage devices, and other hardware that needs real-time data access.

Connecting FireWire devices together enables them to communicate. Running a FireWire cable between two PCs, for example, creates an instant point-to-point network for sharing files. You can connect up to 63 FireWire devices together in a daisy chain, although you would need devices that came with their own power supply to use that many. One cool feature of FireWire chains is that you can use a device somewhere down the chain even if one or more devices in between the port and device is powered down.

The 6-pin standard FireWire 400 ports are slightly taller than USB ports and rounded on one end. The connector plugs are of course shaped to fit, as shown in Figure 2-21. Some devices, such as digital camcorders, use a 4-pin mini-FireWire connector, similar to the mini-USB connector, although they are certainly not interchangeable (Figure 2-22). FireWire 800 devices use a square 9-pin connector (Figure 2-23). You can get adapters and two-headed cables to connect a FireWire 400 device into a FireWire 800 port.

FIGURE 2.21 FireWire 400 (IEEE 1394a) connector and port

FIGURE 2.22 Mini-FireWire port and connector

Travel Assistance

For more information regarding FireWire and the IEEE 1394 standard, visit http://www.ieee.org/.

FIGURE 2.23 FireWire 800 (IEEE 1394b) port and connector

SCSI

SCSI—amusingly pronounced "skuzzy"—has been around for a long time. Innovations in SCSI technology have kept SCSI competitive with other enhanced technologies such as USB and FireWire. Many high-end PCs have built-in SCSI connectors, and SCSI controller cards are widely available to add SCSI ports to your system.

SCSI devices have a variety of interfaces—*SCSI-1, SCSI-2, Ultra SCSI, Wide Ultra SCSI,* just to name a few—but the 68-pin female Ultra-320 port shown in Figure 2-24 is the most common today. You may also see 50-pin or 25-pin ports on some older devices or PCs. Note that the very fine port sockets shown in the picture are matched to fine contact pins on the male Ultra-320 connector. Take it from me, these tiny pins bend and break easily, so handle with care!

Data throughput on SCSI varies from around 5 to 80 megabytes per second (MBps) for early incarnations to 320 MBps for many current versions. Chapter 8 covers the amazing variety of SCSI devices and standards.

Travel Assistance

For more information on SCSI, check out the SCSI Trade Organization at http://www.scsita.org/.

FIGURE 2.24 Ultra-320 port

CHECKPOINT

✔ **Objective 2.01: Legacy Multifunction Ports** The 9-pin and 25-pin serial ports and the 25-pin parallel ports are used for connecting serial and parallel devices, respectively, to the PC. Serial devices transfer data 1 bit a time, whereas parallel devices transfer data 8 bits at a time.

✔ **Objective 2.02: Standard Single-Function Ports** Keyboards connect to the motherboard with 6-pin mini-DIN (PS/2) or USB connectors. Mice connect to the 9-pin serial bus in older systems, and PS/2 or USB in newer systems. Make sure you remember the 15-pin, three-row D-sub port is for video, whereas the 15-pin, two-row D-sub port is for MIDI devices or joysticks. Finally, know the difference between the RJ-11 connectors for modems and the RJ-45 connectors for NICs.

✔ **Objective 2.03: Modern Multifunction Ports** USB enables you to hot-swap devices and daisy-chain up to 127 devices in one PC. The Type A connector goes into the USB port; the Type B or mini connector goes into the USB device. USB (a.k.a. normal USB 1.1) is capable of throughput speeds up to 12 Mbps, while Hi-Speed USB is good for up to 480 Mbps. IEEE 1394 is also known as FireWire, iLink, and Lynx. The 1394a version is capable of speeds up to 400 Mbps, and 1394b runs at up to 800 Mbps. Either version of IEEE 1394 enables you to connect up to 63 devices to a single IEEE 1394 port. Finally, the 68-pin ports used by Ultra-320 devices are the most common ones seen on the many SCSI technologies available today, but you might also see 50-pin, 25-pin, or other varieties.

REVIEW QUESTIONS

1. Which of these connectors can you use to connect a keyboard to a PC? (Select two.)

 A. Mini-DIN

 B. 9-pin serial

 C. 25-pin parallel

 D. USB

2. Which of these connectors can you use to connect a CRT monitor to a PC?

 A. 25-pin serial

 B. 9-pin serial

 C. 15-pin D-sub in two rows

 D. 15-pin D-sub in three rows

3. Which of the following ports can be found on network cards?

 A. HDMI

 B. Parallel

 C. RJ-45

 D. USB

4. How many pins does a parallel port have?

 A. 10

 B. 25

 C. 34

 D. 36

5. How is data transferred in serial communications?

 A. 10 bits at a time

 B. 1 bit at a time

 C. 1 byte at a time

 D. 16 bits at a time

6. How is data transferred in parallel communications? (Select two.)

 A. 8 bits at a time

 B. 1 byte at a time

 C. 1 bit at a time

 D. 8 bytes at a time

7. In theory, how many USB devices can you daisy-chain together?

 A. 1

 B. 2

 C. 63

 D. 127

8. Which connector provides high-quality video *and* audio?

 A. HDMI

 B. S/PDIF

 C. S-Video

 D. VGA

9. To what does a Type A USB connector connect?

 A. To a USB port on the PC

 B. To a USB device

 C. To a serial port on the back of your PC

 D. To a USB modem

10. What is the top data transfer speed possible under the IEEE 1394a standard?

 A. 50 megabits per second

 B. 400 megabits per second

 C. 400 megabytes per second

 D. 800 megabits per second

11. How many devices can you daisy-chain on a single FireWire connection?

 A. 63

 B. 65

 C. 127

 D. 1023

REVIEW ANSWERS

1. **A D** Keyboards can use a mini-DIN or USB connector.

2. **D** An CRT monitor cable has a 15-pin D-sub connector in three rows.

3. **C** Most network cards have RJ-45 ports.

4. **B** Parallel ports have 25 pins or contacts.

5. **B** Serial communications transfer data 1 bit at a time.

6. **A B** Parallel communications transfer data 8 bits (1 byte) at a time.

7. **D** You can, in theory, daisy-chain 127 USB devices together.

8. **A** The HDMI connector can handle high-definition video and multiple digital audio signals.

9. **A** The Type A connector on a USB cable connects to the USB ports on the back of your PC. USB devices have a Type B port.

10. **B** The IEEE 1394a FireWire standard enables data transfers of up to 400 megabits per second.

11. **C** You can daisy-chain up to 63 devices on a single FireWire port.

Maintenance and Safety Precautions

	NEWBIE	SOME EXPERIENCE	EXPERT
ETA	3 hours	2 hours	1 hour

There's more to keeping a PC running smoothly than launching an occasional CHKDSK or deleting some temporary Internet files. PCs are machines, and all machines need regular maintenance. This doesn't include changing the oil every 3,000 miles, but it does include things like cleaning and dusting. Yes, *dusting*! Being a PC tech doesn't get you out of housework!

Further, don't be fooled by the benign appearance of a typical PC, monitor, or printer. Underneath that unassuming beige exterior lurk dozens of voltage-carrying wires and circuits. Any one of these can reach out and bite an unwary tech—sometimes with deadly effect.

Finally, you should appreciate that all PCs and PC components have a finite service life. Where do old monitors, batteries, and toner cartridges go to die?

This chapter covers the important cleaning and maintenance routines that you should follow to keep your system in optimal running condition. These routines take you into the very guts of your PC, so to prevent damage to your PC and to you, it's vital that you use the right tools and follow proper safety precautions. This chapter wraps up with a discussion on how to dispose of dead or obsolete PC equipment properly.

Objective 3.01 Cleaning and Maintenance Procedures

To prolong the life of your PC, you must inspect and clean it regularly. Inspecting your PC alerts you to any dangerous or damaging conditions that exist, such as rust and corrosion, damaged connectors, damaged and improperly installed components, frayed cables, loose connections, and heat damage. Cleaning your PC rids it of the dirt, dust, and grime that build up from normal use. This does more than simply maintain a neat appearance; it helps to prevent two of the most damaging conditions: overheating and electrostatic discharge (ESD).

Local Lingo

ESD ESD is a quick electrical charge that occurs when two objects with different electrical potentials come into contact with each other. For more on this subject, see the section "Electrostatic Discharge Precautions and Procedures" later in this chapter.

Your cleaning routine should include the PC and monitor case, the monitor screen, the keyboard and mouse, and any printer, switch, scanner, and other device connected to the PC. Don't forget the inside of the PC case, the motherboard, adapter cards, drives, and power supply.

Following is a look at the safest cleaning compounds and tools you can use to keep your PC looking and running its best, plus steps for properly cleaning and maintaining your PC, monitor, and peripherals.

Exam Tip	

Regular cleaning of the PC will prolong the life of your components, help to prevent ESD, and help to prevent overheating.

Liquid Cleaning Compounds

You can safely use several kinds of liquid cleaners on the PC, from plain water to specially-formulated commercial compounds.

Clean or Soapy Water

Many cleaning chores require nothing more than a cloth dampened with some clean water. Common tap water is usually fine, but some local water is heavy with minerals and may leave a residue. If this is the case in your area, filtered or distilled water is a better choice.

If water alone cannot do the job, use a mild soap solution. Dish soap is best, but make certain that you dilute it thoroughly.

Denatured Alcohol

Use denatured alcohol to clean electrical contacts and components such as the drive heads on removable media drives. Make certain, however, that you never use alcohol on mechanisms such as motors or rubber drive belts. The alcohol dissolves the lubricants in motor bearings, and rubber belts may stretch or become brittle when exposed to alcohol.

Local Lingo

Denatured alcohol Denatured alcohol is alcohol with stuff added to make it poisonous if consumed. That way, manufacturers can sell it to anyone rather than only to people old enough to drink alcohol. Standard rubbing alcohol, mineral spirits, or isopropyl alcohol with a high percentage of alcohol (think 95 percent) work well for computer components.

Glass Cleaner

Glass cleaners such as Windex are usually safe to use on most metal and plastic surfaces on PCs. Ironically, they're not always recommended for use on a PC's glass surfaces such as the monitor screen. Some monitor screens have special coatings that can be damaged by commercial glass cleaners. In particular, you should never use glass cleaner on older LCD screens. You will melt the screens! Instead, use either clean water or a vinegar and water solution. For modern LCD screens, check the user's manual or the manufacturer's Web site for best practices. Each company has different recommendations for its LCDs.

Vinegar and Water Solution

A solution of one part vinegar to four parts water is great for removing dirt, grime, and fingerprints from surfaces such as your monitor screen, LCD screen, or scanner bed. Use plain white vinegar, not the fancier balsamic or red wine vinegar. Save those for your salads!

Commercial Computer Cleaning Solutions

If you want to save yourself the trouble of custom-brewing your own cleaning solution, try commercial products such as ComputerBrite or ComputerBath. These come in spray form and as pre-moistened towelettes (minus the lemon scent). All of these work just fine, although it's debatable whether they work any better than homemade solutions. Still, if you don't want to lug a jug of white vinegar from job to job, commercial cleaners are a good alternative.

As a general rule, remember to read the labels of any commercial cleaning product before applying it to your PC. If you have any doubts about their safety, contact the manufacturer before using.

Cleaning Tools

Along with your trusty Phillips-head screwdriver and multimeter, a complete PC toolkit should contain the following cleaning tools: canned air, lint-free cloths, a small soft-bristled brush and swabs, and a non-static vacuum. Some techs recommend used fabric softening sheets from your dryer to pick up dust, but avoid using the scratchy ones on LCD screens.

Canned Air

Use canned air to loosen dirt and dust from delicate PC components. Canned air comes in a couple of forms: the liquid propellant kind and the kind that uses small cartridges of compressed CO_2. You can find both at computer stores, office supply stores, camera shops, and big box stores that sell electronics.

Follow three rules when using canned air:

1. Never breathe this stuff in. It's not *that* kind of air, and inhaling it can, quite literally, kill you!

2. With regard to the liquid propellant type of canned air, always keep the can upright. Tilting or turning the can upside down causes the liquid inside to come squirting out. This liquid can cause frostbite to the tech and irreparable damage to any PC components that it touches.

3. Don't shake canned air cans. They don't need to be shaken to work, and you run a small but real risk of the can exploding in your hand.

Lint-Free Cloths

Lint-free cloths such as the type used for cleaning eyeglasses or cameras work well for general PC cleaning. These cloths are better than plain paper towels because they don't leave residue and won't scratch plastic surfaces.

> **Travel Advisory**
>
> Make sure you never use "dry dusting" cleaning products in or on your computer. Products such as the *Swiffer Sweeper* use statically-charged cloths to collect the dust. Static electricity and computers don't mix!

Brushes and Swabs

Try using soft-bristled brushes and lint-free swabs to clean dust and dirt from hard-to-reach areas and to wipe grime from electrical contacts.

Some technicians use rubber pencil erasers to clean contacts, but I don't recommend this practice because some erasers contain acids that can leave a residue or destroy your contacts. Plus, they may rub the metal coating completely off of the contacts—a bad thing.

Non-Static Vacuums

Small, hand-held vacuums designed specifically for use on PCs (shown in Figure 3-1) suck up dirt and dust loosened by your brush or canned air. Note that you should definitely *not* use a common household vacuum cleaner. These create static electricity and can toast your PC!

FIGURE 3.1 A non-static vacuum

Cleaning the Outside of the PC, Monitor, and Peripherals

For regular cleaning, wipe down the exterior of your PC, monitor, and peripherals with a lint-free cloth dampened, not soaked, with clean water. Take care not to drip water or anything else onto or into your PC components.

If you're dealing with a buildup of grime, use a mild soap solution. For harder cleaning chores, such as ink, crayon, and tape adhesive, try using a vinegar and water solution, denatured alcohol diluted with water, or commercial cleaners.

Travel Assistance
Chapter 11 covers printer-specific cleaning and maintenance.

Use canned air to blast dust and hair from air vents and other openings. This helps keep the hot air flowing out and cool air flowing in to maintain the appropriate temperature inside the PC or peripheral. This will extend the life of your computer! When using canned air, remember the words of Cpl. Hicks from the *Aliens* movie, and use "short, controlled bursts." If you haven't dusted it in a while, take the computer or peripheral outside before spraying. Otherwise, you'll spread dust everywhere.

Travel Advisory

Read the label on any commercial cleaning solution before using it on your PC. If you have any doubts, contact the manufacturer before using it.

You can use one or more of these solutions to clean the majority of your PC and peripherals safely and effectively. Because they get the majority of the grime, mice, keyboards, and monitor screens warrant a little more discussion.

Mice

Use a damp cloth to clean the mouse cover, buttons, and ball. Use a swab dipped in denatured alcohol to loosen any dirt, lint, and hair wrapped around the tracking rollers. Tweezers are handy for picking the rollers clean, but avoid scratching the rollers. A quick blast of canned air is a good finishing touch.

Optical mice have no ball to clean, but they do have an optical sensor behind a recessed lens. It's important to keep this lens clean for optimal tracking. A lint-free swab dipped in denatured alcohol diluted with water does a good job.

Keyboards

Keyboards tend to accumulate the most grunge of any of your PC's components. Use canned air and a soft-bristled brush to lift out dirt, crumbs, hair, and other unmentionables from between the keys. Wipe down the exterior thoroughly with a dampened lint-free cloth. If necessary, use soapy water or one of the other cleaning solutions to remove stickier messes, but make sure that you disconnect the keyboard from the computer first. Be careful to avoid dripping cleaning liquids onto or into your keyboard. As a general rule, let your keyboard air-dry for 48 hours before plugging it back into the PC.

Monitor Screens

Monitor screens sometimes take a little extra effort to get clean and streak-free. The vinegar and water solution works quite well on both CRT and LCD monitors, as do commercial cleaners (on CRTs, but not LCDs). Make certain that you never spray cleaners directly onto the screen; always put the cleaner onto a lint-free cloth first. Dripping fluid onto a monitor is a bad thing.

Cleaning Contacts, Connectors, Motherboard, and Components

Once you've got the exterior of your PC and components in tip-top shape, it's time to do the same for your computer's contacts, connectors, motherboard, and components. Before you go tugging on cables and removing the cover of your computer, read the "Electrostatic Discharge Precautions and Procedures" and "Safety and Environmental Issues" sections of this chapter to protect your PC and yourself from electrical hazard.

Contacts and Connectors

Start by unplugging and inspecting the cables from the back of the PC. Look for signs of dirt, rust, or corrosion on the contact pins or sockets. Believe it or not, the main culprit in dirty contacts is you! Your skin contains natural oils, and touching the contacts while handling components leaves behind a small amount of oily residue. Given time, this residue leads to dirt and dust buildup, corrosion, and electrical interference.

The best way to protect your electrical components from becoming dirty is to avoid touching the contact pins, connectors, and sockets. If you must touch the contacts or pins, clean them immediately afterward with a lint-free swab dipped in denatured alcohol.

If you see signs of dirt on the contacts, use a lint-free swab dipped in denatured alcohol to loosen and remove it. You can also use a soft-bristled brush. If you see signs of rust or corrosion, you should replace the cable or component.

Motherboards and Components

Next, remove the PC cover to clean accumulated dust, dirt, and hair off the motherboard and adapter cards. Use canned air to loosen the dust and dirt from the delicate electrical components, and use a non-static vacuum to suck it up. Pay particular attention to the case air vents and the power supply intake and exhaust vents. Note also that dust tends to collect in the door openings of the floppy disk drive and optical drives, and inside the CPU heat sink.

Thoroughly clean any fans you can touch. The fans draw cool air into the computer or push hot air away from components, protecting your computer from overheating. Heat kills electrical components, so it's important to do this right. Don't open the power supply to clean the fan inside! Use the tiny straw that comes with canned air to blow out as much dust as possible.

After you've cleaned out the dust and dirt, check to make sure that the adapter cards and drive cables are properly seated. Follow all of the precautions listed in Objective 3.03 of this chapter to prevent ESD damage while working inside the PC case. When you've finished your inspection and maintenance, put the cover back on the computer and reattach the cables. Plug in the computer as the last step.

Turn on the computer and listen. If you placed the fans and plugged the cables in properly, the computer should sound right and boot nicely. If all does not go well, shut down the computer, open the case, and start with a visual inspection to find whatever's not quite connected properly.

Objective 3.02 # Component Protection and Storage

Computers need electricity to work, as you know, but that same juice can kill a PC or its data if it doesn't flow correctly. This section discusses the causes

of power disturbances and goes over steps and tools you can use to protect working equipment. Components not currently in use also run risks, so this section wraps with a bit about properly storing PC components.

Power Problems

Your computer needs good power to run properly, but various factors can take what should be a steady stream of electricity from the wall socket and turn it into a trickle or a fire hose. It's important that you know how to protect your computing environment from electrical power sags and power losses, power spikes, lightning strikes, and electromagnetic interference. Let's start with a look at the causes of these power problems.

A *brownout* occurs when the supply of electricity drops dramatically but does not go out completely. During a brownout, you'll notice lights flickering or growing dim. When the power rises back up to its original level, your computer might not be able to handle the drastic change and damage may occur.

Blackouts occur when power goes out completely. The danger of a blackout is twofold. First, you may have data loss or corruption when the power goes out. Second, your PC may receive electrical damage from the power surge when the electricity comes back on.

Power spikes or *power surges* occur when the voltage on your power line rises suddenly to above-normal levels. Power spikes are extremely dangerous and can destroy PCs, monitors, and any other component plugged in to the affected power line.

Lightning storms are an underrated hazard. Using a computer or even leaving it plugged in during a lightning storm is asking for trouble. Keep in mind that no accessory can completely protect your PC from the damage caused by a lightning strike.

All electrical equipment puts out a certain amount of electrical noise caused by the signal running through wires, cables, and circuits. *Electromagnetic interference* (EMI) occurs when two signals get too close together and the noise of one is picked up by the other. In computers and networking, this can cause problems, such as wavy screens or slow or corrupted data transfers. Long cable runs tend to pick up EMI, especially if a power cable is running alongside a data cable.

Local Lingo	
EMI	Electromagnetic interference (EMI) occurs when two signals are close enough to each other to interfere with each other.

Saving Your PC from Electrical Problems

Many products help protect a computer from power problems, such as a UPS and a surge protector. Plus, you can prevent certain problems by optimizing the computing space.

Uninterruptible Power Supplies

An *uninterruptible power supply* (UPS) protects your PC from brownouts and blackouts. A UPS has built-in batteries that supply power to your PC when the electricity coming through the power line drops below a certain level. They usually have an integrated alarm that tells you when your PC is running on battery power. Many techs call a UPS a *battery backup*. Note that a UPS does not provide unlimited power so you can keep working while the city lights are out! A UPS gives you a short window of opportunity to save your data and shut the PC down properly.

> ### Local Lingo
>
> **Battery backup** Uninterruptible power supplies are sometimes called a *battery backup*.

UPSs come in two main varieties: *standby power systems* (SPSs) and *online* UPSs. Both of these protect your system in the event of a brownout or blackout, but they work differently and provide different levels of protection.

Standby Power Systems

An SPS actively monitors the electricity coming through the power line and begins supplying power as soon as the unit detects a sag. It takes a split second for the SPS to come online, however, and therein lies the main disadvantage. The brief lapse of time can result in data loss or damage before the SPS has kicked in.

Online UPS

An online UPS, in contrast, acts as a power source to the PC, using the electricity from the AC outlet simply to recharge its internal batteries. If you have an electrical brownout or blackout, your PC doesn't even flinch! Of course, as mentioned earlier, you don't have a tremendous amount of time to work while on batteries, but you certainly have a safe window to save your work and shut down properly before the UPS runs out of juice.

As an added bonus, most online UPS boxes act as power conditioners. That is, they regulate the flow of electricity to your PC to even out any fluctuations you might experience from your power line. An online UPS costs more than an SPS, but in the long run its benefits justify the expense.

Exam Tip	
Don't plug a laser printer into a UPS. Printing draws massive amounts of electricity and may interfere with the function of the UPS and prevent you from shutting down safely.	

Surge Suppressors

Surge suppressors help to absorb power surges so that your computer does not feel their effects. They come as either separate modules or are integrated into the UPS. Good surge suppressors come with long-term or lifetime guarantees against damage to your PC. Avoid purchasing or using cheap surge suppressors. These are usually little more than power strips and provide virtually no protection against power spikes.

Unplug Your PC

Even if you have any or all of the layers of protection listed above, the only sure protection against severe threats such as lightning is to shut down and unplug your PC and peripherals. Leave no stone unturned: make sure that you unplug even your modem, because lightning can travel up the telephone line to give your system a shock. (I've seen it happen, folks!)

Exam Tip	
Make sure you know that in the event of an electrical storm, the only way to protect your system is to unplug it completely, plus all peripherals with external power cords.	

EMI Noise Filters

EMI can be controlled by using cables with a Mylar coating and through the use of special EMI noise filters. Noise filters can be purchased as stand-alone products or are sometimes integrated into a UPS. You can also minimize EMI by moving data cables away from power cables and by shortening the cables you use.

Power fluctuations can wreak havoc on an unprotected PC, and not just in the obvious ways. Surges and sags can damage power supplies and components and cause file corruption. The cost of a good UPS or surge suppressor is nothing compared to the cost in time and money caused by lost components or corrupted files that you may have to endure if you don't use either one.

Storing Components for Future Use

If you plan on storing computer components for future use, you need to protect them from ESD, corrosion, and other damage. (Although a direct strike from lightning would still toast them, other electrical hazards don't apply once components aren't connected.)

Storage Environment

Even when your PC is not in use, heat, moisture, and dirt are still hazards. Heat causes plastics to fade and become brittle, moisture encourages rust and corrosion, and dirt is, well, *dirty*. For these reasons, PC components and peripherals should be stored indoors in a climate-controlled environment.

Electrical Precautions

Take precautions to prevent electrical damage when storing PCs and components. Always store PC equipment away from high-voltage devices, and never store batteries of any kind for long periods of time. Old batteries leak or corrode, so if you are not planning on reusing them during their recommended lifetime, recycle them and purchase new ones as needed.

The safest way to store your components for future use and to protect them from ESD is in to put them in antistatic bags (discussed in the section "Electrostatic Discharge Precautions and Procedures"). For the ultimate in component safety, store the components in their manufacturers' original boxes and packaging. That should be encouraging news to the packrats among you!

Exam Tip

The safest way to store components for future use is in their original packaging or in antistatic bags.

Moisture

Moisture and PCs don't mix. You must control moisture to keep rust and corrosion at bay and ensure that your components are still functional when you return them to service. *Silica-gel* packets are available from electronics stores and shipping supply companies. Place one or more small packets inside your component antistatic bags and inside your PC case. Heed the manufacturers' warnings when using this stuff! It is poisonous, so don't eat it, and don't get any in your eyes.

Objective 3.03

Electrostatic Discharge Precautions and Procedures

ESD is one of the main enemies of your computer. To maintain your computer and prolong the life of components, you need to learn about the effects of ESD and how to protect your computer from those effects.

A prime example of ESD is the small shock you receive when you walk across a carpeted floor and then touch a metal doorknob. *Zap!* The small discharge doesn't cause any lasting damage to your body, but such a seemingly harmless shock will destroy computer components. In fact, even discharges well below the level that you can feel can damage or destroy PC components.

Types of ESD

The types of ESDs that affect computers can be placed into three broad categories: catastrophic damage, hidden damage, and gradual degradation.

Catastrophic ESD Damage

Catastrophic ESD causes a computer component to fail immediately. When catastrophic ESD occurs it will be obvious to you, because, in all likelihood, you will be the one who caused it! Picture the scenario described a couple of paragraphs ago with you walking across a carpeted floor. Only this time, in place of the doorknob, picture an expensive RAID controller, video card, or hard disk full of vital data. Are you concerned yet?

Hidden ESD Damage

Dust buildup on PC components causes *hidden ESD* damage. Over time, this buildup creates a small electrical charge. This charge is not enough to cause obvious damage, and in most cases you will not even be aware that a problem exists

until a component begins to behave erratically. By that point, it is extremely difficult or impossible to pinpoint the original source of the problem. Hidden ESD is a good reason to clean your computer regularly.

ESD Degradation

ESD degradation occurs when the effects of ESD are cumulative. This is caused by situations where low levels of ESD occur repeatedly. Damage caused by ESD degradation is not immediately apparent in full force; instead, the effects gradually get more and more noticeable. Like hidden ESD, degradation will cause your components to behave erratically, and it can make the original problem hard to recognize.

Exam Tip
Make sure that you understand what ESD is, how it can damage your PC, and what you can do to protect against it.

Common ESD Protection Devices

ESD protection devices help to ensure a longer and more productive life for your PC components. These devices include antistatic wrist and ankle straps, antistatic mats, antistatic floor mats, and antistatic bags. Antistatic devices make your body's electrical potential the same as the electrical potential of your PC or component.

Local Lingo
Electrical potential Everything has a certain *electrical potential*, or how charged it is relative to the *zero ground* of the Earth. Note the term *relative.* If your body has a +3000-volt charge and you touch a component that also has a +3000-volt charge (working in the International Space Station, perhaps?), no damage will occur. As far as you and the component are concerned, you're at the same electrical potential. Touch a component that has a −3000-volt charge, on the other hand, and watch the sparks fly!

One of the most important steps you can take to prevent the effects of ESD is grounding yourself before you handle PC components. Do this by touching a metal surface such as the exterior of the PC power supply before touching any of your system components.

Antistatic Wrist and Ankle Straps

Antistatic wrist and ankle straps, fondly called "nerd bracelets" by many techs, keep you at the same relative electrical ground level as the computer components on which you're working. Antistatic straps wrap around your wrist or ankle with an elastic strap attached to a long grounding wire. On some models, the grounding wire attaches to a metal clip that you attach to a metal device to ground yourself. Figure 3-2 shows an antistatic wrist strap grounded to a computer chassis. Others have a prong that you plug into the ground wire of an electrical wall outlet.

> **Travel Advisory**
>
> Antistatic wrist and ankle straps use a one-megohm resistor that is suitable for protection against only very low-level static electricity. They are unsuitable as protection against high voltage and can even make high-voltage shocks more dangerous! Make sure that you always remove your antistatic strap before working on or near high-voltage components.

By the way, don't forget to remove your antistatic strap before walking away from your work area! Or, if you forget frequently, try to leave a camcorder running so you'll have something funny to show at your next family reunion.

FIGURE 3.2 An antistatic wrist strap grounded to a computer

Antistatic Mats

Portable antistatic mats provide a work surface that dissipates ESD. They look much like large place mats or those baby-changing mats that come with diaper bags. The thing that distinguishes them is that they have a small metal clip that you can attach to an antistatic strap to ground out ESD. In addition to helping prevent ESD, these mats help keep your work area organized by giving you a place to put your tools and components while you work.

Antistatic Floor Mats

Antistatic floor mats are basically the same as portable antistatic mats, except much larger. Instead of placing them on top of your work area, you place your work area on top of the antistatic floor mat.

Antistatic Bags

Antistatic bags have a special coating or contain small filaments that help dissipate any static charge. Always store adapter cards and drives in antistatic bags when not in use and when transporting—even if you're just going down the hall or across the room. Note that regular plastic or paper bags will *not* protect your components. In fact, plastic baggies conduct static electricity rather than prevent it, so don't use them!

> **Travel Advisory**
>
> Special antistatic sprays dissipate static charges built up in your clothing. Commonly used to prevent unsightly static "cling," they are also good to use before you start working on PCs. Some folks also use these sprays to try to protect their work areas from the effects of ESD, but this is not an effective or recommended procedure. Never use these sprays directly on your components!

Safety and Environmental Issues

Certain factors increase the risk of injury, both to the computer and to the tech. Some factors you can control—such as what you wear when working on PCs—and some you can't, such as the weather. You simply need to know and avoid other issues to stay safe.

Tech-Controlled Factors

Take control of the computing environment to minimize the risk of damage to you or to any computers around you. You make all the difference when it comes to what you wear and how orderly or disorderly the computer space is kept. Plus, you need to use the proper tool for the job at hand and, if anything goes wrong, report it properly.

What to Wear?

What you wear, including your hairdo (I'm serious!), affects both the risk of electrostatic discharge and electrical shorts. Different fabrics have different electrical potentials. Wear natural-fiber clothing, such as cotton or linen, when working on computers. Don't wear silk, though, because it picks up static electricity. Definitely avoid synthetic fabrics. They have a tendency to *produce* static electricity. If you needed an excuse to give the double-knit polyester leisure suit to charity, now you have one! Finally, wear rubber-soled shoes rather than leather-soled shoes.

Keep your hair short or pulled back away from the computer. I've seen techs with long hair shock a computer by brushing it with their hair. That's never fun!

Rings, bracelets, necklaces, watches, and other metal adornments can short out devices if touched on the wrong part of your PC. They can also scratch (or be scratched) by scraping against the PCs surfaces. Remove jewelry and watches before working on or inside of your PC. Just remember to put your wedding ring back on before you head home to the spouse!

Control Those Cords!

A disorderly computing environment invites problems, so successful techs keep it neat. People place computers or peripherals in crazy places: on rickety desks, cardboard boxes, and other places where the chances of dropping are high (Figure 3-3). Arrange your computer and peripherals safely on the floor or a sturdy desk. Tape or cover cords running along the ground to avoid people tripping on

FIGURE 3.3 Don't do this!

them or accidentally ripping a computer off a desk—two very not-funny options. If you see a potential hazard at a work site—even one that's not yours—report it or fix it. You're the expert, so take charge!

Use the Right Tool for the Job

Whenever possible, use the tool designed to do the job at hand. This might seem obvious to most of you, but don't use a knife when you need a screwdriver. Don't use a screwdriver designed for large heads on small-head screws. Using the wrong tool for a job can cost you both in time and equipment. Bleeding all over a motherboard you just sliced into would just add insult to injury, so avoid it!

Incident Reports

When accidents happen—and they will—at the workplace, always provide an *incident report* that details the accident, conditions that contributed, and, if you

know, the cost to replace the equipment damaged. A small company might accept a verbal report; larger companies most likely prefer a formal, written report.

Environmental Factors

The temperature and humidity both in the computing environment and out-side the office can make an impressive impact on the functioning and life of a computer. By and large, computers don't do heat but can handle humidity to a certain point. Even with all fans clean and whirring nicely, a computer in a hot environment can overheat. Overheating causes electrical components to fail, never a good thing! Try to keep any running computer in a temperate or cool environment.

Good techs keep up with weather conditions. Believe it or not, the tem-perature and humidity level *outside* can dramatically affect the risk of ESD *inside*. If the weather is cold and dry, the potential for a PC-killing zap is greatly increased. Take extra precautions to prevent ESD when the weather calls for it.

High-Voltage Equipment

The capacitors in PC power supplies, monitors, and laser printers carry very high voltages that can cause severe injury or death. Fortunately, manufacturers mark high-voltage equipment with a bright yellow warning sticker, making it easy to identify. Watch for these labels and heed them!

Further, any time you work with a piece of high-voltage equipment, make sure the device is unplugged and that you have *removed* your antista-tic wrist strap.

Power Supplies

In the old days, the conventional thinking was that you should leave the PC plugged in while working inside it to ensure electrical grounding. The opposite is true for modern PCs, because modern motherboards always have a small amount of voltage running anytime the PC is plugged in, even if it's not run-ning. Therefore, you should completely unplug the PC before servicing or you'll likely toast something!

Unplugging power supplies does not make them safe enough to work on. The capacitors inside can hold a lethal charge even when unplugged, making them extremely risky to open. As the label says, "There are no user serviceable parts inside." With that in mind, the safest method of repairing power supplies is not to repair them at all. Better to dispose of them properly (as discussed in the

section "Special Disposal Procedures and Environmental Protection Guide-lines" of this chapter) and install a brand-new power supply.

Travel Advisory

As electricians will tell you, it's amperage (the amount of electricity) that's dangerous, not voltage. Power supplies have relatively low voltages, but high amperage. It's not worth the risk to attempt to service a power supply.

Monitors

Let's keep this section short and to the point—*never* open the case of a CRT monitor! As with power supplies, they are not designed to be serviced by field techs. Return damaged or malfunctioning monitors to the manufacturer for servicing or to a qualified monitor repair shop.

Take care when moving CRT monitors. Watch for cords and other tripping factors. Every CRT has a vacuum tube inside that will implode if cracked. Implode or explode, you're still going to be showered with glass if you drop one.

Fires

Thankfully, the risk of fire occurring inside your PC is relatively low. If, however, you do experience a computer fire, or any electrical fire for that matter, never try to extinguish it with water. This can cause the electrical current to travel up and straight into you! Instead, use a fire extinguisher certified for fighting electrical fires. These are type C and type ABC fire extinguishers.

Exam Tip

Make sure that you know that you need to use a type C or type ABC fire extinguisher to put out a fire in a computer.

Objective 3.05

Special Disposal Procedures and Environmental Protection Guidelines

Many computer components, such as batteries, CRTs, chemical solvents, and toner kits, contain harmful ingredients. Don't throw these items in the garbage as this is wasteful and possibly illegal. Recycle, recycle, recycle! If you can't recycle an item, dispose of it properly. We all share the same planet.

Different cities and counties have different requirements for safe disposal of materials such as PC components. Always check with the appropriate authorities before tossing that old Pentium on the curb! Look in the government pages in your local telephone book or your city's official Web site for more information.

Exam Tip

Make sure you know the proper disposal procedures for each of the following items prior to taking the exam.

Batteries

Batteries often contain lithium, mercury, nickel-cadmium, and other hazardous materials. If they are thrown in the garbage and carried off to a landfill, they will contaminate the water and soil. Take batteries to a recycling center or send them back to the manufacturer. Most batteries have disposal instructions printed on them. Familiarize yourself with these instructions and follow them.

CRTs

Many CRT monitors contain lead. Lead is poisonous, so CRTs must be disposed of properly to avoid contamination. To dispose of nonfunctional CRTs, send them to a commercial recycler or contact your city's hazardous waste management department. They will give you the proper procedure for disposing of them.

Toner and Inkjet Cartridges

You have a couple of options when dealing with depleted toner and inkjet cartridges. You can refill them yourself, which saves on environmental wear, but can wreak havoc on your printer if this is not done properly. You can also check the Yellow Pages to see if commercial toner recyclers service your area. Alternately, many toner cartridge manufacturers have a recycling program. Check with your vendor and see if this is an option for you.

Chemical Solvents and Cans

Chemical solvents or canned products for PC use (such as canned air mentioned earlier) contain harmful chemicals that should not be loosed in the environment. Instead, dispose of these through your city's hazardous waste program or by following your local chemical disposal rules.

Material Safety Data Sheet

All batteries, chemicals, and other hazardous materials come with a *Material Safety Data Sheet* (MSDS) that documents any safety warnings about the product, safe methods of transportation, and safe disposal requirements. If you have any doubts or questions about how to handle and dispose of chemicals or compounds, check the MSDS. If an item comes without an MSDS, you can obtain one from the manufacturer or you can locate one on the Internet.

Travel Assistance

For more information about MSDSs, or to search for an MSDS, visit http://www.msdssearch.com/.

CHECKPOINT

✔**Objective 3.01: Cleaning and Maintenance Procedures** You should regularly inspect and clean your PC and peripherals. Plain water or a solution of mild soap and water does a great job of cleaning most PC surfaces. Canned air, non-static vacuums, and soft-bristled brushes help maintain a clean PC. Electrical contacts get dirty from the oily residue from your fingers, so you should exercise care in handling components. Denatured alcohol is the best solution to use for cleaning drive heads and contacts. Keep fans and vents clean and dust free to protect a computer from overheating.

✔**Objective 3.02: Component Protection and Storage** A UPS protects your system against power sags, and a surge suppressor protects your system from power surges. Noise filters help prevent electromagnetic interference. In the event of a lightning storm, make sure you completely unplug the PC and any peripherals with external power cords. When storing components for future use, make sure to store them in a cool, dry place in antistatic bags or in their original packaging.

✔**Objective 3.03: Electrostatic Discharge Precautions and Procedures** To help protect your system from the effects of ESD, always use an antistatic wrist strap or ankle strap unless working around high-voltage devices such as power supplies and CRTs. Antistatic mats, floor mats, and sprays can protect your work area.

✔**Objective 3.04: Safety and Environmental Issues** Wear natural-fiber cloth-
ing and rubber-soled shoes when working on computers. Keep your hair
pulled back and remove excess jewelry. Keep the computing environment
neat, but if accidents happen, file an incident report. The capacitors in power
supplies, monitors, and laser printers carry very high voltages that can cause
severe bodily injuries. Don't touch them! This is especially true for CRT
monitors, which carry *deadly* levels of electricity even after being unplugged.

✔**Objective 3.05: Special Disposal Procedures and Environmental Guidelines**
Batteries contain nasty chemicals, CRTs contain lead, and even innocuous
seeming toner cartridges contain environmentally unfriendly chemicals.
Always be sure to recycle batteries, monitors, and toner cartridges, or have
them picked up as hazardous waste.

REVIEW QUESTIONS

1. What should you use to clean a mouse ball? (Select two.)
 A. Glass cleaner
 B. A damp cloth
 C. Denatured alcohol
 D. Pencil erasers

2. After wiping down your keyboard with a mild cleaning solution, what
 should you do?
 A. Use canned air to dry it out.
 B. Use antistatic spray to give it a protective coating.
 C. Use a pencil eraser to clean the contact pins.
 D. Let it air-dry for 48 hours.

3. Which of the following products will do the best job of completely
 removing the dust from your computer? (Select two.)
 A. Lint-free cloths
 B. Canned air
 C. Non-static vacuums
 D. Paint brushes

4. What type of fire extinguisher should you use to put out a PC fire?
 A. Type A
 B. Type B

 C. Type C

 D. Type D

5. When should you always remove your antistatic wrist strap?

 A. When working around high-voltage devices such as power supplies and CRTs

 B. When cleaning your PC

 C. When changing a toner cartridge in your printer

 D. You should never remove your antistatic wrist strap.

6. If you use an antistatic wrist strap with a prong, where do you attach the prong?

 A. To the grounding wire of a wall outlet

 B. In the slot of a wall outlet

 C. In a special hole that is incorporated into every PC case

 D. Into the back of the power supply

7. If you do not receive an MSDS with a product, where can you obtain one? (Select two.)

 A. The Internet

 B. The outside of the box the product came in

 C. The manufacturer

 D. Any good technical book

8. Which of the following should you avoid using on LCD displays?

 A. Distilled water

 B. Commercial glass cleaners

 C. Mild soap solution

 D. Vinegar and water solution

9. What are two proper ways to dispose of CRTs?

 A. Throw them in the garbage.

 B. Recycle them.

 C. Have them picked up by a hazardous waste program.

 D. There is no proper way to dispose of a CRT.

10. What should the conditions be like in the area where you store computer components? (Select two.)

 A. Cool

 B. Warm

 C. Humid

 D. Dry

11. What weather conditions are most likely to be associated with ESD? (Select two.)

 A. When it is cold

 B. When it is dry

 C. When it is hot

 D. When it is humid

12. How can you protect your PC in the event of a lightning storm?

 A. With a UPS

 B. With a suppressor

 C. By unplugging the PC and all of its components

 D. By turning off the PC

REVIEW ANSWERS

1. **B** **C** Use a damp cloth to clean the mouse cover, buttons and ball. Use a swab dipped in denatured alcohol to loosen any dirt, lint, and hair wrapped around the tracking rollers.

2. **D** Let the keyboard air-dry for 48 hours before plugging it back into the computer.

3. **B** **C** Canned air loosens dirt and dust. Non-static vacuums remove the dust from your system.

4. **C** You would use a type C fire extinguisher to put out a PC or other electrical fire. If a choice on the exam is a type ABC, that type of fire extinguisher can also be used.

5. **A** You should always remove your antistatic wrist strap when working around CRTs and power supplies. The wrist strap provides a connection from the PC to your body, and wearing a wrist strap while working on either of these components could cause your body to absorb extremely high electrical charges, which could harm or kill you.

6. **A** If you are using an antistatic wrist strap with a prong, the prong should be attached in the wire ground of a wall outlet. The wire ground is the round hole—*never* place the prong in one of the slots because they contain electricity.

7. **A C** If you do not receive an MSDS with a product, you can obtain one from the manufacturer or you can find one on the Internet. Technical books won't have MSDS information, and you won't find it on the outside of the box.

8. **B** Commercial glass cleaners such as Windex will melt LCD display screens. Use plain or mildly soapy water or a vinegar and water solution to clean LCDs.

9. **B C** The proper way to dispose of CRTs is to either recycle them or have them picked up by a hazardous waste program. CRTs often contain lead, so you can't throw them in a landfill because they could contaminate the water supply.

10. **A D** The area where you store computer components should be kept cool and dry. PC components do not like extreme heat, and condensation could cause corrosion.

11. **A B** ESD is most likely to occur when it is cold and dry.

12. **C** The only way to protect your system in the event of an electrical storm is to unplug it and all of its components. Simply turning off the machine or using a suppressor will not fully protect your system.

Motherboards, Power Supplies, and Cases

CHAPTER 4

ETA

NEWBIE	SOME EXPERIENCE	EXPERT
5 hours	3 hours	2 hours

At the heart of all personal computers live certain core components. The *motherboard* provides the framework upon which every other component builds. The *power supply* provides DC current to feed the hungry motherboard and components and makes everything chug along happily. The *case* or *system unit* holds it all together. Don't think that all cases are created equal, however, as subtle differences between identical-looking cases can influence how difficult it is to upgrade and service the PC. Every good tech needs to understand these basic ingredients of the PC, including their common variants.

Objective 4.01 Motherboards

E very device in your computer system connects either directly or indirectly to the motherboard. The motherboard, in essence, defines the type of computer you have.

> **Local Lingo**
>
> **System boards, mobos** Many PC techs call motherboards *system boards* or *mobos*.

Manufacturers decide three things when creating a new motherboard. First, they select the set of chips—appropriately called the *chipset*—that provide support for everything that plugs into the motherboard. Second, they select a style of motherboard, the *form factor*, that defines the size and shape, among other things. Finally, manufacturers decide which connectors to include for both internal and external devices.

This section looks at chipsets, form factors, and connections available on motherboards. It wraps with notes on installation and troubleshooting.

Chipsets

Every motherboard has a chipset that determines the type of processor the motherboard accepts, the type and capacity of RAM, and what sort of internal and external devices the motherboard supports. The chips in a PC's chipset serve as electronic interfaces through which the CPU, RAM, and input/output devices interact. Chipsets vary in feature, performance, and stability, so they factor hugely in the purchase or recommendation of a particular motherboard. Most modern chipsets are composed of two primary chips—the *Northbridge* and the *Southbridge* (Figure 4.1).

FIGURE 4.1 Northbridge and Southbridge

The Northbridge chip on Intel-based motherboards helps the CPU work with RAM. On AMD-based motherboards, the Northbridge provides the communication with the video card, rather than memory, because the memory controller is built into the CPU. Current Northbridge chips do a lot and thus get pretty hot, so they have their own heat sink and fan assembly (Figure 4.2).

FIGURE 4.2 Heat sink and fan on a Northbridge

The Southbridge handles some expansion devices and mass storage drives, such as hard drives. Most Southbridge chips don't need extra cooling, leaving the chip exposed or passively cooled with only a heat sink. This makes the Southbridge a great place to see the manufacturer of the chipset, such as Intel Corporation (Figure 4.3).

Most motherboards support old technologies such as floppy drives, parallel ports, and serial ports. Although supporting these old devices was once part of the Southbridge's job, hardly any modern chipsets still support these devices. Motherboard manufacturers add a third chip called the *Super I/O chip* to handle these chores. Figure 4.4 shows a typical Super I/O chip.

Travel Advisory

Super I/O chips work with chipsets but are not part of the chipset. Motherboard makers purchase them separately from chipsets.

FIGURE 4.3 An Intel Southbridge chip on a motherboard

FIGURE 4.4 Super I/O chip on ASUS motherboard

The system ROM chip provides part of the BIOS for the chipset, but only a barebones, generic level of support. The chipset still needs support for the rest of the things it can do, so it requires drivers loaded from a CD or downloaded from the manufacturer.

Travel Assistance

Chapter 7 covers the system BIOS and system ROM chip in detail.

Four companies make the vast majority of chipsets for PCs: Intel, VIA, NVIDIA, and AMD through its ATI brand. With the exception of Intel, every chipset maker has chipsets for Intel and AMD processors, so you need to pay attention when purchasing or recommending a particular motherboard. You can buy an NVIDIA nForce 590-based motherboard that supports an AMD Athlon 64, for example, or an NVIDIA nForce 590-based motherboard that supports an Intel Core 2 Duo processor. They're not interchangeable!

Travel Advisory

Just like most devices, motherboards ship with dated drivers. Smart techs download the updated drivers from the manufacturer's Web site.

Motherboard Form Factors

Most motherboards come in one of two form factors, ATX or BTX, plus you'll see a sprinkling of proprietary and other form factor motherboards out there as well. Each form factor has several varieties.

The form factor defines the motherboard's size, its orientation, the location of built-in sockets and expansion slots, and so on. The motherboard's form factor determines the type of power supply and case a PC can use. Form factors are not interchangeable. That means that ATX motherboards fit into ATX cases, and BTX motherboards fit into BTX cases.

ATX

ATX motherboards, as shown in Figure 4.5, have a central Northbridge chip encircled by the CPU, RAM, drive, and power connections; expansion slots; and connections for external devices. ATX motherboards use mini-DIN (PS/2) connectors for the keyboard and mouse, and most have integrated USB ports. Many also feature onboard modem and NIC ports, FireWire ports, sound, and video. ATX motherboards dominate the PC market.

Two popular variations of the ATX form factor are *microATX* and *FlexATX*. These use the same power connections and have the same basic layout as ATX but are scaled to fit into much smaller ATX cases. Full-sized ATX motherboards will not fit into microATX or FlexATX cases, although most full-sized cases support the smaller motherboards.

FIGURE 4.5 microATX motherboard

BTX

Fast CPUs and powerful graphics cards in today's PCs create phenomenal amounts of heat, which motivated the PC industry to create the "coolest" form factor used today—the Balanced Technology eXtended (BTX) form factor (Figure 4.6). BTX defines three subtypes: standard BTX, microBTX, and picoBTX, designed to replace ATX, microATX, and FlexATX, respectively. At first glance, BTX looks like ATX, but notice that the I/O ports and the expansion slots have switched sides.

Everything in the BTX standard is designed to improve cooling. BTX cases vent in cool air from the front and vent out warm air in the back. CPUs are moved to the front of the motherboard so they benefit from the cool air entering the front of the case. BTX defines a special heat sink and fan assembly called the *thermal unit*. The thermal unit's fan blows the hot CPU air directly out the back of the case, as opposed to the ATX method of just blowing the air into the case and letting the power supply and case fans pull air out.

The BTX standard offers better cooling than ATX, but the PC industry tends to take its time when making big changes like moving to a new form factor. As a result, BTX has not yet made much of an impact in the industry, and BTX motherboards, cases, and thermal units are still fairly rare.

FIGURE 4.6 microBTX motherboard

Proprietary Form Factors

Several major PC makers, including Dell and Sony, make motherboards that work only with their cases. These *proprietary* motherboards enable these companies to create systems that stand out from the generic ones and, not coincidently, push you to get service and upgrades from their authorized dealers. Some of the features you'll see in proprietary systems are riser boards like you see with the NLX form factor—part of a motherboard separate from the main one, but connected by a cable of some sort—and unique power connections. Proprietary motherboards drive techs crazy as replacement parts tend to cost more and are not readily available.

Motherboard Connections

Motherboards today come with connectors to support literally dozens of devices, from the core components of CPU and memory, to sophisticated high-speed networking. You've already seen the most common integrated I/O ports in Chapter 2, which covered serial, parallel, keyboard, mouse, video, audio, multimedia, MIDI/joystick, modem, network, USB, FireWire, and SCSI ports. Six of the next seven chapters of this book cover the rest: CPU, RAM, hard drives, removable drives, and expansion slots. (There's no reason to go through any of these in any detail in this chapter.)

When you upgrade or recommend an upgrade, you must address one question: Can the hardware do the job desired by your client? If your client wants to play the latest and greatest games, for example, you need to look at his or her machine and determine its capability. Can it handle a powerful enough CPU? Does the motherboard have enough RAM slots to install 2+ GB of memory? Does the chipset support that much? Look at the expansion slot for the video card. Is it AGP or PCI Express? Does it have the number and type of expansion slots needed for future growth (Figure 4.7)?

If your client wants to get a new, high-speed scanner—a more mundane example—you need to weigh several factors. If the motherboard has a FireWire port, just recommend a FireWire-capable scanner and the client is set. If the motherboard has USB but not FireWire, on the other hand, you need to determine whether the USB is Hi-Speed or plain vanilla USB. If the latter, buying a Hi-Speed USB–capable scanner and plugging it into the lower speed connection would work, but would the client be getting his money's worth? Of course not! So a good recommendation to overcome this motherboard limitation would be to go for the Hi-Speed scanner and install a Hi-Speed USB controller into an expansion slot. By examining the capabilities and limitations of specific motherboards, you can provide the right experience for your clients.

PCI

PCI Express

FIGURE 4.7 Sweet! A mobo with both PCI Express and PCI!

Installing a Motherboard

Installing or replacing a motherboard requires you to go through a couple of simple steps. First, install the motherboard into a case designed for the motherboard. Most system boards come with an I/O shield that matches the external I/O connectors on the motherboard, so you might have to replace the one that's in the case before you can insert the new motherboard. Second, adjust the standouts on the case to align with the mounting holes in the motherboard. Third, angle the motherboard into the I/O shield (Figure 4.8) and screw it down snugly. Plug in power, CPU, RAM, fans, and video, and you're ready to go.

Troubleshooting Motherboards

Motherboards can go bad over time because of external factors such as power spikes and sags, electrostatic discharge, or excessive heat. A motherboard can be faulty right out of the box, so if you run into a new system that you have trouble getting to work, you can add the new motherboard to the list as a possible culprit.

FIGURE 4.8 Installing a motherboard (note spare I/O shield)

Troubleshooting motherboards—even in a new installation—can drive a tech to distraction, because the symptoms of a failing motherboard range from devices not working to intermittent lockups. What would you suspect first if a network card that worked before a storm didn't work after a storm? The card seems the logical suspect and that's what you'd check first, but the motherboard could have taken a hit from the storm and have a few electrons jangling loose. This is especially true in motherboards with built-in NICs.

Travel Advisory

You can update a motherboard's internal drivers through a process called *flashing the BIOS*. You can also turn a motherboard into an inert piece of wall art easily by flashing the BIOS incorrectly or having an error occur during the flashing process. *There's no recovery* from a flashing failure, so be careful! See Chapter 7, "BIOS and CMOS," for the scoop on flashing the BIOS.

When you suspect a motherboard has gone or is going bad, replace it. A computer must have a rock-solid foundation, and a buggy motherboard is simply not acceptable.

Objective 4.02 Power Supplies

The PC's power supply (Figure 4.9) converts high-voltage alternating current (AC) power into the lower voltage direct current (DC) power that your motherboard and drives need. Its internal fan also provides essential cooling for the PC components and drives. In the United States, standard AC comes in somewhere between 110 and 120 volts, often written as ~115 VAC. Most of the rest of the world uses 220–240 VAC, so many power supplies have a little switch in the back so you can use them anywhere.

Exam Tip	
Remember that the power connector for the AC plug on the back of a power supply is called an *IEC 320* connector.	

Power supplies come in various form factors that determine the physical size and shape, as well as the types of connectors you'll find. Power supplies vary in output and efficiency.

Cooling fan

Power switch

Port for power cord

Cables to deliver power to the system

FIGURE 4.9 Power supply

> ### Exam Tip
>
> Look for the acronym *PSU*, for *power supply unit*, on the CompTIA A+ exams. Most techs refer to power supplies using the full words rather than the acronym.

Power Supply Form Factors

Power supply form factors more or less mirror motherboard form factors. ATX power supplies are the most common, and they plug into all sizes of ATX and BTX motherboards. You can find smaller power supplies that fit microATX, FlexATX, and microBTX motherboards as well. Finally, manufacturers have created all sorts of proprietary power supplies that come in all shapes and sizes (Figure 4.10).

Power Supply Connectors

Power supplies offer several connectors for the motherboard and drives. All have four-wire *mini* and Molex connectors for floppy, parallel ATA (PATA), and small computer system interface (SCSI) drives, and most have serial ATA

FIGURE 4.10 Proprietary power supply

FIGURE 4.11 Mini, Molex, and SATA power connectors (left to right)

(SATA) connectors for SATA drives (Figure 4.11). Better power supplies have a dedicated six-wire *PCIe* connector for PCI Express video cards (Figure 4.12).

Power supplies connect to the motherboard with up to four connectors: the 20- or 24-wire *P1* connector, the primary power circuit; a 4-wire *P4* connector to add another 12-volt circuit (or *rail*, as techs say) to the motherboard to add stability; and a 6-wire auxiliary connector (referred to as an *AUX* connector) that very few motherboards use (Figure 4.13). Table 4.1 lists the common connectors of the *ATX12V* power supplies—the current standard—with their voltages and uses.

Exam Tip

The 5-volt orange wire on the P1 connector is called *power good* and is used in the initial boot sequence. See Chapter 7 for the boot sequence.

FIGURE 4.12 PCIe power connector

FIGURE 4.13 P1, P4, and AUX connectors (left to right)

Travel Advisory

All power connectors are keyed so you can't easily plug them in backward. The mini socket keying on floppy drives is often flimsy, though, so you need to take care with them. Reversing the power on a device will destroy that device, because you're plugging a 12-volt wire into a 5-volt circuit. That's a bad thing!

TABLE 4.1 Power Connectors and Voltages

Connector	Voltages	Common Use
Molex	5 V, 12 V	PATA and SCSI hard drives and optical drives; some PCIe video cards; some PCIe motherboards
Mini	5 V, 12 V	Floppy drives
SATA	5 V, 12 V	SATA drives
PCIe	12 V	PCIe video cards
P1 (20-wire)	3.3 V, 5 V, 12 V	Primary power for older ATX motherboards
P1 (24-wire)	3.3 V, 5 V, 12 V	Primary power for current ATX motherboards
P4	12 V	Secondary power for current ATX motherboards
AUX	3.3 V, 5 V, 12 V	Auxiliary power for motherboards

Output—Wattage and Harmonics

Power supplies provide a certain amount of *wattage* that the motherboard, drives, and fans draw on to run. That's the desired output. Power supplies also produce *harmonics*, the hum you hear when the power supply runs, that can cause problems if not controlled.

Local Lingo
Wattage Wattage is the amount of amperage flowing at a specific voltage, usually written as W=VA.

A PC requires sufficient wattage to run properly. Every device in a PC also requires a certain amount of wattage in order to function. A typical hard drive draws 15 watts of power when accessed, for example, whereas some Athlon 64 X2 CPUs draw a whopping 110 watts at peak usage—with average usage around 70 watts. The total wattage of all devices combined is the minimum you need the power supply to provide.

If the power supply cannot produce the wattage needed by a system, that PC won't work properly. Because most devices in the PC require maximum wattage when first starting, the most common result of insufficient wattage is a paperweight that looks like a PC. The only fixes for this problem are to remove a device from the PC—such as the new hard drive you just plugged in—or get a power supply with more wattage. Today's PCs require 400+ watt power supplies to function.

Good PC power supplies come with *active power factor correction (active PFC)*, extra circuitry that smoothes out the way the power supply takes power from the power company and eliminates harmonics. Older and poorer power supplies don't have this circuitry and should not be used if at all possible.

Most active PFC power supplies are *auto-sensing*, meaning they can detect the voltage coming from the wall and adjust accordingly. You can use an auto-sensing power supply anywhere in the world, from the ~115 VAC in New York City to the ~230 in Hong Kong. This is especially important with portable computers!

Troubleshooting Power Supplies

Power supplies fail in two ways: sudden death and slowly over time. When they die suddenly, the computer will not start and the fan in the power supply will not turn. In this case, verify that electricity is getting to the power supply before you do anything else. Assuming that the system has electricity, the best way to

verify that a power supply is working or not working is to check the voltages coming out of the power supply with a multimeter (Figure 4.14).

The voltages supplied by most PC power supplies can safely vary by as much as ±10 percent of their stated values. This means that the 12-volt line can vary from roughly 10.5 to 12.9 volts without exceeding the tolerance of the various systems in the PC. The 5.0- and 3.3-volt lines offer similar tolerances.

If the power supply fails to provide power, throw it into the recycling bin and get a new one. Do *not* open a power supply and try to service it yourself, because it contains dangerously high-voltage capacitors.

When power supplies die slowly, bad things begin to happen to the computer intermittently. The computer locks up every once in a while, for example, or it takes two tries before it boots up in the morning. Because a Blue Screen of Death (BSoD) in Windows can be caused by a lot of things, diagnosing a lockup as a power supply problem is tough to do. The key is the word *intermittent*. If you run into phantom problems, switch out the power supply to see if that makes a difference. Every tech should have a known-good power supply as a *field replaceable unit* (*FRU*).

Many devices in the computing world use an AC adapter (Figure 4.15) rather than an internal power supply. Even though it sits outside a device, an AC adapter converts AC current to DC, just like a power supply. Unlike power supplies, AC adapters are rarely interchangeable. Although manufacturers of different devices often use the same kind of plug on the end of the AC adapter cable,

FIGURE 4.14 Testing one of the 5-volt DC connections

FIGURE 4.15 AC adapter

these adapters are not necessarily interchangeable. Just because you can plug an AC adapter from your friend's laptop into your laptop does not mean it's going to work!

You need to make sure that three things match before you plug an AC adapter into a device: voltage, amperage, and polarity. If the voltage or amperage output is too low, the device won't run. If the polarity is reversed, it won't work—just like putting in a battery backward in a flashlight. If the voltage or amperage—especially the latter—is too high, on the other hand, you can quickly toast your device. Don't do it! Always check the voltage, amperage, and polarity of a replacement AC adapter before you plug it into a device.

 Objective 4.03 # Cases

Cases come in six basic sizes: slimline, desktop, mini-tower, mid-tower, tower, and cube. Slimline and desktop models generally sit on the desk, beneath the monitor. The various tower cases usually occupy a bit of floor space next to the desk. The mini-tower and mid-tower cases are the most popular choices. Make sure you get a case that will fit your motherboard—many microATX and all FlexATX cases are too small for a regular ATX motherboard. Cube cases generally require a specific motherboard, so be prepared to buy both pieces at once. A quick test fit before you buy saves a lot of return trips to the supplier.

Exam Tip

The six case sizes listed here apply only to consumer or workstation PCs. Server PCs come in several different varieties, such as huge dual-power supply behemoths and rack-mounted systems too svelte to handle a normal expansion card. The CompTIA A+ certification exams test you only on the consumer or workstation models.

The typical case has four screws on the back, two of which you remove with a Phillips-head screwdriver. This releases the side panel and enables access to the interior of the case. Panels slide into a slot so they should fit snugly.

Vendors such as Alienware offer myriad colors and exotic body styling. More important, these cases are outfitted with detailing that enhances the PC's function, such as additional cooling fans or liquid cooling systems, high-output power supplies, cable management systems, roomier interiors, screwless body panels (these require no tools to remove), and such welcome touches as front-mounted USB, FireWire, and sound ports.

Other design features that separate better PC cases from lower-quality models are finished edges (these prevent nasty scrapes both to your knuckles and to cables), quick-release drive bays (Figure 4.16), a detachable mother-board mount tray, and a removable front *bezel*, or faceplate. The more you work on PCs, the more you'll appreciate how these small features make it easier for you to service them.

If you're looking for pure aesthetic flash, case modification (mod) kits are available to trick out your boring beige box with neon and fiber-optic lighting, see-through acrylic panels, special LED speed and temperature displays, and fancy multimedia control panels. These do nothing to enhance a PC's perfor-

FIGURE 4.16 PC case with quick-release drive bays

mance or reliability, nor do they make them easier for techs to service, but they sure are cool to look at!

CHECKPOINT

✔ **Objective 4.01: Motherboards** All motherboards have a chipset—Northbridge and Southbridge, plus Super I/O—to provide support for everything that plugs into the motherboard, including the CPU, RAM, drives, and integrated I/O devices. The ATX form factor—including full-sized, microATX, and FlexATX—dominates the PC market, but BTX is on the horizon. Motherboards support literally dozens of device types through integrated I/O and expansion slots. Installing is a matter of placing standouts properly and screwing down the motherboard. Troubleshooting is tough, though, because of all the variables in the computer, but the fix for a bad motherboard is simple: replace it.

✔ **Objective 4.02: Power Supplies** The PSU converts AC power into the DC power that your motherboard and drives need. Its internal fan also provides essential cooling for the PC components and drives. ATX power supplies dominate the market and plug into all three ATX and both BTX form factor motherboards. You'll find up to seven connectors on power supplies—Molex, mini, SATA, PCIe, P1, P4, and AUX—for drives, video cards, and motherboards. Power supplies are rated in wattage, such as 400-watt or 1-kilowatt; plus better PSUs employ active PFC to stop harmonics. Power supplies die suddenly or slowly over time. With the latter, the clue is intermittent problems. Replace, don't try to fix, a dead or dying power supply.

✔ **Objective 4.03: Cases** PC cases come in six basic sizes: slimline, desktop, mini-tower, mid-tower, tower, and cube. Make sure you get a case that will fit your motherboard—many microATX and all FlexATX cases are too small for a regular ATX motherboard. Cube cases generally require a specific motherboard, so be prepared to buy both pieces at once.

REVIEW QUESTIONS

1. What part of the PC is the framework on which everything builds?

 A. I/O buses

 B. Expansion slots

 C. CPU

 D. Motherboard

2. Which of the following motherboards are you most likely to see in modern PCs? (Select two.)

 A. AT

 B. ATX

 C. Baby ATX

 D. microATX

3. If you have a PC with an ATX motherboard and case and you decide you would like to upgrade the motherboard, can you replace it with a BTX motherboard?

 A. No

 B. Yes, if you reset the jumpers

 C. Yes, if you add more screw holes

 D. Yes, if you remove the integrated ports

4. If you have a PC with a full-sized ATX motherboard and case and you decide you would like to upgrade the motherboard, can you replace it with a microATX motherboard? (Select the best answer.)

 A. No

 B. Yes, if you reset the jumpers

 C. Yes, if you add more screw holes

 D. Most likely, if you move the standouts

5. What types of connector attach the ATX power supply to a modern ATX motherboard? (Select two.)

 A. P1

 B. P2

 C. P4

 D. P8

6. What advantage do BTX form factor systems have over ATX systems?

 A. Better device support

 B. Better CPU support

 C. Better sound

 D. Better cooling

7. Mario bought a PCI Express video card. What type of connector might he need to plug into the card? (Select two.)

 A. Molex

 B. P1

 C. P4

 D. PCIe

8. Which motherboard type uses a riser card?

 A. ATX

 B. BTX

 C. microATX

 D. NLX

9. Molex connectors supply electricity to which devices? (Select two.)

 A. Floppy drives

 B. Hard drives

 C. Optical drives

 D. Thumb drives

10. A client notices the 115/230 switch on the back of a power supply you're installing. What's the switch used for?

 A. Powering computers in countries that run at a higher standard voltage than that used in the United States

 B. Powering computers in countries that run a lower standard voltage than that used in the United States

 C. Powering server computers that need double the normal voltage

 D. Overclocking

11. In what circumstance should you open a power supply?

 A. You open a power supply for routine cleaning.

 B. If the computer suddenly won't start up, you can check and replace the fuse inside the power supply.

 C. If you see a flash of light or see smoke coming out, you should open the power supply.

 D. Never open a power supply. It's not safe.

12. Which voltages does a power supply provide through a mini connector?

 A. 3.3 V, 5 V

 B. 5 V, 12 V

 C. 3.3 V, 12 V

 D. 115 V, 230 V

13. After installing an additional drive into a working computer, the computer won't power up at all—no lights, no spinning drives, nothing. What's most likely the problem?

 A. Dead hard drive

 B. Dead power supply

 C. Insufficient DC wattage provided by the power supply

 D. Insufficient AC wattage provided by the electrical outlet

14. What's another name for a computer case?

 A. Brick

 B. Bucket

 C. System unit

 D. System support

15. What feature do you find on better power supplies that eliminates harmonics?

 A. Active PFC

 B. Active scan

 C. Passive PFC

 D. Passive scan

REVIEW ANSWERS

1. **D** The motherboard can be considered the cornerstone of the PC. All your system devices are either directly or indirectly attached to the motherboard, making it the most important part of your PC.

2. **B** **D** You'll find primarily ATX and microATX motherboards in modern systems. AT motherboards are old and baby ATX motherboards don't exist.

3. **A** You cannot replace an ATX motherboard with a BTX motherboard using the same case. ATX motherboards go into ATX cases, and BTX motherboards go into BTX cases.

4. **D** Most full-sized ATX cases support microATX motherboards.

5. **A** **C** Modern ATX motherboards use P1 for primary power and P4 for secondary power.

6. **D** BTX systems offer better cooling than ATX systems. Both offer similar device, CPU, and sound support.

7. **A** **D** Some PCIe video cards use a Molex connector, although most require a PCIe connector.

8. **D** NLX motherboards use a riser card.

9. **B** **C** Molex connectors supply power for hard drives and optical drives.

10. **A** When powering up computers in countries that use ~230 VAC, you simply flip the switch from ~115 to ~230.

11. **D** Don't open that power supply as the capacitors can bite. Hard.

12. **B** Mini connectors provide 5 V and 12 V.

13. **C** If a power supply does not have enough DC wattage to power up the computer, you'll get a completely inert computer.

14. **C** Many techs call computer cases "system units."

15. **A** Active power factor correction (PFC) helps smooth out those nasty harmonics.

CPUs

	NEWBIE	SOME EXPERIENCE	EXPERT
ETA	3 hours	2 hours	1 hour

The microprocessor, or as most techs call it, the *central processing unit (CPU)*, is the thing that enables a computer to compute. Everything else on the computer can be considered part of the CPU's life-support system. So what does the CPU do? If you believe the hyperbole of popular culture, the CPU is some sort of machine brain that's always on the verge of declaring "I think, therefore I am" and trying to take over the world. Don't let them kid you—computers don't think! What the CPU does, and does amazingly well, is add numbers. The CPU is really just a super-fast, super-powerful calculator.

As simple as that may sound, keep in mind that a CPU churns out *billions* of calculations every second. These calculations make possible everything that your PC does: displaying your operating system (OS) desktop, processing print jobs, grabbing Web pages, and doing everything else that you ask it to do. Of all the whiz-bang pieces of engineering that go into the PC, the CPU is by far the most impressive. The CPU has gone through many evolutions since its introduction more than 20 years ago, but even the most advanced CPUs still operate in much the same manner as the old Intel 8088 that powered the first IBM PC.

Today's desktop CPU market is dominated by two vendors, Intel and American Micro Devices (AMD). Intel's CPU offerings include the Pentium, Celeron, Core, Core 2, Xeon, and Itanium processors. AMD gives us the Athlon XP, Sempron, Turion, and Athlon 64 product families, and the server-oriented Opteron processor.

Travel Advisory

Over the years, other companies have tried to get into the CPU business. Companies such as Cyrix, IDC, VIA, and Transmeta have all made CPUs, but they've been met with limited success and minor market share.

The CompTIA A+ certification exams concentrate on the aspects of the CPU that a tech has to know to service PCs in today's business world. First, you need to understand the basic internal components of a CPU and what they do so that you can make informed decisions and recommendations on CPUs. Second, you need to know how to install a CPU and its cooling system. Finally, you need to handle the relatively simple troubleshooting CPUs require.

Objective 5.01 CPU Technology

Modern CPUs are composed of multiple distinct components, from processing to memory, and the variations among them can give you pause when you look at the price. Why is one Intel processor so much more expensive than another? How do you compare between AMD and Intel CPUs? This section looks at components shared by all CPUs and variations in computing processes, and then finishes with a discussion of technology innovations.

Inside the CPU

Ancient CPUs operated pretty much like simple calculators, able to do simple arithmetic, but modern CPUs have dedicated circuitry to process amazingly complex things. Here's a brief look at those circuits (Figure 5.1). You can't fix any of this stuff, but it's good to know how processors work because the knowledge enables you to see differences among CPUs.

(Registers)

FIGURE 5.1 Inside the CPU

Arithmetic Logic Unit

The *arithmetic logic unit (ALU)* processes data and is the primary processing component of the CPU. The ALU takes data from the CPU *registers*, processes it, and copies it back into the registers before moving on to the next batch of data.

Registers

Registers are memory circuits located inside the CPU that hold data before and after processing. In essence, the registers are the ALU's workbenches. Early Intel Pentium CPUs (Pentium I and Pentium MMX) used primarily 32-bit registers; modern CPUs use 64- and 128-bit register sizes.

Floating-Point Unit

The *floating-point unit (FPU)* handles complex calculations for applications that require it, such as graphics programs and 3-D games. The FPU on today's PC is integrated with the CPU. Ancient, pre-Pentium CPUs relied on a separate FPU chip, sometimes called the *math coprocessor,* to handle FPU mathematics.

Cache Memory

Modern CPUs have two sets of ultra-fast *static RAM (SRAM)* memory built in, called *cache.* Normal system RAM is called *dynamic RAM (DRAM),* because it can hold data for a very short duration before it needs to be *refreshed*—that is, so a 1 stays a 1 rather than draining to become a 0. (It's all just binary, after all!) SRAM, in contrast, never needs to be refreshed and is therefore much faster than DRAM. The *Level 1 (L1)* cache memory is the first and fastest and built into the processor. *Level 2 (L2)* cache memory is the second cache, placed on the CPU package with a special bus connecting it to the processor, called the *backside bus.* It is always larger than the L1 cache (around 256 KB to 1 MB) and is usually slower.

> ### Local Lingo
>
> **Package and Die** The ceramic casing that holds the CPU is called the *package.* The silicon wafer that has all the transistors is called the *die.* Components that are incorporated into the silicon, such as L2 cache memory, are referred to as being *on-die.*

Since SRAM is so much faster, why don't PCs use it for system RAM instead of DRAM? The answer is simple: cost. SRAM is roughly 10 times more expensive than DRAM.

> ### Exam Tip
>
> Remember that DRAM is fast, cheap, and must be refreshed; SRAM is much faster, very expensive, and requires no refreshing.

The *frontside bus* connects the CPU to RAM or to the Northbridge chip of the chipset. The frontside bus usually runs at 2× or 4× the speed of the system crystal, so it is referred to as a double-pumped or quad-pumped frontside bus. Every CPU since the Intel Pentium has a 64-bit frontside bus. Figure 5.2 shows the relationship of the CPU, cache, backside bus, and frontside bus.

FIGURE 5.2 The CPU in the center

Address Space

The number of wires on the address bus defines the maximum amount of RAM a CPU can theoretically address. This is called the *address space*. With a 32-bit address bus, for example, the maximum amount of memory the CPU can address is 2^{32}, or 4,294,967,296 bytes (4 GB).

Concepts

Techs use certain concepts and terms to differentiate among CPUs, so you can judge pretty quickly which specific make and model fits your client's needs. Specifically, the pipeline, clock speed, and clock multipliers give you a good indication of the caliber of the CPU.

Pipeline

The term *pipeline* refers to the discrete series of steps that the CPU follows to process commands. Think of a pipeline in terms of doing laundry. Doing laundry follows an ordered series of steps: sort, wash, dry, iron, and fold or hang up. Early, pre-Pentium CPUs had only a single pipeline and thus could process only a single command at a time. With a complex mathematical command, for example, the FPU might be working hard and the ALU sitting idle. The Pentium introduced dual pipelines that enabled the CPU to process two commands simultaneously. Current CPUs have many more pipelines and can thus process more commands at once.

Clock Speed

The CPU clock speed tells you how many calculation cycles a CPU can (in theory) execute per second. One calculation cycle per second is equal to 1 hertz (Hz). Of course, nobody measures clock cycles in hertz, but rather in millions of calculation cycles per second, or megahertz (MHz). These days, it's more common to see clock speed measured in billions of cycles per second, or gigahertz (GHz).

Two things determine clock speed: the maximum speed of the CPU itself and the maximum speed that the motherboard can handle. The CPU speed is determined by the manufacturer and is set at the factory. The *system crystal*—a quartz crystal circuit that oscillates at a fixed frequency when fed current—sets the motherboard's clock speed.

Multipliers

Early CPUs took the beat set by the clock and simply doubled it, thus enabling the CPU to run internally at twice the speed of the motherboard. Modern CPUs multiply the signal many times. A CPU running at 2 GHz on a 200-MHz system

bus, for example, uses a ×10 clock multiplier. Because CPUs do so much more work processing than any other component, it makes sense for them to do 10 things while some other processor—such as a sound card processor—would do a single thing.

The system bus speed and the multiplier on CPUs had to be manually configured via jumpers on the motherboard in the old days. Today's CPUs actually report to the motherboard through a function called *CPUID* (CPU identifier), and the system bus speed and multiplier are often set automatically. Many motherboards offer manual configuration, but this is primarily for tweaking systems. See the section on "Overclocking" later in this chapter for more details.

Performance Ratings

Intel has traditionally been able to produce CPUs that run faster than CPUs from AMD, and its marketing reflected this aspect of CPUs. AMD, in contrast, has argued that speed is less important than processing efficiency and has concentrated on the latter for its CPUs. Unfortunately for AMD, Intel has a great marketing force and most consumers bought the erroneous line that raw speed is the most important aspect of a CPU.

To overcome this marketing, AMD marks its CPUs with a *performance rating* in addition to a clock speed, to advertise that a slower AMD CPU performs on par with a much faster Intel CPU. An AMD Athlon 64 X2 5400+ might run at only 2.8 GHz, for example, but according to AMD can compete head to head with a 5.4-GHz Intel CPU. With the Pentium M and the more recent Core and Core 2 processors, Intel has conceded the point and has removed raw speed as the primary factor in CPU quality and performance.

CPU Packages

All current CPUs come in a square package called a *pin grid array (PGA)*, like that shown in Figure 5.3, but variations exist within and among manufacturers. Collectively, Intel and AMD have used close to 100 variations of the PGA package over the years for hundreds of different CPU models with names like staggered-PGA, micro-PGA, ball grid array (which uses tiny balls instead of pins), and land grid array (which uses flat pads instead of pins).

Many different varieties of PGA CPUs are based on the number of pins sticking out of the CPU. These CPUs snap into special sockets on the motherboard, with each socket designed to match the pins (or balls or pads) on the CPU.

To make CPU insertion and removal easier, these sockets—officially called *zero insertion force (ZIF) sockets*—use a small arm on the side of the socket (Figure 5.4) or a cage that fits over the socket to hold the CPU in place. ZIF sockets are easily identified by their squarish shape. Many sockets today have names

FIGURE 5.3 Typical PGA CPU

like Socket 939 and Socket 775 to reflect the number of pins, although AMD's
Socket AM2 is the exception.

Exam Tip

For a short time, Intel and AMD produced large, rectangular-shaped
CPU packages called *single edge cartridges (SECs)* that fit into a slot,
kind of like an expansion card. The first was the Intel Pentium II.

FIGURE 5.4 ZIF socket (arm up)

Voltage Regulator Modules

CPUs vary greatly in the amount of voltage they need to run. With the many variations among CPUs you can install into a single motherboard, motherboards need to have some mechanism to accommodate the different voltages. Older motherboards used an add-on device called a *voltage regulator module* that you could replace or adjust via jumpers or switches to handle CPU varieties. Modern motherboards do this automatically.

Variations

Several innovations have created a great divide between CPUs on the high end and all the rest. Technology innovations include enhanced registers, hyper-threading, 64-bit processors, multi-core CPUs, and mobile CPU varieties.

Enhanced Registers

Starting with later versions of the Intel Pentium, manufacturers have improved some of the registers inside the CPU, adding specific-use and general-use 128-bit registers. The first were called *multimedia extensions (MMX)*. Later Intel options were *streaming SIMD extensions (SSE)*, SSE2, and SSE3. AMD added 3DNow! to the mix.

Hyper-threading

Most desktop CPUs handle multiple *processes*—opening a file, playing an MP3, and so on—nearly simultaneously by switching rapidly back and forth between those processes. Intel introduced *hyper-threading* with the Pentium 4, a way to run multiple processes or *threads* truly simultaneously. A single Intel Pentium 4 with hyper-threading looks like two CPUs to the operating system (Figure 5.5). Currently, only the Pentium 4 with hyper-threading comes with the technology. Intel's more advanced processors—like the Core and Core 2—do not.

Local Lingo

Process and Thread Although the words *process* and *thread* are used interchangeably, they're not quite the same thing all the time. Think of a process as the big task, such as running Word or playing World of Warcraft. When a programmer designs the application, he or she can create side tasks or make the program *multi-threaded*, to accomplish multiple things within the program without interrupting the main program flow. Think of Word auto-saving while you're typing and you get the idea of a classic thread—a task that needs doing but isn't the main task.

FIGURE 5.5 Dual CPU Usage History graphs for a hyper-threaded Pentium 4

64-bit Processors

A 64-bit CPU has general-purpose, floating-point, and address registers that are 64 bits wide, meaning they can handle 64-bit-wide code in one pass—twice as wide as a 32-bit processor. And they can address much, much more memory. Both AMD and Intel currently produce 64-bit CPUs.

With the 32-bit address bus of the Pentium and later CPUs, the maximum amount of memory the CPU can address is 2^{32} (4 GB), as you know. With a 64-bit address bus, CPUs can address 2^{64} bytes of memory, or more precisely, 18,446,744,073,709,551,616 bytes of memory—that's a lot of RAM! This number is so big that gigabytes and terabytes are no longer convenient, so we now go to an exabyte (2^{60}). A 64-bit address bus can address 16 exabytes of RAM.

The current consumer-oriented 64-bit processors are the AMD Athlon 64 family (Figure 5.6) and the Intel Core 2 family. Both are designed to run either 32-bit or 64-bit operating systems, so they support 64-bit Windows Vista out of the box.

FIGURE 5.6 AMD Athlon 64

Multicore CPUs

CPU clock speeds hit a practical limit of roughly 4 GHz around the years 2002–2003, motivating the CPU makers to find new ways to get more processing power for CPUs. Although Intel and AMD had different opinions about 64-bit CPUs, both decided at virtually the same time to combine two CPUs into a single chip, creating a *dual-core* architecture (Figure 5.7). Dual core isn't just two CPUs on the same chip. A dual-core CPU has two execution units—two sets of pipelines—but the two sets of pipelines share caches (how they share caches differs between Intel and AMD) and RAM. Both AMD and Intel also produce *multicore CPUs* of four or eight cores on a single chip. Now that's firepower!

FIGURE 5.7 Intel Core 2 Duo

Travel Advisory

What makes a dual-core CPU better than a hyper-threaded CPU? The hyper-threaded Pentium 4 shares a single ALU but splits out the FPU for multiple threads. If two processes both need the ALU, then the hyper-threading doesn't do much. A dual-core CPU has two distinct processors and could handle multiple processes more efficiently.

Mobile CPUs

The inside of a laptop PC is a cramped, hot environment, where no self-respecting CPU should ever need to operate. Since the mid-1980s, CPU manufacturers have endeavored to make specialized versions of their processors to function in the rugged world of laptops. These are called *mobile processors*. Over the years, a number of CPU laptop solutions have appeared. Virtually every CPU made by Intel or AMD has come in a mobile version. You can usually tell a mobile version by the word *mobile* or the letter *M* in its name. Here are a few examples:

- Mobile Intel Pentium III
- Intel Pentium M
- Mobile AMD Athlon 64
- AMD Turion 64 (All Turions are mobile processors but don't use *mobile* or *M* in their name. AMD usually adds *mobile technology* as part of the Turion description.)
- Intel Core Duo (a dual-core CPU)

A mobile processor uses less power than an equivalent desktop model. This provides two advantages. First, it enables the battery in the laptop to last longer. Second, it makes the CPU run cooler, and the cooler the CPU, the fewer cooling devices you need.

Almost every mobile processor today runs at a lower voltage than the desktop version of the same CPU. As a result, most mobile CPUs also run at lower speeds—it takes juice if you want the speed! Mobile CPUs usually top out at about 75 percent of the speed of the same CPU's desktop version.

Throttling

Modern CPUs have the capability to reduce their processing cycles and lower their clock speeds when they reach a certain temperature; this feature is called *throttling*. This is incredibly important with mobile processors because the heat dissipation method for portable PCs is wimpy compared with that of desktop PCs. It's also essential when you have a catastrophic fan failure—either through

animal hair gunking up the works or technician error when installing a fan. Rather than overheating and destroying the CPU and most likely the mother-board (the way it worked in the old days), modern CPUs simply throttle down to the point where they can survive. You'll recognize serious throttling by the amazingly slow response times when trying to do anything on the PC.

Recommending a CPU

The CPU that's right for a specific situation depends entirely on the computing needs of your client. For a workstation that does primarily documents, e-mail, and the Web, *any* modern processor will do. In fact, slapping in the latest dual-core, 64-bit CPU isn't going to provide much of a different experience at all from its single-core, 32-bit little brother running the same low-end applica-tions. Save your clients some money and recommend a lower-end CPU in such a situation.

Where you see the great benefits of high-end processors is in 3-D modeling programs, high-end photograph and video editing, and 3-D games. Plus you provide a bit of future-proofing for the client, so he or she can upgrade software but not have to worry about hardware for a few years. Aside from raw comput-ing power providing a little burst, though, few applications take full advantage of multicore CPUs, so ask your clients what kind of applications they use and then do some research online at the application-makers' Web sites. If the appli-cations kick into overdrive on multicore CPUs, then recommend them.

Objective 5.02 # Installing CPUs

Installing a CPU successfully requires three steps. First, do your homework so you know what CPU works with your motherboard. Second, practice proper electrostatic discharge (ESD) avoidance techniques during the install. Finally, install a cooling solution, generally a heatsink and fan assembly.

Compatibility Issues

The key to a successful CPU installation is making sure that the processor and motherboard are compatible. The motherboard's documentation is the best source for compatibility information. The motherboard manual should contain some sort of chart listing the CPUs that it supports. You can also check the Web site of the motherboard manufacturer for details.

Because Intel and AMD CPUs are not pin-compatible, all motherboards made since the mid-1990s support *either* Intel CPUs *or* AMD CPUs—not both. Once you know which brand of processor your motherboard takes, the next step is to match the model. The type of CPU socket that the motherboard uses (PGA or BGA) determines which model of Intel or AMD CPU you can install. Many motherboards accept more than one model of CPU into a compatible socket; for example, most Intel motherboards will take either a Pentium 4 or Celeron processor. Remember that some CPU models use more than one socket type. For instance, the Athlon 64 CPU comes in three socket varieties: Socket 754, Socket 939, and Socket AM2. Make certain that you know which one you need before you make a decision! Table 5.1 shows typical processors and their socket types.

Travel Advisory

Table 5.1 leaves out a lot of the old or less mainstream products, so it is by no means a complete listing of what you'll find in the field. You'll find Pentium 4 CPUs in Socket 423 varieties, for example, and Intel and AMD make server-oriented CPUs in the Xeon and Opteron processors, respectively.

Once you've narrowed down your choices to a particular brand and model, you need to determine which CPU speed your system can support. The maximum speed of a particular CPU that a motherboard can handle is determined by the chipset and BIOS and is listed along with the other information in the

TABLE 5.1 Typical Processors and Sockets

Manufacturer	Processor	Socket
Intel	Pentium 4	Socket 478, Socket T (LGA 775)
Intel	Celeron (Pentium 4)	Socket 478
Intel	Celeron D	Socket 478, Socket T (LGA 775)
Intel	Pentium D	Socket T (LGA 775)
Intel	Core 2 Duo	Socket T (LGA 775)
AMD	Athlon XP	Socket A
AMD	Duron	Socket A
AMD	Sempron	Socket 754, Socket AM2
AMD	Athlon 64	Socket 754, Socket 939, Socket AM2
AMD	Athlon 64 FX	Socket 939, Socket 940, Socket F / Socket 1207
AMD	Athlon 64 X2	Socket 939, Socket AM2

motherboard documentation. Sometimes you can upgrade the speed of CPU that a motherboard can handle by updating (flashing) the BIOS. Your motherboard maker's Web site is the best place to find out whether this is an option for you.

CPU Physical Installation

Once you have the preliminaries out of the way, you can install the CPU. If you plan to upgrade the CPU, first power down the PC and unplug the power cable. Put the PC case on your antistatic mat, if you have one. Make sure you've got enough room and light to work and remove the cover from the case. Strap on your nerd bracelet and ground yourself, and then skip to "Installing the Cooling System" for steps on removing the heatsink and fan assembly. Then come back here.

Once you've removed the heatsink and fan or if you plan to install a CPU onto an uninstalled motherboard, just leave the motherboard on the antistatic map and follow these steps to install:

1. Lift the CPU release lever arm (Figure 5.8).

2. Locate the orientation mark on the corner of the CPU and socket. They are usually marked with an arrow or raised dot. Double-check the orientation by looking at the pin configuration—the CPU and socket should be oriented so that the corner (or corners) with missing pins align (Figure 5.9).

FIGURE 5.8 Lifting the arm

FIGURE 5.9 CPU orientation marks

3. Holding the CPU by its edges, position it over the socket and gently set it in place. If the pins and socket holes are oriented correctly, the CPU should drop right in without any force (*zero* insertion force—get it?). If the CPU doesn't fit easily into the socket, you're doing it wrong! Make certain that it's oriented correctly and try again. When seated, the CPU package should sit flush with the socket mount with no pins showing.

4. Lower and lock the release lever into place.

That's all there is to it. Your next step is to install the cooling system.

Installing the Cooling System

CPUs have no moving parts (that you can see with the naked eye), but they nonetheless generate considerable heat. Excessive heat to the CPU leads to system instability, lockups, and dead CPUs. CPU packages are made from high-tech thermal plastics and ceramics that dissipate heat, but they still can't provide enough relief without help. This help comes in the form of heatsink and fan assemblies (Figure 5.10) and from liquid cooling systems.

Heatsink and fan assemblies take a bit of force and finesse to mount properly—more than you might think! A small, straight-slot screwdriver will help.

Heatsink and fan assemblies for PGA-packaged CPUs usually come as a unit, but if not, you should attach the fan to the heatsink before installing them onto the CPU.

FIGURE 5.10 Retail heatsink and fan assembly

1. If your CPU has thermal paste pre-applied, remove and discard the protective tape. If not, then apply a thin film of thermal paste to the raised center of the CPU package (Figure 5.11).

2. Align the mounting bracket hardware on the heatsink and fan assembly with the mounting notches on the CPU socket.

3. Attach the mounting bracket to one side of the CPU socket.

FIGURE 5.11 Applying thermal compound

4. Using your screwdriver as a lever, press down on the mounting bracket on the other side of the CPU socket and snap the bracket into place (Figure 5.12). If this makes you nervous, don't worry—that's normal. Most techs are surprised by the amount of force needed to mount the heatsink and fan assembly into place.

5. The last step is to plug the fan's power cable into the appropriate socket or header on the motherboard. Check your motherboard documentation for information.

Installing a Liquid Cooling System

Despite all the differences between traditional heatsink and fan assemblies and the more modern liquid cooling systems, the essential installation steps are similar.

1. Follow the manufacturer's instructions to attach the hoses from the coolant reservoir tank to the CPU cooling element and the heat exchanger unit. Make certain that all hoses are secure and crimped properly.

FIGURE 5.12 Using a straight-slot screwdriver to move the mounting bracket

2. Fill the coolant reservoir with the recommended amount of distilled water.

3. Apply a small amount of thermal compound to the CPU.

4. If your liquid cooling system uses a separate CPU temperature sensor on the cooling element, attach it to the appropriate slot or groove and secure it with the supplied metal tape.

5. Mount the cooling element to the CPU with the attached bracket and secure it in place with the tension screw (Figure 5.13). Be careful not to over-tighten the screw.

6. You're ready to go!

Exam Tip

You don't have to know how to install a water cooling system in a PC for the CompTIA A+ certification exams. You simply need to know that the option is available. This information has been added here simply for a quick reference.

FIGURE 5.13 Cooling element mounted on CPU

Overclocking

Most modern systems use the CPUID to set the clock speed and clock multiplier automatically for any CPU you install, so all but true enthusiasts are done with installation at this point. Boot up the PC and watch the screen. Assuming you've done everything correctly, your system will start without any undue alarms or errors. If, however, something has gone wrong, you need to turn to trouble-shooting.

Some motherboards enable you adjust CPU settings manually by moving a jumper, changing a CMOS setting, or using software. So many enthusiasts deliberately change these settings to enhance performance; this is called *overclocking*. You can make a couple of adjustments to overclock successfully. First, increase the bus speed for the system. Second, you often have to increase the voltage going into the CPU just a little to provide stability. You do that by changing a jumper or CMOS setting. Always do only one thing at a time, document your change, and then reboot.

Overriding the defaults can completely lock up your system, to the point where even removing and reinstalling the CPU doesn't bring the motherboard back to life. (There's also a slight risk of toasting the processor, although all modern processors have circuitry that shuts them down quickly before they overheat.) Most motherboards have a jumper setting called *CMOS clear* (Figure 5.14) that makes the CMOS go back to default settings. Before you try overclocking on a modern system, find the CMOS clear jumper and make sure you know how to use it.

FIGURE 5.14 CMOS clear jumper, marked JCMOS1 JCI1

Objective 5.03 Troubleshooting CPUs

CPUs are pretty robust beasts and rarely have problems after they're installed. You're most likely to encounter problems with installation, although heat issues can become a big deal at a later time.

Installation Problems

Look (and listen) for the following signs of installation problems:

- It's normal for the CPU fan speed to fluctuate, but if the fan doesn't spin at all for more than 5 seconds or so, turn the system off and make sure that the fan is plugged in correctly.
- If the fan is spinning but the PC doesn't boot, make certain that any jumpers governing speed or voltage are set correctly.
- If, after a few minutes, you hear a loud alarm, this is an indication that the system is overheating. Turn it off immediately and check your fan installation to make sure you've got good CPU/heatsink contact and that the fan is functioning properly.
- If the system does not boot and the fan does not spin, check to ensure that the CPU is seated properly and that no other components or cables have been unseated or disturbed.

Heat Issues

Excessive heat can cause serious damage to your CPU and to any other components inside your computer. The fan on the CPU pushes hot air away from the CPU and into the case; case fans and power supply fans push hot air out the back of the case. Front case fans pull cool air into the case.

The problems start with ribbon cables that impede airflow and clogged or dying fans. Incautious drive installation can leave ribbon cables strewn all over the case (Figure 5.15). Dirt, dust, hair, and age can slow down fans to the point where they can't do the job.

The warning signs will be there: spontaneous reboots, especially on warmer days or with the heat blasting in winter time; occasional alarms from the tinny PC speaker; lockups; excessively loud fans. The fix is easy. Check the fans and replace when necessary.

FIGURE 5.15 Messy cables

Travel Assistance

Installing good fans in a case can make a world of difference to the user experience. No one wants to use a new or upgraded PC that sounds like a helicopter! I always install the quietest fans I can get, generally as big as I can get into a case. If you have a case with options for 80-mm or 120-mm fans, for example, go for the latter. Bigger fans move more air at lower speeds. Check out the "Quiet Fans" at one of my favorite online retailers, Directron: www.directron.com/quietfans.html. I recommend Papst, but all the top brands listed (Zalman, Cooler Master, Antec, Panaflo) produce excellent products.

CHECKPOINT

✔**Objective 5.01: CPU Technology** CPUs are composed of multiple distinct components, such as the ALU, registers, and FPU for processing, and L1 and L2 cache of SRAM for quick data access. Modern CPUs use multiple

processing pipelines and run at a clock speed that's some multiple of the system bus speed. Every current processor comes in some form of PGA package. Advances in CPUs include enhanced registers; hyper-threading; 64-bit processing; dual-core and multicore processors; and cool, energy sipping mobile processors.

✔**Objective 5.02: Installing CPUs** Motherboards are made to accommodate a narrow range of CPU types. The CPU's form factor must be compatible with the socket on the motherboard. Installing a CPU is simple, but you must be careful not to damage the CPU pins or package. Proper cooling is absolutely essential. Use thermal compound between the CPU and the heatsink and fan assembly, or between the CPU and cooling element if using a liquid cooling system. You can deliberately push the CPU to run faster than recommended through overclocking.

✔**Objective 5.03: Troubleshooting CPUs** Installation errors and heat build-up over time are the two biggest problem areas for CPUs. Look and listen for erratic fan noise, no fan noise, or alarms. Crashing PCs and lockups on warm days are also good clues. Check your installation; clean or replace your fans to fix.

REVIEW QUESTIONS

1. Which component inside the CPU holds data before and after processing?
 A. ALU
 B. FPU
 C. Pipeline
 D. Registers

2. Which component inside the CPU is the primary processing component?
 A. ALU
 B. FPU
 C. Pipeline
 D. Registers

3. What type of memory is an L1 cache?
 A. DRAM
 B. ROM

 C. SRAM

 D. VRAM

4. Which component sets the clock speed of the motherboard?

 A. Cache

 B. CPU

 C. System crystal

 D. ZIF crystal

5. What form factor do modern CPUs have?

 A. EGA

 B. SVGA

 C. PGA

 D. VGA

6. What function enables motherboards to set up BIOS for CPUs automatically?

 A. BIOS

 B. CPUID

 C. CPUNow!

 D. Processor ID

7. What technology enables a single-core CPU to appear as two CPUs?

 A. Dual-core

 B. Hyper-threading

 C. Multicore

 D. Z-core

8. The Intel Core Duo is an example of what sort of processor? (Select two.)

 A. Dual-core

 B. Hyper-threaded

 C. Mobile

 D. SEC

9. Which of the following must you do to install a CPU successfully?

 A. Align the orientation marks on the CPU with the marks on the socket.

 B. Push hard to seat the CPU properly.

 C. Lift the socket arm to lock the CPU into place.

 D. Plug in the power cable.

10. Which tool would help attach or remove a heatsink and fan assembly?

 A. Knife

 B. Phillips-head screwdriver

 C. Straight-slot screwdriver

 D. Torx wrench

11. Intentionally increasing the clock speed of a CPU beyond the manufacturer's recommendation is called _____.

 A. CMOS clear

 B. Overclocking

 C. SpeedStep

 D. Underclocking

12. John installed a new CPU. When he boots the system, it comes up for a few seconds and then shuts down. What could be the problem?

 A. John forgot to plug in the fan and the CPU is overheating.

 B. John installed an AMD CPU in an Intel motherboard.

 C. John installed an Intel CPU in an AMD motherboard.

 D. John failed to raise the arm on the socket to lock down the CPU.

REVIEW ANSWERS

1. **D** The registers hold data before and after processing.

2. **A** The arithmetic logic unit (ALU) handles the primary processing duties.

3. **C** The L1 cache uses SRAM.

4. **C** They system crystal sets the motherboard clock speed.

5. **C** Modern CPUs use the pin grid array (PGA) form factor.

6. **B** The motherboard scans the CPUID to set up BIOS automatically.

7. **B** Hyper-threading makes a single CPU appear to be a dual-core CPU.

8. **A C** The Intel Core Duo is a dual-core mobile CPU.

9. **A** To install a CPU, align the orientation marks on the CPU with the marks on the socket.

10. **C** A straight-slot screwdriver is an essential tool for most heatsink and fan installation or removal.

11. **B** Although you might need to use the CMOS clear jumper in case it fails, overclocking is the term for cranking up your CPU speed.

12. **A** Starting and closing down at boot is a classic sign of overheating. Plug in that fan!

RAM

ETA	NEWBIE	SOME EXPERIENCE	EXPERT
	1.5 hours	1 hour	45 minutes

PC users are curious people, and before long one of them is going to ask you, the learned PC tech, "Where do my programs actually run?" Without hesitation, you might answer, "In your system RAM, of course!" If you're like most techs, you might continue to talk about how RAM works until her eyes glaze over and she asks you to go away.

Many PC users are under the misapprehension that programs run directly off of the PC's hard drive. This is, of course, impossible, because even the fastest hard drive simply can't keep up with even the slowest CPU. Instead, programs must be copied to a super-fast medium that's capable of supplying the CPU with the data that it needs to run an application at a speed that it can use: this is the function of RAM. Launching an application loads the necessary files from the hard disk into RAM, where the CPU can grab the specific data that it needs to run the program.

Not long ago, RAM was a precious commodity in the PC world, and even a small upgrade would set you back hundreds of dollars. Things have changed dramatically for the better, so nowadays adding more RAM is often the best upgrade option for a sluggish PC. This doesn't mean that you can just grab any type of RAM that you can get your hands on and stick it in your system. You've got to match the motherboard with the right type of RAM, running at the right speed.

In most cases, installing RAM is literally a snap, but don't take the installation procedure for granted. RAM is perhaps the most sensitive component on the system when it comes to the dreaded electrostatic discharge (ESD). Safe handling is absolutely vital. Once you've successfully installed RAM, you may find that your work isn't done. Memory errors come in many shapes and sizes, and when things go wrong with RAM, you can pretty much plan on canceling any appointments you had for the rest of the day if you don't know what to do.

In this chapter, you'll learn how to identify types of RAM, how to handle RAM safely, how to install RAM correctly, what to look for when you suspect a RAM error, and what steps you can take to correct RAM errors.

Objective 6.01 RAM Overview

RAM has been available in a wide variety of physical form factors (sometimes called *packages*) and technologies over the years. This section looks at what you might find in the field today.

RAM Form Factors

RAM form factors have gone through several evolutionary steps since the introduction of the first PC. Manufacturers originally installed RAM directly onto the motherboard, as shown in Figure 6.1, but this took up too much room and made upgrading difficult.

The next step was to put RAM memory chips onto special removable circuit boards, called RAM *sticks,* that fit into sockets on the motherboard. These RAM sticks are what we use today: the SIMM, the DIMM, and the RIMM.

SIMM

Single inline memory modules (SIMMs) used to be the most common form of memory, but you won't see them on any PCs manufactured in the last few years. SIMM RAM sticks come in either 30-pin or 72-pin layouts. There's no real significance to the number of pins as far as PC techs are concerned. You might occasionally find an older printer that needs 72-pin SIMMs, but that's about it today. Figure 6.2 shows two SIMMs.

FIGURE 6.1 RAM soldered onto an ancient motherboard, now part of the Total Seminars Tech Museum

| **FIGURE 6.2** | 72-pin and 30-pin SIMMs |

DIMM

Dual inline memory modules (DIMMs) are the sticks you're most likely to run into these days, including two popular variants used in laptops, *MicroDIMMs* and *small outline DIMMs (SO-DIMMs)*. DIMMs for desktop PCs look similar to SIMMs but are wider and longer. DIMMs have 168, 184, or 240 pins; are 64 bits wide; and have a capacity of up to 1 GB at this writing. Figure 6.3 shows 184-pin and 240-pin DIMMs.

| **FIGURE 6.3** | 184-pin (top) and 240-pin DIMMs |

MicroDIMM RAM comes in 144-pin packages. The SO-DIMM variant comes in 72-pin, 144-pin, and 200-pin configurations. You can find MicroDIMMs and SO-DIMMs of the same capacities as their full-sized counterparts.

RIMM

The other RAM package you might see is the *RIMM*. Technically, the term RIMM doesn't stand for anything, but most techs use it as an acronym for *Rambus inline memory module*. RIMMs come in capacities of up to 512 MB. RIMM sticks look like DIMMs but have 184 pins. Figure 6.4 shows a typical RIMM stick. Note that the memory chips themselves are covered by a thin metal shield called a *heat spreader*. This shield helps dissipate heat generated by the RIMM memory chips.

RAM Packaging

RAM manufacturers produce an amazing variety of RAM packages. You'll find sticks that offer the same capacity, for example, but vary in number or location of memory chips. One 256 MB stick, for example, might have four chips on the front and four on the back—a double-sided stick—whereas another might have eight chips on the front only—a single-sided stick. A third might be single sided with only four chips and a fourth, double sided with 16 chips!

Individual memory chips come in different capacities and in how many bits they can put on the bus at one time. A ×32 chip, for example, puts four bytes on the bus at once, whereas a ×16 chip does two and a ×8 only one. Manufacturers use different combinations to make their sticks.

The general rule on memory packaging is *never mix packages* if you can help it. It leads to overall system instability in enough cases that a prudent tech uses uniform RAM sticks.

FIGURE 6.4 184-pin RIMM

> ### Exam Tip
>
> I know that many techs will shake their heads about this and say they've been mixing RAM packages for years and never had any problems. I had a Windows Me box that ran for years without problems, too, but that doesn't mean there aren't problems with mixing RAM or running Windows Me! More to the point for this discussion is that CompTIA's subject matter experts (SMEs), as well as I, think it's a problem to mix RAM packages, so look for a question on the topic and get it right.

RAM Types

RAM comes in two forms: static RAM (SRAM) and dynamic RAM (DRAM). SRAM is faster than DRAM, because it never needs to be refreshed; however, it is also much more expensive. SRAM is therefore reserved for special purposes, such as L1, L2, and L3 system cache memory. DRAM is used for system memory and needs to be refreshed every few nanoseconds (ns). During this time it is inaccessible to the CPU. This interval is called a *wait state*. Faster RAM has a shorter wait state. The paragraphs that follow describe the popular types of DRAM available on the PC market today.

> ### Exam Tip
>
> Remember that SRAM doesn't need to be refreshed, but it costs more than other RAM solutions and so is used primarily for cache. DRAM requires periodic refreshing and is used for system memory.

EDO

Extended data out RAM (EDO RAM) works by grabbing large chunks of data to feed to the CPU. EDO RAM is asynchronous, meaning that it runs at a speed independent of the system clock speed. EDO RAM is sold in 72-pin SIMMs and (rarely) in 168-pin DIMMs and has access times of 50 to 60 ns.

SDRAM

Synchronous dynamic RAM (SDRAM) delivers data in high-speed bursts. SDRAM runs at the speed of the system bus (thus, *synchronously*) and has access times in the 8 to 10 ns range. Manufacturers don't rate SDRAM speeds in nanoseconds, however, but rather in megahertz (MHz). SDRAM is rated according to the highest speed data bus it runs on, such as 66, 100, or 133 MHz. Hence, we have PC66, PC100, and PC133 SDRAM. To avoid confusion, most RAM

manufacturers label SDRAM with both nanosecond and megahertz ratings. SDRAM DIMMs have a special chip called the *serial presence detect* (SPD) chip that identifies a DIMM's capacity, speed, and *latency*—the latter being a measurement of how long the RAM takes to respond to the memory controller.

Exam Tip
Know that SDRAM transfers data in high-speed bursts and is measured in megahertz, not in nanoseconds.

The most common form of SDRAM uses a 168-pin DIMM (Figure 6.5). SDRAM for laptops comes in two reduced-size varieties, 72-pin and 144-pin SO-DIMMs, and MicroDIMMs.

RDRAM

When Intel developers were working on the Pentium 4 chip, they knew that regular SDRAM just wasn't going to be fast enough to handle the quad-pumped 400-MHz frontside bus. Intel announced plans to replace SDRAM with a faster, new type of RAM developed by Rambus, Inc., called *Rambus DRAM*, or simply *RDRAM*. Hailed by Intel as the next great leap in DRAM technology, RDRAM could handle speeds up to 800 MHz, which gave Intel plenty of room to improve the Pentium 4.

RDRAM was greatly anticipated by the industry for years, but industry support for RDRAM proved less than enthusiastic due to significant delays in development plus a price many times that of SDRAM. From a tech's standpoint, RDRAM shares almost all of the characteristics of SDRAM. RDRAM came only on RIMMs. RDRAM also had a speed rating: 600 MHz, 700 MHz, 800 MHz, or 1066 MHz. RDRAM employed an interesting dual-channel architecture. Each RIMM was 64 bits wide, but the Rambus memory controller chip (MCC)

FIGURE 6.5 SDRAM DIMM

alternated between two sticks to increase the speed of data retrieval. You were required to install RIMMs in pairs to use this dual-channel architecture.

RDRAM motherboards also required that all RIMM slots be populated. Unused pairs of slots needed a passive device called a *continuity RIMM* (CRIMM) installed in each slot to enable the RDRAM system to terminate properly. Figure 6.6 shows a CRIMM.

RDRAM offered dramatic possibilities for high-speed PCs, but it is effectively dead in today's market.

DDR SDRAM Many motherboards support *double data rate (DDR) SDRAM*, usually referred to as simply *DDR*. DDR operates in a similar fashion to modern CPUs, taking the base bandwidth speed of the system bus and multiplying it. DDR ranges from 266 MHz (PC2100) to 400 MHz (PC3200)—the top end of the official standard—to well beyond. DDR comes in a 184-pin DIMM package for desktops or either a 200-pin SO-DIMM or a 172-pin MicroDIMM for laptops.

Travel Advisory

The *PC####* that often follows the name of a DDR stick—such as *DDR 333 (PC2700)*—refers to the data throughput possible with that particular stick. A DDR 333 stick, therefore, has a bandwidth of 2.7 GB per second (GBps).

Manufacturers have released motherboards with memory controllers that support dual-channel architecture using DDR. *Dual-channel* DDR motherboards use regular DDR sticks, although manufacturers often sell RAM in matched pairs, branding them as dual-channel RAM. Dual-channel DDR works like RDRAM in that you must have two identical sticks of DDR and they must snap into two paired slots. Unlike RDRAM, dual-channel DDR doesn't require any additional devices like CRIMMs.

FIGURE 6.6 CRIMM

DDR2

The faster versions of DDR RAM run at a blistering PC4800. That's 4.8 GBps of data throughput! You'd think that kind of speed would satisfy most users, and to be honest, DRAM running at approximately 5 GBps really is plenty fast—for now. However, the ongoing speed increases ensure that even these speeds won't be good enough in the future. Knowing this, the RAM industry came out with DDR2, the successor to DDR. *DDR2* is DDR RAM with some improvements in its electrical characteristics, which enable it to run even faster than DDR while using less power. The big speed increase from DDR2 comes by clock doubling the input/output circuits on the chips. This does not speed up the core RAM— the part that holds the data—but speeding up the input/output and adding special buffers (sort of like a cache) makes DDR2 runs much faster than regular DDR. DDR2 uses a 240-pin DIMM that's not compatible with DDR. You'll find motherboards running both single-channel and dual-channel DDR2.

Error-checking RAM: Parity and ECC

High-end, mission-critical systems often use special *parity* or *error-correcting code (ECC)* RAM. These types of RAM use special circuitry to detect and, in some cases, correct errors in data. Parity RAM, the older technology, used a dedicated parity chip mounted on the RAM stick that added an extra bit—the parity bit—to each byte of data. Parity checking was useful in the early days of desktop computers when DRAM had a relatively high failure rate, but today's DRAM is so dependable that few PCs still support parity.

ECC RAM contains circuitry that not only detects errors but corrects it on the fly without causing interruption to system processes. ECC RAM is common on performance-enhanced workstations and server systems.

Note that the PC's motherboard and BIOS must be designed to support either parity or ECC RAM. Most motherboards that are designed for parity or ECC RAM can be configured in BIOS to disable error checking, thus enabling you to install RAM that is not parity or ECC RAM.

Memory Addressing

RAM is made up of millions of individual storage circuits, similar to the cells of a spreadsheet table. Each cell stores one bit of data, and any cell that holds data is charged into the "on" position, or in the binary terms that the PC understands, it's set to 1. Cells that don't have any data are "off," represented as a 0. This binary numbering scheme is the key to how the CPU uses RAM.

CPUs read data 1 byte at a time, so it takes eight individual cells to equal one addressable block of memory. Referring back to Chapter 5, you know that the number of wires on the address bus determines how much RAM a CPU can address, the formula being 2^x, with X being the number of wires on the address bus. Modern CPUs use 32 or more wires on the address bus.

Handling and Installing RAM

It's important that you follow the proper RAM handling and installation procedures to prevent damage to your PC. In this section, you will learn the proper way to handle RAM, how to install RAM, and how to confirm RAM installation.

Handling RAM

RAM is extremely sensitive to ESD, so take precautions while transporting, handling, and installing RAM. Always store RAM in antistatic bags or sleeves when it's not installed on a PC. If you have spare RAM lying around, always keep it labeled with the type, size, and speed so that you can identify it later. Don't take a RAM stick out of its bag before you actually need to install it. Handle RAM by the edges, and avoid touching the contacts or circuits.

Installing RAM Modules

DIMM and RIMM sticks need to go into their sockets vertically. You'll note on the motherboard that the guide notches on the sockets match up to the notches on the RAM to prevent you from inserting it the wrong way. Glance back up at Figures 6.3 and 6.4. All three RAM sticks pictured are the same size—roughly 5 inches wide—but the notches enable you to install each only in the proper slot.

Before you install a DIMM or RIMM into a slot, power down the computer and unplug it from the AC outlet. Make sure that the RAM retention clips at either end of the socket are pushed completely outward. Holding your RAM stick by the edges, position it above the RAM socket and press it straight down into the slot with gentle pressure. When the RAM is fully inserted, the retention clips will swing up and engage the retention notches in the outside edges of the RAM. Snap the clips firmly into place, and you're done. Figure 6.7 shows a properly seated DIMM RAM.

FIGURE 6.7 Properly seated DIMM

Barring ESD, not a lot can go wrong with installing DIMMs or RIMMs. The main thing to look for is improper seating. If the retention clip doesn't engage fully, your RAM stick isn't inserted completely. Double-check your positioning, and insert the RAM again. If it doesn't go in easily, you're not in the right position.

To remove a DIMM or RIMM, push the retention clips on the socket outward. These clips act as levers to raise the RAM stick out of the socket so that you can then pull it all the way out.

Confirm RAM Installation

Once you've installed your RAM, confirm that your PC recognizes it by booting up and checking the RAM count message (see Figure 6.8). Modern systems automatically detect the RAM size and configure the system accordingly. You rarely need to reconfigure BIOS RAM settings.

FIGURE 6.8 Confirming RAM installation by checking RAM count at startup

Objective 6.03 Troubleshooting RAM Errors

Your first task is to determine whether or not the error is, indeed, RAM- related. Once you've done that, you can begin the process of pinpointing the cause and taking corrective measures. The following sections list symptoms of false and genuine RAM errors, causes of errors, and corrective measures that you should take.

False Memory Errors

A lot of system errors get blamed on memory when they don't really have anything to do with RAM. If you've used any version of Windows prior to Windows 2000, you've surely seen the infamous *Out of memory* error pop up. "How can this be?" you may have asked yourself, "I've got *plenty* of RAM!"

As you may have guessed, that particular error doesn't have anything to do with the amount of RAM your PC has. It's actually Windows' way of telling you that your system resources are running low, which is a different matter altogether.

Other errors that mimic RAM errors are things such as page faults, exception errors, the dreaded Blue Screen of Death, the system slowdown or freeze, and the ever-popular spontaneous reboot. These are often tied to other factors, such as a badly fragmented hard disk, an overtaxed CPU, or a faulty application or driver. Overheating as a result of dust and dirt accumulated inside the PC case or a failed cooling fan is also a common culprit. Finally, a dying power supply can cause any or all of these random types of errors.

Common Symptoms of RAM Errors

The majority of genuine memory errors happen after you've made a change to your PC's hardware and restart the system and it goes through the power-on self test (POST) routine. Common startup errors include the following:

- System won't boot, accompanied by a loud, continuously repeating beep
- System boots, but the display screen is blank
- System boots, misreports RAM size
- System boots, reports memory or address error

Once you've determined that the error you're getting is a genuine RAM error, you can determine the cause and take corrective measures.

Common Causes of RAM Errors

Genuine RAM-related system errors are generally the result of one of two things: a RAM installation error or a faulty RAM component.

Improper installation is pretty common, though most techs don't like to admit it! This can mean you didn't fully seat or snap a RAM stick into its socket, or it can mean that some other related factor, such as dirt, dust, or corrosion on the RAM contact pins or socket, is causing a problem. Installation errors may also mean that while you were installing RAM, you accidentally unseated another hardware component or cable. Remove and inspect the RAM and RAM sockets for dirt or corrosion, and clean as necessary. Then reinstall the RAM and test the system again.

Faulty RAM is less common, but it does happen. Sometimes it comes out of the factory that way, but it's more likely that the RAM was damaged somehow during transport or storage. Don't forget that our old enemy ESD can cause good RAM to go bad in no time flat.

To test for bad RAM, remove and replace the RAM. Try to use RAM that you know is good, such as RAM taken from another working system of the same configuration. If the error recurs after you've installed known good RAM, you know that it's unlikely that the RAM is at fault. If the error goes away after you swap RAM sticks, you've probably got bad RAM.

You may wonder if there's a better way to test RAM sticks than swapping them around from PC to PC. Practically speaking, that's the only way to do it. Dedicated RAM testing devices exist, but they cost as much as a whole new PC system. Until a cheaper alternative comes along, you're stuck with doing it the old-fashioned way.

CHECKPOINT

✔ **Objective 6.01: RAM Overview** DRAM requires periodic refreshing, unlike SRAM, but it costs substantially less. SDRAM improves on EDO RAM by running at the speed of the data bus and moving data in high-speed bursts. Current systems sport DDR or DDR2 RAM on 184-pin or 240-pin

DIMMs. The two most common styles of error-checking RAM are parity and error-correcting code (ECC).

✔**Objective 6.02: Handling and Installing RAM** RAM is very sensitive to ESD, so always keep it in an antistatic bag or package until you're ready to install it. Make certain that you orient the RAM sticks properly using the motherboard socket's guide notches, and be sure to lock the RAM into place. Following installation, confirm the RAM count during bootup.

✔**Objective 6.03: Troubleshooting RAM Errors** Many errors that are not directly related to memory mimic RAM errors. Genuine RAM errors are caused by improper RAM installation or faulty or damaged RAM. Make certain that RAM is properly seated and banked, and that you don't accidentally unseat other components or cables during RAM installation. If you suspect faulty or damaged RAM, swap it out with known good RAM of the same type and speed.

REVIEW QUESTIONS

1. Which type of RAM never needs periodic refreshing?
 A. SRAM
 B. DRAM
 C. FPM RAM
 D. EDO RAM

2. Which type of RAM module has 168 pins?
 A. SIMMs
 B. DIMMs
 C. RIMMs
 D. None

3. Which RAM modules are available in two different pin packages?
 A. SIMMs
 B. DIMMs
 C. RIMMs
 D. SRAM

4. What RAM module was created to work specifically with RDRAM?
 A. SIMMs
 B. DIMMs

 C. RIMMs

 D. EDO RAM

5. Which type of RAM is used mainly for cache memory?

 A. SRAM

 B. DRAM

 C. EDO RAM

 D. SDRAM

6. What is stored in RAM?

 A. Currently running programs

 B. Programs that aren't running

 C. Nothing is stored in RAM

 D. Hardware information

7. Which type of RAM requires the use of Rambus channels?

 A. SRAM

 B. DRAM

 C. SDRAM

 D. RDRAM

8. Which type of RAM is measured in megahertz?

 A. SRAM

 B. SDRAM

 C. DRAM

 D. VRAM

9. What were parity chips used for?

 A. Error checking for RAM

 B. To increase the speed of RAM

 C. To increase the capacity of RAM

 D. To speed up Windows

10. What is a CRIMM used for?

 A. Error-checking

 B. Termination

 C. To synchronize RAM with the system clock

 D. To identify the RAM to the system BIOS

REVIEW ANSWERS

1. **A** SRAM requires no refreshing and, thus, incurs no CPU wait states.

2. **B** Dual inline memory modules (DIMMs) have 168 or 184 pins. SIMMs have 30 or 72 pins, and RIMMs have 184 pins.

3. **A** SIMMs are available in both 30-pin and 72-pin sizes.

4. **C** RIMMS were created for the insertion of RDRAM. RDRAM requires the use of Rambus channels and RIMM slots on the motherboard.

5. **A** SRAM is used mainly for cache memory because it's extremely expensive, but it doesn't need to be refreshed.

6. **A** Currently running programs are stored in RAM. When you start a program, part of the program is taken from the hard drive and placed into RAM to make access speeds quicker.

7. **D** RDRAM requires the use of Rambus channels. RDRAM also requires you to have RIMM slots on your motherboard.

8. **B** SDRAM is measured in megahertz. Manufacturers started including a nanosecond access speed setting after confusion occurred regarding the speed of SDRAM.

9. **A** Parity chips were used to check RAM for errors.

10. **B** CRIMMs are used to terminate RDRAM.

BIOS and CMOS

	NEWBIE	SOME EXPERIENCE	EXPERT
ETA	2 hours	1.5 hours	1 hour

In the seconds between the time that you press the power button and the desktop appears on your monitor, your PC goes through a series of ordered steps called the *boot process.* The vital components that drive the boot process are the system ROM, the system *basic input/output system (BIOS),* and the *complementary metal-oxide semiconductor (CMOS)* memory chip and setup utility. The system ROM—for *read-only memory*—is the special memory chip that stores the BIOS programs. System BIOS is the collective name for the hundreds of tiny programs that tell your computer everything from what time it is to what *kind* of computer it is. The CMOS memory chip and the setup utility enable you to control important aspects of your PC configuration such as the boot device sequence.

All PCs share these components in common and follow the same process when booting up. Understanding the boot process on one computer enables you to troubleshoot the boot process on any computer. Likewise, with only slight variations, BIOS and CMOS work the same on practically any PC. You will find yourself entering CMOS many times in your career as a PC technician, and the CompTIA A+ certification exams expect you to demonstrate an understanding of the system ROM, system BIOS, and CMOS setup utility functions.

Objective 7.01 Boot Process and POST

The three main stages of the boot process are the power-on, *power-on self test (POST),* and operating system (OS) loading steps.

Power-on/CPU Wakes

You start the process by powering the system on, sending current to the motherboard and drives. Assuming your power supply is in good working order, a special wire on the CPU called the *power good* wire is charged, telling it to wake up. The CPU then communicates with the system ROM chip and starts the BIOS programs.

POST

Unlike a person who wakes up knowing who they are and how many fingers they have, a computer literally rediscovers itself every time it powers up. This is done via the POST process. During POST, the system BIOS communicates with

all essential hardware and, in essence, tells them all to identify themselves. The devices—the keyboard, mouse, disk drives, RAM, display adapter, and so on—then run internal diagnostic routines and report back to the BIOS. If one of the devices reports an error condition back to the BIOS, the BIOS reports this back to the user by using special POST *error codes*.

POST Error Codes

As you may have guessed, the POST process is the most vital of the steps in the boot process. It's during POST that any serious low-level hardware errors come to light. The way that the PC communicates POST errors is through special sound codes called *beep codes* and through text or numeric messages displayed on your monitor.

Beep Codes

Beep codes vary according to the PC's BIOS manufacturer, although you'll find certain codes are common on most PCs. A single, happy-sounding chirp at bootup signals that all is well. A long, repeating beep signals a problem with RAM. A series of beeps—one long and three short—usually points to a problem with the video card.

Numeric and Text Codes

POST may also display numeric or text errors indicating the nature of a hardware problem. Numeric error codes are somewhat standardized into certain code *ranges*. For instance, an error code in the range 100–199 indicates a motherboard error, 200–299 indicates a RAM error, and 300–399 indicates a keyboard error.

Text errors tend to be fairly direct statements, such as "Floppy drive failure" or "Keyboard error or no keyboard present," that display on your monitor and usually require you to press a key such as F1 to continue.

Some hardware problems prevent any POST errors from properly appearing on the display screen or coming through the system speaker. In these cases, a special hardware tool called a *POST card* comes in handy.

POST Cards

POST cards aren't the kind you use to send snail-mail holiday greetings. A POST card, shown in Figure 7.1, is a dedicated hardware component that plugs into a PCI slot and displays POST codes coming from the system BIOS.

The POST card uses an LED display to present special POST code listings that the technician then interprets. Most POST cards come with documentation explaining the various error codes in general, but different BIOS manufacturers

POST card error code readout

use different codes. You should visit the motherboard manufacturer's Web site for information on the specific motherboard you're testing. You can also check the BIOS maker's Web site for error code explanations.

OS Loads

During POST, the BIOS also locates the system boot device—such as the floppy disk, CD-ROM, or hard drive—that contains the OS. Once the POST process completes successfully, the BIOS then passes control of the boot process over to the PC's OS. The exact loading process differs from one OS to the next, but in general, one or more vital system files such as NTLDR (pronounced "NT loader") load into memory and start the ball rolling. Things move fast from there, as the OS load its core files, drivers, and services into RAM. The next thing you know, you're looking at your desktop and hearing the soothing strains of the Windows logon sound file.

 Objective 7.02 System ROM

The system ROM chip stores the system BIOS routines and CMOS setup utility. System ROM is distinctively labeled with the BIOS maker's name, as shown in Figure 7.2. On older PCs, the BIOS routines were hard-coded onto the

FIGURE 7.2 System ROM chip

system ROM chip, meaning that the BIOS were unchangeable without replacing the entire ROM chip. Current motherboards use writable ROM chips such as *flash ROM*. Writable ROM chips enable you to install updated BIOS information without physically replacing the chip.

Exam Tip

Many techs refer to the system BIOS as the *ROM BIOS*, and the CompTIA A+ certification exams may use either term.

There's a big difference between system ROM chips and RAM that you need to appreciate. RAM is called *volatile* memory because RAM stores data only while the PC is powered on. System ROM memory, on the other hand, is *non-volatile* memory and retains data even with the system is powered off.

From a technician's standpoint, you don't need to do much to maintain the system ROM. System ROM requires no servicing beyond the usual blowing-out-the-dust type of PC case maintenance that should be a part of your routine. Nor does the system ROM itself ever need to be updated, although the BIOS programs residing on it sometimes do. The only type of maintenance that you'll ever undertake on the system ROM is replacing the CMOS battery (described in the next section). Let's take a closer look at the system BIOS and CMOS setup utility.

System BIOS and CMOS Setup Utility

Objective 7.03

Y̶ou never deal directly with the many BIOS routines, but instead interact with them only peripherally through the CMOS setup utility. Motherboard manufacturers don't actually write their own BIOS routines. Instead, they buy BIOS from third-party BIOS makers; among the largest makers are American Megatrends (AMI) and Phoenix Technologies. The latter produces BIOS under both the Phoenix and Award brands. A great deal of uniformity exists among brands of BIOS software, however, so from a technician's point of view, there's not all that much of a difference between them.

System BIOS

The system BIOS contains many routines—called services—to initialize and support the many devices that make up a modern PC. Services control things as mundane as whether the NUM LOCK key is engaged at startup, to things as exotic-sounding as the *SDRAM precharge control,* and beyond.

Unlike most types of PC software, BIOS routines rarely change. BIOS makers update BIOS routines only to fix known bugs (thus enhancing stability) and to add important functions such as compatibility with new hardware or hardware standards.

Travel Advisory

Motherboard manufacturers make new BIOS routines available to enhance stability and to add new functions.

Updating the System BIOS

Techs refer to updating system BIOS as *flashing the BIOS*. It's a simple procedure, but you must take care to ensure that it's done correctly and without interruption. A BIOS flash procedure that gets interrupted usually results in a PC that won't boot and a motherboard that's rendered completely useless! Before flashing your BIOS, back up your important documents and update any system repair discs or emergency rescue diskettes. Do your best to make certain that the process isn't disturbed once you start.

Travel Advisory

If something goes wrong during a system BIOS flashing and you turn a motherboard into a paperweight, *sometimes* the motherboard manufacturer can help you. If it's a mission-critical system and the board is out of warranty, it's worth a shot.

BIOS makers provide updating utilities for their BIOS on their Web sites. The correct steps to update a system BIOS are as follows:

1. Obtain the flashing program from the manufacturer's Web site.
2. Turn off your system.
3. Insert a valid boot disk and boot to the A: prompt.
4. Insert the disk containing the flashing program and new BIOS into the floppy drive.
5. Run the flashing program according to your BIOS manufacturer's instructions, making certain to back up your current BIOS when prompted.
6. Restart your system when the update is complete.

That's all there is to it! A lot of current motherboards come with a Windows-based utility that will go to the Web, download an updated BIOS, and enable you to flash the BIOS from within Windows. When it works, it's sweet.

CMOS Setup Utility

The CMOS setup utility, stored in the system ROM, enables you to configure important system BIOS settings stored in the CMOS chip that's a part of the *Southbridge* on most PCs. These settings include CPU setup, boot device sequence, power management, and a number of others, as described here.

Travel Advisory

The *chipset* is the circuitry built onto the motherboard that acts as the conduit between the CPU and the rest of the components on the PC. Chipset technology changes frequently, but in general, the chipset is split into two distinct pathways. The *Northbridge* connects the CPU to the system RAM (Intel and older AMD only) and the PCI Express, accelerated graphics port (AGP), and peripheral component interconnect (PCI) buses, while the *Southbridge* links the CPU to the "secondary" buses—universal serial bus (USB), IDE, PS/2, and so on.

Entering the CMOS Setup Utility

You can't enter the CMOS setup utility from within your OS; you must do it during the early stages of the boot process. Different BIOS makers specify different methods for entering CMOS (Figure 7.3). The instructions for entering CMOS appear on your monitor during bootup. Watch the messages carefully and press the proper key when prompted. Typically, AMI and Award BIOS makers have you press the DEL key when prompted. Phoenix might have you press CTRL-ALT-ESC, or possibly F2. Check your motherboard documentation for the exact method on your PC.

Once you enter CMOS, navigate with the keyboard (AMI provides mouse support). Use the TAB and arrow keys to move around and the ENTER key to make selections. This also varies according to which BIOS is installed on your PC. Navigation instructions should be prominent in the display somewhere. If you get stuck, press the F1 key to bring up a Help menu.

Let's take a look at some of the more important CMOS settings.

SoftMenu The SoftMenu enables you to change the voltage and multiplier settings on the motherboard for the CPU from the defaults. Motherboards that cater to overclockers tend to have this option. Usually you just set this to Auto or Default and stay away from this screen (Figure 7.4).

Standard CMOS Features The Standard CMOS Features screen (Figure 7.5) enables you to change floppy drive and hard drive settings, as well as the system's

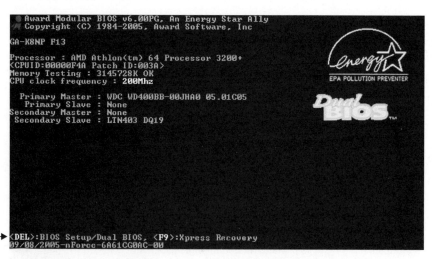

Instructions for entering CMOS

FIGURE 7.3 Each BIOS maker provides instructions for entering CMOS at bootup

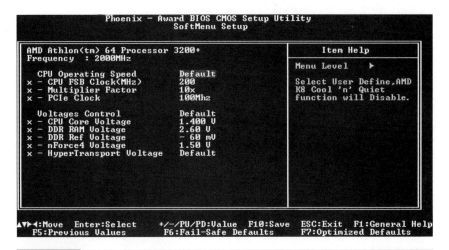

FIGURE 7.4 SoftMenu Setup screen

date and time. Most systems display the hard drives and optical drives here automatically.

Advanced BIOS Features The Advanced BIOS Features screen is the dumping ground for all the settings that aren't covered in the Standard menu but don't fit nicely under any other screen. This screen varies wildly from one system to the next. You most often use this screen to select the boot options (Figure 7.6).

FIGURE 7.5 Standard CMOS Features screen

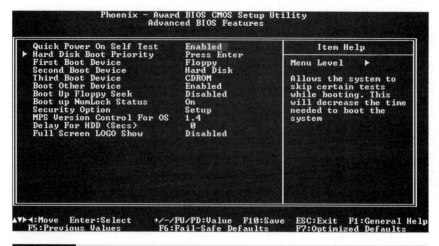

FIGURE 7.6 Advanced BIOS Features screen

Advanced Chipset Features The Advanced Chipset Features screen strikes fear into most everyone because it deals with extremely low-level chipset functions. Avoid this screen unless a high-level tech (like a motherboard maker's support tech) explicitly tells you to do something in here (Figure 7.7).

Integrated Peripherals You will use the Integrated Peripherals screen quite often (Figure 7.8). Here, you configure, enable, or disable the onboard ports, such as the serial and parallel ports.

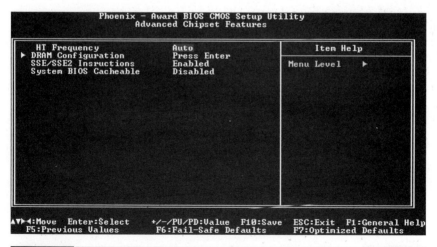

FIGURE 7.7 Advanced Chipset Features screen

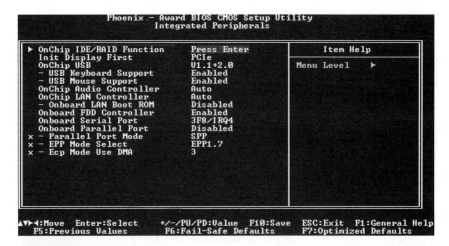

FIGURE 7.8 Integrated Peripherals screen

Power Management As the name implies, you can use the Power Management screen to set up the power management settings for the system. These settings work in concert (sometimes in conflict) with Windows' power management settings to control how and when devices turn off and back on to conserve power (Figure 7.9).

PnP/PCI Configurations All CMOS setup utilities come with menu items that are for the most part no longer needed, but no one wants to remove. PnP/PCI is

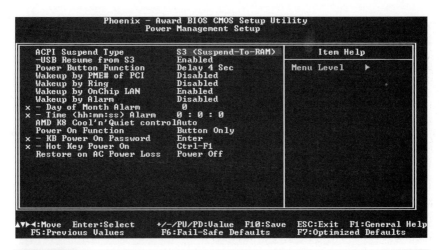

FIGURE 7.9 Power Management screen

a perfect example. Plug and Play (PnP) is how devices automatically work when you snap them into your PC. PCI is a type of slot used for cards. Odds are very good you'll never deal with this screen (Figure 7.10).

Other Options Some of the other options you'll find in CMOS, such as the PC Health Status, enable you to see the active temperature of the computer or how fast the fans are spinning. Other options don't even have their own screens. Rather, these simply use small dialog boxes that pop up, usually asking, "Are you sure?" The Load Fail-Safe/Optimized defaults options keep you from having to memorize all those weird settings you'll never touch. Fail-Safe sets everything to simple settings—you might occasionally use this setting when low-level problems like freeze-ups occur and you've checked more obvious areas first. Optimized sets the CMOS to the best possible speed/stability for the system. You might use this option after tampering with the CMOS so much so that you need to put it back like it was!

- **Set Password** A user-CMOS password enables you to set a degree of low level security on the PC. With this setting configured, the user is required to enter a password during the early stages of the boot process. The PC will not boot without the correct password. In most CMOS utilities, you can also set supervisor passwords that prevent unauthorized persons from accessing the CMOS. This is especially important if the PC is accessible by the public, such as at a trade show or in a library. Remember, however, that if you forget or lose the password, you'll be unable to access the CMOS.

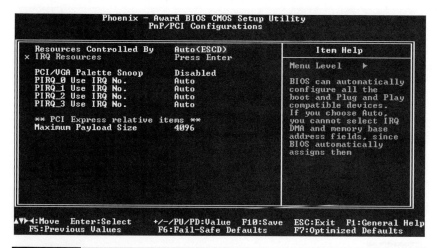

FIGURE 7.10 PnP/PCI Configurations screen

Should you wind up locking yourself out of your PC by losing the CMOS password, you have a couple of ways to get access. You can use the CMOS clear jumper, as discussed in Chapter 5. Check the motherboard's documentation for the exact instructions for your particular motherboard. The other method is to disconnect the AC power cable (remember that ATX systems always have a 5-V trickle charge on the motherboard when plugged in) and unplug the CMOS battery for a few seconds. This clears your CMOS of all settings, including the offending password.

Exam Tip

Remember that setting a jumper on the motherboard or removing and replacing the CMOS battery can clear CMOS passwords.

- **Save & Exit Setup** This option will make any changes you've configured in CMOS setup permanent. Use it with caution! Typically, selecting this option brings up a confirmation prompt along the lines of "Are you really, really sure you want to make these changes? Y/N." Don't make any changes unless you're absolutely certain what will be the effect.
- **Exit Without Saving** Of all the options on the CMOS setup menu, this one is your best friend. Exit Without Saving undoes any changes that you've made. Choosing this option brings up another "Are you sure? Y/N" type of confirmation prompt. Choose Y to take your leave of CMOS setup without doing any damage.

Replacing the CMOS Battery

When CMOS batteries fail, they do so gradually. The first and best indicator that a PC's CMOS battery is dying is that the PC starts to lose time. If you notice that your PC's clock is running slow, or if you're consistently prompted to enter the date and time when you boot the PC, it's time to replace the CMOS battery.

Replacing the CMOS battery is as simple as sliding the old one out of the bracket and slipping the new one in its place. Figure 7.11 shows a CMOS battery.

A built-in capacitor preserves your current BIOS configuration during the battery-swapping process, but you may be prompted to reconfigure the date and time settings manually after swapping a CMOS battery.

FIGURE 7.11 CMOS battery

It's vitally important that the voltage of the replacement battery match the original. Newer systems run on 3.6-V batteries, while older ones typically use the 6-V variety. Check your motherboard's documentation to determine the correct battery for your system.

CHECKPOINT

✔**Objective 7.01: Boot Process and POST** After the CPU powers up, the system BIOS loads and runs the POST to test all the built-in and common devices in the PC. The POST sounds a beep code or displays numeric or text error messages in the event of hardware failure. POST cards enable you to interpret POST error codes and troubleshoot a dead PC. At the end of the POST the operating system loads.

✔**Objective 7.02: System ROM** The system ROM chip stores the system BIOS programs and CMOS setup utility. System ROM is flash ROM memory that maintains data even while the PC is turned off through the use of a CMOS battery.

✔**Objective 7.03: System BIOS and CMOS Setup Utility** The system BIOS includes hundreds of small programs that establish communication between your PC hardware and the OS. System BIOS can be updated (*flashed*) to fix bugs or add new functions. The CMOS setup utility enables you to modify settings for built-in and common devices, such as floppy and hard drives. You access CMOS by entering a key combination that's specific to the manufacturer of the BIOS on your OS. You should write down your CMOS settings before making any changes.

REVIEW QUESTIONS

1. Which of the following can you configure in the CMOS? (Select three.)
 - **A.** Parallel ports
 - **B.** Serial ports
 - **C.** Hard drive
 - **D.** Video resolution

2. When should you update your system BIOS?
 - **A.** When you upgrade your OS
 - **B.** Every time you boot your computer
 - **C.** Every time you defragment your computer
 - **D.** To add functionality or fix known bugs

3. What should you do before making any changes to your CMOS settings?
 - **A.** Reboot your computer.
 - **B.** Write down the current settings.
 - **C.** Remove all the cables from your PC.
 - **D.** Replace the BIOS.

4. What do you need to do if the clock on your PC starts losing time?
 - **A.** Replace your BIOS.
 - **B.** Replace the CMOS battery.
 - **C.** Replace your hard drive.
 - **D.** Reinstall Windows.

5. If a user password has been set in the CMOS, what will happen?

 A. An unauthorized person will be unable to enter the CMOS settings program.

 B. The user must enter the correct password to boot the system.

 C. Nothing will happen.

 D. Only certain settings in the CMOS will be available to unauthorized users.

6. If you've set and forgotten a supervisor password for your CMOS, how can you get into the CMOS settings program? (Select two.)

 A. Reboot the PC and press F1.

 B. Set a jumper on your motherboard to clear the password.

 C. Reinstall Windows.

 D. Remove and reinstall the CMOS battery.

7. At startup, where does your PC receive its first set of instructions?

 A. Operating system

 B. RAM BIOS

 C. ROM BIOS

 D. CMOS

8. If you're using Windows and set your Plug and Play BIOS so the BIOS configures your PnP devices, what will happen?

 A. Your BIOS will configure the devices.

 B. Windows will configure the devices.

 C. The devices will need to be configured manually.

 D. None of the above.

9. If you boot your computer and receive a 301 error code, which of the following devices has a problem?

 A. Floppy drive

 B. Hard drive

 C. Video

 D. Keyboard

10. You get a tech call from a distraught field tech. He was upgrading a client's PC and now it won't boot at all. When he applies power, the

fans and drives spin, but the computer screen stays blank and the PC just beeps, over and over and over. What's most likely the problem?

A. He installed a video card incorrectly.

B. He installed RAM incorrectly.

C. He installed a CPU incorrectly.

D. Nothing's wrong. It sometimes takes a PC a few reboots to work after performing upgrades.

REVIEW ANSWERS

1. **A** **B** **C** Parallel ports, serial ports, and your hard drive are all configurable in the CMOS settings program.

2. **D** System BIOS should be updated only when a new BIOS version will fix a problem or add new functions.

3. **B** Before making any changes in the CMOS, you should write down the current CMOS settings. Taking the time to do this can save you from having to retrace your steps later.

4. **B** If the clock on your PC starts losing time, this is a good indication that it's time to change the CMOS battery.

5. **B** If a user password is set in the CMOS, the computer won't fully boot until the correct password is entered by the user.

6. B D If you've set and forgotten a supervisor password in the CMOS, you can still enter the CMOS by setting a jumper on the motherboard to clear the password or by removing and reinstalling the CMOS battery.

7. **C** At startup, your PC receives its first set of instructions from the system BIOS, also called ROM BIOS. There's no such thing as RAM BIOS, a fact you should remember for the exam.

8. **B** If you're using a PnP operating system, regardless of the settings made for the PnP BIOS, the operating system will override the settings.

9. **D** All 300 series error codes refer to the keyboard; therefore, if you receive a 301 error code, this means you're experiencing a keyboard problem.

10. **B** The repeating beep at boot and a "dead" PC are classic indicators of improperly seated RAM.

Hard Drives

	NEWBIE	SOME EXPERIENCE	EXPERT
ETA	4 hours	3 hours	1.5 hours

159

Hard drives enable you to store operating systems, applications, and data so that they're available when the PC powers up. Because they store the data, hard drives hold a central place in the computer. If the drive dies, all the data dies, too, and that's not a good thing!

This chapter looks at five aspects of hard drives in the PC. First, you'll read about various hard drive technologies so you can readily make the proper recommendation for your clients. Second, you'll learn the installation steps for ATA and SCSI drives. Third, the chapter talks about preparing a drive to hold data. Fourth, you'll learn about setting up drives for data redundancy. Finally, you'll read about essential tools and practices to maintain and troubleshoot hard drives.

Objective 8.01 Hard Drive Technologies

Hard drives store data magnetically onto spinning platters, using a fast-moving actuator arm with read-write heads. Figure 8.1 shows the inside of a hard drive. Although almost all hard drives look similar on the outside, their mechanical nature reveals wide variations among drives in three categories: capacity, seek time, and bandwidth. The key for recommending a drive is to understand that a 200-GB drive is smaller than a 500-GB drive; a 5400-rpm drive is slower than a 7200-rpm drive (but perhaps a little quieter) and will have a corre-

FIGURE 8.1 Inside a hard drive

spondingly slower seek time; and a drive with a 2-MB cache won't have the sustained throughput of a drive with a 16-MB cache.

All hard drives connect to a hard drive controller of some sort with a ribbon cable. All drives need 5-V and 12-V power from the power supply, though connectors differ among the various technologies. All desktop hard drives have the same 3.5-inch rectangular shape.

For all the similarities, two distinctly different hard drive technologies have been used in PCs: ATA and SCSI. They connect to their own type of controller and use cabling unique to themselves. Both technologies have been around for many years so you'll find lots of variation in the hardware out in the field and in the marketplace.

ATA

The *Advanced Technologies Attachment (ATA)* drives have been around since the beginning of the PC, though they've advanced a lot since the early days. Two styles exist in modern PCs, *parallel ATA (PATA)* and *serial ATA (SATA)*, with the latter rapidly replacing the former as the hard drive of choice in most systems. Techs often refer to ATA drives as *integrated drive electronics (IDE)* or *Enhanced IDE (EIDE)*. Any of the terms are acceptable.

PATA

The latest (and most likely last) PATA standard, called ATA/ATAPI-7, provides support for very large hard drives (144 petabytes, a number greater than 144 million GB) at speeds up to 133 MB per second (MBps). All PATA drives use a standard Molex power connector (Figure 8.2). Slower PATA drives (33 MBps and slower) can get by with a 40-pin ribbon cable. Drives that go 66 MBps or faster require an 80-wire cable. Figure 8.3 shows both types of cables, and Table 8.1 shows the types of PATA drives you might see in the field.

FIGURE 8.2 Molex connector

| **FIGURE 8.3** | 40-pin and 80-wire PATA cables |

You can connect up to two PATA drives—including hard drives, optical drives, and tape drives—to a single ATA controller.

Exam Tip

You should know that the technologies that enabled steadily larger drive size are Logical Block Addressing (LBA) (up to 8 GB), INT 13 extensions (up to 137 GB), and ATA/ATAPI-6 (up to 144 PB).

SATA

For all its longevity as the mass storage interface of choice for the PC, parallel ATA has problems. First, the flat ribbon cables impede airflow and can be a pain to insert properly. Second, the cables have a limited length, only 18 inches. Third, you can't hot-swap PATA drives. You have to shut down completely before installing or replacing a drive. Finally, the technology has simply reached the limits of what it can do in terms of throughput.

Serial ATA addresses these issues. SATA creates a point-to-point connection between the SATA device—hard disk, CD-ROM, CD-RW, DVD-ROM, DVD-RW, and so on—and the SATA controller. At a glance, SATA devices look identical to standard PATA devices. Take a closer look at the cable and power connectors, however, and you'll see significant differences (Figure 8.4).

| **TABLE 8.1** | Common PATA Drive Types |

Name	Transfer Mode	Speed	Cable Type
ATA/33	Ultra DMA mode 2	33 MBps	40-pin
ATA/66	Ultra DMA mode 3	66 MBps	80-wire
ATA/100	Ultra DMA mode 4	100 MBps	80-wire
ATA/133	Ultra DMA mode 5	133 MBps	80-wire

Data port
Power port
Data cable
Power cable

FIGURE 8.4 SATA power and data connectors

Because SATA devices send data serially instead of in parallel, the SATA interface needs far fewer physical wires—seven instead of the 80 wires typical of PATA—resulting in much thinner cabling. This might not seem significant, but the benefit is that thinner cabling means better cable control and better airflow through the PC case, resulting in better cooling.

Further, the maximum SATA device cable length is more than twice that of a PATA cable—about 40 inches (1 meter) instead of 18 inches. Again, this might not seem like a big deal, unless you've struggled to connect a PATA hard disk installed into the top bay of a full-tower case to a PATA connector located all the way at the bottom of the motherboard.

SATA does away with the entire master/slave concept. Each drive connects to one port, so no more daisy-chaining drives. Further, there's no maximum number of drives—many motherboards are now available that support up to eight SATA drives. Want more? Snap in a SATA host card and load 'em up.

The big news, however, is in data throughput. As the name implies, SATA devices transfer data in serial bursts instead of parallel, as PATA devices do. Typically, you might not think of serial devices as being faster than parallel, but in this case, that's how it works. A SATA device's single stream of data moves much faster than the multiple streams of data coming from a PATA device—theoretically up to 30 times faster. SATA drives come in two common varieties, the 1.5Gb and the 3Gb, that have a maximum throughput of 150 MBps and 300 MBps, respectively.

SATA's ease of use has made it the choice for desktop system storage, and its success is already showing in the fact that more than 90 percent of all hard drives sold today are SATA drives.

eSATA

External SATA (eSATA) extends the SATA bus to external devices, as the name implies. The eSATA drives use similar connectors to internal SATA, but they're keyed differently so you can't mistake one for the other. Figure 8.5 shows eSATA connectors on the back of a motherboard. eSATA uses shielded cable lengths up to 2 meters outside the PC and is hot-pluggable. The beauty of eSATA is that it extends the SATA bus at full speed, so you're not limited to the meager 50 or 60 MBps of FireWire or USB.

SCSI

Many specialized server machines and enthusiasts' systems use the *small computer system interface (SCSI)* technologies for various pieces of core hardware and peripherals, from hard drives to printers to high-end tape backup machines. SCSI is different from ATA in that SCSI devices connect together in a string of devices called a *chain*. Each device in the chain gets a SCSI ID to distinguish it from other devices on the chain. Last, the ends of a SCSI chain must be terminated. Let's dive into SCSI now and see how SCSI chains, SCSI IDs, and termination all work.

FIGURE 8.5 eSATA connectors

SCSI is an old technology dating from the late 1970s, but it has been continually updated. SCSI is faster than ATA (though the gap is closing fast), and until SATA arrived, SCSI was the only choice for anyone using RAID (see the "Protecting Data with RAID" section a little later). SCSI is arguably fading away, but it still deserves some mention.

SCSI Chains

SCSI manifests itself through a *SCSI chain*, a series of SCSI devices working together through a host adapter. The *host adapter* provides the interface between the SCSI chain and the PC. Figure 8.6 shows a typical PCI host adapter. Many techs refer to the host adapter as the *SCSI controller,* so you should be comfortable with both terms.

All SCSI devices can be divided into two groups: internal and external. Internal SCSI devices are attached inside the PC and connect to the host adapter through the latter's internal connector. Figure 8.7 shows an internal SCSI device, in this case a CD-ROM drive. External devices hook to the external connector of the host adapter. Figure 8.8 is an example of an external SCSI device.

FIGURE 8.6 SCSI host adapter

FIGURE 8.7 Internal SCSI CD-ROM

Internal SCSI devices connect to the host adapter with a 68-pin ribbon cable (Figure 8.9). This flat, flexible cable functions precisely like a PATA cable. Many external devices connect to the host adapter with a 50-pin high density (HD) connector. Figure 8.10 shows a host adapter external port. Higher end SCSI devices use a 68-pin HD connector.

FIGURE 8.8 Back of external SCSI device

FIGURE 8.9 Typical 68-pin ribbon cable

Multiple internal devices can be connected together simply by using a cable with enough connectors. Figure 8.9, for example, shows a cable that can take up to three SCSI devices, plus the host adapter.

Assuming the SCSI host adapter has a standard external port (some controllers don't have external connections at all), plugging in an external SCSI device is as simple as running a cable from device to controller. The external SCSI connectors are D-shaped, so you can't plug them in backward. As an added bonus,

FIGURE 8.10 50-pin HD port on SCSI host adapter

FIGURE 8.11 Internal SCSI chain with two devices

some external SCSI devices have two ports, one to connect to the host adapter and a second to connect to another SCSI device. The process of connecting a device directly to another device is called *daisy-chaining*. You can daisy-chain up to 15 devices to one host adapter. SCSI chains can be internal, external, or both (see Figures 8.11 and 8.12).

FIGURE 8.12 Internal and external devices on one SCSI chain

SCSI IDs

If you're going to connect a number of devices on the same SCSI chain, you must provide some way for the host adapter to tell one device from another. To differentiate devices, SCSI uses a unique identifier called the *SCSI ID*. The SCSI ID number can range from 0 to 15. SCSI IDs are similar to many other PC hardware settings in that a SCSI device can theoretically have any SCSI ID, as long as that ID is not already taken by another device connected to the same host adapter.

SCSI IDs follow some conventions, but nothing's set in stone. Typically, most people set the host adapter to 7 or 15, but you can change this setting. Aside from the host adapter, it does not matter which device gets which number, and you can skip numbers. Many folks give ID 0 to a bootable hard drive, but in reality, the ID simply has to match what the controller has as the ID for a bootable drive. Restrictions on IDs apply only within a single chain. Two devices can have the same ID, in other words, as long as they are on different chains (Figure 8.13).

Every SCSI device has some method of setting its SCSI ID. The trick is to figure out how as you're holding the device in your hand. A SCSI device may use jumpers, dip switches, or even tiny dials; every new SCSI device is a new adventure as you try to determine how to set its SCSI ID.

Termination

Whenever you send a signal down a wire, some of that signal reflects back up the wire, creating an echo and causing electronic chaos. SCSI chains use *termination*

SCSI device
SCSI ID 6

SCSI device
SCSI ID 1

SCSI host adapter
SCSI ID 7

SCSI host adapter
SCSI ID 7

FIGURE 8.13 IDs don't conflict between separate SCSI chains

to prevent this problem. Termination simply means putting something on the ends of the wire to prevent this echo. Terminators are usually pull-down resistors and can manifest themselves in many different ways. Most of the devices within a PC have the appropriate termination built in. On other devices, including SCSI chains and some network cables, you have to set termination during installation.

The rule with SCSI is that you *must* terminate *only* the ends of the SCSI chain. You have to terminate the ends of the cable, which usually means that you need to terminate the two devices at the ends of the cable. Do *not* terminate devices that are not on the ends of the cable. Figure 8.14 shows some examples of where to terminate SCSI devices.

Because any SCSI device might be on the end of a chain, most manufacturers build SCSI devices that can self-terminate. Some devices will detect that they are on the end of the SCSI chain and will automatically terminate themselves. Most devices, however, require that you set a jumper or switch to enable termination (Figure 8.15).

FIGURE 8.14 Location of the terminated devices

FIGURE 8.15 Termination settings

Objective 8.02 Installing Hard Drives

Installing a drive is a fairly simple process if you take the time to make sure you've got the right drive for your system, you've configured the drive properly, and you've made a few quick tests to see if it's running properly. Since PATA, SATA, and SCSI have different cabling requirements, we'll look at each of these separately.

Choosing Your Drive

First, decide where you're going to put the drive. Look for an open ATA connection. Is it PATA or SATA? Is it a dedicated RAID controller? (See "Protecting Data with RAID," later in the chapter.) Many motherboards with built-in RAID controllers have a CMOS setting that enables you to turn the RAID on or off (Figure 8.16). Do you have the right controller for a SCSI drive?

Second, make sure you have room for the drive in the case. Where will you place it? Do you have a spare power connector? Will the data and power cables reach the drive? A quick test fit is always a good idea.

Jumpers and Cabling on PATA Drives

If you have only one hard drive, set the drive's jumpers to master or standalone. If you have two drives, set one to master and the other to slave. Figure 8.17 shows a close-up of a PATA hard drive showing the jumpers.

FIGURE 8.16 Settings for RAID in CMOS

At first glance, you might notice that the jumpers aren't actually labeled *master* and *slave*. So how do you know how to set them properly? The easiest way is to read the front of the drive; most drives have a diagram on the housing that explains how to set the jumpers properly. Figure 8.18 shows the front of one of these drives, so you can see how to set the drive to master or slave.

Hard disk drives may have other jumpers that may or may not concern you during installation. One common set of jumpers is used for diagnostics at the

FIGURE 8.17 Master/slave jumpers on a hard drive

MDL : WD200EB — 00CPF0
DATE: 09 APR 2002
DCM : DSBANV2C

Product of Malaysia

WD P/N: WD200EB — 00CPF0

J8 JUMPER SETTINGS
9 7 5 3 1
40 Pin
Conn.
POWER
10 8 6 4 2
CABLE SELECT SETTING

Standard Settings
Master Single
w/ Slave or
Slave Present Master

Product warranty will be void if seal,
label or cover is removed or damaged

FIGURE 8.18 Drive label showing master/slave settings

manufacturing plant or for special settings in other kinds of devices that use hard drives. Ignore them. They have no bearing in the PC world. Second, many drives provide a third setting, which is used if only one drive connects to a controller. Often, master and single drive are the same setting on the hard drive, although some hard drives require separate settings.

Travel Advisory
The name for the single drive setting varies among manufacturers. Some use *Single*; others use *1 Drive* or *Standalone*.

Many current PATA hard drives use a jumper setting called *cable select,* rather than master or slave. As the name implies, the position on the cable determines which drive will be master or slave: master on the end, slave in the middle. For cable select to work properly with two drives, both drives must be set as cable select and the cable itself must be a special cable-select cable. If you see a ribbon cable with a pinhole through one wire, watch out! That's a cable-select cable.

If you don't see a label on the drive that tells you how to set the jumpers, you have several options. First, look for the drive maker's Web site. Every drive manufacturer lists its drive jumper settings on the Web, although it can take a while to find the information you want. Second, try phoning the hard drive maker directly. Unlike many other PC parts manufacturers, hard drive producers tend to stay in business for a long period of time and offer great technical support.

Hard drive cables have a colored stripe that corresponds to the number-one pin—called *Pin 1*—on the connector. You need to make certain that Pin 1 on the controller is on the same wire as Pin 1 on the hard drive. Failing to plug in the drive properly will also prevent the PC from recognizing the drive. If you incorrectly set the master/slave jumpers or cable to the hard drives, you won't break anything; it just won't work.

Finally, you need to plug a Molex connector from the power supply into the drive. All modern PATA drives use a Molex connector.

Cabling SATA Drives

Installing SATA hard disk drives is even easier than installing PATA devices because there's no master, slave, or cable select configuration to mess with. In fact, there are no jumper settings to worry about at all, as SATA supports only a single device per controller channel. Simply connect the power and plug in the controller cable as shown in Figure 8.19—the OS automatically detects the drive and it's ready to go. The keying on the SATA controller and power cables makes it impossible to install either incorrectly.

The biggest problem with SATA drives is that many motherboards come with four or more. Sure, the cabling is easy enough, but what do you do when it comes time to start the computer and the system is trying to find the right hard drive to boot up? That's where CMOS comes into play. By default, boot order and drive letter priority follows SATA controller ID, so SATA 0 in a single drive system would be C:, SATA 1 would be D:, and so on.

FIGURE 8.19 Properly connected SATA cable

Travel Advisory

Most CMOS setup utilities enable you to change the boot order quite easily, which is great for multiple–operating system computers. Just put one OS on one drive and the other OS on the other. A simple reboot and quick trip to CMOS and you can switch from one drive to the other.

Connecting SCSI Drives

Connecting SCSI drives requires three things: You must use a controller that works with your drive. You need to set unique SCSI IDs on the controller and the drive. Finally, you need to connect the ribbon cable and power connections properly. With SCSI, you need to attach the data cable correctly. You can reverse a PATA cable, for example, and nothing happens except the drive doesn't work. If you reverse a SCSI cable, however, you can seriously damage the drive. Just as with PATA cables, Pin 1 on the SCSI data cable must go to Pin 1 on both the drive and the host adapter.

 Objective 8.03 # Partitioning and Formatting

*P*artitioning establishes the framework upon which your file system is built. *Formatting* creates the file system.

Partitioning

Windows 2000 and XP support two different partitioning methods: the older but more universal master boot record (MBR) partitioning scheme and the newer (but proprietary to Microsoft) dynamic storage partitioning scheme. Microsoft calls a hard drive that uses the MBR partitioning scheme a *basic disk* and a drive using the dynamic storage partitioning scheme a *dynamic disk*. A single Windows system with two hard drives may have one of the drives partitioned as a basic disk and the other as a dynamic disk, and the system will run perfectly well.

Basic Disks

Basic disk partitioning creates two very small data structures on a drive, the master boot record (MBR) and a partition table, and stores them on the first sector of the hard drive—called the *boot sector*. The MBR is nothing more than a tiny bit of code that takes control of the boot process from the system BIOS. When the computer boots to a hard drive, BIOS automatically looks for MBR code on the boot sector. The MBR has only one job: to look in the partition table for a partition with a valid OS (Figure 8.20).

Travel Advisory

Only one MBR and one partition table exist per basic disk.

All basic disk partition tables support up to four partitions. The partition table supports two types of partitions: primary partitions and extended partitions. *Primary partitions* are designed to support bootable operating systems. *Extended partitions* are not bootable. A single basic disk may have up to three primary partitions and one extended partition. If your disk does not have an extended partition, it may have up to four primary partitions.

Partitioning enables multiple operating systems. You can install up to four different operating systems, each installed on its own primary partition, and boot to your choice each time you fire up the computer.

Every primary partition on a single drive has a special setting called *active* stored in the partition table. This setting is either on or off on each primary partition. At boot, the MBR uses the active setting in the partition table to determine which primary partition to choose to try to load an OS.

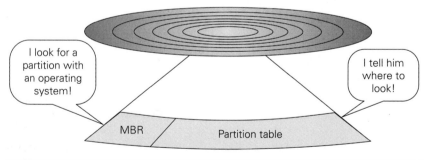

FIGURE 8.20 Functions of the MBR and partition table

Each partition must have some unique identifier to enable users to recognize it as an individual partition. Microsoft operating systems (DOS and Windows) traditionally assign primary partitions a drive letter from C: to Z:. Extended partitions do not get drive letters.

After you create an extended partition, you must create logical drives within that extended partition. A logical drive traditionally gets a drive letter from D: to Z:.

Windows 2000 and XP partitions are not limited to drive letters. With the exception of the partition that stores the boot files for Windows (which will always be C:), any other primary partitions or logical drives may get either a drive letter or a folder on a primary partition.

Instead of assigning drive letters, you can mount logical drives as folders on an existing drive. It's easy to make a logical drive and call it C:\STORAGE, for example. If the C:\STORAGE folder fills up, you could add an extra hard drive, make the entire extra drive an extended partition with one logical drive, unmount the old C:\STORAGE drive, and then mount the new huge logical drive as C:\STORAGE—as though you made your C: drive bigger without replacing it.

Dynamic Disks

With the introduction of Windows 2000, Microsoft defined an entirely new type of partitioning called *dynamic storage partitioning*, better known as *dynamic disks*. Dynamic disks drop the word *partition* and instead use the term *volume*. There is no dynamic disk equivalent to primary versus extended partitions. A volume is still technically a partition, but it can do things a regular partition cannot do, such as spanning. A *spanned volume* goes across more than one drive. Windows allows you to span up to 32 drives under a single volume. Dynamic disks also support RAID 0 in Windows 2000 Professional and Windows XP Professional. Windows 2000 Server and Windows Server 2003 support RAID 0, 1, and 5. See "Protecting Data with RAID" later in this chapter for more details.

Travel Advisory

Windows XP Home and Windows Media Center do not support dynamic disks.

How to Partition Using Disk Management

This example assumes that you want to create a partition on a new, second hard drive installed on a system that has an operating Windows 2000 OS. Follow these steps to create a new partition:

1. To access the Disk Management console, select Start | Programs | Administrative Tools | Computer Management.

2. Expand the Storage branch in the left-hand pane to access the storage management tools, and then highlight the Disk Management folder icon to connect to the Local Disk Management service.

3. Right-click an unallocated section of the disk and select Create Partition to start the Create Partition Wizard (see Figure 8.21). Then follow the prompts from the wizard to select a partition type (primary, extended, or logical), specify partition size, assign a drive letter or path (mount the partition to a folder), and format the partition with a file system.

FIGURE 8.21 The Create Partition Wizard in Windows 2000 Disk Management

Formatting

Formatting creates a file system for the drive—essentially a big spreadsheet that tracks what piece of data is stored in which location. As described earlier, Windows supports three different file systems—FAT, FAT32, and NTFS. Each of these file systems has its own benefits and drawbacks, as described in the sections that follow.

FAT

FAT's strength is that it is supported by all Microsoft operating systems, but aside from that, FAT has some considerable limitations. For instance, FAT does not support disk partitions larger than 2.1 GB, and it offers no local, file-level security. The main reason to keep FAT around is for backward compatibility with older operating systems.

FAT32

FAT32 is the improved, 32-bit version of FAT that was introduced with Windows 95 OSR2. FAT32 supports partitions as large as 2 TB. FAT32 is also more efficient at storing data than FAT16. However, like FAT16, FAT32 has no mechanism for controlling local security.

NTFS

Windows 2000/XP operate well on FAT- and FAT32-formatted disks, but to get the full benefits of these operating systems, you need NTFS. Put simply, NTFS is the way to go in Windows 2000/XP. Why? How about the fact that NTFS supports partitions as large as 2 TB? How about built-in compression and encryption capabilities that enable you to conserve disk space and secure files against prying eyes? How about support for *disk quotas*—a method of limiting the amount of disk space a user can use—and dynamic disk configurations that enable you to add space to existing partitions on the fly? Oh, and the last three big reasons to use NTFS:

1. Security
2. Security!
3. *Security!!!*

NTFS supports local security, and without that, you have no true control over your resources. That reason alone is worth the price of admission!

Compression NTFS enables you to compress individual files and folders to save space on a hard drive. Compression makes access time to the data slower, because the OS has to uncompress files every time you use them, but in a space-limited environment, sometimes that's what you have to do.

Encrypting File System One of the big draws with NTFS is file encryption, the black art of making files unreadable to anybody who doesn't have the right key. You can encrypt a single file, a folder, and a folder full of files. Microsoft calls the encryption utility in NTFS the *encrypting file system (EFS)*, but it's simply an aspect of NTFS, not a stand-alone file system. To encrypt a file or folder, right-click it in My Computer and select Properties to open the folder Properties dialog box. Click the Advanced button to open the Advanced Attributes dialog box. As you can see in Figure 8.22, encryption (and compression) is simply a selectable check box. Click the box next to *Encrypt contents to secure data* and then click the OK button—instantly your file is safe from prying eyes!

Encryption does not hide files; it simply makes them unreadable to other users. Figure 8.23 shows a couple of encrypted image files. Note that in addition to the pale green color of the filenames (that you can't tell are pale green in this black-and-white image), the files seem readily accessible. Windows XP can't

FIGURE 8.22 Options for compression and encryption

FIGURE 8.23 Encrypted files

provide a thumbnail, however, even though it can read the type of image file (JPEG) easily.

Travel Advisory

Windows XP Home and Media Center editions do not support EFS.

Disk Quotas

NTFS supports *disk quotas,* enabling administrators to set limits on drive space usage for users. To set quotas, you must log in as an Administrator, right-click the hard drive name, and select Properties. In the Local Disk Properties dialog box, select the Quota tab and make changes. Figure 8.24 shows configured quotas for a hard drive. While rarely used on single-user systems, setting disk quotas on multi-user systems prevents any individual user from monopolizing your hard disk space.

How to Format a Partition

Windows enables you to format partitions either from the command line, using the FORMAT command, or from within the OS using My Computer. You can also use the Disk Management console in Windows 2000/XP.

Using FORMAT Syntax for FORMAT is as follows: format *drive* [*/v:label*]. For example, to format a hard drive with the letter D:, open a command line window

Hard drive quotas in Windows XP

and type **format d:**. You are warned that all data will be lost; press the Y key to proceed or N to cancel (see Figure 8.25). Note that the *label* parameter switch is

Using the FORMAT command from a Windows 2000 command line window

optional but useful if you want to assign the drive a distinct, user-friendly name in addition to its drive letter. Windows 2000/XP also offers the /fs: *file system* parameter switch, which enables you to specify whether to format the partition with FAT or NTFS. Note that Windows 2000 automatically formats partitions of 2 GB or less with FAT, and greater than 2 GB with FAT32.

Using My Computer All versions of Windows enable you to right-click a partition in My Computer or Windows Explorer and choose Format from the drop-down menu to open a Format dialog box (see Figure 8.26).

Using Disk Management Windows 2000/XP offer a third way to format a partition—the Disk Management utility. Access the Disk Management Console as described earlier, and right-click an unformatted partition to open the Format dialog (shown in Figure 8.27). Then select Format from the pop-up menu, enter a volume label (optional), select a file system from the drop-down menu, and specify any other options. Then click OK.

FIGURE 8.26 Using My Computer in Windows 2000 to format

Format G: ? ✕

Volume label:	New Volume
File system:	NTFS ▼
Allocation unit size:	Default ▼

☐ Perform a quick format
☐ Enable file and folder compression

OK Cancel

FIGURE 8.27 Windows 2000 Disk Management Format dialog box

Objective 8.04

Protecting Data with RAID

A few sharp guys in Berkeley back in the 1980s organized the many techniques for using multiple drives for data protection and increasing speeds as the *redundant array of independent (or inexpensive) disks (RAID)*. They outlined seven levels of RAID, numbered 0 through 6.

Local Lingo

Array An *array* in the context of RAID refers to a collection of two or more hard drives.

- **RAID 0—Disk Striping** Disk striping requires at least two drives. It does not provide redundancy to data. If any one drive fails, all data is lost.

- **RAID 1—Disk Mirroring/Duplexing** RAID 1 arrays require at least two hard drives, although they also work with any even number of drives. RAID 1 is the ultimate in safety, but you lose storage space since the data is duplicated—you need two 100-GB drives to store 100 GB of data.

- **RAID 2—Disk Striping with Multiple Parity Drives** RAID 2 was a weird RAID idea that never saw practical use. Unused, ignore it.

- **RAID 3 and RAID 4—Disk Striping with Dedicated Parity** RAID 3 and RAID 4 combined dedicated data drives with dedicated parity drives. The differences between the two are trivial. Unlike RAID 2, these versions did see some use in the real world but were quickly replaced by RAID 5.

- **RAID 5—Disk Striping with Distributed Parity** Instead of dedicated data and parity drives, RAID 5 distributes data and parity information evenly across all drives. This is the fastest way to provide data redundancy. RAID 5 is by far the most common RAID implementation and requires at least three drives. RAID 5 arrays effectively use one drive's worth of space for parity. If, for example, you have three 200-GB drives, your total storage capacity is 400 GB. If you have four 200-GB drives, your total capacity is 600 GB.

Exam Tip

If you get a question on "disk striping with parity" on the CompTIA A+ certification exams, always assume the question is asking about RAID 5.

- **RAID 6—Disk Striping with Extra Parity** If you lose a hard drive in a RAID 5 array, your data is at great risk until you replace the bad hard drive and rebuild the array. RAID 6 is RAID 5 with extra parity information. RAID 6 needs at least five drives, but in exchange you can lose up to two drives at the same time. RAID 6 is gaining in popularity for those willing to use larger arrays.

Local Lingo

RAID 0+1 and RAID 10 After the first RAID levels were defined, some manufacturers came up with ways to combine different RAID arrays. For example, if you mirror two pairs of striped drives, you get what is called RAID 0+1. Or (read this carefully now) if you take two pairs of mirrored drives and stripe the pairs, you then get RAID 1+0, or what is often called RAID 10. Combinations of different types of single RAID are called Multiple RAID solutions. Multiple RAID solutions, while enjoying some support in the real world, are quite rare when compared to single RAID solutions RAID 0, RAID 1, and RAID 5.

> ### Local Lingo
>
> **JBOD**　*JBOD* stands for Just a Bunch of Disks (or Drives). It's a term used for a storage system composed of multiple independent disks, rather than disks organized using RAID.

Implementing RAID

All RAID implementations break down into either hardware or software methods. Software is often used when price takes priority over performance. Hardware is used when you need speed along with data redundancy. Software RAID does not require special controllers—you can use the regular ATA controllers or SCSI host adapters to make a software RAID array. But you do need "smart" software. The most common software implementation of RAID is the built-in RAID software that comes with Windows 2000 and 2003 Server. The Disk Management program in these Windows Server versions can configure drives for RAID 0, RAID 1, or RAID 5, and it works with ATA and or SCSI (Figure 8.28). Disk Management in Windows 2000 Professional and Windows XP Professional, in contrast, can only configure RAID 0.

FIGURE 8.28　Disk Management in Windows 2003 Server

Travel Advisory

You can use Disk Management in Windows 2000 and Windows XP Professional to create RAID 1 and RAID 5 arrays, but you can use Disk Management only remotely on a Windows 2000 or 2003 Server OS. In other words, the capability is there, but Microsoft has limited the OS. If you want to use software RAID in Windows 2000 or XP (Home or Professional), you need to use a third-party tool to set it up.

Software RAID means the operating system is in charge of all RAID functions. It works for small RAID solutions but tends to overwork your OS easily, creating slowdowns. When you *really* need to keep going, when you need RAID that doesn't even let the users know a problem has occurred, hardware RAID is the answer.

Hardware RAID centers around an *intelligent* controller—either a SCSI host adapter or an ATA controller that handles all the RAID functions (Figure 8.29). Unlike a regular ATA controller or SCSI host adapter, these controllers have chips that know how to "talk RAID."

Most RAID setups in the real world are hardware-based. Almost all of the many hardware RAID solutions provide *hot-swapping*—the ability to replace a bad drive without disturbing the OS. Hot-swapping is common in hardware RAID.

Hardware-based RAID is invisible to the OS and is configured in several ways, depending on the specific chips involved. Most RAID systems have a special configuration utility in flash ROM that you access after CMOS but before the OS loads. Figure 8.30 shows a typical firmware program used to configure a hardware RAID solution.

FIGURE 8.29 Serial ATA RAID controller

```
FastBuild <tm> Utility <c> 2004-2005 Promise Technology, Inc.
================[ View Drives Assignments ]================

   Channel:ID        Drive Model       Capacity <MB>  Assignment
        1:Mas  HDT722525DLA380            250059
               Extent 1                   249992       LD  1-1
        2:Mas  HDT722525DLA380            250059
               Extent 2                   249992       LD  1-2
        3:Mas  HDT722525DLA380            250059
               Extent 3                   249992       LD  1-3
        4:Mas  HDT722525DLA380            250059
               Extent 4                   249992       LD  1-4

==========================[ Keys Available ]==========================

  [↑] Up    [↓] Down    [ESC] Exit
```

FIGURE 8.30 RAID configuration utility

Objective 8.05 Maintaining and Troubleshooting Hard Drives

Hard drives are complex mechanical and electrical devices. With platters spinning at thousands of rotations per minute, they also generate heat and vibration. All of these factors make hard drives susceptible to failure. In this section, you will learn some basic maintenance tasks that will keep your hard drives healthy. For those inevitable instances when a hard drive fails, you will learn what you can do to repair it.

Maintenance

Hard drive maintenance can be broken down into two distinct functions: checking the disk occasionally for failed clusters, and keeping data organized on the drive so that it can be accessed quickly.

Error Checking

Individual clusters on hard drives sometimes go bad. There's nothing you can do to prevent this from happening, so it's important that you check occasionally for bad clusters on the drives. The tools used to perform this checking are generically called *error-checking utilities*, although the terms for two older Microsoft tools—ScanDisk and CHKDSK (pronounced "checkdisk")—are often used. Microsoft calls the tool Error-checking in Windows XP. Whatever the name of

the utility, each does the same job: when the tool finds bad clusters, it puts the electronic equivalent of orange cones around them so that the system won't try to place data in those bad clusters.

Most error-checking tools do far more than just check for bad clusters. They go through all the drive's filenames, looking for invalid names and attempting to fix them. They look for clusters that have no filenames associated with them (we call these *lost chains*) and erase them. From time to time, the underlying links between parent and child folders are lost, so a good error-checking tool checks every parent and child folder. With a folder such as C:\TEST\DATA, for example, they make sure that the folder DATA is properly associated with its parent folder, C:\TEST, and that C:\TEST is properly associated with its child folder, C:\TEST\DATA.

To access Error-checking on a Windows 2000 or Windows XP system, open My Computer, right-click the drive you want to check, and choose Properties to open the drive's Properties dialog box. Select the Tools tab and click the Check Now button (Figure 8.31) to display the Check Disk dialog box, which has two options (Figure 8.32). Check the box next to *Automatically fix file system errors*, but save the option to *Scan for and attempt recovery of bad sectors* for times when you actually suspect a problem, because it takes a while on bigger hard drives.

FIGURE 8.31 The Tools tab in the Local Disk Properties dialog box in Windows XP

FIGURE 8.32 Check Disk dialog box options

Now that you know how to run Error-checking, your next question should be, "How often do I run it?" A reasonable maintenance plan would include running it about once a week. Error-checking is fast (unless you use the *Scan for and attempt recovery* option), and it's a great tool for keeping your system in top shape.

Defragmentation

Fragmentation of clusters can make your drive access times increase dramatically. It's a good idea to defragment—or *defrag*—your drives as part of your monthly maintenance. You access the defrag tool, called Disk Defragmenter, on Windows 2000 and XP the same way you access Error-checking—right-click a drive in My Computer and choose Properties—except you click the Defragment Now button on the Tools tab to open the Disk Defragmenter (Figure 8.33).

Defragmentation is interesting to watch—once. From then on, schedule it to run late at night. You should defragment your drives about once a month, although you could run it every week, and if you run it every night it takes only a few minutes. The longer you go between defrags the longer it takes. If you don't run Disk Defragmenter, your system will run slower. If you don't run Error-checking, you may lose data.

FIGURE 8.33 Disk Defragmenter in Windows XP

Disk Cleanup

Did you know that the average hard drive is full of trash? Not the junk you intentionally put in your hard drive, like the 23,000 e-mail messages that you refuse to delete from your e-mail program. This kind of trash is all the files that you never see that Windows keeps for you. Here are a few examples:

- **Files in the Recycle Bin** When you delete a file, it isn't really deleted. It's placed in the Recycle Bin in case you decide you need the file later. I just checked my Recycle Bin and found 3 GB worth of files (Figure 8.34). That's a lot of trash!

- **Temporary Internet files** When you go to a Web site, Windows keeps copies of the graphics and other items on the page so that the page will load more quickly the next time you access it. You can see these files by opening the Internet Options applet on the Control Panel. Figure 8.35 shows my temporary Internet files.

- **Downloaded program files** Your system always keeps a copy of any Java or ActiveX applets that it downloads. You can see these in the Internet Options applet. You'll generally find only a few tiny files here.

FIGURE 8.34 Mike's Recycle Bin

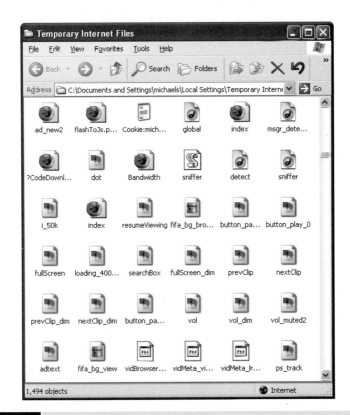

FIGURE 8.35 Lots of temporary Internet files

- **Temporary files** Many applications create temporary files that are supposed to be deleted when the application is closed. For one reason or another, these temporary files sometimes aren't deleted. The location of these files varies with the version of Windows, but they always reside in a folder called TEMP.

Every hard drive will eventually become filled with lots of unnecessary trash. All versions of Windows tend to act erratically when the drives run out of unused space. Fortunately, all versions of Windows have a powerful tool called Disk Cleanup (Figure 8.36). You can access Disk Cleanup in all versions of Windows by choosing Start | Program | Accessories | System Tools | Disk Cleanup.

Disk Cleanup gets rid of the four types of files just described (and a few others). Run Disk Cleanup once a month or so to keep plenty of space available on your hard drive.

Troubleshooting

There's no scarier computer problem than an error that points to trouble with a hard drive. This section looks at some of the more common problems that occur with hard drives and how to fix them. These issues fall into three broad categories: installation, data corruption, and dying hard drives.

FIGURE 8.36 Disk Cleanup dialog box

Installation Errors

Installing a drive and getting to the point at which it can hold data requires four distinct steps: connectivity, CMOS, partitioning, and formatting. If you make a mistake at any point during any of these steps, the drive won't work. The beauty of this is that if you make an error, you can walk back through each step and check for problems.

Connectivity A connectivity error means something isn't plugged in correctly or something has managed to unplug itself. These problems virtually always show themselves at boot time. Here are some classics:

- Hard drive error
- No fixed disks present
- HDD controller failure
- No boot device available
- Drive not found

If you plug the data cable in backward for a PATA drive, for example, the computer simply won't see the drive—it's a famous error, and everyone who has ever installed a hard drive has done it. Just reinsert the cable properly and turn the machine back on. The power connectors aren't nearly as forgiving. If you install the power cable backward, you will destroy the drive in a dazzling display of sparks and smoke. Fortunately, the chamfers on Molex connectors make this mistake difficult to do.

You can usually conquer connectivity errors by carefully inspecting the entire connection system (including electricity) and finding the silly mistake (welcome to the club). Always remove and reseat the controller (if it's on an expansion card) if you get an HDD controller failure, as the controllers are prone to static buildup. It is also a good idea to keep an extra controller around to verify whether a controller is bad or good. Cables can go bad, but it is rare unless the cable is obviously ripped or pinched. If your BIOS has an autodetection function, use it. It will not detect a drive unless everything is installed correctly. It's a great, quick connectivity verifier.

If you've just installed the drive, check the jumper settings. You can't have two masters or two slaves on a single controller. And don't forget the 1 Drive or Standalone setting on some drives.

Installing two drives on the same controller increases the chances of errors dramatically. For example, adding a slave drive to an existing single drive requires that you check the first drive to see if its jumper needs to change from single to master. You need to make sure to install the slave drive properly or neither

drive will work, causing the system to fail on boot. Additionally, some ATA drives are simply incompatible and will not work on the same controller. I've worked on many systems where I had to add a second drive to the secondary controller since it would not work with the existing drive.

CMOS Modern systems rarely get CMOS errors, because the autodetection feature handles most drives. The errors that do occur generally fall into two groups: forgetting to run Autodetect and selecting the wrong sector translation in Autodetect. Two rules apply here: Always run Autodetect and *always* select LBA (logical block addressing).

Older systems could lose CMOS data for a variety of reasons, including static electricity, inserting an expansion card, and blinking with too much force. It takes nothing to do a quick CMOS check to verify that the drive's geometry is correct using autodetection. Here are some of the more common errors that might point to CMOS problems:

- CMOS configuration mismatch
- No boot device available
- Drive not found
- Missing OS

If Autodetect fails to see the drive in question, it's probably a connectivity problem. Grab a screwdriver and look inside the system. This is also the one time where your hard drive's S.M.A.R.T. (Self-Monitoring, Analysis, and Reporting Technology) functions may help. Unplug the drive and make it an extra drive on a working system. Go to the hard drive manufacturer's Web site and download its diagnostic tool and run it. If you get a failure, the drive is dead and there's nothing you can do except be really happy that you back up your data all the time.

Partitioning Partitioning errors generally fall into two groups: failing to partition at all and making the wrong size or type of partition. You'll recognize the former type of error the first time you open My Computer after installing a drive. If you forgot to partition it, the drive won't even show up in My Computer. If you made the partition too small, that'll become painfully obvious when you start filling it up with files.

The fix for partitioning errors is simply to open Disk Management and do the partitioning correctly. If you've added files to a drive you're going to repartition, don't forget to back them up before you repartition.

Formatting Failing to format a drive makes the drive unable to hold data. Accessing the drive in Windows will result in a drive "is not accessible" error, and from a C:\ prompt, you'll get the famous "Invalid media" type error. Format the drive unless you're certain that the drive is already formatted. Corrupted files can create the "Invalid media" type error. Check the sections on corrupted data later in this chapter for the fix.

Most of the time, formatting is a slow, boring process. But sometimes the drive makes "bad sounds" and you start seeing errors like the one shown in Figure 8.37 at the bottom of the screen.

An *allocation unit* is Windows' term for a cluster. The drive has run across a bad cluster and is trying to fix it. For years, I've told techs that seeing this error a few (610) times doesn't mean anything, because every drive comes with a few bad spots. This is no longer true. Modern ATA drives actually hide a significant number of extra sectors that they use to replace bad sectors automatically. If a new drive gets a lot of "Trying to recover lost allocation unit" errors, you can bet that the drive is dying and needs to be replaced. Get the hard drive maker's diagnostic to be sure. Bad clusters are reported by S.M.A.R.T.

Mental Reinstall Focus on the fact that all of these errors share a common thread—you just installed a drive! Installation errors don't show up on a system that has been running correctly for three weeks; they show up the moment you try to do something with the drive you just installed. If a newly installed drive fails to work, do a "mental reinstall." Does the drive show up in the CMOS Autodetect? No? Then recheck the cables, master/slave settings, and power. If it does show up, did you remember to partition and format the drive? Did it need

```
A:\>format C:/s

WARNING:   ALL DATA ON NON-REMOVABLE DISK
DRIVE C:   WILL BE LOST!
Proceed with Format  (Y/N)?y

Formatting  30709.65M

Trying to recover lost allocation unit 37,925
```

FIGURE 8.37 The "Trying to recover lost allocation unit" error

to be set to active? These are commonsense questions that come to mind as you march through your mental reinstall. Even if you've installed thousands of drives over the years, you'll be amazed at how often you do things such as forget to plug in power to a drive, forget CMOS, or install a cable backward. Do the mental reinstall—it really works!

Data Corruption

All hard drives occasionally get corrupted data in individual sectors. Power surges, accidental shutdowns, corrupted installation media, and viruses, along with hundreds of other problems, can cause this corruption. In most cases, this type of error shows up while Windows is running. Figure 8.38 shows a classic example.

You may also see Windows error messages saying one of the following:

- The following file is missing or corrupt
- The download location information is damaged
- Unable to load file

If core boot files become corrupted, you may see text errors at boot, such as the following:

- Cannot find COMMAND.COM
- Error loading operating system
- Invalid BOOT.INI

On older programs, you may see a command prompt open with errors such as this one:

```
Sector not found reading drive C: Abort, Retry, Fail?
```

The first fix for any of these problems is to run the Error-checking utility. Error-checking will go through and mark bad clusters and hopefully move your data to a good cluster.

FIGURE 8.38 A corrupted data error

Extract/Expand If Error-checking fails to move a critically important file—such as a file Windows needs in order to load, you can always resort to the command line and try to extract the file from the Windows cabinet files. Most Windows programs store all files in a compressed format called CAB (short for cabinet file). One CAB file contains many files, and most installation disks have lots of CAB files (see Figure 8.39).

To replace a single corrupt file this way, you need to know two things: the location of the CAB file that contains the file you need, and how to get the file out so you can copy it back to its original spot. Microsoft supplies the EXPAND program to enable you to get a new copy of the missing file from the CAB files on the installation CD-ROM. Also notice how they are numbered—that's the secret to understanding these programs.

In most cases, all the CAB files for a program are piled into some folder, as shown in Figure 8.39. Let's say you need a file called OLEPRO32.DLL. (I have no idea what this file does. I only know that Windows can't find it and you need to

FIGURE 8.39 CAB files

put it back!) Get to a command prompt within Windows and tell EXPAND to check *all* the CAB files on your installation CD (drive E: in this example) with this command:

```
EXPAND e:\I386\*.CAB -F:OLEPRO32.DLL
```

EXPAND goes through all the CAB files and finds the file. If you want to see details on the EXPAND command, use Windows Help or type **EXPAND /?** at a command prompt.

Corrupted Data on Bad Sectors If the same errors continue to appear after running the Error-checking utility, there's a chance that the drive has bad sectors.

Almost all drives today take advantage of built-in error correction code (ECC) that constantly checks the drive for bad sectors. If the ECC detects a bad sector, it marks the sector as bad in the drive's internal error map. Don't confuse this error map with a FAT. The partitioning program creates the FAT. The drive's internal error map was created at the factory on reserved drive heads and is invisible to the system. If the ECC finds a bad sector, you will get a corrupted data error as the computer attempts to read the bad sector. Error-checking utilities fix this problem most of the time.

Dying Hard Drive

Physical problems are rare but devastating when they happen. If a hard drive is truly damaged physically, there is nothing that you or any service technician can do to fix it. Fortunately, hard drives are designed to take a phenomenal amount of punishment without failing. Physical problems manifest themselves in two ways: either the drive works properly but makes a lot of noise, or the drive seems to disappear.

All hard drives make noise—the hum as the platters spin and the occasional slight scratching noise as the read/write heads access sectors are normal. If your drive begins to make any of the following sounds, however, it is about to die:

- Continuous high-pitched squeal
- Series of clacks, a short pause, and then another series of clacks
- Continuous grinding or rumbling

Back up your critical data and replace the drive. Windows comes with great tools for backing up data.

You'll know when a drive simply disappears. If it's the drive that contains your OS, the system will lock up. When you try to restart the computer, you'll see this error message:

```
No Boot Device Present
```

If it's a second drive, it will simply stop showing up in My Computer. The first thing to do in this case is to fire up the System Setup program and see if Autodetect sees the drive. If it does, you do not have a physical problem with the drive. If Autodetect fails, shut off the system and remove the ribbon cable, but leave the power cable attached. Restart the system and listen to the drive. If the drive spins up, you know that the drive is getting good power. In most cases, this is a clue that the drive is probably good. In that case, you need to look for more mundane problems such as an unplugged power cord or jumpers incorrectly set. If the drive doesn't spin up, try another power connector. If it still doesn't spin up and you've triple-checked the jumpers and ribbon cable, you have a problem with the onboard electronics, and the drive is dead.

Travel Advisory

Most hard drives have three-year warranties. Before you throw away a dead drive, check the hard-drive maker's Web site or call the manufacturer to see if the drive is still under warranty. Ask for a return material authorization (RMA). You'll be amazed how many times you get a newer, usually larger, hard drive for free! It never hurts to check!

CHECKPOINT

✔**Objective 8.01: Hard Drive Technologies** You'll find three types of hard drives in personal computers today: PATA, SATA, and SCSI. PATA drives use either a 40-wire or 80-wire ribbon cable and a Molex power connector. SATA drives use an 8-wire ribbon cable and SATA power. SCSI drives differ according to the type of SCSI used, but most require a 68-pin ribbon cable and a Molex connector.

✔**Objective 8.02: Installing Hard Drives** PATA controllers can handle up to two drives on each cable. Set the jumpers on the drives as master, slave, or

standalone, depending on the configuration of the system. SATA drives are point to point, whereas SCSI drives differ by technology. You can have up to 16 SCSI drives connected to a single controller as long as all the drives have unique SCSI IDs.

✔**Objective 8.03: Partitioning and Formatting** Partitioning establishes the framework upon which your file system is built. Formatting creates the file system. In Windows, use dynamic disks and NTFS whenever possible. You can use Disk Management to do both partitioning and formatting.

✔**Objective 8.04: Protecting Data with RAID** The many techniques for using multiple drives for data protection and increasing speeds are called the redundant array of independent disks (RAID). In the field, you're likely to run into three types of RAID. RAID 0 is called disk striping, using two drives as a single unit. RAID 1 is mirroring, where two drives contain matching content for data redundancy. RAID 5 is disk striping with parity. Three drives provide data redundancy, but this requires the equivalent of one drive's capacity.

✔**Objective 8.05: Maintaining and Troubleshooting Hard Drives** Maintaining hard drives requires three pieces of software. Error-checking or scandisk checks the physical disk for problems. Disk Defragmenter does exactly what it sounds like, taking files and folders fragmented on the drive and putting them back together. Disk Cleanup completes the triumvirate, enabling you to empty temporary files and other debris from your drive quickly and easily.

REVIEW QUESTIONS

1. What kind of cable fully supports a PATA drive running at 100 MBps?

 A. 7-wire

 B. 40-pin

 C. 68-pin

 D. 80-wire

2. What is the maximum data cable length for a SATA drive?

 A. 18 inches

 B. 36 inches

 C. 1 meter

 D. 2 meters

3. Which hard drive technology offers the best airflow?

 A. EATA

 B. PATA

 C. SATA

 D. SCSI

4. How does the controller differentiate among devices on a SCSI chain?

 A. Cable select

 B. Master/slave

 C. RAID number

 D. SCSI ID

5. Where do you terminate the SCSI chain? (Select the best answer.)

 A. Only at the ends

 B. Always at the controller

 C. Only on external devices

 D. Never on the controller

6. John has two hard drives set to cable select. Where should he place the drive he wants to be the C: drive?

 A. In the center of the cable, closest to the controller.

 B. At the end of the cable.

 C. It doesn't matter.

 D. This does not apply. He needs to jumper the drive's master and slave.

7. What partitioning method creates an MBR?

 A. Dynamic storage

 B. Master boot record

 C. Volume boot record

 D. Dynamic volume

8. What must a partition be to be bootable?

 A. Basic disk, active

 B. Dynamic disk, active

 C. Primary partition, active

 D. Extended partition, active

9. When do you format extended partitions?

 A. Immediately after you create them

 B. After you create a primary partition

 C. After you create a dynamic partition

 D. You don't format extended partitions; you create logical drives in the extended partition and then format those

10. Eileen has been called in to look at a client's machine and discovers that the computer has a second hard drive, but it doesn't have a drive letter. Instead, to access that drive she clicks a drive icon that says "My Stuff." What kind of partition is the "My Stuff" drive?

 A. Basic disk

 B. Extended partition

 C. Mounted volume

 D. Primary partition

11. What advantage does FAT have over FAT32?

 A. Larger partition size

 B. Better security

 C. Better compression

 D. None

12. Which format offers local file security?

 A. FAT

 B. FAT32

 C. NTFS

 D. NTFS32

13. How many drives minimum are required for disk striping with parity?

 A. One

 B. Two

 C. Three

 D. Four

14. What tool enables you to create a RAID 0 array in Windows?

 A. Disk Management

 B. FDISK

 C. RAID Management

 D. SCSI configuration utility

15. What tool scans and corrects hard drive problems?

 A. Disk Management

 B. Disk Defragmenter

 C. Error-checking

 D. File Checker

REVIEW ANSWERS

1. **D** PATA drives running at 100 MBps need an 80-wire cable.

2. **C** SATA cables can be up to 1 meter long.

3. **C** The thin and narrow SATA cables offer the best airflow of the technologies mentioned.

4. **D** The controller uses the SCSI IDs to differentiate different devices on the SCSI chain.

5. **A** Only terminate SCSI chains on the ends of the chain.

6. **B** With cable select, the drive on the end of the cable will get a drive letter before the one in the middle. Since C: is the first possible drive letter, he's got to place that drive on the end of the cable.

7. **B** A master boot record partitioning method creates an MBR.

8. **C** You need a primary, active partition to be bootable.

9. **D** Format the logical drives in an extended partition.

10. **C** "My Stuff" is a mounted volume.

11. **D** FAT32 pretty much blows FAT away.

12. **C** NTFS supports local file security.

13. **C** You need at least three drives to support a RAID 5 array.

14. **A** Disk Management is the tool for creating a software striped (RAID 0) array.

15. **C** Error-checking is the official name for the tool that scans and fixes hard drive problems.

Removable Media

	NEWBIE	SOME EXPERIENCE	EXPERT
ETA	3 hours	2 hours	1 hour

Removable media is any type of mass storage device that you may use in one system and then physically remove from that system and use in another. As a PC technician, you'll not only need to install, maintain, and troubleshoot removable media on users' systems, but you'll also find yourself turning to removable media as a way to store and run software tools to perform all types of PC support.

This chapter covers the most common types of removable media used today. For the sake of organization, all removable media fall into these groups:

- **Floppy drives** The traditional floppy drive
- **Flash memory** From USB thumb drives to flash memory cards
- **Optical media** Any shiny disc technology from CD-ROMs to DVDs
- **Tape drives** Drives that use removable Mylar tape cassettes
- **External drives** Any hard drive, optical drive, or tape drive that connects to a PC via an external cable

Objective 9.01 Floppy Drives

When you insert a *floppy disk* into a *floppy drive*, the protective slide on the disk opens, revealing the magnetic media inside the plastic casing. A motor-driven spindle snaps into the center of the drive to make it spin. A set of read/write heads then moves back and forth across the disk, reading or writing tracks on the disk as needed. The current floppy disks are 3.5 inches wide and store 1.44 MB (Figure 9.1). You use a 3.5-inch floppy drive to access the contents of the disk.

Whenever your system accesses a floppy disk in a floppy drive, a read/write LED on the outside front of the drive flashes on. You should not try to remove the floppy disk from the drive when this light is lit. That light means that the read/writes heads are accessing the floppy drive, and pulling the disk out while the light is on can damage the floppy disk. When the light is off, you can push in the small release button on the front of the drive to eject the floppy disk.

Installing Floppy Drives

All Windows systems reserve the drive letters A: and B: for floppy drives. You cannot name them anything other than A: or B:, but you can configure a floppy drive to get either drive letter. However, convention dictates that if you have only one floppy drive, you should call it A:. The second floppy drive will then be called B:.

FIGURE 9.1 External floppy drive and floppy disk

Floppy drives connect to the computer via a *34-pin ribbon cable*. If the cable supports two floppy drives, it will have a seven-wire twist in the middle, used to differentiate electronically between the A: and B: drives (Figure 9.2). Given that the majority of users do not want two floppy drives, many system makers have dropped the twist and saved a couple of pennies on a simpler cable.

Inserting Ribbon Cables

Look at the floppy cable shown in Figure 9.2 and notice the connector on the left side. This connector, identical to the other connectors on the same cable, plugs

Floppy B

Floppy A

Floppy controller plug

FIGURE 9.2 Floppy cable that supports two drives

into the floppy controller on the motherboard, as shown in Figure 9.3. Notice how clearly the motherboard has Pin 1 marked in Figure 9.3. Not all motherboards are so clear. Make sure to orient the cable so that the colored stripe is aligned with Pin 1.

After you insert the floppy ribbon cable into the floppy controller, you need to insert the ribbon cable into the floppy drive, also properly orienting Pin 1.

Exam Tip
In the past, the CompTIA A+ certification exams have been focused on the pins on cables. Know the number (34) and orientation (Pin 1 to Pin 1) for the pins on the floppy drive ribbon cable.

If the floppy drive is installed on the end connector, it becomes the A: drive; if the drive is installed on the middle connector, it is the B: drive. If you're installing only one floppy drive, make sure you install it in the A: drive position.

If you install the ribbon cable incorrectly, the floppy drive won't work. If you reverse one end of the cable, the floppy drive LED will come on and stay on, a classic signal. You won't hurt anything, so just put the cable on correctly and check that the drive works.

Power

Floppy drives need electricity to work, just like every other device in the PC. Modern 3.5-inch floppy drives use a mini power connector. Be careful! It is

FIGURE 9.3 Plugging a floppy cable into a controller, Pin 1 labeled at left

easy to insert a mini connector incorrectly, and if you install it incorrectly, you'll destroy the floppy drive and experience what we call "The Nasty Smell." In Figure 9.4, note the bottom view of a properly installed mini connector—note the chamfers (beveled edges) that show correct orientation. The problem lies in the plastic used to make the connector. The plastic connector bends easily, giving even the least brawny techs the ability to put the plug in a mini backward or to hit only three of the four pins.

CMOS

After the floppy drive is installed, your next step is to configure the CMOS settings, which must correspond to the capacities of the drives. Look in your CMOS for a menu called "Standard CMOS Features" (or something similar to that) to see your floppy settings. Most CMOS setups configure the A: drive by default as a 3.5-inch, 1.44-MB drive, so in most cases the floppy is already configured. Simply double-check the setting in CMOS; if it's okay, exit without changing anything.

Floppy Drive Maintenance and Troubleshooting

The key preventative maintenance to perform on floppy drives is cleaning. You can find floppy drive cleaning kits at some electronics stores, or you can use a cotton swab and some denatured alcohol to scour gently inside the drive for dust and other particles.

FIGURE 9.4 Properly installed mini connector

Repairing Floppy Drives

When a floppy drive stops working, follow these steps to resolve the problem:

1. Check for a bad floppy disk. If you run into a disk that doesn't work, try a known good disk to see if the problem is the disk or the drive.

2. Check for data errors on the disk. You can run Error-checking on floppy disks, just as you would on a hard drive.

3. Check the CMOS settings. CMOS errors generally occur only with installation. If you install and the system won't recognize that the floppy drive is attached, make certain that the controller is enabled in CMOS.

4. Check the cable. This is a problem only on installation. Make certain your cabling is on properly, Pin 1 to Pin 1.

5. Replace the floppy drive. There's no "fix" for a truly broken floppy drive. Just replace it.

Objective 9.02 # Flash Memory

Flash memory, the same flash memory that replaced CMOS technology for your system BIOS, found another home in PCs in the form of removable mass storage devices. Flash memory comes in two different families: USB thumb drives and memory cards. *USB thumb drives* are flash devices that contain a standard USB connection. *Memory cards* is a generic term for a number of different tiny cards that are used in cameras, PDAs, and other devices. Both of these families can manifest themselves as drives in Windows, but they usually perform different jobs. USB thumb drives have replaced virtually all other rewritable removable media as the way people transfer files or keep copies of important programs.

USB Thumb Drives

Moving data between computers is always a pain, and even more so since digital photography and multimedia storage has littered hard drives with huge files that won't fit on a single floppy disk. The latest entry into the floppy disk replacement sweepstakes is a winner: the USB flash memory drive, also known as the *USB thumb drive, jump drive,* or *flash drive.* These tiny new drives (Figure 9.5) are incredibly popular. For a low price, you can get a 2-GB thumb

FIGURE 9.5 USB thumb drives

drive that holds as much data as 1400 standard 3.5-inch floppy disks and it's much faster.

The smallest thumb drives are slightly larger than an adult thumbnail, whereas others are larger and more rounded. The drives are hot-swappable in all modern operating systems.

Flash Cards

Flash cards are used to store data on small appliances. Every digital camera, virtually every PDA, and many cell phones come with slots for some type of memory card. Memory cards come in a number of different incompatible formats, such as CompactFlash (CF), Secure Digital (SD), and Extreme Digital (xD) Picture Card. Figure 9.6 shows typical cards. Keep in mind that most devices only use a single format, and with very few exceptions, the cards are not interchangeable.

FIGURE 9.6 Typical flash memory cards

Card Readers

Whatever type of flash memory you use, your PC must have a *card reader* to access the data on the card directly. A number of inexpensive USB card readers are available (Figure 9.7), and some PCs, especially those tuned to home theater use, often come with built-in readers—handy to have when someone pulls out an SD card and says "Let's look at the pictures I just took!"

Of course, if the person just happened to bring his or her camera and the usually-proprietary USB cable along, you could connect the camera to the PC and pull pictures in that way. Just make sure you have spare batteries. Wouldn't a card reader be a more elegant solution?

Whichever type of flash memory you have, understand that it acts exactly like a hard drive. If you want, you can format a memory card as well as copy, paste, and rename files stored on the card.

Maintaining and Troubleshooting Flash Media

Aside from keeping the media clean, there's not much to do with flash media. Don't send it through the wash in your jeans (I've done this more than once) and don't touch the contacts on flash memory cards with your fingers. When flash media dies, there's no fix, so you have to replace it.

FIGURE 9.7 USB card reader

Objective 9.03 # Optical Drives

CD- and DVD-media discs and drives come in a variety of flavors and formats, enabling you to back up data, record music, master a home video, and much, much more. Generically, we call them *optical discs* and the drives that support them *optical drives.*

Optical discs come in several formats—the two most common being *compact disc (CD)* and *digital versatile disc (DVD)*—and three main styles: read-only, write-once, and rewritable. Sounds simple enough, and it is for CD-media, but DVD is a whole different story. There are no fewer than 11 competing standards of sizes and formats of DVD-media.

Optical drives can read and write specific formats and styles—that is, a CD-ROM drive can read CD-ROM, CD-R, and CD-RW discs, but it can't write to any format. Many optical drives support multiple media types. Most modern DVD drives, for example, are known as combo drives and can read and write to any optical format, including all of the CD formats. Here's a list of the common optical formats:

- CD-ROM
- CD-R
- CD-RW
- DVD-ROM
- DVD-Video
- DVD-R
- DVD-R DL
- DVD-RW
- DVD-RW DL
- DVD+R
- DVD+R DL
- DVD+RW
- DVD+RW DL
- DVD-RAM

Travel Advisory

Manufacturers label DVD drives that can read and write multiple DVD formats as *DVD±RW*. There's no ± format, just – and +.

The formats that end in *ROM* are read-only. The formats that end in *R* are recordable once. The formats of *RW* are rewritable many times. The DVD-Video is a DVD-ROM movie, like the latest copy of *Lord of the Rings* you got for your birthday. DVD-RAM is just different, an RW format that requires a special cartridge. The DL stands for *dual-layer* and requires a bit more explanation about capacity.

Capacity

Optical discs vary in capacity a lot between CDs and DVDs, and even more among various DVD types. Most CDs come in either 650-MB or 700-MB capacity, though you can occasionally find 800-MB and 900-MB varieties. DVDs vary according to how many layers manufacturers use—single or dual—and whether they're single or double sided (the latter meaning you have to flip the disc over to get the second half of the data). Table 9.1 shows the various DVD capacities.

Note two things about DVD capacity: First, unlike CD-media, DVD capacity is rated in billions of bytes, not the binary number you'd think. So a 4.7-GB disc holds 4,700,000 bytes of data, which translates to a mere 4.38 gigabytes. You don't need to know this for the CompTIA A+ certification exams, but a client might query you about the discrepancy. Second, you need a special dual-layer–capable DVD drive to burn a dual-layer disc.

Local Lingo

Gigabyte and Gigibyte The computer industry has always used the term gigabyte (GB) with an *a* to refer to the binary number 2^{30}, or 1,073,741,824 bytes. The DVD industry has chucked that consensus, claiming that the term *gigabyte* specifically refers to the decimal number 10^9, or 1,000,000,000, and that the binary number 2^{30} is 1 *gigibyte* (GiB). Outside of Wikipedia and the DVD industry, nobody in the PC industry uses the term *gigibyte* and you won't find it on the CompTIA A+ certification exams.

Exam Tip

The CompTIA A+ certification exams use the DVD-industry term *GB* to denote the capacity of a DVD disc. According to the exams, therefore, a single-sided, single-layer DVD has a capacity of 4.7 GB.

TABLE 9.1	Standard DVD Capacities	
	Single Layer	**Dual Layer**
Single Sided	4.7 GB	8.5 GB
Double Sided	9.4 GB	17.1 GB

Speed

Though woefully slow compared with hard drive speeds, optical drive throughput has improved through the years from the 150 MBps speed of the original CD-ROM drive. Modern drives have up to three speeds listed for each action: read, write, and rewrite, listed in that order. CD-media drives use a "number times" designation, such as 40×, to denote the speeds. It's simple math, so if you see a 40× think (40 × 150) and you'll come up with 6000 KBps throughput. A CD-RW will have three speeds, such as 40×16×24× for the read, write, and rewrite.

DVD drives read, write, and rewrite DVDs 9 times faster than CD drives, so a 1× DVD drive and disc has a throughput of 1.32 MBps. They read and write CDs faster than that, though, so they often have multiple speeds listed, just like CD-R and CD-RW drives.

Installing Optical Drives

Most optical drives use parallel ATA (PATA) or serial ATA (SATA) connections and support the ATAPI (AT Attachment Packet Interface) standard. (Other connections, such as SCSI and USB, are possible but less common.) ATAPI treats an optical drive exactly as though it were an ATA drive. PATA optical drives have regular 40-pin ATA connectors and master/slave jumpers. SATA optical drives use standard SATA cables. You install them the same way you would install any ATA hard drive. Figure 9.8 shows a typical DVD installation using PATA. The

FIGURE 9.8 Typical DVD installation

DVD is configured as slave with a master hard drive on a system's primary ATA controller. Optical drives require no CMOS changes as part of the install process.

A regular CD-ROM drive installation involves no applications. You install it, Windows sees it, and you're done. CD-R and CD-RW drives, in contrast, require that you install applications to enable their burning features. DVD-media drives need software to enable you to watch movies, burn DVDs, and so on. As of this writing, Nero Burning ROM (www.nero.com) and Roxio's Easy Media Creator (www.roxio.com) suites of programs share the crown as the most popular CD-burning software programs.

ISO Files

Ever wanted to make a perfect copy of a CD so that you can keep your original in a safe place? You can do so using a special file type called an ISO file. An *ISO file* is a complete copy—an ISO image as we say—of a CD. As you might imagine, they are huge files, but they are also very important to techs. Techs use ISO images to send each other copies of bootable utility CDs. For example, if you want a copy of the Ultimate Boot CD (an excellent utility for techs), you go to the Ultimate Boot Web site and download an ISO image. You then take your third-party burning program (Windows XP built-in burning software can't do this) and go through a special process called *burning an ISO image*. Learn how to burn ISO images with your burning program, because you'll use it all the time.

Troubleshooting Optical Drives and Discs

Optical drives are extremely reliable and durable PC components. At times, however, a reliable and durable device decides to turn into an unreliable, non-durable pile of plastic and metal frustration.

The single biggest problem with optical drives, especially in a new installation, is the connection. Your first guess should be that the drive has not been properly installed in some way. A few of the common culprits are forgetting to plug in a power connector, inserting a cable backward, and misconfiguring jumpers/switches. Although you need to know the type of drive, the test for an improper physical connection is always the same: using BIOS to see whether the system can see the optical drive.

The way in which a BIOS detects an optical drive depends on the system. Most BIOS makers have created intelligent BIOS software that can see an installed CD-media drive. Figure 9.9 shows a modern Award Software, Inc., BIOS recognizing a CD-RW during startup.

If the device is detected in BIOS, Windows will recognize the drive and you'll see it in My Computer and Device Manager.

```
 Award Modular BIOS v6.00PG, An Energy Star Ally
 Copyright (C) 1984-2003 Phonix Technologies, LTD

Main Processor : AMD Athlon(tm) 64 Processor 3200+
Memory Testing : 1048576K OK
CPU0 Memory Information: DDR 400 CL:3 ,1T Dual Channel, 128-bit

IDE Channel 1 Master : WDC WD1200JB-75CRA0 16.06V16
IDE Channel 1 Slave  : None
IDE Channel 2 Master : TOSHIBA CD=DVDW SDR5372V TV11
IDE Channel 2 Slave  : None
```

FIGURE 9.9 BIOS recognizing an optical drive at boot

If the drive won't read a CD-R or CD-RW disc, first try a commercial CD-ROM disc that is in good condition. CD-R and CD-RW discs sometimes have compatibility issues with CD-ROM drives. The same goes for a DVD-RW or any other writable DVD disc in your DVD drive. As noted earlier, DVD drives have issues with media incompatibility. Also, no optical drive will read badly scratched discs.

If the drive still does not see a disc, try cleaning the drive. Most modern optical drives have built-in cleaning mechanisms, but from time to time, you need to use a commercial optical-drive cleaning kit (see Figure 9.10).

FIGURE 9.10 Optical-drive cleaning kit

Optical drives are not cleaned too often, but the discs are. Although a number of fine optical disc cleaning kits are available, most discs can be cleaned quite well with nothing more than a damp soft cloth. Occasionally, a mild detergent can be added. Always wipe from the center of the optical disc to the edge—never clean a CD or DVD using a circular motion!

> **Travel Advisory**
>
> A common old tech's tale about cleaning optical discs is that they can be washed in a dishwasher! Although this may seem laughable, the tale has become so common that it requires a serious response. This is *not true* for two reasons: First, the water in most dishwashers is too hot and can cause the discs to warp. Second, the water pushes the discs around, causing them to hit other objects and get scratched. Don't do it!

The final problem with optical drives—stuck discs—comes from *technician* error and is not actually the fault of the drives. I can't tell you the number of times I've pulled an optical drive out of a system to replace it, only to discover that I or my customer left an essential disc inside the now-powerless drive. Luckily, most optical drives have a small hole in the front, usually just below the drive opening, into which you can insert a wire—an unbent paper clip is the standard tool for this purpose—and push on an internal release lever that will eject the disc. Try it!

> **Travel Advisory**
>
> At the time of this writing, two optical standards are duking it out to determine which will become The Next Great Thing in optical media: HD DVD and Blu-ray Disc. HD DVD (High-Density DVD) offered the initial salvo, coming out with 30-GB optical discs that could contain eight hours of high-definition video. Blu-ray Disc (no special meaning aside from using blue lasers rather than red lasers) responded with 50-GB discs, and the gloves were off. Right now it appears that HD DVD will be the eventual winner on the video front, but Blu-ray Disc might win on the data-storage front. Time will tell. For more information, check out the respective camps' Web sites: www.thelookandsoundofperfect.com (I am not making this up!) and www.blu-raydisc.com.

Objective 9.04 Tape Drives

Tape drives connect to the ATA or SCSI bus, just like optical drives, but rather than using a shiny CD-R or DVD+R disc, you have to back up to magnetic tape (Figure 9.11).

Tape drive manufacturers have done pretty much everything they can do to make tape backups as fast as possible, but the technology suffers from two huge drawbacks. First, it's tape, which means all data must be stored and restored in *sequential access*. The drive has to go through files 1 and 2 before reaching file 3; in other words, it's unlike any other removable media. Second, tape is painfully slow in comparison to hard drives, optical drives, or flash-media drives.

The only great benefit to tape is that it's relatively cheap to buy multiple tapes with a lot of storage capacity. With hard drive and recordable DVD prices at rock bottom today, though, tape's days are numbered.

Tape drives require periodic cleaning, just like the old audio cassette players you use at home or in your car. You can get special cleaning tapes or do it manually, using a cotton swab and some denatured alcohol. Don't use water to clean inside a tape drive, and make certain the system is unplugged before you clean.

FIGURE 9.11 Backup tapes

Objective 9.05 # External Drives

Almost all new PCs have USB or FireWire external expansion buses, and the makers of optical drives have quickly taken this fact to heart. Many manufacturers have released external versions of optical drives, both readers and burners. Of the two expansion options, I prefer FireWire simply because it's the standard for most digital video cameras and the 400 Mbps *sustained* data transfer rate easily trumps the Hi-Speed USB 480 Mbps burst rate for transferring huge files. This is especially true for external hard drives. FireWire completely spanks USB.

The only benefit to the USB versions is that USB is still more common than FireWire, particularly on portable computers. In fact, quite a few super-light laptops don't have an optical drive built in; the only way to load an OS on them is through an external drive! (Note that some external drives for laptops connect via the IEEE 1284 DB 25 parallel port.) If you can't decide which expansion type to use, several manufacturers have taken pity on you.

You can also find eSATA connections on newer motherboards, as mentioned in Chapter 8, and external SCSI ports on some systems as well. Both are quite a bit less common than USB or FireWire for external drives.

CHECKPOINT

✓**Objective 5.01: Floppy Drives** Modern floppy disks store 1.44 MB of data and require a properly installed floppy disk drive. Internal floppy drives connect to a floppy drive controller using a 34-pin ribbon cable with a twist to distinguish drive A: (end of cable) from drive B: (middle of cable). Orient the cable Pin 1 to Pin 1. Floppy drives use a mini power connector.

✓**Objective 5.02: Flash Memory** Flash memory comes in two different families: USB thumb drives and memory cards. USB thumb drives are flash devices that contain a standard USB connection. *Memory cards* is a generic term for a number of different tiny cards that are used in cameras, PDAs, and other devices.

✔**Objective 5.03: Optical Drives** Optical discs and drives come in several formats—the two most common being CD and DVD—and three main styles: read-only, write-once, and rewritable. The different media offer dramatically different capacities, with the typical CD holding 650 MB, whereas the lowest-capacity DVD holds 4.7 GB of data. Optical drives connect the same way as hard drives, following the rules of PATA, SATA, SCSI, and so on.

✔**Objective 5.04: Tape Drives** Tape drives connect to the ATA or SCSI bus, just like optical drives, but rather than using a shiny CD-R or DVD+R disc, you have to back up to magnetic tape.

✔**Objective 5.05: External Drives** External drives are standard drives that connect to one of four buses: FireWire, USB, eSATA, or SCSI. Of the four, FireWire and Hi-Speed USB are the most common.

REVIEW QUESTIONS

1. You installed a floppy drive that you want to function as the A: drive, but your system won't boot to it. What is the most likely cause of this problem?

 A. You attached the drive to the middle connector on the cable.

 B. You attached the drive to the end connector on the cable.

 C. You forgot to configure the CMOS settings for drive A:.

 D. You forgot to configure the CMOS settings for a single floppy drive.

2. You just installed a floppy drive and you notice that the floppy drive LED stays on. What is most likely the problem?

 A. You attached the floppy drive to the wrong connector on the ribbon cable.

 B. You forgot to configure the floppy drive through the CMOS setup.

 C. You did not attach the colored stripe on the ribbon cable to Pin 1 at the drive or at the controller.

 D. You forgot to attach the power cable to the floppy drive.

3. What is the minimum capacity of a DVD?

 A. 650 MB

 B. 3.47 GB

 C. 4.7 GB

 D. 9.4 GB

4. What type of device must be installed on your system in order to access data on a flash memory card?

 A. Scanner

 B. Card reader

 C. Floppy drive

 D. Zip drive

5. A copy of a CD or DVD can be saved as what type of file?

 A. ISO

 B. ISO-9660

 C. INF

 D. CDDA

6. Both CD and DVD drive speeds are based on multiples of the original CD-ROM drive speed. What is that speed?

 A. 100 KBps

 B. 150 KBps

 C. 100 MBps

 D. 150 MBps

7. A CD-RW has a speed rating of 12×10×32. What do the three numbers refer to, in order?

 A. Write, rewrite, read

 B. Read, write, rewrite

 C. Rewrite, read, write

 D. Write, read, rewrite

8. What settings in the CMOS setup must you change to install an optical drive?

 A. Number of heads and cylinders the drive has

 B. Whether the drive is installed on the primary or secondary IDE channel

 C. Whether the jumpers on the drive are set to master or slave

 D. None, because an optical drive is not configured through the CMOS setup

9. What type of DVD can store 17.1 GB of data or more than eight hours of video?

 A. Double-sided, single-layered

 B. Single-sided, single-layered

 C. Single-sided, dual-layered

 D. Double-sided, dual-layered

10. Which of the following technologies requires sequential access?

 A. Flash drives

 B. Floppy drives

 C. Optical drives

 D. Tape drives

REVIEW ANSWERS

1. **A** When you install a floppy drive that you want to function as the A: drive, you should attach it to the end connector.

2. **C** If you just installed a floppy drive and you notice that the floppy drive LED stays on, you most likely reversed the cable on one end, so the colored stripe on the ribbon cable did not go to Pin 1.

3. **C** A DVD holds a minimum of 4.7 GB.

4. **B** A card reader must be installed on your system in order to access data on a flash memory card.

5. **A** CDs and DVDs can be copied as ISO files.

6. **B** Both CD and DVD drive speeds are based on multiples of 150 KBps, the speed of the original CD-ROM drives.

7. **A** If a CD-RW has a speed rating of 12×10×32, the three numbers refer, in order, to the write, rewrite, and read speeds.

8. **D** You do not have to change any CMOS settings when you install an optical drive because it is not configured through the CMOS setup.

9. **D** For a DVD to store 17.1 GB of data or over eight hours of video, the disc must be double-sided, dual-layered.

10. **D** Tape drives require sequential access, unlike all other removable media technologies.

Adapter Cards and Peripherals

	NEWBIE	SOME EXPERIENCE	EXPERT
ETA	4 hours	3 hours	1.5 hours

At this point in the book you know about ports, processing, and storage, so it's time for you to learn about the final step in the computing process—input/output (I/O). Most input devices plug into ports built into the motherboard, as do some of the common output devices, notably speakers. Other output devices plug into expansion cards that you need to add and configure. This chapter looks at input devices, expansion cards, and output devices.

Objective 10.01 Input Devices

Input devices enable you to interact with the computer and give it commands through typing, clicking, speaking, and more. Windows supports common devices, such as a basic keyboard, straight out of the box, but some fancier or specialty input devices require drivers and configuration. Finally, you should understand how to troubleshoot input devices.

Common I/O Devices

Most PCs have two or more common input devices. The mouse and keyboard are two of the most basic, necessary, and abused input devices on a computer. Another fairly common input device that's been around a long time is the scanner. To these oldsters, you can add relative newcomers to the world of common devices: digital cameras and Web cameras.

Keyboards and Mice

The Control Panel has two applets that handle basic configuration for keyboards and mice, such as setting the repeat delay or the cursor acceleration, appropriately named Keyboard and Mouse. More advanced devices, such as the keyboard shown in Figure 10.1, require drivers as well.

> ### Travel Advisory
> Wireless keyboards provide wonderful convenience, because they remove the cable between you and the PC, but make sure that you keep a complete set of spare batteries around. Most wireless keyboards eat batteries!

Currently, two types of mouse technologies dominate the market: ball mice and optical mice. Ball mice use a small round ball while optical mice use LEDs or lasers and a camera to track their movements.

FIGURE 10.1 Fancy keyboard

The key for maintaining and troubleshooting both keyboards and mice is to keep them clean. Remove dirt and grime from the keys using a cloth dampened with a little water, or if the water alone doesn't do the job, use a bit of isopropyl alcohol on a cloth (Figure 10.2).

The problem with ball mice is that the ball inside the mouse picks up dirt over time and deposits the dirt on internal rollers that contact the ball. Dirt builds up to the point that the mouse stops responding smoothly. If you are struggling with your mouse to point at objects on your screen or your cursor skips on movement, you need to clean the mouse (Figure 10.3). Few mice manufacturers still make ball mice, as they tend to require far more maintenance than optical mice.

FIGURE 10.2 Cleaning keys

FIGURE 10.3 Dirty mouse internals

Scanners

A scanner enables you to make digital copies of existing paper photos, documents, drawings, and more. Better scanners give you the option of copying directly from a photographic negative or slide, providing images of stunning visual quality—assuming the original photo was halfway decent, of course.

All consumer level scanners—called *flatbed scanners*—work the same way. You place a photo or another object facedown on the glass, close the lid, and then use software to initiate the scan. The scanner runs a bright light along the length of the glass tray once or more to capture the image. Figure 10.4 shows an open scanner.

FIGURE 10.4 Scanner open with photograph facedown

The scanning software that controls the hardware can be manifested in a variety of ways. Nearly every manufacturer will have some sort of drivers and other software to create an interface between your computer and the scanner. When you push the front button on an Epson Perfection scanner, for example, the Epson software opens the Photoshop program as well as its own interface (Figure 10.5).

You can also open your favorite image-editing software first and choose to acquire a file from a scanner. Figure 10.6 shows the process of acquiring an image from a scanner in the popular shareware image-editing software Paint Shop Pro. As in most such software, you choose File | Import and then select a source. In this case, the scanner uses the traditional TWAIN drivers. *TWAIN* stands for *Technology Without an Interesting Name* and has been the default driver type for scanners for a long time.

FIGURE 10.5 Epson software interface with Photoshop open in the background

FIGURE 10.6 Acquiring an image in Paint Shop Pro

Almost all modern scanners plug into the USB port on your PC, although some high-end models offer FireWire as well. Older scanners come in SCSI and parallel varieties.

If you travel a lot, you'll want to make sure to use the locking mechanism for the scanner light assembly (Figure 10.7). Just be sure to unlock it before you try to use it or you'll get a light that's stuck in one position. That won't make for very good scans!

Digital Cameras

Another input option available for those not-yet-taken pictures is to put away your point-and-shoot film camera and use a digital camera. Digital cameras are a wonderful tool for capturing a moment and then sending it to friends and relatives.

FIGURE 10.7 Scanner lock

Digital cameras use flash memory—like Secure Digital (SD)—to store pictures and connect to PCs via a cable. These days, almost all digital cameras plug directly into a USB port (Figure 10.8). Another common option, though, is to connect only the camera's storage media to the computer, using one of the many digital media readers available.

Web Cameras

PC cameras, often called *webcams*, enable you to chat over the Internet with video. Webcams measure their resolution in pixels. You can find webcams with resolutions of as few as 100,000 pixels and webcams with millions of pixels. Most people who use webcams agree that 1.3 million pixels (1 megapixel) is pretty much the highest resolution quality you can use before your video becomes so large it will bog down even a broadband connection.

Most people who use online video will also want a microphone. Many cameras come with microphones, or you can use a separately purchased device. Those who do a lot of video chatting may prefer to get a camera without a microphone, and buy a good quality headset with which to speak and listen.

Almost all webcams use USB connections. Windows comes with a limited set of webcam drivers, so always make sure to install the drivers supplied with the camera before you plug it in. Most webcams use Hi-Speed USB, so make sure you're plugging your webcam into a Hi-Speed USB port.

The biggest challenge to using webcams is getting your webcam applications to recognize that your webcam is available and configured for use. Every pro-

FIGURE 10.8 Camera connecting to USB port

gram does this differently, but conceptually the steps are basically the same (with plenty of exceptions):

1. Tell the program you want to use a camera.
2. Tell the program whether you want the camera to turn on automatically when you chat.
3. Configure the image quality.
4. Test the camera.

If you're having problems with a camera, always go through the general I/O problems first, as this will clear up most issues. If you're still having trouble getting the camera to work in a program, be sure to turn off all other programs that may also be using the camera. Windows allows only one program at a time to use a webcam.

Specialty I/O Devices

The CompTIA A+ certification exams want to make sure you're aware of three other types of I/O devices: biometric scanners, bar code readers, and touch screens. Let's look at these fairly specialized devices.

Biometric Devices

PCs use biometrics for security. Biometric security devices scan and remember unique aspects of various body parts such as your retina, iris, head image, or fingerprint, using some form of sensing device such as a retinal scanner. This information is used as a key to prevent unauthorized people from accessing whatever the biometric device is securing. Most biometric devices currently used in PCs secure only themselves. The USB thumb drive in Figure 10.9 has a tiny finger-

FIGURE 10.9 USB thumb drive with fingerprint scanner (courtesy of Lexar Media, Inc.)

print scanner. You slide your finger (any finger, you choose) over the drive to unlock the contents of the thumb drive.

Less common are biometric security devices that secure entire computers. The Microsoft fingerprint scanner is a USB device that replaces standard user name and password security. Figure 10.10 shows the scanner built into a keyboard. When a program or Web site asks for a user name and password, you simply press your finger against the fingerprint scanner. It will confirm your identity (assuming your fingerprint matches), and then special software that comes with the scanner will supply the program or Web site with your stored user name and password.

No matter what biometric device you use, you follow the same steps to make it work:

1. Install the device.

2. Register your identity with the device by sticking your eye, finger, or other unique body part (why are you snickering?) into the device so it can scan you.

3. Configure its software to tell the device what to do when it recognizes your scanned identity.

Bar Code Readers

Bar code readers are designed to read standard Universal Product Code (UPC) bar codes (Figure 10.11). You would read bar codes for only one reason—to track inventory. Bar code readers enable easy updating of inventory databases stored on PCs. Bar code readers are just about the oldest "specialty" I/O device used with PCs.

FIGURE 10.10 Microsoft fingerprint scanner on a keyboard

Neo HE430

0 761345 284301

FIGURE 10.11 Typical UPC read by bar code readers

Touch Screens

A *touch screen* is a monitor with some type of sensing device across its face that detects the location and duration of contact, usually by a finger or stylus. All touch screens then supply this contact information to the PC as though it were a click event from a mouse. Touch screens are used in situations for which conventional mouse/keyboard input is either impossible or impractical. Here are a few places you'll see touch screens at work:

- Information kiosks
- PDAs
- Point-of-sale systems
- Tablet PCs

Touch screens can be separated into two groups: built-in screens like those in PDAs, and stand-alone touch screen monitors like those used in many point-of-sale systems. From a technician's standpoint, you can think of a stand-alone touch screen as a monitor with a built-in mouse. All touch screens will have a separate USB or PS/2 port for the "mouse" part of the device, along with drivers that you install just as you would for any USB mouse.

Objective 10.02 Adapter Cards

A*dapter cards* enable you to add functions to the PC and, in the case of video cards, install and configure an essential output signal, video. Also called *expansion cards*, these fit into expansion slots in the expansion bus, the wires that connect those cards to the CPU and chipset. Modern motherboards have one or two general-purpose internal expansion buses, peripheral component interconnect (PCI) or PCI Express (PCIe). Older motherboards have an accelerated graphics port (AGP) slot dedicated to video.

PCI

Intel introduced the PCI bus architecture (Figure 10.12) in the early 1990s, and the PC expansion bus was never again the same. Intel made many smart moves with PCI, not the least of which was releasing PCI to the public domain to make it very attractive to manufacturers. PCI provided a wider, faster, more flexible alternative than any previous expansion bus. The exceptional technology of the new bus, combined with the lack of a price tag, made manufacturers quickly drop ISA and the other alternatives and adopt PCI.

PCI really shook up the PC world with its capabilities. The original PCI bus was 32 bits wide and ran at 33 MHz, which was superb, but these features were expected and not earth-shattering. The coolness of PCI came from its ability to coexist with other expansion buses. When PCI first came out, you could buy a motherboard with both PCI and ISA slots. This was important because it enabled users to keep their old ISA cards and slowly migrate to PCI. Equally impressive was that PCI devices were (and still are) self-configuring, a feature that led to the industry standard that became known as Plug and Play (PnP). Finally, PCI had a powerful burst mode feature that enabled very efficient data transfers.

Travel Advisory

Before PCI it was rare to see more than one type of expansion slot on a motherboard. Today this is not only common—it's expected!

AGP

Shortly after Intel invented PCI, the company presented a specialized, video-only version of PCI called the *accelerated graphics port (AGP)*. An AGP slot is a

FIGURE 10.12 PCI expansion bus slots

PCI slot, but one with a direct connection to the Northbridge. AGP slots are only for video cards—don't try to snap a sound card or modem into one. Figure 10.13 shows a typical AGP slot. An AGP slot is almost universally brown in color, making it easy to spot.

PCI-X

PCI-X, already available in systems such as the Macintosh G5, is a huge enhancement to the current PCI technology that is also fully backward-compatible, in terms of both hardware and software. PCI-X is a 64-bit-wide bus (see Figure 10.14). Its slots will accept regular PCI cards. The real bonus of PCI-X is its much enhanced speed. The PCI-X 2.0 standard features four speed grades (measured in MHz): PCI-X 66, PCI-X 133, PCI-X 266, and PCI-X 533.

Mini-PCI

PCI has even made it into laptops in the specialty Mini-PCI format (Figure 10.15). You'll find Mini-PCI in just about every laptop these days. Mini-PCI is designed to use low power and to lie flat— both good features for a laptop expansion slot. Mini-PCI returns in Chapter 12.

PCI Express

PCI Express (PCIe) is the latest, fastest, and most popular expansion bus in use today. As its name implies, PCI Express is still PCI, but it uses a point-to-point serial connection instead of PCI's shared parallel communication. Consider a single 32-bit chunk of data moving from a device to the CPU. In PCI parallel communication, 32 wires each carry 1 bit of that chunk of data. In serial communication, only one wire carries those 32 bits. You'd think that 32 are better than 1, correct? Well, first of all, PCIe doesn't share the bus. A PCIe device has its own direct connection (a point-to-point connection) to the Northbridge, so it does not wait for other devices. Plus, when things start going really fast (think gigabits per second), it's difficult to get all 32 bits of data to go from one device to another at the same time because some bits get there slightly faster than

FIGURE 10.13 AGP slot

FIGURE 10.14 PCI-X slots

others. That means you need some serious, high-speed checking of the data when it arrives to verify that it's all there and in good shape. Serial data doesn't have this problem, as all the bits arrive one after the other in a single stream. When data is really moving fast, a single point-to-point serial connection is faster than a shared, 32-wire parallel connection.

And is PCIe fast! A PCIe connection uses one wire for sending and one for receiving. Each of these pairs of wires between a PCIe controller and a device is called a *lane*. Each lane runs at 2.5 Gbps. Better yet, each point-to-point connection can use 1, 2, 4, 8, 12, 16, or 32 lanes to achieve a maximum bandwidth of 160 Gbps. The effective data rate drops a little bit because of the *encoding*

FIGURE 10.15 Mini-PCI

scheme—the way the data is broken down and reassembled—but full duplex data throughput can go up to a whopping 12.8 GBps on a ×32 connection.

The most common PCIe slot is the 16-lane (×16) version most commonly used for video cards, as shown in Figure 10.16. The first versions of PCIe motherboards used a combination of a single PCIe ×16 slot and a number of standard PCI slots. (Remember that PCI is designed to work with other expansion slots, even other types of PCI.)

Local Lingo

PCIe When you talk about the lanes, such as ×1 or ×8, say "by" rather than "ex" for the multiplication mark. So "by 1" and "by 8" are the correct pronunciations. You'll probably hear it referred to as "ex 8" and "8 ex" for the next few years until the technology has become a household term.

The bandwidth generated by a ×16 slot is far more than anything other than a video card would need, so most PCIe motherboards also contain slots with fewer lanes. Currently ×1 (Figure 10.17) and ×4 are the most common general-purpose PCIe slots, but PCIe is still pretty new—so expect things to change as PCIe matures.

FIGURE 10.16 PCIe ×16 slot (black) with PCI slots (white)

FIGURE 10.17 PCIe ×1 slots

Installing Expansion Cards

Installing an expansion card successfully—another one of those bread-and-butter tasks for the PC tech—requires at least four steps. First, you need to know that the card works with your system and your operating system. Second, you have to insert the card in an expansion slot properly and without damaging that card or the motherboard. Third, you need to provide drivers for the operating system—that's *proper* drivers for the *specific* OS. Fourth, you should always verify that the card functions properly before you walk away from the PC.

Travel Advisory

Some manufacturers insist on a different order for device installation than the traditional one listed here. The most common variation requires you to install the drivers and support software for an expansion card *before* you insert the card. Failure to follow the manufacturer's directions with such a card can lead to hours of frustration while you uninstall the card and reinstall the drivers, sometimes manually removing some drivers and software from the system. The bottom line? Read the instructions that come with a particular card. Later chapters provide more specific examples of problem devices.

Step 1: Knowledge

Learn about the device you plan to install. For Windows systems, your best resource for this knowledge is the Windows Marketplace. This used to be called the Hardware Compatibility List (HCL), and you'll still hear lots of people refer to it as such. You can check out the Web site (http:// testedproducts.windowsmarketplace.com) to see if your product is listed, but most people just look on the box of the device in question (Figure 10.18) — all Windows-certified devices will proudly display that they work with Windows.

Step 2: Physical Installation

To install an expansion card successfully, you need to take steps to avoid damaging the card, the motherboard, or both. This means knowing how to handle a card and avoiding electrostatic discharge (ESD) or any other electrical issue. You also need to place the card firmly and completely into an available expansion slot.

Optimally, a card should always be in one of two places: in a computer or in an antistatic bag. When inserting or removing a card, be careful to hold the card only by its edges. Do not hold the card by the slot connectors or touch any components on the board (Figure 10.19).

Use an antistatic wrist strap if possible, properly attached to the PC, as noted in Chapter 3. If you don't have a wrist strap, you can use the tech way of avoiding ESD by touching the power supply after you remove the expansion card from its antistatic bag. This puts you, the card, and the PC at the same electrical potential and thus minimizes the risk of ESD.

Modern systems have a trickle of voltage on the motherboard at all times when the computer is plugged into a power outlet. Chapter 4 covers power for the PC and how to deal with it in detail, but here's the short version: *Always*

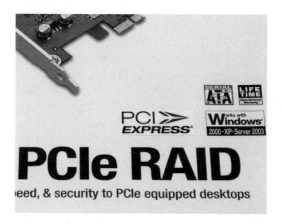

FIGURE 10.18 Works with Windows

FIGURE 10.19 Where to handle a card

unplug the PC before inserting an expansion card! Failure to do so can destroy the card, the motherboard, or both. It's not worth the risk!

Never insert or remove a card at an extreme angle. This may damage the card. A slight angle is acceptable and even necessary when removing a card. Always screw the card to the case with a connection screw. This keeps the card from slipping out and potentially shorting out against other cards. Also, many cards use the screw connection to ground the card to the case (Figure 10.20).

FIGURE 10.20 Always screw down all cards

Step 3: Device Drivers

Installing device drivers is fairly straightforward. You should use the correct drivers—kind of obvious, but you'd be surprised by how many techs mess this up—and, if you're upgrading, you might have to unload current drivers before loading new drivers. Finally, if you have a problem, you may need to uninstall the drivers you just loaded or, with Windows XP, roll back to earlier, more stable drivers.

To be sure you have the best possible driver you can get for your device, you should always check the manufacturer's Web site. The drivers that come with a device may work well, but odds are good that you'll find a newer and better driver on the Web site. How do you know that the drivers on the Web site are newer? First, take the easy route: look on the CD. Often the version is printed right on the CD itself. If it's not printed there, you're going to have to load the CD in your CD-ROM drive and poke around. Many driver discs have an AutoRun screen that advertises the version. If there's nothing on the pop-up screen, look for a Readme file (Figure 10.21).

Not all driver makers use the Windows Certification program. When Windows runs into such a driver, it brings up a scary-looking screen (Figure 10.22) that says you're about to install an unsigned driver.

The fact that a company refuses to use the Windows Certification doesn't mean that its drivers are bad—it simply means that they haven't gone through Microsoft's exhaustive quality-assurance certification procedure. If I run into this, I usually check the driver's version to make sure I'm not installing something outdated, and then I just take my chances and install it. (I've yet to encounter a problem with an unsigned driver that I haven't also seen with Windows Certified drivers.)

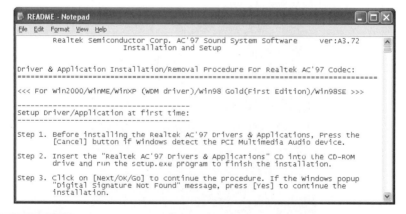

FIGURE 10.21 Part of a Readme file showing the driver version

FIGURE 10.22 Unsigned driver warning

Windows XP offers the nifty feature of rolling back to previous drivers after an installation or driver upgrade. If you decide to live on the edge and install beta drivers for your video card, for example, and your system becomes frightfully unstable, you can back up to the drivers that worked before you installed the betas. (Not that I've ever had to use that feature, of course!) To access the rollback feature, simply open the Device Manager and access the properties for the device you want to adjust. On the Driver tab (Figure 10.23), you'll find the Roll Back Driver button.

FIGURE 10.23 Driver rollback feature

Step 4: Verify

As a last step in the installation process, inspect the results of the installation and verify that the device works properly. Immediately after installing, you should open the Device Manager and verify that Windows sees the device (Figure 10.24). Assuming that Device Manager shows the device working properly, your next check is to put the device to work by making it do whatever it is supposed to do. If you installed a printer, print something; if you installed a scanner, scan something. If it works, you're done!

Troubleshooting Expansion Cards

A properly installed expansion card rarely makes trouble—it's the botched installations that produce headaches. Chances are high that you'll have to troubleshoot an expansion card installation at some point, usually from an installation that you botched personally.

The first sign of an improperly installed card usually shows up the moment you first try to get that card to do whatever it's supposed to do and it doesn't do it. When this happens, your primary troubleshooting process is a reinstallation—after checking in with Device Manager.

FIGURE 10.24 Device Manager shows the device working properly

Device Manager

The Device Manager provides the first diagnostic and troubleshooting tool in Windows. After you install a new device, Device Manager gives you many clues if something has gone wrong.

Occasionally, Device Manager may not even show the new device. If that happens, verify that you inserted the device properly and, if needed, that the device has power. Run the Add/Remove Hardware Wizard and see if Windows recognizes the device. If the Device Manager doesn't recognize the device at this point, you have one of two problems: either the device is physically damaged and you must replace it, or the device is an onboard device, not a card, and is turned off in CMOS.

It's rare that Device Manager completely fails to see a device. More commonly, device problems manifest themselves in the Device Manager via error icons—a black "!" or a red "X" or a blue "i."

- A black "!" on a yellow circle indicates that a device is missing, that Windows does not recognize a device, or that there's a device driver problem. A device may still work even while producing this error.

- A red "X" indicates a disabled device (Figure 10.25). This usually points to a device that's been manually turned off or a damaged device. A device producing this error will not work.

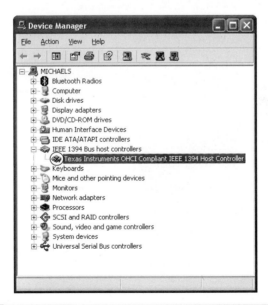

FIGURE 10.25 An "X" in Device Manager, indicating a problem with the selected device

- A blue "i" on a white field indicates a device on which someone has configured the system resources manually. This occurs only on non-ACPI systems. This symbol merely provides information and does not indicate an error with the device.

The "!" symbol is the most common error symbol and is usually the easiest to fix. First, double-check the device's connections. Second, try reinstalling the driver with the Update Driver button. To get to the Update Driver button, right-click the desired device in the Device Manager and select Properties. In the Properties dialog box, select the Driver tab. On the Driver tab, click the Update Driver button to launch the Hardware Update Wizard (Figure 10.26).

A red "X" error strikes fear into most technicians. If you see one, first check that the device isn't disabled. Right-click the device and select Enable. If that doesn't work (it often will not), try rolling back the driver (if you updated the driver) or uninstalling (if it's a new install). Shut down the system and make triple-sure you have the card physically installed. Then redo the entire driver installation procedure, making sure you have the most current driver for that device. If none of these procedures works, return the card—it's almost certainly bad.

FIGURE 10.26 Updating the driver

As you look at the errors in Device Manager, you'll notice error codes for the device that does not work properly. Windows has about 20 error codes, but the fixes still boil down to the same methods just shown. If you really want to frustrate yourself, try the Troubleshooter. It starts most fixes the same way—by reinstalling the device driver.

Objective 10.03 Output Devices

O utput devices enable you to see or hear feedback from the computer. You've done your input; the computer processes that information and then provides output. Output devices come in three main categories: sound, video, and hard copy. Printing gets its own chapter, so this section concentrates on sound and video.

Sound

Sound output in the PC has two basic components, the sound card and speakers. Most PCs use sound cards built into the motherboard, though these are not as good as stand-alone cards.

Most built-in sound lacks a dedicated sound processor, relying on the CPU for the processing power. This eats into CPU time and reduces overall performance. Built-in sound usually picks up interference from the rest of the motherboard, thus leading to a noticeable hiss, especially when listening through headphones.

A dedicated sound card—particularly in Windows 2000 and Windows XP—offers an inexpensive performance enhancing upgrade that should be done for most systems. Windows Vista offers a different story, though, because it lacks support (at least at this writing) for dedicated sound processors. Vista requires sound processing through the OS and thus through the CPU.

Speakers, much more than the sound card—built-in or dedicated—make a huge difference in customer satisfaction. This won't show up on the CompTIA A+ certification exams, but it is useful information nonetheless. Spend the extra small amount of money to get better speakers. If you can fit only a 2.1 set, then go for the big subwoofer and nice satellites, like those shown in Figure 10.27.

Sound cards install and configure like every other expansion device. Install the card, and then install updated drivers. Plug things into the right ports and they'll work fine.

FIGURE 10.27 Klipsch 2.1 speaker set

Video

The video system in PCs is composed of two complex pieces, the video card and the monitor. The video card handles the commands from the CPU and OS and then sends commands to the monitor to update and change what it displays.

Video Cards

As far as the CompTIA A+ certification exams go, you can treat a video card—whether stand-alone or built into the motherboard—just like any other expansion card. It goes into the appropriate slot, AGP or PCIe, for the most part, and you install drivers. Use the Device Manager when you set it up to make sure everything works right. The Display Control Panel applet (Figure 10.28) enables you to make changes to the function of the video card (or *display adapter*).

Just giving you the CompTIA A+ certification line on video cards would be a disservice, even in a cram-style book, because a properly chosen and set up video card can make an amazing difference in the performance of a computer, especially when it comes to gaming, image editing, and 3-D modeling. Plus, Windows Vista uses 3-D video card processing extensively, so you need to know about video cards in the real world.

The video card is composed of two major pieces: the video RAM and the video processor circuitry. The video RAM stores the video image. On the first video cards, this RAM was good old dynamic RAM (DRAM), just like the RAM

FIGURE 10.28 Display applet

on the motherboard. Today's video cards often have better RAM than your system has. The video processing circuitry takes the information on the video RAM and shoots it out to the monitor. While early video processing circuitry was little more than an intermediary between the CPU and the video RAM, modern video processors are more powerful than all but the latest CPUs! It's not at all uncommon to see video cards that need fans to cool their onboard processors (see Figure 10.29).

Video card discussion, at least among techs, almost always revolves around the graphics processor they use and the amount of RAM onboard. A typical video card might be called an ATI Radeon X1950 XTX 512 MB, so let's break that down. ATI is the manufacturer, Radeon X1950 XTX is the model of the card as well as the graphics processor, and 512 MB is the amount of video RAM.

Your choice of graphics processor is your single most important decision in buying a video card. Low-end graphics processors will usually work fine for the run-of-the-mill user who wants to write letters or run a Web browser. High-end graphics processors are designed to support the beautiful 3-D games that are so popular today.

FIGURE 10.29 Video card with a cooling fan

The two major video processor makers, NVIDIA and ATI, are extremely competitive, and both companies introduce multiple models of graphics processors (and therefore new models of cards) every year. However, unless you're using the Vista Aero glass desktop, all of these extra features you see in video cards are really only for the true driving force in video cards: 3-D gaming. Your PC is capable of providing you with hours of incredible entertainment via a huge number of popular games that immerse you in 3-D environments full of light, shadows, explosions, and other amazing effects that create a fun and beautiful gaming experience.

Drivers Because of the complexity of modern video cards, manufacturers constantly tweak their drivers to make them work better with Windows. With almost no exception, when you take a video card out of the box, the drivers on the CD bundled with the card are outdated. Always hit the manufacturer's Web site as soon as possible and download the latest non-beta drivers. You and your clients will be much better served than if you installed the bundled drivers.

DirectX and Video Cards In the old days, many applications communicated directly with much of the PC hardware and, as a result, could crash your com-

puter if not written well enough. Microsoft tried to fix this problem by placing all hardware under the control of Windows, but programmers balked because Windows added too much work for the video process and slowed down everything. For the most demanding programs, such as games, only direct access of hardware would work.

This need to "get around Windows" motivated Microsoft to unveil a new set of protocols called *DirectX*. Programmers use DirectX to take control of certain pieces of hardware and to talk directly to that hardware; it provides the speed necessary to play more of today's advanced games. The primary impetus for DirectX was to build a series of products to enable Windows to run 3-D games. That's not to say that you couldn't run 3-D games in Windows *before* DirectX; rather, it's just that Microsoft wasn't involved in the API rat race at the time and wanted to be. Microsoft's goal in developing DirectX was to create a 100-percent stable environment, with direct hardware access, for running 3-D applications and games within Windows.

DirectX is not only for video; it also supports sound, network connections, input devices, and other parts of your PC. Each of these subsets of DirectX has a name like DirectDraw, Direct3D, or DirectSound.

- **DirectDraw** Supports direct access to the hardware for 2-D graphics.
- **Direct3D** Supports direct access to the hardware for 3-D graphics— the most important part of DirectX.
- **DirectInput** Supports direct access to the hardware for joysticks and other game controllers.
- **DirectSound** Supports direct access to the hardware for waveforms.
- **DirectMusic** Supports direct access to the hardware for MIDI devices.
- **DirectPlay** Supports direct access to network devices for multiplayer games.
- **DirectShow** Supports direct access to video and presentation devices.

Microsoft constantly adds and tweaks this list. As almost all games need DirectX and all video cards have drivers to support DirectX, you need to verify that DirectX is installed and working properly on your system. To do this, use the DirectX diagnostic tool in the System Information program. After you open System Information (it usually lives in the Accessories | System Tools area of the Start menu), click the Tools menu and select DirectX Diagnostic Tool (see Figure 10.30).

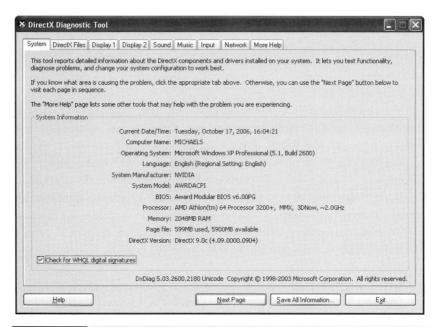

FIGURE 10.30 The DirectX Diagnostic Tool

Monitors

Video displays for PCs come in three varieties: CRT, LCD, and projectors. The first two you'll see on the desktop or laptop; the last you'll find in boardrooms and classrooms, splashing a picture onto a screen. Figure 10.31 shows an LCD and a CRT.

LCD CRT

FIGURE 10.31 LCD and CRT

CRT Monitors

Cathode ray tube (CRT) monitors contain a large, airtight vacuum tube. One end of this tube is a slender cylinder that contains three electron guns. The other end of the tube, which is fatter and wider, is the display screen.

The inside of the display screen has a phosphor coating. The monitor displays video data as the electron guns make a series of horizontal sweeps across the screen, energizing the appropriate areas of the phosphor coating. The sweeps start at the upper-left corner of the monitor and move across and down to the lower-right corner.

The speed at which the electron beam moves across the screen is known as the *horizontal refresh rate (HRR)*. The monitor draws a number of lines across the screen, eventually covering the screen with glowing phosphors. The number of lines is not fixed, unlike television screens, which have a set number of lines. After the guns reach the lower-right corner of the screen, they turn off and point back to the upper-left corner. The amount of time it takes to draw the entire screen and get the electron guns back to the upper-left corner is called the *vertical refresh rate (VRR)*.

If the video card is set to push at too low a VRR, the monitor produces a noticeable flicker, causing eyestrain and headaches for users. Pushing the monitor at too high of a VRR, however, causes a definite distortion of the screen image and will damage the circuitry of the monitor and eventually destroy it. Set the VRR in the Display Control Panel applet, Advanced tab.

Resolution

Monitor *resolution* is always shown as the number of horizontal pixels times the number of vertical pixels. A resolution of 640×480, therefore, indicates a horizontal resolution of 640 pixels and a vertical resolution of 480 pixels. Figure 10.32 shows the relationship between resolution and pixels.

Some common resolutions are 640×480, 800×600, 1024×768, 1280×960, 1280×1024, and 1600×1200. Notice that most of these resolutions match a 4:3 ratio. This is called the *aspect ratio*. Many monitors are shaped like television screens, with a 4:3 aspect ratio, so most resolutions are designed to match—or at least be close to—that shape. Many monitors, generically called *wide-screen monitors*, have a 16:9 or 16:10 ratio. Two of the common resolutions you'll see with these monitors are 1366×768 and 1920×1200.

LCD Monitors

Liquid crystal displays (LCDs) are the most common type of display technology for PCs. LCD monitors have many advantages over CRTs. They are thinner and

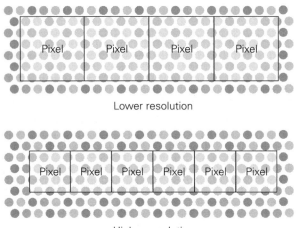

FIGURE 10.32 Resolution and pixels

lighter, use much less power, are virtually flicker free, and don't emit potentially harmful radiation.

A color LCD screen is composed of a large number of tiny liquid crystal molecules (called *sub-pixels*) arranged in rows and columns between polarizing filters. A translucent sheet above the sub-pixels is colored red, green, or blue. Each tiny distinct group of three sub-pixels—one red, one green, and one blue—forms a physical pixel, as shown in Figure 10.33.

FIGURE 10.33 LCD pixels and resolution

LCD Resolution

All LCD monitors have a *native resolution,* such as 1680×1050, that enables them to display the sharpest picture possible. As mentioned earlier, the pixels are fixed. You simply cannot run an LCD monitor at a resolution higher than the native one. Worse, because LCDs have no equivalent to a shadow mask, they can't run at a *lower* than native resolution without severely degrading image quality. A CRT can simply use more dots and the filtering and smoothing of the shadow mask to make a picture at a lower resolution look as good and crisp as the same picture at a higher resolution, but an LCD cannot. The LCD has to use an edge-blurring technique called *anti-aliasing* to soften the jagged corners of the pixels when running at lower than native resolution, which simply does not look as good. The bottom line? Always set the LCD at native resolution.

> **Travel Advisory**
>
> Two LCD panels that have the same physical size may have different native resolutions.

LCD Technologies

Two technologies dominate the LCD market. PC monitors and portable computers use *active matrix* or *thin film transistor (TFT)* technology to provide a responsive, color-saturated display. You'll find *passive matrix* technology in use on the little monochrome screens like point-of-sale machines and automated teller machines.

LCD Components

The typical LCD projector is composed of three main components: the LCD panel, the backlight(s), and the inverters. The *LCD panel* creates the image, the *backlights* illuminate the image so you can see it, and the *inverters* send power to backlights. Figure 10.34 shows a typical layout for the internal components of an LCD monitor.

Response Rate

An LCD panel's *response rate* is the amount of time it takes for all of the sub-pixels on the panel to go from pure black to pure white and back again. This is roughly the same concept as the CRT refresh rate, but with one important difference. Once the electron gun on a CRT lights a phosphor, that phosphor begins to fade until it is lit again. Individual LCD sub-pixels hold their intensity until the LCD circuitry changes that sub-pixel, making the problem of flicker nonexistent on LCDs.

FIGURE 10.34 LCD internals

Manufacturers measure LCD response rates in milliseconds, with lower being better. A typical lower end or older LCD will have a response rate of 20 to 25 ms. The screens look fine, but you'll get some ghosting if you try to watch a movie or play a fast-paced video game. In recent years, manufacturers have figured out how to overcome this issue, and you can find many LCD monitors with a response rate of 6 to 8 ms.

Contrast Ratio

A big drawback of LCD monitors is that they don't have nearly the color saturation or richness of contrast of a good CRT monitor—although LCD technology continues to improve every year. A good contrast ratio—the difference between the darkest and lightest spots that the monitor can display—is 450:1, although a quick trip to a computer store will reveal LCDs with lower levels (250:1) and higher levels (1000:1).

Projectors

Projectors shoot the image out the front and count on you to put up a screen at the proper distance. Front-view projectors connected to PCs running Microsoft PowerPoint have been the cornerstone of every meeting almost everywhere for years (Figure 10.35).

FIGURE 10.35 Front-view projector (photo courtesy of Dell, Inc.)

The bane of every projector is the lamp. Lamps work hard in your projector, as they must generate a tremendous amount of light. As a result, they generate quite a bit of heat, and all projectors come with a fan to keep the lamp from overheating. When you turn off a projector, the fan will continue to run until the lamp is fully cooled. Lamps are also very expensive, which comes as a nasty shock to someone who's not prepared for the price when his or her lamp dies.

Common Features

For all the radical differences among monitor technologies, they have several aspects in common. They're the classic visual output device, of course, but you can make adjustments to how they appear and apply techniques to minimize their power consumption.

Adjustments

Most adjustments to the monitor take place at installation, but for now, let's just make sure you know what they are and where they are located. Clearly, all monitors have an On/Off button or switch. Also, see if you can locate the Brightness and Contrast buttons. Beyond that, most monitors (at least the only ones you should buy) have an onboard menu system, enabling a number of adjustments. Every monitor maker provides a different way to access these menus, but they all provide two main functions: physical screen adjustment (bigger, smaller, move to the left, right, up, down, and others) and color adjustment. The color adjustment lets you adjust the red, green, and blue guns to give you the best color tones. All these settings are a matter of personal taste. Make sure the person who will use the computer understands how to adjust these settings (see Figure 10.36).

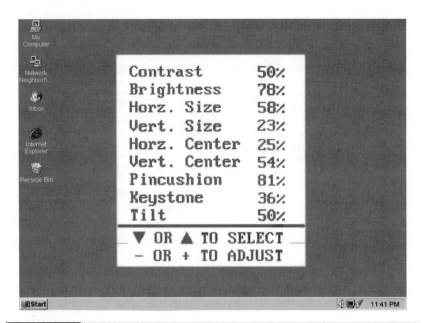

Contrast	50%
Brightness	78%
Horz. Size	58%
Vert. Size	23%
Horz. Center	25%
Vert. Center	54%
Pincushion	81%
Keystone	36%
Tilt	50%

▼ OR ▲ TO SELECT
– OR + TO ADJUST

FIGURE 10.36 Typical menu controls

Power Conservation

CRT and LCD monitors differ greatly in the amount of electricity they require. The bottom line is that CRTs use a lot and LCDs use a lot less. Here's the scoop.

Approximately half the power required to run a desktop PC is consumed by the CRT monitor. Monitors that meet the Video Electronics Standards Association (VESA) specification for *display power-management signaling (DPMS)* can reduce monitor power consumption by roughly 75 percent. This is accomplished by reducing or eliminating the signals sent by the video card to the monitor during idle periods. By eliminating these pulses, the monitor essentially takes catnaps. The advantage over simply shutting off the monitor is in the time it takes to restore the display.

A typical CRT monitor consumes approximately 120 watts. During a catnap or power-down mode, the energy consumption is reduced to below 25 watts, while enabling the screen to return to use in less than 10 seconds. Full shutoff is accomplished by eliminating all clocking pulses to the monitor. Although this reduces power consumption to below 15 watts, it also requires anywhere from 15 to 30 seconds to restore a usable display.

A typical LCD monitor, in contrast, uses less than half the electricity that a CRT uses. A 19-inch, 4:3 aspect-ratio flat panel, for example, uses around 33 watts at peak usage and less than 2 watts in DPMS mode. Larger LCDs use more power at peak usage than smaller ones. A 21-inch wide-screen model, for exam-

ple, might draw about 75 watts at peak, but still drop down to less than 2 watts in DPMS mode. Swapping out CRTs with LCDs is a great way to save on your electric bill.

CHECKPOINT

✔**Objective 10.01: Input Devices** Input devices enable you to interact with the computer and give it commands through typing, clicking, speaking, and more. Windows supports common devices, such as a keyboard or mouse, straight out of the box, but some fancier or specialty input devices require drivers and configuration. Other common input devices include scanners, digital cameras, and webcams. Specialty input devices include biometric scanners, bar code readers, and touch screens.

✔**Objective 10.02: Adapter Cards** Adapter or expansion cards come in several varieties, such as PCI, AGP, PCI-X, Mini-PCI, and PCI Express. Installing an expansion card successfully requires at least four steps: knowledge of the proper device, physical installation, device driver installation, and verification of success.

✔**Objective 10.03: Output Devices** Output devices enable you to see or hear feedback from the computer. Output devices come in three main categories: sound, video, and printing. Sound manifests as a sound card and speakers. Video manifests as video card or display adapter and monitor. Monitors come in three types: CRT, LCD, and projectors.

REVIEW QUESTIONS

1. Which of the following devices enables you to input a picture into a computer easily?
 A. Keyboard
 B. Mouse
 C. Printer
 D. Scanner

2. John's cursor keeps "skipping" as he moves it across the screen. What should he do?
 A. Clean the keyboard.
 B. Clean the mouse.

 C. Check the Keyboard applet settings.

 D. Check the Mouse applet settings.

3. Which of the following devices enables voice and video connection over the Internet?

 A. Digital camera

 B. Printer

 C. Scanner

 D. Webcam

4. Which of the following is an example of a biometric device?

 A. Digital camera

 B. Flatbed scanner

 C. Retina scanner

 D. Webcam

5. What device enables you to enter data directly to a computer using only your fingers?

 A. Bar code reader

 B. Flatbed scanner

 C. Touch screen

 D. Webcam

6. A "32-bit parallel expansion bus" describes which of the following technologies?

 A. AGP

 B. PCI

 C. PCI Express

 D. PCI-X

7. Which expansion bus enables you to add devices to a portable computer?

 A. Micro-PCI

 B. Mini-PCI

 C. PCI

 D. PCI Express

8. Which of the following technologies provides a serial expansion bus?

 A. AGP

 B. PCI

 C. PCI Express

 D. PCI-X

23 Wilson St.
Skowhegan, Me.
04796

OPERATING FUND RECONCILIATION

Reconciled by: _____ Date _____

Authorized Vault Fund $ _____

Authorized Register Fund $ _____

Total $ _____

ACTUAL COIN _____

ACTUAL BILLS _____

TOTAL _____

OVER/SHORT _____

Attach to Daily Cash Report.
Call Sales Audit before 12:00/noon if there is a
discrepancy of $10.00 or more

9. Mary wants to add a new sound card to a client's system. What should she do before inserting the card into the motherboard? (Select two.)

 A. Isolate the card.

 B. Install the drivers.

 C. Ground herself.

 D. Unplug the PC.

10. After installing an updated sound card driver, Tiffany's Windows XP system boots but now no sound comes out of the speakers. She has the speakers plugged in properly and powered up. What can she do to get the sound working again?

 A. Roll back the drivers.

 B. Reinstall the drivers.

 C. Reload Windows.

 D. Unsign the drivers.

11. Which of the following devices is an example of an output device? (Select two.)

 A. Keyboard

 B. Mouse

 C. Monitor

 D. Speaker

12. Which monitor technology offers the least power consumption?

 A. AMD

 B. CRT

 C. DirectX

 D. LCD

13. Akili gets a tech call about a new LCD that's "fuzzy." What might he check first?

 A. Check the resolution and set it at the native resolution.

 B. Check the refresh rate and increase the vertical refresh rate.

 C. Check the refresh rate and increase the horizontal refresh rate.

 D. Check the lamp and replace if necessary.

14. What's a typical adjustment you can make on a monitor?

 A. Increase the brightness.

 B. Increase the inverter.

 C. Increase the lamp.

 D. Increase the response rate.

15. What do you use in Windows XP to adjust the resolution of a monitor?
 A. Display applet
 B. Monitor applet
 C. Resolution applet
 D. Video applet

REVIEW ANSWERS

1. **D** You can import or input pictures easily into a computer using a scanner.

2. **B** A skipping cursor usually indicates a dirty ball mouse. Clean it!

3. **D** A webcam enables you to chat with both voice and video over the Internet.

4. **C** A retinal scanner is an example of a biometric device.

5. **C** A touch screen enables direct input of data using your fingers or a stylus.

6. **B** A PCI is a 32-bit, parallel expansion bus.

7. **B** Many portable computers have a Mini-PCI slot that enables you to add a device.

8. **C** PCI Express (PCIe) provides a serial, rather than parallel, expansion bus.

9. **C D** Mary should both ground herself to the PC and unplug it to turn off the trickle charge on the motherboard before inserting the card.

10. **A** The quickest fix here would be to reinstall the old card and do a driver rollback.

11. **C D** Monitors and speakers are the two most common output devices on the PC, with the printer (not an option here) being the third.

12. **D** LCDs have far lower power demands than CRTs.

13. **A** A fuzzy LCD often is just running in a resolution that's not its native resolution. That's the first thing to check in such a situation.

14. **A** All monitors have some option to increase or decrease the brightness.

15. **A** You can use the Display applet in Windows XP to adjust the resolution of a monitor.

Printers

	NEWBIE	SOME EXPERIENCE	EXPERT
ETA	6 hours	4 hours	2 hours

A good twenty-first century tech understands the various types of printers and printer connections and can diagnose and troubleshoot printing problems to keep users up and running with all those paper documents. In most office and repair situations, you (as a tech) almost always get tagged, not as the PC repair person, but as the *computer person,* and *everyone* knows that printers are included in that description!

Objective 11.01 Types of Printers

Printers create print output, usually on paper, but also on other materials such as transparencies and cloth. The CompTIA A+ certification exams have traditionally tested on printer types and configuration. This chapter helps you identify the different printer types, connections, configurations, and common troubleshooting issues.

Dot-Matrix Printers

Dot-matrix technology uses a series or matrix of pins to create printed dots arranged to form characters on a piece of paper. The speed at which a dot-matrix printer prints is measured in the number of characters it can produce per second. The print head mechanism pushes each pin into the ribbon, which then strikes the paper. The original dot-matrix print heads had 7 pins, while newer, letter-quality print heads use 24 pins to produce near letter quality (NLQ) documents. Figure 11.1 shows a typical dot-matrix printer.

Dot-matrix printers are called *impact* printers because the printing mechanism physically strikes the page. The continual motion of the pins through the print head creates a ton of heat, so avoid touching the print head after printing a handful of pages or more. A hot print head can give you a nasty burn.

Paper moves through a dot-matrix printer using a *tractor-feed* mechanism, as shown in Figure 11.2. Spoked wheels located on each side of the paper feed mechanism move the paper. The spokes on the outer edges of the wheels fit into holes on the sides of specially designed *continuous form* paper. As the wheels turn, they pull the paper through the printer.

Because impact printers physically strike the page, you can use them to create multipart forms with ease. Many offices and government agencies use them for that very reason. Although impact printers have been replaced in most homes and offices by newer, sexier inkjet and laser printers (discussed in the sections that follow), they still retain a substantial portion of the market in their niches.

FIGURE 11.1 Dot-matrix printer

Inkjet Printers

Inkjet printers create printouts by squirting ink out of special inkjet cartridges. They use both black and colored ink cartridges, and they can combine ink colors to create a wide range of hues. Inkjet printers use either liquid ink cartridges or solid, wax-based ink cartridges. Figure 11.3 shows a typical inkjet printer.

An inkjet printer is a *non-impact* printer because its print mechanism never actually touches the paper. Because an inkjet printer processes an entire page at

FIGURE 11.2 Tractor-feed mechanism in a dot-matrix printer

FIGURE 11.3 Typical inkjet printer

a time before starting to print it, it is referred to as a *page* printer. The inkjet printer uses a *friction-feed* mechanism to feed paper through the printer. Sheets of paper are stacked in the paper tray, where small rollers press down to create friction and pull a sheet of paper through the printer.

Most liquid inkjet printers and all solid inkjet printers use a thermal process to eject ink onto the paper. The printing element heats up, boiling the ink in the case of liquid inkjet printers, and melting it in the case of solid inkjet printers. A tiny bubble of ink forms on the end of the print nozzle. Once the bubble becomes sufficiently enlarged, it pops, at which point electrically charged plates deflect the ink onto the paper. Sounds kind of messy, but it's actually precise. An inkjet print head contains between 300 and 600 nozzles, each about the diameter of a human hair. Figure 11.4 illustrates a typical inkjet print head. When the inkjet cartridge is not in use, pump pressure keeps the ink from leaking out the nozzle.

Epson printers use a different, proprietary inkjet technology featuring a special crystal at the back of the ink reservoir that flexes when an electric current is applied to it. When the crystal flexes, it forces a drop of ink out of the nozzle. The way it flexes determines the size and placement of the resulting drop.

A common problem with inkjet printers is the tendency for the ink inside the jets to dry out when the printer is not used, even for a relatively short time. To counter this problem, all inkjet printers move the print head to a special park position that keeps the ink from drying. Except for replacing the inkjet cartridges and print heads, you don't need to do much maintenance. In some cases, you may need to replace the rubber paper rollers or tracking belts, but for the

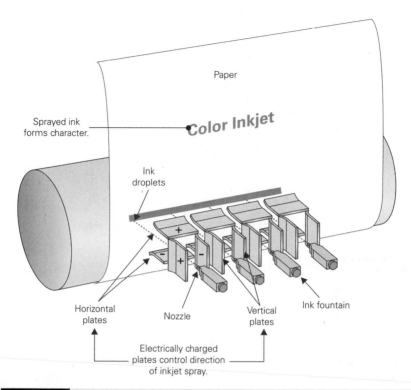

Paper

Sprayed ink
forms character.

Color Inkjet

Ink
droplets

+

+ −

Horizontal
plates

Nozzle

Vertical
plates

Ink fountain

Electrically charged
plates control direction
of inkjet spray.

FIGURE 11.4 Detail of an inkjet print head

most part any serious repairs are simply not cost-effective. The low cost of new inkjet printers makes them candidates for replacement rather than repair.

Dye-Sublimation Printers

The term *sublimation* means to cause something to change from a solid form into a vapor and then back into a solid. This is exactly the process behind *dye-sublimation* printing (sometimes called *thermal dye transfer* printing).

The dye-sublimation technique uses a roll of heat-sensitive plastic film embedded with page-sized sections of cyan, magenta, and yellow dye (some also have a section of black dye). A print head containing thousands of heating elements capable of precise temperature control moves across the film, vaporizing the dyes and causing them to soak into specially coated paper underneath before cooling and reverting to a solid form. The process requires one pass per page for each color. Some printers also utilize a final finishing pass that applies a protective laminate coating to the page. Figure 11.5 shows how a dye-sublimation printer functions.

Dye-ribbon roll

Thermal print head

Vaporized dye

FIGURE 11.5 Dye-sublimation printing process

Documents printed through dye-sublimation display *continuous tone* images, meaning that each pixel dot is a blend of the different dye colors. This is in contrast to the *dithered* images of other print technologies, which use closely packed, single-color dots to simulate blended colors. Dye-sublimation printers produce high-quality color output that rivals professional photo lab processing. They are used mainly for photo printing, high-end desktop publishing, medical and scientific imaging, or other applications for which fine detail and rich color is more important than cost and speed. Smaller, specialized printers called snapshot printers use dye-sublimation to print photos at a reduced cost (compared to their full-sized counterparts). Still, when you can get a high-end inkjet printer for the same price and have the versatility to print documents with speed and low expense and high-quality photographs, the snapshot printers become less desirable.

Thermal Printers

You'll see two kind of thermal printers in use: the *direct thermal* printer and the *thermal wax transfer* printer.

Direct thermal printers use a heated print head to burn dots into the surface of special heat-sensitive paper. If you remember the first generation of fax machines, you're already familiar with this type of printer. You don't see many fax machines of the direct thermal type in the workplace anymore, but you will often see this type of printer used in retail point-of-sale areas as receipt printers.

Thermal wax transfer printers work similarly to dye-sublimation printers, except that instead of using rolls of dye-embedded film, the film is coated with colored wax. The thermal print head passes over the film ribbon and melts the wax onto the paper. Unlike dye-sublimation printers, however, thermal wax printers don't require special papers and so are more flexible and somewhat cheaper to use.

Also in contrast to dye-sublimation printers, thermal wax printers don't offer continuous tone output, using color dithering instead. This means that their output isn't quite as good as dye-sublimation printers, but it is still quite good.

Laser and LED Printers

Laser printers rely on the photoconductive properties of certain organic compounds. *Photoconductive* means that particles of these compounds, when exposed to light (that's the *photo* part), will conduct electricity. Laser printers use lasers as a light source because of their precision. *LED* printers work exactly the same way laser printers work, except that they use tiny LEDs as a light source instead of lasers. Both types of printer are usually simply called a laser printer. Unlike inkjet printers, the relatively high initial cost of laser printers makes their repair a practical and popular option. Figure 11.6 shows a typical laser printer.

Like inkjet printers, laser printers are non-impact page printers. The print mechanism never touches the paper, and the entire page is imaged before being transferred to paper. Some laser printers support *duplex* printing, which enables

FIGURE 11.6 Typical laser printer

printing on both sides of the paper, either through a built-in mechanism or an add-on duplexing tray device. Modern laser printers are capable of resolutions as high as 2400×2400 dots per inch (dpi).

Until recently, one of the limitations of laser printing was that color wasn't available—at least, not without spending prohibitively big bucks! Lately, however, the price of laser printing in color has dropped dramatically, so you can expect to see full-color laser printers deployed in the workplace and referenced on the CompTIA A+ certification exams.

Laser Printer Parts

Laser printers have many components, and the CompTIA A+ certification exams expect you to know them. Here's the list.

Toner Cartridge Components Many manufacturers incorporate laser printer components such as the image drum and fuser assembly (both described in the text that follows) into the toner cartridge (see Figure 11.7). While this makes replacement of individual parts nearly impossible, it also greatly reduces maintenance costs. Those parts most likely to break are replaced every time you replace the toner cartridge.

Travel Assistance

If you're looking for a company that sells laser printer parts, try The Printer Works, a large mail-order outfit with knowledgeable sales folks. Like experts at an auto parts store, they can often help you determine the source of a problem and then sell you the necessary part to fix it. The Printer Works is on the Web at www.printerworks.com.

FIGURE 11.7 Laser printer's toner cartridge

Toner The *toner* in a laser printer is a fine powder that's made up of plastic particles bonded to iron particles. The reservoir in the toner cartridge where the toner is stored is called the *hopper*. The *toner cylinder* charges the toner with a negative charge of between ~200 and ~500 volts. Because that charge falls between the original uniform negative charge of the photosensitive image drum (~600 to ~1000 volts) and the charge of the particles on the drum's surface hit by the laser (~100 volts), particles of toner are attracted to the areas of the photosensitive drum that were hit by the laser—that is, they're attracted to the areas with a positive charge *relative to* the toner particles.

Travel Advisory
Watch out for toner spills, as the super-fine toner particles make quite a mess. They'll stain your clothes as badly and permanently as ink and, worse, can prove toxic if inhaled. Don't sniff any toner!

Photosensitive Drum The *photosensitive drum* (sometimes called the *image drum*) is an aluminum cylinder coated with particles of photosensitive compounds (see Figure 11.8). The drum itself is grounded to the power supply, but the coating is not. When light hits these particles, whatever electrical charge they may have had drains out through the grounded cylinder.

As noted previously, most printer component manufacturers incorporate the image drum into the toner cartridge, so that both components are replaced when the cartridge runs out of toner. Some makers, such as Okidata, use long-life image drum components that are replaced separately from the toner cartridge.

FIGURE 11.8 Toner cartridge with photosensitive drum exposed

The photosensitive image drum is extremely light-sensitive and should not be exposed for longer than a few seconds. Bright lights such as direct sunlight can permanently damage an image drum. Image drums sometimes become dirty from dust or spilled toner. In these cases, the drum can be wiped clean with a dry, lint-free cloth. Keep in mind, however, that if you scratch the drum, the scratch will appear on every page printed from that point on!

Erase Lamp The *erase lamp* exposes the entire surface of the photosensitive drum with light, making the photosensitive coating conductive. Any electrical charge present in the particles bleeds away into the grounded drum, leaving the surface particles electrically neutral.

Primary Corona Wire The *primary corona wire,* located close to the photosensitive drum, never touches the drum. When the wire is charged with an extremely high voltage, an electric field (or corona) forms, allowing voltage to pass to the drum and charge the photosensitive particles on its surface. The *primary grid* regulates the transfer of voltage, ensuring the surface of the drum receives a uniform negative charge of between ~600 and ~1000 volts.

Transfer Corona Wire To transfer the image from the photosensitive drum to the paper, the paper must be given a charge that will attract the toner particles off the drum and onto the paper. The *transfer corona wire* applies a positive charge to the paper, drawing the negatively charged toner particles to the paper. The paper, with its positive charge, is also attracted to the negatively charged drum. To prevent the paper from wrapping around the drum, a *static charge eliminator* removes the charge from the paper.

Transfer corona wires are prone to grime buildup and should be cleaned regularly using a special tool supplied with your printer. You should never touch the transfer corona wire with your bare fingers, as oils from your skin attract dirt and cause corrosion.

Laser or LED The *laser* is the printer's writing mechanism. Any particle on the drum struck by the laser becomes conductive, allowing its charge to be drained away into the grounded core of the drum. In this way, the laser *writes* a positive image onto the drum. Particles struck by the laser are left with a ~100 volt negative charge, compared to the ~600 to ~1000 volt negative charge of the rest of the drum surface.

Some printers use an array of powerful LEDs in place of a laser beam to write the image onto the photosensitive image drum. Otherwise, LED printers work identically to laser printers.

Fuser In most printers, the *fuser* assembly (sometimes called the *fuser pad*) is outside the toner cartridge, but it can be an integrated component. After the static charge eliminator has removed the paper's static charge, the toner is still merely resting on top of the paper. The toner must be fused to the paper to make the image permanent. Two rollers—a pressure roller and a heated roller—work together to fuse the toner to the paper. The pressure roller presses against the bottom of the page, while the heated roller presses down on the top of the page, melting the toner into the paper. The heated roller has a nonstick coating to prevent the toner from sticking to it.

Travel Advisory

Laser printers' fuser pad assemblies have probably been responsible for more burned fingers than any other PC components. Use caution when working around the fuser assembly of a laser printer.

The Laser Printing Process

You can put these steps together to see how a typical laser printer does its job. Remember that some brands of laser printers may depart from this exact process, although most do work in exactly this order. The printing process contains six steps, in this order:

1. Clean
2. Charge
3. Write
4. Develop
5. Transfer
6. Fuse

Exam Tip

Know the order of a laser printer's printing process. To help you keep the steps in order, remember this: Careful Computer Weenies Don't Trade Files!

Step 1: Clean the Drum Before printing each new page, the drum must be returned to a clean, fresh condition, so the printing process begins with the physical and electrical cleaning of the photosensitive drum. All residual toner left

over from printing the previous page is removed, usually by a rubber cleaning blade that scrapes the surface of the drum. If residual particles remain on the drum, they appear as random black spots and streaks on the next page. The physical cleaning mechanism either deposits the residual toner in a debris cavity or recycles it by returning it to the toner cartridge hopper. Damage to the drum during the physical cleaning process causes a permanent mark to be printed on every page.

The image drum must also be electrically cleaned, as shown in Figure 11.9. One or more erase lamps bombard the surface of the drum with the appropriate wavelengths of light, causing the surface particles to discharge into the grounded drum. After the cleaning process, the drum should be completely free of toner and have a neutral electrical charge.

Step 2: Charge the Drum Electrically charging the drum makes it receptive to new images. The corona wire applies a uniform negative charge to the entire surface of the drum, normally between ~600 and ~1000 volts.

Step 3: Write the Image Next the laser writes a positive image on the surface of the drum, as shown in Figure 11.10.

Step 4: Develop the Image Every particle on the drum hit by the laser will release most of its negative charge into the drum. Those particles are then posi-

FIGURE 11.9 Cleaning and erasing the drum

Primary corona

Imaging laser

Toner

FIGURE 11.10 Writing the image

tively charged relative to the toner particles and will attract them, creating a developed image on the drum.

Step 5: Transfer the Image To transfer the image from the drum onto the paper, the transfer corona charges the paper with a positive charge. Once in proximity to this positive charge, the negatively charged toner particles leap from the drum to the paper. Then the static charge eliminator removes the paper's positive charge, leaving the particles resting on the paper.

Step 6: Fuse the Image For the final step in the process, the fuser melts the toner onto the paper (see Figure 11.11). The printer then ejects the final printed copy, and the process begins again with the physical and electrical cleaning of the printer.

> **Travel Advisory**
>
> The heated roller of the fuser produces enough heat to melt some types of plastic media, particularly overhead transparency materials. Never use transparencies in a laser printer unless they are specifically designed for use in laser printers. Use of non-approved materials can seriously damage a laser printer and void the warranty!

Static eliminator

Fuser rollers

Transfer corona

FIGURE 11.11 Fusing the image

Other Laser Printer Components

Although the majority of the printing activity takes place within the toner cartridge, many other parts of the laser printer are hard at work outside the cartridge, as you can see in Figure 11.12.

Printer memory

System board

Toner cartridge

High-voltage power supply

Gearbox/motors

Fuser assembly

Sublogic board

Paper tray

Primary power supply

FIGURE 11.12 Inside a laser printer

Power Supplies All laser printers have at least two separate power supplies. The first power supply is called the *primary power supply* or sometimes just the *power supply*. The primary power supply powers the motors that move the paper, the system electronics, the laser, and the transfer corona.

The second power supply is the *high-voltage* power supply. It usually powers only the primary corona. The extremely high voltage of this power supply makes it one of the most dangerous devices in the world of PCs! Therefore, it's imperative that—except when inserting a new toner cartridge or paper—you *always turn off* a laser printer before you open it.

Turning Gears A laser printer performs many mechanical operations. The paper must be picked up, fed through, and kicked out of the printer. The photosensitive roller must be turned, and the laser, or a mirror, must be moved from left to right. The toner must be evenly distributed, and the fuser assembly must squish the toner into the paper. All these functions are performed by complex gear systems. In most laser printers, these gear systems are packed together in discrete units powered by their own solenoid motors. These units are generically called *gear packs* or *gearboxes*. Most laser printers have two or three gearboxes. These are relatively easy to remove and replace in the rare case when one of them fails.

System Board Every laser printer has at least one electronic board containing the main processor, the printer's ROM, and the RAM it uses to store the image before it's printed. Many printers divide these functions among two or three boards dispersed around the printer. The printer may also have an extra ROM chip and/or a slot where you can install an extra ROM chip, usually for special functions such as PostScript printing. When the printer doesn't have enough RAM to store the image before it prints, it generates a Memory Overflow error. Solve this condition by adding more RAM.

> **Travel Advisory**
>
> Adding RAM is usually a simple job—just snapping in a SIMM stick or two—but getting the *right* RAM is important. Call the printer manufacturer and ask what type of RAM it needs. Although most printer companies will happily sell you their expensive RAM, most printers can use generic dynamic RAM (DRAM) like the kind you use in your PC.

Network Interface Recognizing that most offices share networked printers, many manufacturers include integrated network interface cards (NICs) on some printers. These printers have built-in print server software that enables

them to be plugged directly into an available network plug instead of attached to a PC.

Ozone Filter The coronas inside laser printers generate *ozone* (O_3). While the amount generated isn't harmful to humans, high concentrations of ozone will damage printer components. To counter this problem, most laser printers have a special ozone filter that must be replaced periodically. The best time is when you replace the toner cartridge, and in fact many toner cartridges come packaged with a new ozone filter.

Sensors and Switches Every laser printer contains a large array of sensors and switches. The sensors are used to detect a broad range of conditions such as paper jams, empty paper trays, or low toner levels. Many sensors are really tiny switches that detect conditions such as open printer doors. Most of the time, these sensors and switches work reliably, but they can occasionally become dirty or broken and send a false signal to the printer. Simple inspection is usually sufficient to determine whether a problem is real or just the result of a faulty sensor or switch.

Duplexer *Duplexers* are mechanical paper-feeding devices that enable you to print on both sides of a sheet of paper. If your printer doesn't have a built-in duplexing mechanism, you can usually purchase one as an add-on component. Depending on the make and model of your printer, the duplexer may attach onto the front or back of the printer, or it may take the place of the paper tray.

Finishers Some printers also include components called *finishers* that do things like collate, staple, and bind printed documents. Typically, these functions are beyond the capabilities of all but high-end, commercial printers.

Exam Tip	
Know and understand the various laser printer components.	

Objective 11.02 Installing Printers

Y ou need to take a moment to understand how Windows 2000 and Windows XP handle printing, and then you'll see how to install and configure printers for use with these operating systems.

To Windows 2000/XP, a "printer" is not a physical device; it is a *program* that controls one or more physical printers. The *physical* printer is called a "print device" to Windows (although I continue to use the term "printer" for most purposes, just like almost every tech on the planet). Printer drivers and a spooler are present, but in Windows 2000/XP they are integrated into the printer itself (Figure 11.13). This arrangement gives Windows 2000/XP amazing flexibility. For example, one printer can support multiple print devices, enabling a system to act as a print server. If one print device goes down, the printer software automatically redirects the output to a working print device.

Printer Languages

Printers are designed to accept predefined printer languages that handle both characters and graphics. Your software must use the proper language when communicating with your printer, so that your printer can output documents onto a piece of paper. Most printers use the *graphical device interface (GDI)* component of Windows to handle print functions. Some might use the *Adobe PostScript* language, while others use the Hewlett-Packard developed *Printer Control Language (PCL)*. The bottom line for installation purposes is that you need to install the proper drivers for the printer.

Physical Connection

Print devices connect through a multipurpose port, such as USB, FireWire, or parallel, or wirelessly through Bluetooth, Wi-Fi, or infrared. You might encoun-

Printer

Print device

Spooler

Printer driver

FIGURE 11.13 Printer driver and spooler in Windows 2000/XP

ter a dedicated serial printer or a SCSI (small computer systems interface) printer, but these are so rare as to be almost not worth mentioning. Some printers have a slot for an add-on network card, so you can connect them directly to a network switch, just like a PC. Finally, you can connect to a print server on a LAN and install a networked printer rather than a local printer.

Setting Up Printers

Setting up a printer is so easy that it's almost scary. Most printers are Plug and Play, so installing a printer is reduced simply to plugging it in and loading the driver if needed. If the system does not detect the printer or if the printer is not Plug and Play, click Start | Printers and Faxes in Windows XP to open the Printers applet; in Windows 2000, click Start | Settings | Printers. The icon for this applet can also be found in the Control Panel.

As you might guess, you install a new printer by clicking the Add a Printer icon. This starts the Add Printer Wizard. After a pleasant intro screen, you must choose to install either a printer plugged directly into your system or a network printer (Figure 11.14). You can use the *Automatically detect and install my Plug and Play printer* option in many cases when installing a USB printer.

If you choose a local printer, the applet next asks you to select a port (Figure 11.15); select the port in which you installed the new printer. Once you select the port, Windows asks you to specify the type of printer, either by selecting the type from the list or using the Have Disk option, just as you would for any other device. When you click Next on this screen, Windows installs the printer.

FIGURE 11.14 Choosing local or network printer in Windows XP

FIGURE 11.15 Selecting a port in Windows XP

Figure 11.16 shows a typical Windows XP Printers and Faxes screen on a system with one printer installed. Note the small check mark in the icon's corner; this shows that the device is the default printer. If you have multiple printers,

FIGURE 11.16 Installed default printer in the Printers and Faxes applet

you can change the default printer by selecting the printer's properties and checking Make Default Printer.

Optimizing Print Performance

Although a quality printer is the first step toward quality output, your output relies on factors other than the printer itself. What you see on the screen may not match what comes out of the printer, so calibration is important. Using the wrong type of paper can result in less than acceptable printed documents. Configuring the printer driver and spool settings can also affect your print jobs.

Calibration

If you've ever tweaked a digital photograph so it looks perfect on screen, only to discover that the final printout was darker than you had hoped, consider calibrating your monitor. *Calibration* matches the print output of your printer to the visual output on your monitor and governs that through software. All three parts need to be set up properly for you to print what you see consistently.

Computer monitors output in RGB—that is, they compose colors using red, green, and blue pixels—while printers mix their colors differently to arrive at their output. The CMYK method, for example, composes colors from cyan (blue), magenta (red), yellow, and black.

The upshot of all this is that the printer tries to output using CMYK (or another technique) what you see on the screen that uses RGB. Because the two color modes do not create color the same way, you see color shifts and not-so-subtle differences between the onscreen image and the printed image. By calibrating your monitor, you can adjust the setting to match the output of your printer. This can be done manually through "eyeballing" it or automatically using calibration hardware.

To calibrate your monitor manually, obtain a test image from the Web (try sites such as www.DigitalDog.net) and print it out. If you have a good eye, you can compare this printout to what you see on the screen and make the adjustments manually through your monitor's controls or display settings.

Objective 11.03 Troubleshooting Printers

It's the rare business that has a dedicated printer technician on staff. As a CompTIA A+ certified PC tech, most businesses expect your problem-

solving skills to extend beyond the computer to the printer. Printer-related errors come in a variety of forms, and troubleshooting them can range from pleasingly simple to headache-inducingly complex. When troubleshooting printers, try the obvious fix first, and then graduate to more advanced troubleshooting techniques. This section describes common printer errors and solutions.

Exam Tip	
Know the basic troubleshooting procedures for all printer types.	

Feed and Output

Printers often develop problems with the paper-feed mechanism. When paper-feed problems occur, the paper can become jammed in the feed mechanism, halting the printing process.

Problems with Friction-Feed Mechanisms

The most common problem with friction-feed mechanisms is usually caused by user error: too much paper in the paper tray. This causes the feed mechanism to pick up several sheets of paper and try to send them through the printer at the same time, resulting in a paper jam. Most paper trays have a line or symbol on the edge to show the maximum allowed paper in the paper tray at one time.

Another cause of this type of error is static electricity. Static buildup in friction-feed mechanisms causes pages to stick together, which again results in several pages being fed through the printer at the same time. To prevent paper jams caused by static, fan the stack of papers on a desk or other surface before placing it in the paper feed tray. This loosens the pages and reduces the static cling.

Believe it or not, having too little paper in the paper tray also causes feed errors. If the paper level is too low, the rollers can have trouble catching hold of the top sheet. If sufficient paper seems to be in the tray, check to see whether you're using recycled paper, which can sometimes be thinner than normal paper and harder for the rollers to grab.

To fix a paper jam, turn off the printer, and then open it and gently extract the paper. Whenever possible, move the paper in the direction it would normally go. Remember your physics, and pull slowly and gently. This minimizes the likelihood that you'll rip off the exposed part of the paper. Also, pulling too hard can damage the rollers in the feed mechanism. Some printers won't continue printing after you fix the problem until you press the online or reset button.

Problems with Tractor-Feed Mechanisms

Impact printers' tractor-feed mechanisms require you to line up the spokes on the wheels with the holes in the paper. If the holes on either side of the paper aren't lined up evenly, the text might print diagonally on the page. If the holes are uneven, the paper will crease, wrinkle, and jam.

Because they use continuous form paper, tractor-feed printers can require a bit of skill to position the paper properly. Each model of printer has its own special way of positioning the paper vertically, making trial and error an essential part of this process. If you get this wrong, your top and bottom margins will be off, and sometimes lines of text will even split across two sheets of paper.

Printer Errors

Printing errors centered on the printer itself can be a bit more complicated to troubleshoot than paper-feed errors. Sometimes printer errors are accompanied by error messages from either the PC or the printer itself. Other times, you'll have to investigate a bit further to get to the root of the problem.

Out-of-Paper Errors

The cause of a *paper out* error should be pretty obvious: no paper is in the printer. To correct this problem on a tractor-feed printer, lift the printer's lid and carefully feed the first sheet onto the tractor wheels. To fix this problem on a friction-feed printer, simply add paper to the paper tray.

Input/Output Errors

Input/output errors occur when the computer is unable to communicate with the printer. When troubleshooting an input/output error, start with these possibilities:

- Is the printer plugged in?
- Is the printer turned on?
- Are all cables firmly connected?
- Is the proper driver for your printer installed? If so, could it have become corrupted?
- Are the IRQ and I/O settings for the printer correct?

If all these check out, try restarting the printer, the PC, or both. Simply restarting can sometimes fix a multitude of problems. If the printer still produces the input/output error, connect the printer to another computer. If the printer does not work on the other computer, you know you have a printer problem. If it works fine on the other computer, you have a configuration problem.

Incorrect Port Mode Errors

An *incorrect port mode* error indicates the parallel port to which you connected the printer isn't using the correct port mode. If you receive this error, use the CMOS settings program to change the port mode to one that's compatible with your printer.

No Default Printer Errors

A *no default printer* error indicates that no printer has been installed or that you haven't set a default printer. Here's how to set a default printer:

1. Click the Start button.
2. Select Settings.
3. Select Printers. The Printers dialog box will open.
4. Right-click the icon of the printer you want to set as the default.
5. Select Set As Default from the Shortcut menu.

If no printer has been installed, follow these steps:

1. Click the Start button.
2. Select Settings.
3. Select Printers. The Printers dialog box will appear.
4. Double-click the Add Printer icon and follow the instructions.

Toner Low and Ink Low Errors

When the toner cartridge in a laser printer runs low, it issues a warning before the cartridge runs out completely. Replace the cartridge as soon as you see the error to avoid half-finished or delayed print jobs. You should also replace inkjet cartridges promptly to prevent clogged print nozzles.

Consumable Refills Ink and toner refill kits are much less expensive than purchasing new cartridges and may seem like an economic solution to the consumable problem. Because you're reusing the original cartridge components, however, such as the pump and heating element, you risk damaging your printer. Purchasing new cartridges is more economical than fixing your laser printer because of damage caused by old cartridges.

Remanufactured laser toner cartridges, however, are usually safe to use and reliable. Many laser toner manufacturers even have their own recycling programs.

Print Quality

Depending on the printer type you're using, several factors might affect print quality.

Dot-Matrix Print Quality Issues

One downside to dot matrix is the need for ongoing maintenance. Keep the *platen* (the roller or plate on which the pins impact) and the print head clean. Be sure to lubricate gears and pulleys according to the manufacturer's specifications. Never lubricate the print head, however, because the lubricant will smear and stain the paper.

White Bars on Text White bars through the text point to a dirty or damaged print head. Try cleaning the print head with a little denatured alcohol. If the problem persists, replace the print head. Print heads for most printers are readily available from the manufacturer.

Chopped Text If the characters look chopped off at the top or bottom, the print head probably needs to be adjusted. Follow the manufacturer's instructions for proper adjustment.

Pepper Look If the paper is covered with dots and small smudges—the "pepper look"—the platen is dirty. Clean the platen with a soft cloth.

Faded Image If the image is faded and you know the ribbon is good, try adjusting the print head closer to the platen.

Light to Dark If the image is okay on one side of the paper but fades on the other, the platen is out of adjustment. Platens are difficult to adjust, so your best plan is to send it to the manufacturer's local warranty/repair center. The money you'll spend is far cheaper than the frustration of trying to do it yourself.

Inkjet Print Quality Issues

Inkjet printers are more complicated than dot-matrix printers, which also means more things can go wrong.

Unclear Images If an inkjet printer is producing unclear images, the ink cartridges are probably running low on ink and need to be replaced.

Blank Printouts If an inkjet printer is producing blank printouts, either the ink level is low or the nozzles have become clogged. First check the ink and

replace the cartridge if it's low. If the ink is at an acceptable level, the nozzles have probably become clogged. To unclog the nozzles, dip a cotton swab in denatured alcohol and gently wipe away any dried ink.

Confetti Printouts Printouts with ink speckles, or *confetti,* always indicate an ink problem. Over time, ink can escape into the body of an inkjet printer, eventually finding its way onto subsequent printouts. To fix or prevent speckling, clean the insides of the printer with a damp cloth.

Wrong Colors in Printouts If an inkjet produces printouts using the wrong colors, check for low ink in one or more cartridges, or a dirty nozzle. First check the ink cartridges. If they're full, clean the nozzles with a cotton swab dipped in denatured alcohol.

Smudges on Printouts Smudges on printouts are most often caused by the user touching the printout before the ink has completely dried. Other causes include dirty printers and worn-out nozzles. Worn-out nozzles cannot be fixed. You must replace the ink cartridges if the nozzles have become worn out.

Laser Print Quality Issues

Laser printers usually manifest problems by creating poor output. One of the most important tests you can do on any printer—not only a laser printer—is called a *diagnostic print page* or an *engine test page.* You can print a test page by holding down the Online button as the printer is started or by selecting the menu option on the printer's operator panel. You can also select Start | Settings | Printers in Windows and issue the test page command from the printer's Properties dialog box.

Exam Tip
The CompTIA A+ certification exams are *very* concerned that you understand laser printer maintenance. Make sure you know the causes and solutions for various maintenance problems.

Blank Paper Blank sheets of paper usually mean the printer is out of toner. If the printer does have toner and nothing prints, print a diagnostic print page. If that's also blank, remove the toner cartridge and look at the imaging drum inside. If the image is still on the drum, you know the transfer corona or the high-voltage power supply has failed. Check the printer's maintenance guide to see how to zero in on the bad part and replace it.

Ghosting Sometimes ghost images appear at regular intervals on the printed page. Either the imaging drum hasn't fully discharged and is picking up toner from a previous image, or a previous image has used up so much toner that either the supply of charged toner is insufficient or the toner hasn't been adequately charged.

Light Ghosting vs. Dark Ghosting A variety of problems can cause both light and dark ghosting, but the most common source of *light ghosting* is *developer starvation.* If you ask a laser printer to print an extremely dark or complex image, it can use up so much toner that the toner cartridge won't be able to charge enough toner to print the next image. The proper solution is to use less toner by doing the following:

- Lowering the resolution of the page (print at 300 dpi instead of 600 dpi)
- Using a different pattern
- Avoiding 50 percent gray scale and dot-on/dot-off patterns
- Changing the layout, so grayscale patterns don't follow black areas
- Making dark patterns lighter and light patterns darker
- Adjusting print density and Resolution Enhancement Technology (RET) settings
- Printing a completely blank page immediately prior to the page with the ghosting image and as part of the same print job

Low temperature and low humidity can aggravate ghosting problems. Check your users' manual for environmental recommendations.

Dark ghosting can sometimes be caused by a damaged drum. It can be fixed by replacing the toner cartridge. Light ghosting cannot be solved in this way. Switching other components usually won't fix ghosting problems because they're a side effect of the entire printing process.

Vertical White Lines Vertical white lines are usually caused by clogged toner. Clogs prevent the proper dispersion of toner on the drum. Try shaking the toner cartridge from side to side to dislodge the clog, or, if that doesn't work, replace the toner cartridge.

Blotchy Print This is most commonly because of uneven dispersion of toner—especially if the toner is low. Try shaking the toner from side to side. Also be sure the printer is level. Finally, make sure the paper isn't wet in spots. If the blotches are in a regular order, check the fusing rollers and the photosensitive drum for foreign objects.

Spotty Print If spots appear at regular intervals on the printout, the printer's drum may be damaged or toner may be stuck to the fuser rollers. Try wiping off the fuser rollers. Check the drum for damage. If the drum is damaged, you must get a new toner cartridge.

Embossed Effect If your prints have an embossed effect (like putting a penny under a piece of paper and rubbing it with a pencil), a foreign object is almost certainly on a roller. Use regular water with a soft cloth to try to remove it. If the foreign object is on the photosensitive drum, you'll have to use a new toner cartridge.

Incomplete Characters Incompletely printed characters on laser-printed transparencies can sometimes be corrected by adjusting the print density. Remember to use only materials approved for use in laser printers.

Creased Pages Laser printers have up to four rollers. In addition to the heat and pressure rollers of the fusing assembly, rollers are designed to move the paper from the source tray to the output tray. These rollers crease the paper to avoid curling, which would cause paper jams in the printer. If the creases are noticeable, try using a different paper type. Cotton bond paper is usually more susceptible to noticeable creasing than other bonds. You might also try sending the output to the face-up tray, which eliminates one roller. No hardware solution exists for this problem. This is simply a side effect of the process.

Warped, Overprinted, or Poorly Formed Characters Poorly formed characters can indicate either a problem with the paper (or other media) or a problem with the hardware.

Incorrect media causes a number of problems. Avoid paper that is too rough or too smooth. Paper that's too rough interferes with fusing of characters and their initial definition. If the paper is too smooth (like some coated papers, for example), it might feed improperly, causing distorted or overwritten characters. Although you can purchase laser printer–specific paper, all laser printers will run acceptably on standard photocopy paper. Because paper picks up humidity from the air, don't open a ream of paper until you're ready to load it into the printer. Always fan the paper before loading it into the printer—especially if the paper has been left out for more than a few days.

The durability of a well-maintained laser printer makes hardware a rare source of character-printing problems, but it is a possibility. Fortunately, checking the hardware is easy. Most laser printers have a self-test function, often combined with a diagnostic printout, that's quite handy to verify those "Is it the

printer or is it the computer?" questions. Run the self-test to check for connectivity and configuration problems. Following are possible solutions:

- Replace the toner cartridge, especially if you hear popping noises.
- Check the cabling.
- Replace the data cable, especially if bends or crimps exist or objects are resting on the cable.
- If you have a Front Menu Panel, turn off Advanced Functions and High Speed Settings to determine whether they aren't working properly or aren't supported by your current software configuration (check your manuals).

If these solutions don't work, the problem might not be user serviceable. Contact an authorized service center.

General Print Quality Issues

Now that you understand some of the print quality issues that can affect the individual printer types, you need to understand the print quality issues that can affect all three types. Let's look at the most common print problems in Windows.

Print Job Never Prints If you click the Print button and nothing comes out of the printer, check the obvious things first. Is the printer turned on? Is it connected to the computer and to a power source? Is it online? Does it have paper? Assuming the printer is physically in good order, the next step is to check the print server's print *spooler* status.

The print spooler is the hard disk space reserved for channeling print jobs from the PC to the printer. You can see the spooler status either by double-clicking the printer's icon in the Printers applet or by clicking the tiny printer icon in the system tray if it's present (if you're having a problem, it's almost always there).

Print spoolers can overflow or become corrupt because of a lack of disk space or too many print jobs in the queue. The Printers window shows all the pending print jobs and enables you to delete, start, or pause jobs. The best answer is usually to delete the print jobs and try again.

You might also run into a situation where the print jobs seem to spool, but then just vanish or "despool" as the jargon goes. The print spooler shows print jobs for a brief moment, but then nothing prints. Check the printer driver. An incorrect driver for the attached printer can cause this issue.

Incorrect Page Size A print job that comes out sized incorrectly usually points to a user mistake in setting up the job. Check the Print dialog box for incorrect print parameters. Also check the Page Setup option in the relevant application. Make sure the user is setting up the page properly.

If you know the page is set up correctly, recheck the printer drivers. If necessary, uninstall and reinstall the print drivers. If the problem persists, the printer's print engine may be causing the trouble, but that is a possibility only when you continually get the same strangely sized printouts using a number of different applications.

Garbage Characters in Printout Misaligned or garbage printouts invariably point to a corrupted or incorrect driver. Make sure you're using the appropriate printer driver and then uninstall and reinstall the driver. If the problem persists, it's possible that you're asking the printer to do something it cannot do. For example, you might be printing to a PostScript printer with a PCL driver. Check the printer type to verify you haven't installed the wrong type of driver for that printer. Try some of these diagnostic avenues:

- Make sure the printer cables are attached firmly and haven't become loose.
- Turn off the power to the printer, and then turn it on again.
- To check the basic communication between the PC and the printer, try printing a plain text file—Notepad is excellent for this.
- Restart your computer. Many Windows and application problems can be resolved simply by restarting your system.
- Reinstall your printer drivers. Drivers occasionally become corrupted and might need reinstalling.
- Check your resource settings for the parallel or USB port to verify no resource conflicts exist.
- Connect the printer to a different computer. If the printer continues producing garbage characters on the second computer, you know the problem lies within the printer.
- Try printing a smaller document. If you can print a smaller document, the problem may be insufficient memory in the printer. Insufficient memory can be remedied by adding more RAM to the printer.

Printer Not Responding If the printer isn't responding, check the easy things first. Make sure the printer is turned on and the cables are securely and correctly attached. Make sure the printer is online. Make sure the application you're printing from is sending the print job to the correct printer. Make sure you have

the correct print driver installed for the printer. Try to print a test page. Try attaching the printer to a new computer. If nothing works, your printer might have to go to a printer repair facility.

Objective 11.04 Preventive Maintenance

Printers are more mechanical in nature than most PC components and so require regular maintenance to stay in top running form. Paper dust, toner, and ink deposits are the root of many printer problems. Paper dust can jam gears and causes ESD. Excess ink or toner causes poor-quality printouts. Cleaning your printer regularly can prevent many problems from occurring.

This section describes the procedures for cleaning dot-matrix, inkjet, and laser printers. On all types of printers, be sure to turn the power off and unplug all cables from the printer before servicing. You should also wait a few minutes after shutting down the printer to allow the print heads and fuser components to cool down and the onboard capacitor circuits to discharge.

Exam Tip	
Know the proper cleaning procedures for all printer types.	

Cleaning Dot-Matrix Printers

Follow these steps to clean a dot-matrix printer:

1. Remove the plastic casing and carefully pull the print head away from the platen.
2. Inspect the ribbon and replace it, if necessary.
3. Loosen paper dust from the printer by using compressed air and remove it with an antistatic vacuum.
4. Clean the print head with denatured alcohol.
5. Remove paper from the platen.
6. Inspect the carriage belt and replace it if it's worn or cracked.

After you finish cleaning the printer, lubricate the gears and pulleys—*not* the print head itself! Never lubricate the print head, or your printouts will appear stained. Reassemble the printer in reverse order and run a test printout.

Cleaning Inkjet Printers

To clean liquid or solid inkjet printers, follow these steps:

1. Remove the plastic housing and ink cartridges.
2. Loosen paper dust from the printer by using compressed air and remove it with an antistatic vacuum.
3. Wipe off the ink cartridges with a damp cloth.
4. Wipe excess ink from the inside of the printer with a damp cloth.
5. Clean the platen.
6. Inspect the carriage belt and replace it, if necessary.

Once you're finished, reassemble the printer and run a test printout.

Cleaning Thermal and Dye-Sublimation Printers

To clean thermal-based printers such as thermal wax and dye-sublimation printers, follow these steps:

1. Remove the wax or dye ribbon cartridge.
2. Loosen paper dust from the printer by using compressed air and remove it with an antistatic vacuum.
3. Wipe off the ribbon cartridges with a damp cloth.
4. Wipe excess ink residue from the inside of the printer with a damp cloth.
5. Use compressed air to loosen dust from the drive gears and remove it with an antistatic vacuum.
6. Be careful not to disturb the thermal print head!

Once you're finished, reassemble the printer and run a test printout.

Cleaning Laser Printers

To clean a laser printer, follow these steps:

1. Remove and wipe off the toner cartridges.
2. Loosen paper dust from the printer by using compressed air and remove it with an antistatic vacuum.

3. Use the special tool supplied with the printer to clean the transfer corona wire. You can also wipe the wire with a swab and denatured alcohol.

4. On LED printers, use a clean, lint-free cloth to clean the LED array window. Many toner kits come with a special one-use cleaning pad for this purpose.

5. Clean the fusing rollers and replace the roller pad.

6. Replace the ozone filter.

7. Clean the rubber guide rollers with clean water.

When you finish, carefully reassemble and reconnect the printer and run a test printout.

CHECKPOINT

✔ **Objective 11.01: Types of Printers** Know the types of printers—dot-matrix, inkjet, dye-sublimation, thermal, and laser—and how each one works. Understand the laser printing process and know its six discrete steps in the order they occur.

✔ **Objective 11.02: Installing Printers** Installing printers involves a few steps. First, you need to connect the print device to your system through parallel, USB, FireWire, NIC, or wirelessly. You need to install the proper driver, such as a GDI driver for Windows or a PCL driver for some HP printers.

✔ **Objective 11.03: Troubleshooting Printers** Common printer problems include paper jams and problems with paper-feed mechanisms, I/O errors, low toner/ink, a huge variety of print quality issues, and non-responsive printers.

✔ **Objective 11.04: Preventive Maintenance** The CompTIA A+ certification exams expect you to know the proper cleaning procedures for each printer type, including dot-matrix, inkjet, and laser. In general, you will vacuum up small particles; clean appropriate surfaces and mechanisms; and, where needed, replace certain parts such as ribbons, belts, and filters.

REVIEW QUESTIONS

1. What are the six steps of the laser printer process?

 A. Paper in, Charge, Develop, Transfer, Fuse, Paper out

 B. Clean, Charge, Write, Develop, Transfer, Fuse

 C. Charge, Clean, Write, Transfer, Print, Fuse

 D. Clean, Charge, Develop, Transfer, Write, Fuse

2. What type of feed mechanism do dot-matrix printers use?

 A. Tractor feed

 B. Friction feed

 C. Paper feed

 D. Spoke feed

3. Which printer types use friction-feed mechanisms? (Select two.)

 A. Dot-matrix

 B. Laser

 C. Inkjet

 D. Impact

4. Garbage characters are appearing in a printout. What's the problem?

 A. The printer is old and needs to be replaced.

 B. You have the wrong language set up for the printer.

 C. The printer needs to be cleaned.

 D. The computer isn't communicating correctly with the printer.

5. What does the primary corona wire in a laser printer do?

 A. Cleans the drum

 B. Charges the drum

 C. Creates the image on the drum

 D. Transfers the image from the drum to the paper

6. What do inkjet printers use to deflect ink onto a page?

 A. A print head

 B. Electrically charged plates

 C. Fusers

 D. Rollers

7. Dye-sublimation printers use what to transfer ink to the paper surface?

 A. Impact print head

 B. Thermal print head

 C. Electrically charged plates

 D. Print nozzles

8. What can cause ghosted images to appear in printouts from a laser printer?

 A. The writing stage of the laser printer process has failed.

 B. The charging stage of the laser printer process has failed.

 C. The transferring stage of the laser printer process has failed.

 D. The cleaning stage of the laser printer process has failed.

9. Which part of a dot-matrix printer is most dangerous?

 A. The print head

 B. The ribbon

 C. The feed mechanism

 D. The wheels

10. Which part of a laser printer is the most dangerous?

 A. Laser

 B. Primary corona

 C. Fuser

 D. High-voltage power supply

11. Which type of printer can create carbon copies?

 A. Laser

 B. Inkjet

 C. USB

 D. Dot-matrix

12. What component of a laser printer transfers the image from the drum to the paper?

 A. Primary corona

 B. Fusing rollers

 C. Transfer corona

 D. Friction feed

REVIEW ANSWERS

1. **B** The steps of the laser printer process are Clean, Charge, Write, Develop, Transfer, Fuse.

2. **A** Dot-matrix printers use a tractor-feed mechanism.

3. **B** **C** Both laser and inkjet printers use a friction-feed mechanism.

4. **D** Garbage characters in a printout mean the computer isn't communicating correctly with the printer. One possible reason for this is incorrect or corrupted drivers.

5. **B** The primary corona wire charges the drum after it has been cleaned.

6. **B** Electrically charged plates deflect ink onto the paper.

7. **B** Dye-sublimation printers use a thermal print head to vaporize dyes and transfer them to paper.

8. **D** Ghosted images in laser printer printouts indicate the cleaning stage of the laser printer process has failed.

9. **A** The print head on a dot-matrix printer gets very hot and can burn you.

10. **D** The high-voltage power supply inside the laser printer can pack a lot of punch and give you a terrible shock. Be very careful inside a laser printer!

11. **D** Dot-matrix printers are impact printers and can create carbon copies.

12. **C** The transfer corona in laser printers transfers the image from the drum to the paper.

Portable
Computers

	NEWBIE	SOME EXPERIENCE	EXPERT
ETA	3 hours	2 hours	1 hour

The computing world today differs vastly from that of earlier years; this is perhaps most evident in the world of portable computers. The term *portable* acts as an umbrella term describing a number of different devices. Generally speaking, *portable* refers to any of the three most common types of mobile computing devices: *laptop computers, handheld computers,* and *personal digital assistants* (*PDAs*). Advances in display screen technology, battery life, CPU muscle, and networking capabilities have prompted many folks to opt for portables in addition to, and sometimes instead of, desktop PCs.

Laptops range in size from sleek and thin so-called *ultra-portables* with displays around 11 inches across and weighing only 5 pounds or so, to gigantic *desktop replacement* systems with displays of 17 inches or more and tipping the scales at more than 15 pounds. You'll also hear some laptop computer models described as *notebook* or *subnotebook* computers, but these are marketing terms and not really cut-and-dried official definitions.

Handheld computers, such as Tablet PCs (Figure 12.1), are smaller and lighter than laptops, with display screens usually no more than about 10 inches across and weighing in at around 3 to 5 pounds. Handheld computers use a specialized version of the Windows OS such as Windows CE.

FIGURE 12.1 Tablet PC

PDAs are the smallest form factor. Once considered mere gadgets that only hardcore geeks could love, PDAs are now powerful and sport enough features to make them truly useful. Sometimes called *palmtop computers,* PDAs fit literally into the palm of your hand with display screens no more than about 3 inches across and weighing only a few ounces. The CompTIA A+ certification exams expect you to be familiar with the special quirks and support requirements for all of these devices, and you should know how to get them to interact with each other seamlessly.

Objective 12.01 Components

For years, portable PC makers engineered entirely proprietary components for each system model they developed. For the most part, this proprietary attitude still prevails, but some standardization makes it easier to repair or upgrade the system using parts from third-party vendors instead of sometimes-expensive OEM (original equipment manufacturer) parts. The following sections highlight the most common components.

RAM

Stock factory portable PCs almost always come with a minimal amount of RAM, so one of the first laptop upgrades you'll be called on to do is to add more RAM. Economy laptops running Windows XP Home routinely sit on store shelves and go home to consumers with as little 256 MB of RAM, an amount guaranteed to limit the use and performance of the laptop. The OS alone will consume more than half of the RAM! Luckily, every decent laptop has upgradeable RAM slots. Laptops use one of four types of RAM. Most older laptops use either 72-pin or 144-pin small outline DIMMs (SO-DIMMs) with synchronous dynamic RAM (SDRAM) technology (Figure 12.2). Double data rate (DDR) and DDR2 systems primarily use 200-pin SO-DIMMs although some laptops use MicroDIMMs.

Some laptops (and desktops) support *shared memory*, a means of reducing the cost of video cards by reducing the amount of memory on the video card itself. Instead of a video card with 256 MB of RAM, it might have only 64 MB of RAM but can borrow 192 MB of RAM from the system. This equates to a 256 MB video card. The video card uses regular system RAM to make up for the loss.

FIGURE 12.2 72-pin SO-DIMM stick (front and back)

Adding more system RAM to a laptop with shared memory will improve laptop performance. Although it might appear to improve video performance, that doesn't tell the true story. It will improve overall performance because the OS and CPU get more RAM to work with. On some laptops, you can improve video performance as well, but that depends on the CMOS setup. If the shared memory is not set to maximum by default, increasing the overall memory and upping the portion reserved for video will improve video performance specifically.

Hard Drives

ATA hard drives in the 2.5-inch drive format now rule in laptops. Although much smaller than regular 3.25-inch desktop ATA drives, 2.5-inch hard drives use the same features and configurations. Figure 12.3 shows a laptop's hard drive (left) compared to a standard 3.25-inch desktop hard drive.

Some manufacturers might use special settings, such as requiring the drive to use the cable select setting instead of master or slave configuration, but otherwise these 2.5-inch ATA hard drives are installed, partitioned, and formatted in exactly the same way as their larger 3.25-inch brethren.

FIGURE 12.3 A 2.5-inch laptop hard drive (left) and a standard desktop hard drive

CPUs

Both Intel and AMD have long sold specialized, modular CPUs for laptops. These CPUs consume a lot less wattage and produce less heat than their desktop cousins. Lots of folks don't realize they can easily upgrade many systems by removing the old module and replacing it with a new one, as shown in Figure 12.4. (Always follow the manufacturer's specifications when upgrading a laptop CPU.)

FIGURE 12.4 Modular laptop CPU

Input Devices

Portable computers come with a variety of input devices. Bigger portables come with specialized keyboards. Most enable you to interact with the desktop using a built-in *touchpad* (Figure 12.5). Handheld computer users may input data and interact with the desktop either using a scaled-down keyboard or through a pen-like *stylus* or a *digitizer* and touch-sensitive screen with specialized hand-writing recognition software. PDAs use stylus-based input, although some also have tiny keyboards.

External Connections

You can connect all sorts of devices to a portable computer, especially the full-sized variety of laptops. Most offer dedicated mouse or keyboard connections, USB and parallel ports, and an external monitor port. Some offer a FireWire port. You can plug in devices just as you would to the back of a PC. The only thing you might need to do differently is press a function key to activate an external monitor. This provides support for projectors, for example, when you're doing a PowerPoint presentation.

Wireless NICs and Mini-PCI

Many laptops now come with integrated wireless networking support by way of a built-in Wi-Fi adapter that's usually installed in a Mini-PCI slot on the laptop motherboard. The *Mini-PCI* bus is an adaptation of the standard PCI bus and was developed specifically for integrated communications peripherals such as modems and network adapters. Built-in networking support means you don't need an additional PC Card to provide a network adapter. The Mini-PCI bus

FIGURE 12.5 Touchpad

also provides support for other integrated devices such as Bluetooth, modems, audio, or hard-drive controllers. One great aspect of Mini-PCI is that if some new technology eclipses the current wireless technology or some other technology that uses the bus, you can upgrade by swapping a card.

Exam Tip

You should know that a typical reason to upgrade a Mini-PCI Wi-Fi NIC is to gain access to improved security options such as better encryption.

Officially released in 1999, Mini-PCI is a 32-bit, 33-MHz bus and is basically PCI v2.2 with a different form factor. Like PCI, it supports bus mastering and direct memory access (DMA). Mini-PCI cards are about a quarter the size of a regular PCI card. They can be found in small products such as laptops, printers, and set-top boxes.

To extend battery life, built-in communication devices such as Wi-Fi and Bluetooth adapters can be toggled on and off without powering down the computer. Many laptops come with a physical switch along the front or side edge that enables you to power on or off the communications adapter. Similarly, you can often use a keyboard shortcut for this, generally by pressing the Function (FN) key along with some other key. The FN key, when pressed, allows other keys to accomplish specific tasks. For example, on my laptop, pressing FN-F2 toggles my Wi-Fi adapter on and off; pressing FN-F10 ejects the disc from my CD-ROM drive.

Travel Assistance

Chapter 14, "Networks: Wireless Networking," covers wireless networking in great detail (as you might guess from the title).

PC Cards

The *Personal Computer Memory Card International Association (PCMCIA)* establishes standards involving portable computers, especially when it comes to expansion cards, which are generically called *PC Cards*. PC Cards are roughly credit card–sized devices that enhance and extend the functions of a portable PC. PC Cards are as standard on today's mobile computers as the hard drive. PC Cards are easy to use, inexpensive, and convenient. Figure 12.6 shows a typical PC Card.

FIGURE 12.6 PC Card

Exam Tip

The CompTIA A+ certification exams use the older term *PCMCIA cards* to describe PC Cards. Don't be shocked if you see that as an option on your exams. You'll hear many techs use the phrase as well, though the PCMCIA trade group has not used it for many years.

Almost every portable PC has one or two PC Card slots, into which you insert a PC Card. Each card will have at least one function, but many have two, three, or more. You can buy a PC Card that offers connections for removable media, for example, such as combination Secure Digital (SD) and CompactFlash (CF) card readers. You can also find PC Cards that you can plug into multiple types of networks. All PC Cards are *hot-swappable*, meaning you can plug them in without powering down the PC.

Exam Tip

Many manufacturers use the term *hot-pluggable* rather than hot-swappable to describe the ability to plug in and replace PC Cards on the fly. Look for either term on the exams.

The PCMCIA has established two versions of PC Cards, one using a parallel bus and the other using a serial bus. Each version, in turn, offers two technology variations as well as several physical varieties. This might sound complicated at first, but here's a map to help you sort it all out.

Parallel PC Cards

Parallel PC Cards come in two flavors, *16-bit* and *CardBus*, and each flavor comes in three different physical sizes, called Type I, Type II, and Type III. The 16-bit PC Cards, as the name suggests, are 16-bit, 5-V cards that can have up to two distinct functions or devices, such as a modem/network card combination. CardBus PC Cards are 32-bit, 3.3-V cards that can have up to eight (!) different functions on a single card. Regular PC Cards will fit into and work in CardBus slots, but the reverse is not true. CardBus totally dominates the current PC Card landscape, but you might still run into older 16-bit PC Cards.

Type I, II, and III cards differ only in the thickness of the card (Type I being the thinnest and Type III the thickest). All PC Cards share the same 68-pin inter-face, so any PC Card will work in any slot that's high enough to accept that card type. Type II cards are by far the most common. Therefore, most laptops will have two Type II slots, one above the other, to enable the computer to accept two Type I or II cards or one Type III card (Figure 12.7).

Although PCMCIA doesn't require that certain sizes perform certain func-tions, most PC Cards follow the PCMCIA recommendations. Table 12.1 lists the sizes and typical uses of each type of PC Card.

Travel Advisory

Most PC Cards normally come with a hard plastic storage case. Always be sure to use this case to store the cards when you're not using them. If dust, dirt, or grime gets into the array of contacts at the end of the card, the card won't work when you try to use it next. Also, be careful when using PC Cards that extend out of the PC Card slot past the edge of your laptop. One dark night I set my laptop on the floor with a PC Card NIC sticking out of it while I went to get a drink of water. On my way back, I accidentally stepped on the card sticking out of my laptop and nearly snapped it in half. Luckily, my laptop wasn't damaged, but the card was toast!

FIGURE 12.7 PC Card slots

TABLE 12.1	PC Card Types and Their Typical Uses			
Type	**Length**	**Width**	**Thickness**	**Typical Use**
Type I	85.6 mm	54.0 mm	3.3 mm	Flash memory
Type II	85.6 mm	54.0 mm	5.0 mm	I/O (modem, NIC, and so on)
Type III	85.6 mm	54.0 mm	10.5 mm	Hard drives

ExpressCard

ExpressCard, the high-performance serial version of the PC Card, has begun to re-place PC Card slots on newer laptop PCs. While ExpressCard offers significant performance benefits, keep in mind that ExpressCard and PC Cards are incom-patible. You cannot use your PC Card in your new laptop's ExpressCard socket. The PC Card has had a remarkably long life in portable PCs, and you can still find it on some new laptops, but get ready to replace all your PC Card devices. ExpressCard comes in two widths: 54 mm and 34 mm. Figure 12.8 shows a 34-mm ExpressCard. Both cards are 75-mm long and 5-mm thick, which makes them shorter than all previous PC Cards and the same thickness as a Type II PC Card.

ExpressCards connect to either the Hi-Speed USB 2.0 bus or a PCI Express (PCIe) bus. These differ phenomenally in speed. The amazingly slow-in-comparison USB version has a maximum throughput of 480 Mbps. The PCIe version, in contrast, roars in at 2.5 Gbps in unidirectional communication. Woot!

Table 12.2 shows the throughput and variations for the parallel and serial PC Cards currently or soon to be on the market.

© 2003 PCMCIA
www.expresscard.org

| FIGURE 12.8 | 34-mm ExpressCard *(photo courtesy of PCMCIA)* |

TABLE 12.2 PC Card Speeds	
Standard	**Maximum Theoretical Throughput**
PC Card using 16-bit bus	160 Mbps
CardBus PC Card using PCI bus	1056 Mbps
ExpressCard using USB 2.0 bus	480 Mbps
ExpressCard using PCIe bus	2.5 Gbps

Software Support for PC Cards

The PCMCIA standard defines two levels of software drivers to support PC Cards. The first, lower level is known as *socket services*. Socket services are device drivers that support the PC Card socket, enabling the system to detect when a PC Card has been inserted or removed and providing the necessary I/O to the device. The second, higher level is known as *card services*. The card services level recognizes the function of a particular PC Card and provides the specialized drivers necessary to make the card work.

In today's laptops, the socket services are standardized and are handled by the system BIOS. Windows itself handles all card services and has a large preinstalled base of PC Card device drivers, although most PC Cards come with their own drivers.

> **Travel Advisory**
>
> ExpressCards don't require either socket or card services, at least not in the way PC Cards do. The ExpressCard modules automatically configure the software on your computer, which makes them truly Plug and Play.

 Objective 12.02 **Power Management**

In early portable computers, every component drew power continuously, whether or not the system needed that device at that time. The hard drive would continue to spin whether or not it was being accessed, for example, and

the screen would continue to display, even when nobody was actively using the system. Modern systems use specialized hardware, the BIOS, and the OS itself to enable *power management* functions.

System Management Mode

Intel's 386SX CPU was the first to employ power management features. These new features, collectively called *System Management Mode (SMM)*, allowed the CPU to slow down or stop its clock without erasing the register information and supported power saving in peripherals. From its humble beginnings in the 386SX, SMM slowly started to show up in more CPUs and is now common.

Using only a power-saving CPU meant power management was relegated to special sleep or doze buttons that would stop the CPU and all the peripherals on the laptop. To take real advantage of SMM, you must also have a specialized BIOS and operating system. To this end, Intel proposed the Advanced Power Management (APM) specification in 1992 and the Advanced Configuration and Power Interface (ACPI) standard in 1996.

Requirements for APM/ACPI

APM and ACPI require four features to function fully:

- The first requirement is an SMM-capable CPU, which all CPUs now are.
- The second requirement is an *APM-compliant BIOS,* which enables the CPU to shut off the peripherals as desired.
- The third requirement is devices that will accept being shut off. These devices are usually called *Energy Star* devices, which signals their compliance with the EPA's Energy Star standard. To be an Energy Star device, a peripheral must have the ability to shut down without actually turning off.
- Finally, the system's operating system must know how to request that a particular device be shut down and the CPU's clock be slowed down or stopped.

ACPI goes beyond the APM standard by supplying support for hot-swappable devices, always a huge problem with APM. This feature aside, it's a challenge to tell the difference between an APM system and an ACPI system at first glance.

APM/ACPI Levels

The APM specification defines five different power usage operating levels for a system: Full On, APM Enabled, APM Standby, APM Suspend, and Off. These levels are left intentionally fuzzy to give manufacturers considerable leeway in their use.

- **Full On** Everything in the system running at full power. No power management.
- **APM Enabled** CPU and RAM running at full power. Power management enabled. An unused device may or may not be shut down.
- **APM Standby** CPU is stopped. RAM still stores all programs. All peripherals are shut down, although configuration options are still stored, so you won't have to reinitialize the devices to get back to APM Enabled state.
- **APM Suspend** Everything in the PC is shut down or at its lowest power consumption setting. Many systems use a special type of Suspend called *hibernation,* where critical configuration information is written to the hard drive. Upon a wake-up event, the system is reinitialized and the data is read from the drive to return the system to the APM Enabled mode. The recovery time between Suspend and Enabled states is much longer than the time between Standby and Enabled states.
- **Off** When in the Off state, your computer or device is powered down and inactive. Data and operational parameters may or may not be preserved.

ACPI handles all these levels, plus a few more, such as *Soft Power On/Off,* which enables you to define the function of the power button.

Configuration of APM/ACPI

You configure APM/ACPI via CMOS settings or through Windows. Windows settings will override CMOS settings. Although the APM/ACPI standards permit a great deal of flexibility, which can create some confusion among different implementations, certain settings apply generally to CMOS configuration. First is the ability to initialize power management; this enables the system to enter the APM Enabled mode. Often CMOS will then present time frames for entering

Standby and Suspend modes, as well as settings to determine which events take place in each of these modes. Also, many CMOS versions will present settings to determine wake-up events, such as directing the system to monitor a modem or a particular interrupt request (IRQ) (Figure 12.9). A true ACPI-compliant CMOS provides an ACPI setup option. Figure 12.10 shows a typical modern BIOS that provides this setting.

APM/ACPI settings can be found in the Windows 2000/XP Control Panel's Power Options applet. The Power Options applet has several built-in *power schemes* such as Home/Office and Max Battery (Figure 12.11) that put the system into Standby or Suspend mode after a certain interval. You can also require the system to go into Standby mode after a set period of time or turn off the monitor or hard drive after a time, thus creating your own custom power scheme.

Travel Advisory

You can also access Power Options by right-clicking the desktop and choosing Properties, and then opening the Screen Saver tab. Click the Power button in the Monitor Power section of the Screen Saver tab.

Another feature, Hibernate mode, takes everything in active memory and stores it on the hard drive just before the system powers down. When the PC

```
               Phoenix - AwardBIOS CMOS Utility
                            Power

         APM Configuration                          Select Menu

   Restore on AC Power Loss     [Power-Off]     Item Specific Help►►
   PWR Button < 4 secs          [Instant-Off]
   Power Up On PCI/PCIE Devices [Disabled]      Set the Data, Time
   USB Resume from S5           [Disabled]      resume by Alarm.
   Power On By RTC Alarm        [Enabled]
   Date(of Month) Alarm         [ 5]
   Alarm Time(hh:mm)             2 :  9 :  5
   Power Up By PS/2 Mouse       [Disabled]
   Power Up By PS/2 Keyboard    [Disabled]

   F1:Help      ↑↓:Select Item    -/+: Change Value      F5:Setup Defaults
   ESC:Exit     ►◄:Select Menu    Enter: Select SubMenu  F10:Save and Exit
```

FIGURE 12.9 Setting a wake-up event in CMOS

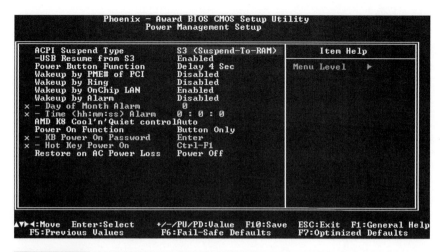

```
            Phoenix - Award BIOS CMOS Setup Utility
                     Power Management Setup

  ACPI Suspend Type        S3 (Suspend-To-RAM)       Item Help
  -USB Resume from S3      Enabled
  Power Button Function    Delay 4 Sec          Menu Level    ►
  Wakeup by PME# of PCI    Disabled
  Wakeup by Ring           Disabled
  Wakeup by OnChip LAN     Enabled
  Wakeup by Alarm          Disabled
x - Day of Month Alarm       0
x - Time (hh:mm:ss) Alarm    0 : 0 : 0
  AMD K8 Cool'n'Quiet controlAuto
  Power On Function        Button Only
x - KB Power On Password   Enter
x - Hot Key Power On       Ctrl-F1
  Restore on AC Power Loss Power Off

▲▼►◄:Move  Enter:Select   +/-/PU/PD:Value  F10:Save  ESC:Exit  F1:General Help
  F5:Previous Values      F6:Fail-Safe Defaults      F7:Optimized Defaults
```

FIGURE 12.10 CMOS with ACPI setup option

comes out of hibernation, Windows reloads all the files and applications into RAM. Figure 12.12 shows the Power Options Properties screen's Hibernate tab in Windows XP.

FIGURE 12.11 Power Options Power Schemes tab

FIGURE 12.12 Power Options Hibernate tab

Objective 12.03 Power

The thing that makes portable computers portable is their mobile power source: the battery. But all portables come with some sort of AC adapter to charge the battery and to provide primary power when the battery is depleted, missing, or simply not desired. Three types of batteries are commonly used in portable PCs, handhelds, and PDAs: nickel-cadmium, nickel-metal hydride, and lithium-ion.

Nickel-Cadmium

Nickel-Cadmium (Ni-Cd) batteries were the first type of battery able to provide portable computers with the steady supply of voltage that they need and were widely used in early portable PCs. However, Ni-Cds were far from an ideal solution. For one thing, they weren't capable of holding a sufficient charge to power the computer for more than a couple of hours even under the best of conditions. Real-life usage with frequent hard drive and CD-ROM activity drained Ni-Cd batteries in about half that time. Another problem that plagued Ni-Cds is something called *battery memory*.

Battery memory is a tendency for Ni-Cd batteries to "remember" the level at which they are usually discharged before they are recharged. For example, if you consistently use up a battery's charge to about 70 percent of its capacity before hooking it up to a charger, eventually the battery will start behaving as if it *needs* to be recharged at 70 percent capacity, thereby wasting the remaining 30 percent!

To prevent memory problems, a Ni-Cd battery had to be discharged completely before each recharging. Another fix was to purchase a *conditioning* charger, which would first totally discharge the Ni-Cd battery and then generate a special reverse current that electrically cleaned the internal parts of the battery.

Another knock against Ni-Cd batteries is that they're not very robust. They would, at best, last for about 1000 charges, and far fewer if they were subjected to rough use. Ni-Cds were also sensitive to overcharging—a very real danger because Ni-Cd chargers aren't very "smart" about determining how much of a charge the battery requires. Ni-Cds were also extremely susceptible to high temperatures, so storing your laptop in the trunk of a car for more than a few hours would usually result in a dead battery.

Ni-Cd batteries didn't stop causing trouble after they died. The highly toxic metals inside the battery made it unacceptable to throw them in the trash. Ni-Cd batteries must be disposed of via specialized disposal companies—most recycling centers and many battery manufacturers and distributors are glad to take them. For the most part, Ni-Cd batteries aren't used in computer devices much anymore, although you'll still find them in many consumer electronics devices.

Nickel Metal Hydride

Nickel Metal Hydride (NiMH) batteries were the next generation of mobile PC batteries and are still quite common today. Basically, NiMH batteries are similar to Ni-Cd batteries, but without most of the headaches. NiMH batteries are much less susceptible to memory problems, are less susceptible to overcharging (because they take advantage of *smart battery* technology, explained in the next section), and last longer between rechargings. Like Ni-Cd batteries, however, NiMH batteries don't tolerate heat well and have limited capacity.

While they're considered nontoxic to the environment, it's still a good idea not to dispose of them in the trash. Unlike Ni-Cds, NiMH batteries usually respond best to shallow recharges, or *topping off*, as opposed to a complete discharge/recharge. NiMH batteries are popular replacement batteries for Ni-Cd systems.

Lithium Ion

The most common type of battery used today is *Lithium Ion (Li-Ion)*. These batteries are extremely powerful, are completely immune to memory problems, and provide power for twice as long on a charge as Ni-Cd or NiMH batteries (up to four hours on systems using power management). They also carry a charge longer than Ni-Cd or NiMH batteries when not in use, and it's not unusual to be able to power up a laptop that's been sitting idle for days or even weeks.

Li-Ion batteries are susceptible to overcharging damage and in fact will explode if they're overcharged! For this reason, all Li-Ion batteries use *smart battery* technology (explained next) and have built-in circuitry to prevent accidental overcharging. Lithium batteries can be used only on systems designed to use them, and they can't be used as replacement batteries for the older types.

Smart Batteries

To provide better maintenance for laptop batteries, manufacturers have developed a new type of battery technology called the *smart battery*. NiMH and Li-Ion batteries incorporate smart battery technology. With previous, non-smart batteries, the computer had to make a guess at the battery's capacity and charge state. Smart batteries contain built-in circuitry that communicates with the computer to tell it when they need to be charged, conditioned, or replaced.

Battery Maintenance Guidelines

Remember the following five basic rules to extend the life of your portable computer's battery in a safe manner:

1. Always store batteries in a cool place. Although a freezer might sound like an excellent storage place, moisture, metal racks, and foodstuff make it a bad idea.

2. Use only conditioning chargers for your Ni-Cd and NiMH batteries—they'll last longer.

3. Keep battery contacts clean with a little alcohol or a dry cloth.

4. *Never* handle a battery that has ruptured or is broken—battery chemicals are extremely dangerous.

5. Always recycle old batteries; don't throw them in the trash.

AC Adapters

AC adapters for portable devices offer the same function that power supplies offer desktop PCs: converting AC to DC for the devices to run properly. The typical laptop computer AC adapter has a big power brick in the middle—that's the transformer. Although many AC adapters offer similar connections, you have to use the proper adapter for your device. If you plug in a device that provides too much AC, for example, you could toast something on the portable. One that provides not enough can cause a perfectly good device to be a poorly functioning nightmare. (See Objective 12.05 for more details on AC adapters.)

Objective 12.04

Docking Stations and Port Replicators

U ntil recently, it was almost always true that a person who owned a portable PC also had a desktop PC. You could take your portable to a job site or on a trip—and that was cool—but when you wanted to get real work done, you used your desktop computer. To keep these multiple-PC users on the near side of sanity, Microsoft and other vendors provide a number of handy tools such as the Microsoft Briefcase to assist you in synchronizing the data on your laptop with the data on your PC.

The power of laptops has gotten great enough, and the cost low enough, to tempt many people to forgo the desktop PC entirely and replace it with a laptop. While simple on the surface, this solution presents a number of challenges. For example, a laptop computer selected for its light weight and portability might be uncomfortable to work on for extended periods because of its small screen and keyboard. It may also be inconvenient to have to reattach printers, network cables, modem cables, scanners, and other devices to the portable computer every time you want to transport it.

Recognizing this problem, manufacturers of portable PCs provide devices called *docking stations* and *port replicators*. The docking station is a base that sits on your desk and has connections for printers, mice, display monitors, and so on. Further, many docking stations have integrated hardware devices that might not exist on the laptop, such as floppy disk drives, CD or DVD media drives, additional hard drives, network connections, and so on. A special port connector on the back or bottom of the laptop, shown in Figure 12.13, matches up to a connector on the docking station.

FIGURE 12.13 Docking station port connector

Simply lock the laptop into place and the attached peripherals come to life. Figure 12.14 shows a typical laptop connected to a docking station.

Port replicators are similar in function and design to docking stations, except that they don't offer any additional devices or connections. Port replicators are simply a convenient way of collecting all of your I/O port connectors— keyboard, mouse, printer, and so on—into a single device that connects to the appropriate piece of hardware on your desktop.

Hardware Profiles

Docking stations provide fantastic convenience, but with a catch—the laptop has to know what hardware is available on the docking station and be able to use

FIGURE 12.14 Laptop computer in a docking station

that equipment. By the same token, once the laptop is disconnected, it must know what hardware *isn't* available anymore. Windows handles this problem via *hardware profiles.*

A hardware profile is a preconfigured list of devices Windows automatically enables or disables in the Device Manager, depending on what devices the system detects. The user can also manually choose a profile from a list at bootup, as shown in Figure 12.15.

The manual method has become less prominent because smarter laptops can detect their current state and easily choose the proper profile via the Plug and Play process. Both Windows 2000 and Windows XP configure their hardware profiles in the System Properties applet. Figure 12.16 shows the hardware profiles for a laptop running Windows XP. One profile is for what this user calls *Standalone*—not connected to the docking station. The other hardware profile is used when the laptop is connected to the docking station.

In theory, you can create hardware profiles for any system, but in reality, hardware profiles are for laptops. In fact, the hardware profiles features in Windows 2000/XP simply assume that if you use hardware profiles, you're using a laptop. The only trick to hardware profiles is that some devices show as disabled in the Device Manager, depending on which profile is active. Don't panic if you see a red "X" on a device in Device Manager on a laptop—this might mean only that a particular device isn't being used by the current profile.

```
            Hardware Profile/Configure Recovery Menu

    This menu allows you to select a hardware profile
    to be used when Windows 2000 is started.

    If your system is not starting correctly, then you may switch to a previous
    system configure, which may overcome startup problems.

    IMPORTANT: System configure changes made since the last successful
    startup will be discarded.
    DOCKED
    UNDOCKED

    Use the up and down arrow keys to move the highlight
    to the selection you want.  Then press ENTER.

    To switch to the Last Known Good configuration, press 'L' .
    To Exit this menu and restart your computer, press F3.

    Seconds until highlighted choice will be started automatically:20
```

FIGURE 12.15 Bootup hardware profile list

System Properties

General | Device Manager | Hardware Profiles | Performance

You can create hardware profiles to select different hardware configurations at startup.

Most computers do not need separate hardware profiles. For more information, see Help.

Original Configuration
Standalone

Copy... | Rename... | Delete

OK | Cancel

FIGURE 12.16 Hardware profiles

Objective 12.05

Maintaining and Troubleshooting Portables

Most portable PCs come from the factory solidly built and configured. Manufacturers know that few techs outside their factories know enough to work on them, so they don't cut corners. From a tech's standpoint, your most common work on maintaining portables involves taking care of the batteries and extending the battery life through proper power management, as discussed earlier. You also need to keep the machine clean, avoid excessive heat, and be careful about physical damage.

Everything you normally do to maintain a PC applies to portable PCs. You need to keep current on Windows patches and Service Packs, and use stable, recent drivers. Run Error-checking with some frequency, and definitely defragment the hard drive. Disk Cleanup is a must if the laptop runs Windows XP. That said, let's look at issues specifically involving portables.

For troubleshooting, portables have distinctive issues regarding power and networking. Plus, you can run into issues with the screen and input devices.

Cleaning

Most portable PCs take substantially more abuse than a corresponding desktop model. Constant handling, travel, airport food on the run that accidentally crumbled into the keyboard, and so on can radically shorten the life of a portable if you don't take action. One of the most important things you should do is clean the laptop regularly. Use an appropriate screen cleaner (not a glass cleaner!) to remove fingerprints and dust from the fragile LCD panel.

If you've had the laptop in a smoky or dusty environment where the air quality alone causes problems, try compressed air for cleaning. Compressed air works great for blowing out the dust and crumbs from the keyboard and for keeping PC Card sockets clear. Don't use water on your keyboard! Even a minor amount of moisture inside the portable can toast a component.

Heat

To manage and maintain a healthy portable PC, you need to deal with issues of heat. Every portable has a stack of electronic components crammed into a very small space. Unlike their desktop brethren, portables don't have lots of freely-moving air space that enables fans to cool everything down. Even with lots of low-power-consumption devices inside, portable PCs still crank out a good deal of heat. Excessive heat can cause system lockups and hardware failures, so you should handle the issue wisely. Try this as a starter guide.

- Use power management, even if you're plugged into the AC outlet. This is especially important if you're working in a warm (more than 80 degrees Fahrenheit) room.
- Keep air space between the bottom of the laptop and the surface on which it rests. Putting a laptop on a soft surface like a pillow on your lap, for example, creates a great heat retention system—not a good thing. Always use a hard, flat surface.
- Don't use a keyboard protector for extended amounts of time.
- Listen to your fan, assuming the laptop has one. If it's often running very fast—you can tell by the high-pitched whirring sound—examine your power management settings and your environment and change whatever is causing heat retention.

- Speaking of fans, be alert to a fan that suddenly goes silent. Fans do fail on laptops, causing overheating and failure. All laptop fans can be replaced easily.

Protect the Machine

While prices continue to drop for basic laptops, a fully loaded system is still pricey. To protect your investment, you'll want to adhere to certain best practices. You've already read tips in this chapter to deal with cleaning and heat, so let's look at the "portable" part of portable computers.

Tripping

Pay attention to where you run the power cord when you plug in a laptop. One of the primary causes of laptop destruction is people tripping over the power cord and knocking the laptop off a desk. This is especially true if you plug in at a public place such as a café or airport. Remember that the life you save could be your portable PC's!

Storage

If your laptop or PDA isn't going to be used for a while, storing it safely will go a long way toward keeping it operable when you do power it up again. It's worth the extra few dollars to invest in a quality case—preferably one with ample padding. Smaller devices such as PDAs are well protected inside small shock-resistant aluminum cases that clip on to your belt, while laptops do fine in well-padded cases or backpacks. Not only will this protect your system on a daily basis when transporting it from home to office, but it will keep dust and pet hair away as well. Lastly, remove the battery if you'll be storing your device for an extended period of time to protect it from battery leakage.

Travel

If traveling with a laptop, take care to protect yourself from theft. If possible, use a case that doesn't look like a computer case. A well-padded backpack makes a great travel bag for a laptop and appears less tempting to would-be thieves. Don't forget to pack any accessories you might need, such as modular devices, spare batteries, and AC adapters. Make sure to remove any disks, such as CD/DVD or floppies, from their drives. Most importantly—back up any important data before you leave.

Make sure to have at least a little battery power available. Heightened security at airports means you might have to power on your system to prove it's really a computer and not a transport case for questionable materials. And never let

your laptop out of your sight. If you're going through an x-ray machine, request a manual search. The x-ray won't harm your computer like a metal detector will, but if the laptop gets through the line at security before you do, someone else might walk away with it. If flying, keep your laptop out of the overhead bins and under the seat in front of you where you can keep an eye on it.

Shipping

Much of the storage and travel advice can be applied to shipping. Remove batteries and CD/DVD/floppies from their drives. Pack the portable well and disguise the container as best you can. Back up any data and verify the warranty coverage. Ship with a reputable carrier and always request a tracking number and, if possible, delivery signature. It's also worth the extra couple of bucks to pay for the shipping insurance. And when the clerk asks what's in the box, it's safer to say "electronics" rather than "a new 20-inch laptop computer."

Security

The fact is, if someone really wants to steal your laptop, they'll find a way. You can, however, do a few things to make yourself, and your equipment, a less desirable target. As you've learned, disguise is a good idea. While you don't need to camouflage your laptop or carry it in a brown grocery bag on a daily basis, an inconspicuous carrying case will draw less attention.

Another physical deterrent is a laptop lock. Similar to a steel bicycle cable, it has a loop on one end and a lock on the other. The idea is to loop the cable around a solid object, such as a bed frame, and secure the lock to the small security hole on the side of the laptop. Again, if someone really wants to steal your computer, they'll find a way. They'll dismantle the bed frame if they're desperate. The best protection is to be vigilant and not let the computer out of your sight.

An alternative to securing a laptop physically with a lock is to use a software tracking system. Software makers, such as Computer Security Products, Inc., at www.computersecurity.com, offer tracking software that transmits a signal to a central office if stolen and connected to a phone line or the Internet. The location of the stolen PC can be tracked, and sensitive files can even be deleted automatically with the aid of the stealth signal.

Troubleshooting Portable Computers

Many of the troubleshooting techniques you learned about with desktop systems can be applied to laptops. Additionally, you can try some laptop-specific procedures as well.

Laptop Won't Power On

- Verify AC power by plugging another electronic device into the wall outlet. If the other device receives power, the outlet is good.
- If the outlet is good, connect the laptop to the wall outlet and try to power on. If no LEDs light up, you may have a bad AC adapter. Swap it out with a known-good power adapter.
- A faulty peripheral device might keep the laptop from powering up. Remove any peripherals such as USB or FireWire devices.

Screen Doesn't Come on Properly

- If the laptop is booting (you hear the beeps and the drives), first make sure the display is on. Press the FN key and the key to activate the screen a number of times until the laptop display comes on.
- If the laptop display is very dim, you may have lost an inverter. The clue here is that inverters never go quietly. They can make a nasty hum as they are about to die and an equally nasty popping noise when they actually fail. Failure often occurs when you plug in the laptop's AC adapter, as the inverters take power directly from the AC adapter.

Wireless Networking Doesn't Work

- Check for a physical switch along the front, rear, or side edges of the laptop that toggles the internal wireless adapter on and off.
- Try the special key combination for your laptop to toggle the wireless adapter. You usually press the FN key in combination with another key.
- You might simply be out of range. Physically walk the laptop over to the wireless router or access point to ensure there are no "out of range" issues.

Handwriting Is Not Recognized

- If your PDA or Tablet PC no longer recognizes your handwriting or stylus, you may need to retrain the digitizer. Look for an option in your PDA OS settings to "align the screen." On Windows Tablet PCs, you will find a similar option under Start | Settings | Control Panel.

Keypad Doesn't Work

- If none of the keys work on your laptop, you've probably unseated the keypad connector. These connectors are quite fragile and are

prone to unseating from any physical stress on the laptop. Check the manufacturer's disassembly procedures to locate and reseat the keypad.

- If you're getting numbers when you're expecting to get letters, the number lock (NUMLOCK) function key is turned on. Turn it off.

Touchpad Doesn't Work

- A shot of compressed air does wonders for cleaning pet hair out of the touchpad sensors. You'll get a cleaner shot if you remove the keyboard before using the compressed air. Remember to be gentle when lifting off the keyboard and make sure to follow the manufacturer's instructions.

- The touchpad driver might need to be reconfigured. Try the various options in the Control Panel | Mouse applet.

CHECKPOINT

✔**Objective 12.01: Components** Most portables are made up of proprietary components, although if you look hard enough, you can find modular replacement components. Know how to replace or upgrade RAM, hard drives, modular CPUs, and video cards, as well as PC Cards. Also know the three types of PC Cards and how they differ from one another.

✔**Objective 12.02: Power Management** Understand the APM (Advanced Power Management) and ACPI (Advanced Configuration and Power Interface) standards. The five power usage operating levels defined by the APM specification are Full On, APM Enabled, APM Standby, APM Suspend (Hibernate), and Off. The biggest advantage of ACPI is that it supports hot-swappable devices.

✔**Objective 12.03: Power** Three types of batteries are commonly used in mobile PCs: Nickel-Cadmium (Ni-Cd), Nickel-Metal Hydride (NiMH), and Lithium-Ion (Li-Ion). The most common type used today is Li-Ion. Modern Li-Ion batteries provide about four hours of continuous use and can carry a charge for days or weeks when not in use. AC adapters transform AC electricity from the wall socket to DC electricity the portable device can use. They also recharge the battery.

✔**Objective 12.04: Docking Stations and Port Replicators** Docking stations enable laptops to maintain consistent connections to resources such as networks, printers, and mass storage drives. Laptops that connect to docking stations use hardware profiles to determine what devices are available. A hardware profile is a list of devices that Windows automatically enables or disables in the Device Manager, depending on what devices the laptop detects. Port replicators are similar to docking stations, except that they simply duplicate the ports that exist on your laptop.

✔**Objective 12.05: Maintaining and Troubleshooting Portables** You need to keep the machine clean, avoid excessive heat, and be careful about physical damage. Everything else you normally do to maintain a PC applies to portable PCs. For troubleshooting, portables have distinctive issues regarding power and networking. Plus, you can run into issues with the screen and input devices.

REVIEW QUESTIONS

1. Which of the following is *not* true about PC Cards?

 A. Socket Services need to be set to detect whether a card is installed.

 B. PCMCIA services must be set up in CMOS.

 C. Card Services need to be set up to detect the function of the card installed.

 D. PC Cards are hot-swappable.

2. How many Type III cards can typically fit into a laptop at one time?

 A. 1

 B. 2

 C. 3

 D. 4

3. How do you correct the battery memory condition in a Ni-Cd battery? (Choose two.)

 A. Use a conditioning charger.

 B. Place the battery in a freezer overnight.

 C. Completely discharge the battery before recharging it.

 D. Recharge the battery any time its capacity drops below 50 percent.

4. NiMH batteries can be used as replacements for what type of battery?

 A. Ni-Cd batteries

 B. Li-Ion batteries

 C. DMFC fuel cell batteries

 D. NiMH batteries can be used only as replacements for other NiMH batteries

5. What is the difference between a docking station and a port replicator?

 A. Port replicators can provide connections and devices that don't exist on the laptop; docking stations provide only connections that exist on the laptop.

 B. Docking stations can provide connections and devices that don't exist on the laptop; port replicators provide only connections that exist on the laptop.

 C. Docking stations work only on Windows laptops; port replicators work only on laptops running the Macintosh OS.

 D. There is no difference between docking stations and port replicators.

6. How many Type II cards can typically fit into a laptop at one time?

 A. 1

 B. 2

 C. 3

 D. 4

7. Which of the following is not possible?

 A. Having two Type II cards in a laptop at one time

 B. Having a Type I card and a Type II card in a laptop at one time

 C. Having two Type I cards in a laptop at one time

 D. Having a Type II card and a Type III card in a laptop at one time

8. Which of the following is *not* a recommended maintenance procedure for laptop batteries?

 A. Keep the contacts clean using alcohol or a dry cloth.

 B. Store them in the freezer if they won't be used for a long period of time.

 C. Recycle them according to the manufacturer's specifications.

 D. Store them in a cool place.

9. When shipping a laptop from Boston to Los Angeles, what should you remove?

 A. Floppy drive

 B. Hard drive

 C. Battery

 D. Monitor

10. If you encounter a laptop that doesn't seem to recharge, what might be the problem? Select the best answer.

 A. AC adapter

 B. CPU

 C. RAM

 D. Thermal process

REVIEW ANSWERS

1. **B** There's no need to set up PCMCIA services in CMOS.

2. **A** Only one Type III PC Card can fit into a laptop at a time because of the thickness of these cards.

3. **A C** Use a conditioning charger or completely discharge a battery before recharging to correct battery memory.

4. **A** NiMH batteries can be used as replacements for Ni-Cd batteries.

5. **B** Docking stations enable the laptop to use connections and devices such as removable storage drives and network connections that may not exist on the laptop. Port replicators simply duplicate the existing ports.

6. **B** A typical laptop can fit two Type II cards at the same time.

7. **D** If you use a Type III card, no other card will fit into the socket.

8. **B** Storing batteries in the freezer for a long period of time isn't advisable because of the presence of moisture, metal racks, and food.

9. **C** Remove the battery when shipping.

10. **A** A laptop that doesn't recharge has a problem with either the AC adapter or the battery. The former is the logical choice for this question.

Networks:
Wired Networking

	NEWBIE	SOME EXPERIENCE	EXPERT
ETA	3 hours	2 hours	1 hour

No PC is an island. To experience the power of computers, you have to hook them up to other computers. Networking is the name of the game, and Windows PCs play the game very well indeed! Networking enables different users to share resources such as printers, scanners, files, and Internet connections. Computer networks are an integral part of any business environment. Not only that, but more and more multi-computer homes are using networks to get the most out of their PC investment.

Networks range in size from the smallest and simplest network of all—two computers connected together—to the largest and most complex network of all—the Internet. As a CompTIA A+ certified PC tech, you'll have many opportunities to put your networking knowledge to use. This chapter runs through the basics of networking hardware, topologies, and protocols.

> **Travel Assistance**
>
> This chapter touches briefly on the software components needed for a functional network, but you'll find the majority of that discussion in Chapter 18.

 # Networking Components for the PC

Networks need hardware to move data between computers. The network adapter, or *network interface card (NIC)*, links the PC to the rest of the networking hardware. NICs come in wired and wireless varieties, meaning that they either use physical network cabling (such as Ethernet or Token Ring) or some sort of wireless technology (such as infrared or radio waves) to transfer data. Next, you must install appropriate networking software—a network *client*, and one or more protocols. These enable your PC to access network services and resources.

Installing Network Adapters and Drivers

Installing a NIC into any version of Windows is usually a no-brainer, because most NICs today are completely Plug and Play or simply built into the motherboard. For the most part, this is simply a matter of turning off the PC, installing the card into an available expansion bus slot, and turning the system on again. If you are using a USB or PC Card NIC, you don't even need to turn the system off! Simply insert the NIC into the slot and wait for Windows Plug and Play to do its thing.

After the NIC is detected by Windows, supply the appropriate driver, and you're ready to go. The only trick is to remember that you should use the driver diskette that comes with the NIC, even if Windows offers to use its own drivers. Vendor-supplied NIC drivers are usually more up to date than the versions that ship with Windows.

All the issues discussed with respect to installing devices also hold true for NICs. If the NIC shows up in the Device Manager, you're done with this step. If it doesn't, you follow the normal hardware troubleshooting steps to resolve the problem. Figure 13.1 shows a typical network adapter, nicely installed in Windows XP Device Manager.

The Link Between Networking Hardware and Data Packets

At this point, you've got all of the hardware in place that you need to access a network. There's more to it, of course, but we'll save the rest of this discussion for Chapter 18. Before moving on, however, you need to understand the link between networking hardware and the data packets that they send out.

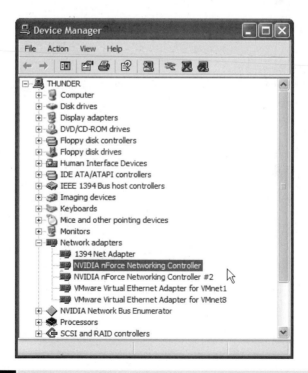

FIGURE 13.1 Windows XP Device Manager showing NICs installed

Every NIC in the world has a built-in identifier called a *media access control (MAC)* address. The MAC address is a binary address that is unique for every network card. Every network card in the world has a unique MAC address. The MAC address is 48 bits long, providing more than 281 *trillion* individual MAC addresses, so there are plenty of MAC addresses to go around. Note that on the vast majority of NICs, the MAC is hard-coded on to the card's circuitry and can't be reset. Some (very few) NICs permit you to configure this value in the card properties.

Local Lingo

Packet A container for data that includes the MAC address of the sending NIC.
Frame A commonly used synonym for packet.

All the many varieties of data packets share certain common features:

- All packets contain the MAC address of the network card to which the data is being sent.
- All packets have the MAC address of the network card that sent the data.
- The data itself (no matter what type) can vary in size depending on the type of packet.
- Some type of data check (such as Cyclic Redundancy Check, or CRC) is in place to enable the receiving network card to indicate whether the data was received in good order (Figure 13.2).

Exam Tip

A detailed understanding of how data packets are assembled, addressed, sent out over the network, and then retrieved and reassembled at the other end isn't necessary for the CompTIA A+ certification exams. That's what the CompTIA Network+ certification exam is for. Just be sure that you understand that each data packet is "tagged" with the physical MAC address of the hardware from which it originates.

At this point, you're ready to plug a piece of network cable into the PC and connect to the network, right? But how does the PC communicate with another PC? You need software for that, specifically client services and software protocols.

FIGURE 13.2 Generic packet

Client Service

The *client service* is the component that enables your computer to see and be seen on the network. If using NetBEUI or TCP/IP, use the *Client Service for Microsoft Networks*. NetWare users need to install the *Client Service for NetWare Networks*. Like the network protocols, the client service is also installed by default when you add a network adapter onto the PC.

Generally, you don't need to do any configuration for the client service, unless your network uses a nonstandard Name Service Provider, such as the DCE Cell Directory Service. This is rare, however, so typically all you have to do with the client service is to install it and let Windows handle it from there.

Software Protocols

Protocols handle the details of data transfer, such as making sure the sending PC packages the data properly in uniformly understood *packets,* and that the receiving PC knows how to put the data back together. Each protocol uses its own unique "language" for a packet, so packets created with one protocol cannot be read by another machine that does not have that protocol installed.

So which protocol should you use? The answer depends on the type of network you're running. For instance, if your network has servers running older versions of Novell's NetWare network operating system, then chances are you'll need the IPX/SPX protocol. Old Windows networks may use Microsoft's NetBEUI protocol, but most modern computer networks use Transmission Control Protocol/Internet Protocol (TCP/IP). Why? All modern computer systems, whether they're Windows, Macintosh, NetWare, or UNIX/Linux, are able to use TCP/IP, so there's no platform-proprietary nonsense to wrestle with. Plus, TCP/IP is the *de facto* standard protocol for the Internet.

In a business environment, you'll typically work with network technicians who can tell you which protocol or protocols to install. Windows also helps by automatically installing TCP/IP when you install a NIC. Should you need to install another protocol, double-click on a network icon in Network Connections in the Control Panel and click the Install button on the General tab. Select Protocol and then click the Add button, as shown in Figure 13.3.

Depending on the protocol you're using, you may also have to configure other settings. For example, IPX/SPX might require you to set the correct *network number* and *frame type*; TCP/IP may require that you configure a unique *IP address* and *subnet mask*. We'll touch on these subjects in Chapter 18.

FIGURE 13.3 Adding a network protocol

Objective 13.02 Network Topologies

Even though most networks share the same basic look and feel, the way the data moves around inside those wires may be quite different from one network to the next. The *topology* of a network describes these different configurations of the cabling between computers.

Networks today use two main types of topologies: *bus* topology and *ring* topology. Other hybrid topologies that are popular are *star ring* and *star bus* topologies. Each of these topologies has advantages and disadvantages. The best topology for a specific situation depends on a variety of factors, including cost, speed, ease of installation, the physical position of the PCs, and the number of PCs in the network.

Bus Topology

The first type of topology was bus topology. In bus topology, all the PCs connect via a *single cable* that runs to all the PCs. Bus topologies look something like Figure 13.4.

Bus topology works like a big telephone party line: all devices must first listen to see if anyone else is sending packets before they can send a packet. If the cable is not being used, the device sends its packet on the line. Every network card on the bus sees and reads the packet. This is called Carrier Sense Multiple Access/Collision Detection (CSMA/CD).

Sometimes two cards do try to talk at the same time. This is called a *collision*, and the cards themselves arbitrate to see who gets to resend its frames first.

Reflection and Termination

Data packets manifest as tiny electrical signals tapped out onto the network wire. Any time a device sends electrical voltage along a wire, some voltage bounces back or reflects when it reaches the end of the wire. This *reflection* poses

FIGURE 13.4 Bus topology

a big problem for a bus topology network. As soon as one PC sends a packet, that packet will bounce off the end and back up the wire, making the cards that want to send data wait for no reason.

Worse, the endlessly reflecting packets create what's called a *packet storm,* which prevents other networked PCs from sending data. To prevent a packet storm, every bus network needs a device called a *terminator* plugged into each end of the bus cable. A terminator is a resistor that absorbs the signal, thus preventing reflection.

This need for termination is a weak spot in bus topology. If the cable breaks anywhere, a packet storm is instantly created and no device can send data, even if the break isn't between the devices exchanging data.

Ring Topology

A *ring topology* connects all the PCs together on a single cable, much like bus topology. As the name implies, however, this bus functions like a ring.

Ring topologies use a transmission method called *token passing.* In token passing, a mini packet, called a *token,* constantly passes from one card to the next in one direction, as shown in Figure 13.5. If one PC wants to talk to another, it must wait until it gets the token. The PC's NIC then attaches data to the token and sends the packet back out the ring. If another PC wants to send data, it must wait until a free token (one that doesn't have an attached packet) comes around.

Because ring topologies use token passing, we tend to use the term *token ring* when describing ring networks. In a few exceptions a ring topology used fea-

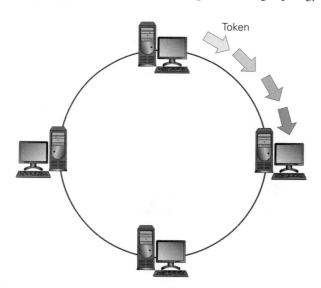

FIGURE 13.5 Ring topology uses token passing scheme

tures other than token passing, but they were few and are long gone. All current ring networks use an IBM-trademarked version of token passing called, rather appropriately, *Token Ring*. So, if it is a ring topology, it's Token Ring.

Star Ring

Token Ring topology was, if not invented, perfected and packaged by IBM. Token Ring actually uses a topology called *star ring*. Instead of running a ring of cable all around the LAN, the ring is stored inside a special box called a multistation access unit (MSAU). We often just call it a *MAU* or *token ring hub* (although Token Ring techs would have a heart attack if you said it within earshot of them). Although Token Ring is a ring, it looks more like a star, as you can see in Figure 13.6.

Star Bus

The star configuration used in Token Ring made it dependable and easy to expand. This led to a variation of the bus topology called *star bus* topology. Imagine if you were to take a bus network and shrink the bus down so that it would fit inside a hub, as in Figure 13.7.

The ring is in the MSAU

FIGURE 13.6 Star ring topology

The bus is in the hub

FIGURE 13.7 Star bus topology

This type of star bus topology is the single most popular topology used today. Cheap and centralized, a star bus network does not go down if a cable breaks. True, the network would go down if the hub itself failed, but that doesn't happen often. Even if a hub fails, replacing a hub in a closet is much easier than tracing a bus running through walls and ceilings trying to find a break.

Objective 13.03 Network Cabling Standards

Now that we've looked at how PCs are made network-ready, we need to examine the connective components of networking. In the vast majority of networks, physical network cabling is the medium by which data packets are moved from one PC to the other. Wireless alternatives exist, as we'll see in Chapter 14, but at some point even wireless networks connect to a wired network "backbone."

Wired (and even wireless) networking hardware—the cabling, hubs, switches, routers, repeaters, and patch panels—must conform to standards defined by the IEEE (Institute of Electrical and Electronics Engineers, pronounced "I-triple-E"). The two predominant standards are *Ethernet* and the previously mentioned *Token Ring*.

Ethernet

Ethernet is, by far, the more popular of the two networking standards. The Ethernet standard—now controlled by the 802 committee of the IEEE standards body—has appeared in several physical forms, such as 10Base5, 100BaseT, 100BaseFX, and 802.11*x* wireless. Significant differences exist among the forms, mainly in terms of cabling media and data throughput, but it's all Ethernet. This means that with the appropriate hardware, you can mix and match without losing the ability to communicate.

Thick Ethernet—10Base5

The original Xerox Ethernet specification defined a specific type of cabling for the first Ethernet networks. This type of cable is called *thick Ethernet*. Thick Ethernet, also known as *ThickNet*, is a thick coaxial cable—about half an inch in diameter—manufactured under the *Belden 9580* standard. Belden is a *big* cable manufacturer, and its internal part number (9580) for thick Ethernet is a popular way to define ThickNet.

Local Lingo

Coaxial cable Coax consists of a center cable (core) surrounded by insulation. This, in turn, is covered with a shield of braided cable. The inner core actually carries the signal, and the shield effectively eliminates outside interference. The entire cable is then sheathed by a protective insulating cover.

ThickNet networks use a true bus topology, which means that all PCs attach to a single cable called the *segment*. ThickNet supports up to 100 devices hooked to one segment. The maximum length of one segment is 500 meters. 10Base5 networks have a maximum data throughput speed of 10 Mbps.

One of the important quirks of ThickNet to keep in mind is that devices must connect to the cable in some multiple of 2.5 meters. This is to reduce noise due to signal oscillation. ThickNet cabling is clearly marked every 2.5 meters to ensure proper device connection. Devices connect to ThickNet by means of a *vampire connector*. The vampire connector has sharp teeth that literally pierce the cable sheathing and contact the cable core when clamped into place.

ThickNet network adapters are different from other types of network adapters. They have both external and internal components: the external *transceiver* is integrated into the vampire connector and passes the network signal to the network adapter card installed in the PC via a cable. The cable from the vampire connector/transceiver to the PC network adapter must be no more than

50 meters. ThickNet connects to a PC's network card via a 15-pin male connector called an *Attachment Unit Interface (AUI)* or *DIX* (Digital, Intel, Xerox) connector. ThickNet uses a bus topology, as mentioned, so it needs terminators. As you might guess, the 50-ohm ThickNet terminator must be placed on each end of the segment.

ThickNet is on its way out for a number of reasons. It's expensive, it's difficult to work with, and it's slow. Nonetheless, ThickNet has an installed user base, which is why it is discussed here.

Thin Ethernet — 10Base2

Thin Ethernet, also known as *ThinNet,* or *802.3,* is an inexpensive alternative to ThickNet. ThinNet cable is much easier to handle than ThickNet cable and is used in many small networks.

ThinNet uses a specific type of coax called RG-58. RG stands for *Radio Grade,* which is an industry standard for measuring coax cables. This type of coax looks similar to the coax used with common cable television boxes, called RG-6, but it's quite different. The RG rating should be clearly marked on the cable. If it isn't, it will say something like ThinNet or 802.3 to let you know you have the right cable.

While ThinNet also runs at 10 Mbps on a true bus topology, it has several big limitations that thick Ethernet doesn't share. Thin Ethernet supports only 30 devices per segment, and each segment can be no more than 185 meters long. On the plus side, cabling with ThinNet is a snap compared with ThickNet. The cable is much thinner and more flexible than for ThickNet. In addition, the transceiver is built into the ThinNet network card, so ThinNet does not require an external transceiver. Each ThinNet network card is simply connected to the bus cable with a T connector.

The ThinNet cable has twist-on, barrel-type connectors, called *British Naval Connectors (BNC),* which attach to the T connector, as shown in Figure 13.8. Termination is handled by twisting small, specialized terminators onto the unused end of the T connector on the machines at the ends of the chain.

When installing ThinNet, it's important that one of the terminators be grounded. Special terminators can be grounded to the case of the PC, but be sure the PC is also grounded. You *must* use a T connector! You cannot simply plug the end of the ThinNet cable into the network adapter.

To add another PC to the network, simply remove the terminator from the last PC, add another piece of cable with another T connector, and add the terminator on the new end. Adding a PC between two systems is also easy: unhook one side of a T connector and add another PC and cable in between.

FIGURE 13.8 BNC connectors plugged into T connector

ThinNet, like its heavyweight cousin, is on its way out. Very popular for a time in *small office/home office (SOHO)* networks, the fact that it uses a bus topology where any wire break means the whole network goes down makes 10Base2 unacceptable in a modern network.

10ˣBaseT

Most modern Ethernet networks employ one of two technologies (and sometimes both), *10BaseT* or *100BaseT*. As the numbers in the names would suggest, 10BaseT networks run at 10 Mbps and 100BaseT networks run at 100 Mbps. Both standards are in the process of being eclipsed by Gigabit Ethernet, or 1000BaseT, which runs at 1 Gbps. The segment length (the distance from the PC to a hub or switch) for all three is limited to 100 meters. All three technologies—collectively abbreviated as *10ˣBaseT* or the clunkier *10/100/1000BaseT*—connect via a type of cable called *unshielded twisted pair (UTP)*.

UTP cables come in categories that define the maximum speed at which data can be transferred (also called *bandwidth*).

Local Lingo

CAT 1–6 levels Experienced network techs refer to the different types of cabling as "*CAT x*," as opposed to "*Category x*," as in, "Yo, Frankie! Toss me that coil o' CAT 5, alright?"

CAT Levels UTP cable comes in seven major categories (CATs) of two-pair cables. You can find the CAT level clearly marked on a cable. Table 13.1 shows the speeds.

These categories are established by the Telecommunication Industry Association/Electronic Industries Alliance (TIA/EIA) and are under the TIA/EIA-568 specification. Currently, just about everybody uses CAT 5 cable (or the slightly superior CAT 5e).

A number of wire makers are pushing UTP with even higher ratings. A good example is Belden Wire and Cable's DataTwist 350 cable, designated to run as fast as 350 Mbps. These new cables tend to get names like "CAT 6a" and "CAT 7," but these are marketing labels and not official CAT designations.

The 10BaseT cabling standard requires two pairs of wires: a pair for sending and a pair for receiving. 10BaseT cables use a connector called an *RJ* connector. The RJ designation was invented by Ma Bell years ago and is still used today. Currently, you see only two types of RJ connectors: *RJ-11* and *RJ-45,* as shown in Figure 13.9.

RJ-11 connectors should look familiar. RJ-11 is the connector that hooks your telephone to the telephone jack. It supports up to two pairs of wires, though most phone lines use only one pair (the other pair is used to support a second phone line). RJ-11 connectors aren't used in any common network installation, although some proprietary "out-of-the-box" network solutions use the telephone lines already installed in a building to transmit data. These types of networks aren't very popular, however.

RJ-45 is the standard for UTP connectors. RJ-45 has connections for up to four pairs of wires and is visibly much wider than RJ-11. The #1 pin on an RJ-45 jack is the first one on the *left* when pointing the jack away from you with the clip facing *down.*

TABLE 13.1	Standard CAT Types

Ethernet Cable Category	Typical Bandwidth Throughput and Usage
CAT 1	Data speeds up to 2 Mbps. Standard phone line.
CAT 2	Data speeds up to 4 Mbps. Rarely used.
CAT 3	Data speeds up to 16 Mbps. Phone and small network use.
CAT 4	Data speeds up to 20 Mbps. Rarely used.
CAT 5	Data speeds up to 100 Mbps. Phone and data. The most common Ethernet network cable in use.
CAT 5e	Data speeds up to 1 Gbps.
CAT 6	Data speeds up to 10 Gbps. Best for new installations.

FIGURE 13.9 RJ-11 (left) and RJ-45 (right)

Exam Tip

Know the 10°BaseT numbers and names—10, 100, or 1000 Mbps data transfers; 100-meter segment length; RJ-45 connectors; and UTP cabling.

Two standards exist for CAT 5/6 cabling: the TIA/EIA *568A* and the TIA/EIA *568B*. Both are acceptable. The only truly critical thing is to use the *same* standard on each end of the cable, but your life will be much simpler if you choose one standard and stick with it. The wires in UTP cabling are color-coded to make standardization easy. Table 13.2 shows the official TIA/EIA standard colors as they correspond to the wire number.

Fiber-Optic Ethernet

Fiber-optic cable is an attractive networking solution for a number of reasons. First, because it uses light instead of electricity, fiber-optic cable is immune to electrical interference and "crosstalk." Second, fiber-optic signals travel much far-

TABLE 13.2 UTP Cabling Color Chart

Pin No.	568A	568B
1	White/green	White/orange
2	Green	Orange
3	White/orange	White/green
4	Blue	Blue
5	White/blue	White/blue
6	Orange	Green
7	White/brown	White/brown
8	Brown	Brown

ther than copper cabling: up to 2000 meters (compared with 100 meters for 10BaseT or 100BaseT). Third, fiber-optic cabling and hardware has become quite affordable in recent years. Last, fiber-optic technology is only slightly more difficult to work with than standard Ethernet, and in some cases it's even easier.

Most fiber Ethernet networks use *62.5/125 multimode* fiber-optic cable. All fiber Ethernet networks that use these cables require two cables. Figure 13.10 shows three of the more common connectors used in fiber-optic networks. Square *SC* connectors are shown in the middle and on the right, and the round *ST* connector is on the left.

Like many other fiber-optic connectors, the SC and ST connectors are half-duplex, meaning data flows only one way—hence the need for two cables in a fiber installation. Other half-duplex connectors you might run into are FC/PC, SMA, D4, MU, and LC. They look similar to SC and ST connectors but offer variations in size and connection. Newer and higher end fiber installations use full-duplex connectors, such as the MT-RJ connectors.

The two most common fiber-optic standards are called *10BaseFL* and *100BaseFX*. As you can guess by the names, the biggest difference is the speed of the network (some important differences occur in the way hubs are interconnected, and so on).

Combining and Extending Ethernet

Because the many technologies involved in Ethernet follow the 802.3 standards, you can get hardware to combine different networks, thus increasing compatibility and range. Many 10BaseT hubs, for example, have a ThinNet BNC connector so that you can hook a small 10Base2 network into a star bus network. That saves you from having to add new NICs and run new cabling for the older network.

FIGURE 13.10 Typical fiber-optic cables with connectors

Combo Cards Because 10BaseT uses the same language as 10Base2 or 10Base5, you can find Ethernet combo network cards that support two or even three different types of connections. Further, most current 100BaseT NICs are actually 10/100 NICs, able to adjust automatically either to 10 Mbps or 100 Mbps speeds, depending on the rest of the network hardware. The same is true for Gigabit cards.

Repeaters Ethernet networks have limited lengths, as noted earlier, but various devices enable you to break that limitation. A *repeater* is an electronic device that amplifies the signal on a line, thus enabling you to extend the useful length of a network segment. Networks use two different types of repeaters.

The first type is a dedicated box that takes input from one segment, amplifies it, and then passes it to another segment. Figure 13.11 shows a photo of a common repeater for 10Base2.

The 10ˣBaseT hub, also a repeater, can enable a maximum separation of 200 meters between PCs on a 10ˣBaseT network.

Hubs and Switches In a 10ˣBaseT network, each PC connects to a 10ˣBaseT hub or switch. These devices have multiple connections called *ports,* one per connected device. To add a device to the network, you simply plug another cable into the hub or switch, shown in Figure 13.12.

The primary functional difference between a hub and a switch is that a switch ends collisions on an Ethernet network, which means that each PC gets to use the full bandwidth available. Bottom line? Swap out your old hubs for newer switches and you'll dramatically improve your network performance.

Networks running 10ˣBaseT use the star bus topology. The hub or switch holds the actual bus and allows access to the bus through the ports. Using a star bus topology creates a robust network: the failure of a single node will not bring down the entire network.

FIGURE 13.11 Ethernet repeater

FIGURE 13.12 Typical switch with several cables connected

The maximum distance from the hub or switch to any device is 100 meters. No more than one PC can be hooked to each segment, and the maximum number of PCs that can be hooked to any one hub or switch is 1024. You'll be hard pressed, though, to find a hub or switch with that many connectors. Most hubs and switches come with 4, 8, 16, 32, or 64 ports. 10BaseT hubs and switches act as repeaters, amplifying the signals between devices hooked into the network. They need power to provide this amplification, so make sure the hubs and switches are plugged in to a good power source.

Although just about every 10ˣBaseT network worth its salt uses a switch of sorts to connect the PCs, in a desperate pinch you can hook two 10ˣBaseT network cards together without a hub. Just connect the two PCs together with a *crossover cable*! Crossover cables work great as a quick way to network two PCs. You can make a crossover cable by making one end TIA/EIA 586A and the other TIA/EIA 568B.

Local Lingo

Patch cable A specific length (usually short, but can be up to 100 feet) of cable terminated at each end with a plug or socket. Also called a patch cord.

To expand a network, technically called *scaling*, you simply add more hubs or switches. Hubs and switches are connected together by a normal patch cable

through an integrated port called an *uplink port*, which performs the same action as a crossover cable.

Token Ring

Token Ring is a confusing term. The problem is that Token Ring refers to two related, but different, things. First, *Token Ring* is a topology. Second, Token Ring is a set of network standards developed by IBM that define a complete network system. Token Ring is completely incompatible with Ethernet and is considered a competitor to Ethernet.

Token Ring runs at either 4, 16, or 100 Mbps, depending on the type of Token Ring network cards you buy. Token Ring was originally based around the IBM Type 1 cable. *Type 1 cable* is a two-pair, *shielded twisted pair (STP)* cable designed to handle speeds up to 20 Mbps. Today, Token Ring can use either STP or UTP.

STP Types

STP cables also have certain categories, called *types,* and are defined by IBM. The most common types are shown in Table 13.3.

Local Lingo

Plenum grade cabling Normal network cabling used for patching network equipment uses a PVC coating—or *cladding*—that gives off toxic fumes when burned. Plenum grade cabling has special cladding that doesn't give off toxic fumes when burned. Plenum grade cabling is usually required by law when stringing cable through ceilings or behind walls. These areas are known as the *plenum space.*

TABLE 13.3 STP Cable Categories

STP Type	Description
Type 1	Standard STP with two pairs—the most common STP cable
Type 2	Standard STP plus two pairs of voice wires
Type 3	Standard STP with four pairs
Type 6	Patch cable—used for connecting hubs
Type 8	Flat STP for under carpets
Type 9	STP with two pairs—Plenum grade

Token Ring Connectors

The Type 1 Token Ring connectors are not RJ-45. Instead, IBM designed a unique *hermaphroditic* connector, called either an IBM-type Data Connector (IDC) or a Universal Data Connector (UDC). These connectors are neither male nor female: they are designed to plug into each other, as shown in Figure 13.13.

Token Ring network cards use a 9-pin female connector. A standard Token Ring cable has a hermaphroditic connector on one end and a 9-pin connector on the other. Token Ring can also be used with CAT 3, 4, 5, 5e, and 6 UTP, or fiber-optic cable. When combined with UTP, Token Ring uses an RJ-45 connector, so from a cabling standpoint, Token Ring UTP and Ethernet UTP look the same. Many Token Ring network cards are combo cards. This means they come with both a 9-pin connection for STP and an RJ-45 connection for UTP.

As discussed earlier, Token Ring uses a star ring topology, so it also uses a hub. A Token Ring hub is *not* interchangeable with an Ethernet hub. IBM has a special name for its hubs. They are called either MAUs or MSAUs. Unfortunately, they are also sometimes just called hubs (usually by Ethernet people who don't know any better).

- Token Ring can support up to 260 PCs using STP and up to 72 PCs using UTP.
- Using UTP, the maximum distance from any MAU to a PC is 45 meters.
- Using STP, the maximum distance from any MAU to a PC is 100 meters.

Token Ring also uses repeaters that can be placed only between MAUs. With a repeater, the functional distance between two MAUs increases to 360 meters (with UTP) and 720 meters (with STP).

FIGURE 13.13 Hermaphroditic IDC/UDC connector

Networking with FireWire and USB

You can connect two computers together using FireWire or USB cables. This creates a compact network but enables you to share between two computers. Apple designed FireWire to be network aware, so the two machines will simply recognize each other and, assuming they're configured to share files and folders, you're up and running.

USB networks require a bit more effort. The most common way is to plug a USB NIC into each PC and then run a UTP crossover cable between the Ethernet ports. You can buy a special USB crossover cable to connect the two machines. Finally, at least one company makes a product that enables you to connect with a normal USB cable, called USB Duet.

Travel Advisory

It would be unfair not to give at least a token nod to the possibility of making direct cable connections using the parallel or serial ports on a pair of PCs. All versions of Windows have complete support for allowing two, and no more than two, systems to network together using either parallel or serial cables. You need crossover versions of IEEE 1284 cables for parallel and RS-232 cables for serial. Given the incredibly slow speeds of parallel and especially serial cable transmission compared to those of Ethernet and Token Ring, direct cable connections should never be used unless there is no other viable alternative.

CHECKPOINT

✔**Objective 13.01: Networking Components for the PC** Network interface cards (NICs) send data on to the network cabling as discrete chunks called data packets, or frames. Every NIC has a unique 48-bit MAC address. PCs also need a client service and a common protocol. Popular protocols include NetBEUI, IPX/SPX, and TCP/IP.

✔**Objective 13.02: Network Topologies** Bus topology refers to a network in which all computers are physically connected by a single length of cable. Each end of the cable must be terminated. Ring topology also refers to a

network in which a single length of cable connects all computers, except the ends are joined, thus making, appropriately, a ring.

✓ **Objective 13.03: Network Cabling Standards** ThickNet (10Base5) supports up to 100 devices attached to a segment of no more than 500 meters. ThinNet (10Base2) uses RG-58 coaxial cables and supports 30 devices attached to a segment of no more than 185 meters. Ethernet (10ˣBaseT) uses UTP cabling (usually CAT 5, 5e, or 6) with RJ-45 connectors. Ethernet hubs and repeaters enable a maximum separation between PCs of 200 meters. Token Ring refers to both the standard star ring topology and the network standards. Token Ring networks use STP, UTP, or fiber-optic cabling and move data at 4, 16, or 100 Mbps.

REVIEW QUESTIONS

1. To provide a computer a physical and electronic connection to a network, what must be installed?

 A. A hub

 B. A router

 C. A NIC

 D. A bridge

2. What is the maximum distance for a 10BaseT segment?

 A. 1000 meters

 B. 330 meters

 C. 185 meters

 D. 100 meters

3. Which of the following is needed to configure a Plug and Play NIC in a Windows 2000 system?

 A. CMOS

 B. Device driver

 C. Configuration software

 D. DMA

4. José wants to extend his 10Base2 network beyond its maximum segment distance. Which of the following does he need?

 A. Converter

 B. Expander

 C. Repeater

 D. Extender

5. Everything worked fine on your 10BaseT star bus topology network yesterday, but today, no one can connect to the server. The server seems to be in good running order. Which of the following is the most likely problem?

 A. A hub is malfunctioning.

 B. Someone changed all the passwords for server access.

 C. Someone's T connector has come loose on the bus.

 D. The server's cable is wired as TIA/EIA 568A, and all the others are wired as TIA/EIA 568B.

6. What is the minimum specification of cable types for 100BaseT networks?

 A. Category 2

 B. Category 3

 C. Category 4

 D. Category 5

7. How far apart can two PCs that share the same 10BaseT hub be placed?

 A. 1000 meters

 B. 330 meters

 C. 200 meters

 D. 100 meters

8. Which component(s) prevent reflection on a bus topology network?

 A. Terminator

 B. Crossover cable

 C. Uplink port

 D. Multiple station access unit

9. What is special about plenum grade network cabling?

 A. Plenum grade cabling doubles bandwidth throughput speed.

 B. Plenum grade cabling increases the maximum length of Ethernet network segments from 100 meters to 185 meters.

 C. Plenum grade cabling does not give off toxic fumes when burned.

 D. Plenum grade cabling has no special qualities: it is simply a marketing term.

10. What must be used to set IRQs on legacy ISA network interface cards with no jumpers?

 A. COMS

 B. Device Manager

 C. Configuration software

 D. DIP switches

REVIEW ANSWERS

1. **C** A system must have a network interface card (NIC) to participate in any type of network.

2. **D** 10BaseT has a maximum distance of 100 meters.

3. **B** A Plug and Play device requires only the proper device driver.

4. **C** José needs a repeater.

5. **A** Although someone might have changed all the passwords or the cables during the night, a bad hub is the most probable answer.

6. **D** 100BaseT requires CAT 5 or better rated cabling.

7. **C** As each system can be 100 meters from the hub, any two systems can be up to 200 meters apart.

8. **A** A terminator is a resistor that absorbs voltage from the bus topology cable to prevent reflection.

9. **C** Unlike normal network cabling, plenum grade cabling doesn't give off toxic fumes when burned. It is usually required by law when stringing cable into a building's plenum space.

10. **C** Although some cards still use jumpers, most NICs use software-based resource settings.

Networks: Wireless Networking

CHAPTER 14

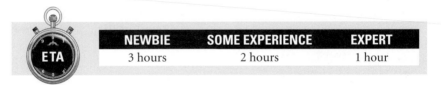

	NEWBIE	SOME EXPERIENCE	EXPERT
ETA	3 hours	2 hours	1 hour

Some of the biggest hurdles to setting up a wired network are the wires. Most businesses frown on having CAT 6 cabling running down every hall and along every wall, so wiring a building for networking means installing cabling up into ceiling crawlspaces and down behind walls and paneling. Any tech who's had to do this more than a few times can tell you that "pulling cable" is an unpleasant chore even under the best conditions. In many cases, installing network cabling is impractical, and in some cases it may even be prohibited, such as in a building that's designated as historical. Thankfully, developments in wireless technology give you a number of alternatives to traditional wired networks.

Objective 14.01 Wireless Networking Basics

A wireless network eliminates the need for the network cabling that connects the PCs to each other in a typical wired network. Instead of a physical set of wires running between networked PCs, servers, printers, or other *nodes,* wireless networks use either radio waves or beams of infrared light to communicate with each other.

Various kinds of wireless networking solutions have come and gone. The types of wireless radio wave networks you'll be supporting these days are those based on the most common implementation of the IEEE 802.11 wireless Ethernet standard—*Wireless Fidelity (Wi-Fi)*—and those based on the *Bluetooth* technology. Wireless networks using infrared light are limited to those that use the *Infrared Data Association* (IrDA) protocol. Finally, the cell phone companies have gotten into the mix and offer access to the Internet through cellular networks.

Wireless devices use the same networking protocols and client that their wired counterparts use, but the basic networking scheme differs. You'll recall from Chapter 13 that Ethernet bus devices use *carrier sense media access/collision detection (CSMA/CD)* to communicate on the same network media without stepping on each other's data packets. Wireless devices use a variation called *carrier sense media access/collision avoidance (CSMA/CA)*.

If two networked systems in a CSMA/CD network attempt to transmit data at the same time, the two packets collide, thereby canceling each other out. This collision is detected by each network node, which responds by generating a random timeout period. When the timeout period expires, the nodes then retransmit the data packet, counting on the randomness of their respective timeouts to prevent another collision. It's not very elegant, but it gets the job done.

Wireless devices use the CSMA/CA networking scheme, so that instead of dealing with collisions after they occur, they proactively take steps to avoid collisions in the first place. Wireless nodes listen in on the wireless medium to see if another node is currently broadcasting data. If so, it waits a random amount of time before retrying.

Wireless Ethernet offers the option of using the *Request to Send/Clear to Send (RTS/CTS)* protocol. When enabled, a transmitting node that determines that the wireless medium is clear to use sends an RTS frame to the receiving node. The receiving node responds with a CTS frame, telling the sending node that it's okay to transmit. Then, once the data is sent, the transmitting node waits for an acknowledgment (ACK) from the receiving node before sending the next data packet. It's very elegant, but keep in mind that using RTS/CTS introduces significant overhead to the process and can impede performance.

Let's look now at the components you need for a wireless network.

Wireless Networking Components

Wireless networking capabilities of one form or another are built into many modern computing devices. Infrared *transceiver* ports have been standard issue on portable computers, PDAs, and high-end printers for years, although they're curiously absent from many of the latest Tablet PCs. Figure 14.1 shows the infrared transceiver ports on a laptop computer and a PDA.

Wireless Ethernet and Bluetooth capabilities are increasingly popular as integrated components, or they can easily be added using USB, PCI, PCI Express, or PC Card adapters. Figure 14.2 shows a PCI card that accepts a wireless PC Card Ethernet card.

FIGURE 14.1 Infrared transceiver ports on a laptop and PDA

FIGURE 14.2 Wireless PC Card NIC inserted into PCI add-on card

You can also add wireless network capabilities using external USB wireless NIC, as shown in Figure 14.3.

Wireless NICs aren't limited to PCs. Many handheld computers and PDAs have wireless built in or available as add-on options. Figure 14.4 shows a PDA accessing the Internet through a wireless NIC.

To extend the capabilities of a wireless Ethernet network, such as by connecting to a wired network or sharing a high-speed Internet connection, you need a

FIGURE 14.3 External USB wireless NIC

FIGURE 14.4 PDA with wireless capability

wireless access point (WAP). A WAP centrally connects wireless network nodes in the same way that a network switch connects wired PCs. Many WAPs also act as high-speed switches and Internet routers, such as the Linksys device shown in Figure 14.5.

FIGURE 14.5 Linksys device that acts as wireless access point, switch, and DSL router

Wireless Networking Software

In terms of configuring wireless networking software, there's very little that you need to do. Wireless network adapters are Plug and Play, so any modern version of Windows will immediately recognize one when installed into a PCI, PCIe, or PC Card slot, or a USB port, prompting you to load any needed hardware drivers.

You will, however, need a utility to set your network name. Windows XP has built-in tools for configuring these settings, but for previous versions of Windows, you need to rely on configuration tools provided by the wireless network adapter vendor. Figure 14.6 shows a typical wireless network adapter configuration utility.

Using this utility, you can determine your link state and signal strength, configure your wireless networking *mode* (discussed in the next section), set security encryption and power saving options, and perform other networking tasks.

Wireless Network Modes

The simplest wireless network consists of two or more PCs communicating directly with each other *sans* cabling or any other intermediary hardware. More complicated wireless networks use a WAP to centralize wireless communication and bridge wireless network segments to wired network segments. These two different methods, or *modes,* are called *ad hoc* mode and *infrastructure* mode.

FIGURE 14.6 Wireless configuration utility

Ad Hoc Mode

In ad hoc mode, sometimes called peer-to-peer mode, each wireless node is in direct contact with every other node in a decentralized free-for-all, as shown in Figure 14.7. Two or more wireless nodes communicating in ad hoc mode form what's called an *Independent Basic Service Set (IBSS)*.

Ad hoc mode networks are easier to configure than infrastructure mode networks and are suited for small groups of computers (less than a dozen or so) that need to transfer files or share printers. Ad hoc networks are also good for temporary networks such as study groups or business meetings.

Infrastructure Mode

Wireless networks running in infrastructure mode use one or more WAPs to connect the wireless network nodes to a wired network segment, as shown in Figure 14.8. If you plan on setting up a wireless network for a large number of PCs or need to have centralized control over the wireless network, you need to use infrastructure mode.

A single WAP servicing a given area is called a *Basic Service Set (BSS)*. This service area can be extended by adding more WAPs. This is called, appropriately, an *Extended Basic Service Set (EBSS)*.

Wireless networks running in infrastructure mode require more planning and are more complicated to configure than ad hoc mode networks, but they also give you finer control over how the network operates. Infrastructure mode

FIGURE 14.7 Wireless ad hoc mode network

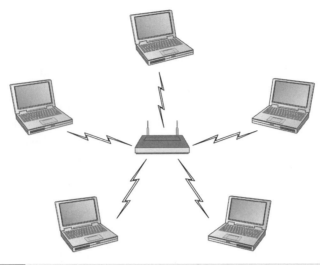

FIGURE 14.8 Wireless infrastructure mode network

is better suited to business networks or networks that need to share dedicated resources such as Internet connections and centralized databases.

Wireless Networking Security

One of the major complaints about wireless networking is that it offers weak security. In many cases, the only thing you need to do to access a wireless network is walk into a WAP's coverage area and turn on your wireless device! Further, data packets float through the air instead of traveling safely wrapped up inside network cabling. What's to stop an unscrupulous PC tech with the right equipment from grabbing those packets out of the air and reading that data?

Wireless networks use three methods to secure access to the network itself and secure the data that's being transferred. The *Service Set Identifier (SSID)* parameter—also called the *network name*—ensures that only wireless network devices configured with the same SSID are permitted access to a particular network. You can tighten security even further by employing *MAC filtering* to create a list of the machines that are permitted to access a network. Enabling wireless encryption through either *Wireless Equivalency Privacy (WEP)*, *Wi-Fi Protected Access (WPA)*, or *WPA2* ensures that the data packets themselves are secure while in transit.

SSID

One of the main security weaknesses with wireless networks is that out of the box, *no* security is configured at all! Wireless devices *want* to be heard, and

WAPs are usually configured to broadcast their presence to their maximum range, welcoming all other wireless devices that respond.

Configuring a unique SSID name is the least that you should to do secure a wireless network. The default SSID names are well-known and widely available online. This is intended to make setting up a wireless network as easy as possible, but conversely it creates a security hole you could drive a bullet train through.

Each node and WAP in a wireless network must be configured with the same unique SSID name. This SSID name is then included in the header of every data packet broadcast in the wireless network's coverage area. Data packets that lack the correct SSID name in the header are rejected.

> **Travel Advisory**
>
> Most WAPs broadcast their SSIDs by default, creating a security breach. Detecting the SSID of a wireless network is a hacker's first step toward using that network without permission. You need additional security to make a wireless network secure.

MAC Filtering

Most WAPs also support MAC address filtering, a method that enables you to limit access to your wireless network using the physical, hard-wired address of the units' wireless network adapters. MAC filtering is a handy way of creating a type of "accepted users" list to limit access to your wireless network. A table stored in the WAP lists the MAC addresses that are permitted to participate in that wireless network. Any data packets that don't contain the MAC address of a node listed in the table are rejected.

WEP

The next step up in wireless security is enabling WEP encryption. Enabling WEP encryption ensures that data is secured while in transit over the airwaves. WEP encryption uses a standard 40-bit encryption to scramble data packets. Many vendors also support 104-bit encryption.

One important consideration is that WEP doesn't provide complete end-to-end encryption, because WEP encryption is stripped from the data packets at the lowest networking levels. For true end-to-end encryption, you need to upgrade to WPA.

WPA

WPA is designed to address the weaknesses of WEP, and it functions as a sort of security protocol upgrade to WEP-enabled devices. WPA offers security enhancements such as an encryption key integrity-checking feature and user

authentication through the industry-standard *Extensible Authentication Protocol (EAP)*. The use of EAP is a huge security improvement over WEP. User names and passwords are encrypted and therefore much more secure. WPA also provides true end-to-end data packet encryption.

Even with these enhancements, WPA is intended only as an interim security solution until the IEEE 802.11i security standard is finalized and implemented.

WPA2

Recent versions of Mac OS X and Microsoft Windows XP Professional support the full IEEE 802.11i standard, WPA2, to lock down wireless networks. WPA2 uses the *Advanced Encryption Standard (AES)*, among other improvements, to provide a secure wireless environment. If you haven't upgraded to WPA2, you should.

Wireless Networking Speed

Wireless networking data throughput speeds depend on several factors. Foremost is the standard used by the networked wireless devices. Depending on the standard used, wireless throughput speeds range from a measly 2 Mbps to a respectable 54 Mbps.

Another factor affecting speed is the distance between wireless nodes (or between wireless nodes and centralized WAPs). Wireless devices dynamically negotiate the top speed at which they can communicate without dropping too many data packets. Speed decreases as distance increases, so the maximum throughput speed is achieved only at extremely close range (less than about 25 feet). At the outer reaches of a device's effective range, speed may d—ecrease to around 1 Mbps before it drops out altogether.

Finally, throughput speed can be affected by interference from other wireless devices operating in the same frequency range, such as cordless phones and baby monitors, as well as by solid objects. So-called *dead spots* occur when something capable of blocking the radio signal comes between wireless network nodes. Large electrical appliances such as refrigerators are *very* effective at blocking wireless network signals. Other culprits include electrical fuse boxes, metal plumbing, and air conditioning units.

Wireless Networking Range

Wireless networking range is hard to define, and you'll see most descriptions listed with qualifiers such as "*around* 150 feet" or "*about* 300 feet." This is simply because, like throughput speed, range is greatly affected by outside factors. Interference from other wireless devices affects range, as does interference from solid objects. The maximum ranges listed in the next section are those presented

by wireless manufacturers as the theoretical maximum ranges. In the real world, you'll see these ranges only under the most ideal circumstances. True effective range is probably about half what you see listed.

Range can be increased in a couple of ways. First, you can install multiple WAPs, to permit "roaming" between one WAP's coverage area and another's—this is the EBSS described earlier in this chapter. Second, you can install a signal booster that increases a single WAP's signal strength, thus increasing its range.

Objective 14.02 Wireless Networking Standards

To help you gain a better understanding of wireless network technology, here is a brief look at the standards that they use. First we'll look at 802.11-based wireless networking and then talk about infrared and Bluetooth.

IEEE 802.11–Based Wireless Networking

The IEEE 802.11 wireless Ethernet standard defines methods by which devices may communicate using spread-spectrum radio waves. *Spread-spectrum* broadcasts data in small, discrete chunks over the different frequencies available within a certain frequency range. All of the 802.11-based wireless technologies broadcast and receive at 2.4 GHz (with the exception of 802.11a, which uses 5 GHz).

Travel Advisory

The 802.11 standard defines two different spread-spectrum broadcasting methods: *direct-sequence* spread-spectrum (DSSS) and *frequency-hopping* spread-spectrum (FHSS). DSSS sends data out on different frequencies simultaneously, while FHSS sends data on one frequency at a time, constantly shifting (or *hopping*) frequencies. DSSS uses considerably more bandwidth than FHSS—around 22 MHz versus 1 MHz, respectively. DSSS is capable of greater data throughput, but it is also more prone to interference than FHSS. HomeRF wireless networks are the only types that use FHSS; all other 802.11-based wireless networking standards use DSSS.

The original 802.11 standard has been extended to the 802.11*a*, 802.11*b*, and 802.11*g* variations used in Wi-Fi wireless networks, and also *hybridized* (combined with another wireless communication technology) to form the *Shared Wireless Access Protocol (SWAP)* used in the short-lived HomeRF networks.

Wi-Fi Wireless Networking Standards

Currently, Wi-Fi is by far the most widely-adopted type of wireless networking. Not only do thousands of private businesses and homes have wireless networks, but many public places such as coffee shops and libraries also offer Internet access through wireless networks.

Technically, only wireless devices that conform to the extended versions of the 802.11 standard—802.11a, 802.11b, and 802.11g—are Wi-Fi certified. Wi-Fi certification comes from the Wi-Fi Alliance (formerly the Wireless Ethernet Compatibility Alliance, or WECA), a nonprofit industry group comprising more than 175 member companies who design and manufacturer wireless networking products. Wi-Fi certification ensures compatibility between wireless networking devices made by different vendors. First-generation devices that use the older 802.11 standard are not Wi-Fi certified, and so may or may not work well with devices made by different vendors.

Wireless devices can communicate only with other wireless devices that use the same standard. The exception to this is 802.11g, which is backward-compatible with 802.11b (although at the slower speed of 802.11b). The following paragraphs describe the important specifications of each of the popular 802.11-based wireless networking standards.

> ### Travel Advisory
>
> Devices that use the original 802.11 (with no letter) standard are rare these days. You're likeliest to find them in service on some brave early wireless adopter's network. The original 802.11 standard was hampered by both slow speeds (2 Mbps maximum) and limited range (about 150 feet). 802.11 employed some of the same features in use in the current wireless standards. 802.11 uses the 2.4 GHz broadcast range, and security is provided by the use of industry-standard WEP and WPA encryption.

802.11a Despite the "a" designation of this extension to the 802.11 standard, 802.11a was actually developed *after* 802.11b. 802.11a differs from the other 802.11-based standards in significant ways. Foremost is that it operates in a different frequency range, 5 GHz. This less-popular frequency range means that 802.11a devices are less prone to interference from other devices. 802.11a also offers considerably greater throughput than 802.11 and 802.11b, reaching speeds up to 54 Mbps. Range, however, suffers somewhat, topping out at about 150 feet. Despite the superior speed of 802.11a, it isn't widely adopted in the PC world.

802.11b Currently the reigning king of wireless networking standards, 802.11b is practically ubiquitous. The 802.11b standard supports data throughput of up

to 11 Mbps—on par with older wired 10BaseT networks—and offers a range of up to 300 feet under ideal conditions. 802.11b networks can be secured though the use of WEP and WPA encryption. The main downside to using 802.11b is, in fact, that it's so popular. The 2.4 GHz frequency is already a crowded place, so you're likely to run into interference from other wireless devices.

802.11g The latest and greatest version, 802.11g, offers data transfer speeds of up to 54 Mbps, equivalent to the 802.11a standard, and the wider 300-foot range of 802.11b. More important, 802.11g is backward-compatible with 802.11b, meaning that an 802.11g WAP can service both 802.11b and 802.11b wireless nodes.

Table 14.1 compares the important differences between the versions of the 802.11 standard.

TABLE 14.1 Comparison of 802.11 Standards

Standard	802.11a	802.11b	802.11g
Max. Throughput	54 Mbps	11 Mbps	54 Mbps
Max. Range	150 feet	300 feet	300 feet
Frequency	5 GHz	2.4 GHz	2.4 GHz
Security	SSID, MAC filtering, industry-standard WEP, WPA	SSID, MAC filtering, industry-standard WEP, WPA	SSID, MAC filtering, industry-standard WEP, WPA
Compatibility	802.11a	802.11b	802.11b; 802.11g
Spread-spectrum method	DSSS	DSSS	DSSS
Communication mode	Ad hoc or infrastructure	Ad hoc or infrastructure	Ad hoc or infrastructure
Description	Products that adhere to this standard are considered Wi-Fi Certified. Eight available channels. Less prone to interference than 802.11b and 802.11g.	Products that adhere to this standard are considered Wi-Fi Certified. Fourteen channels available in 2.4 GHz band (only 11 can be used in the U.S. due to FCC regulations). Three non-overlapping channels.	Products that adhere to this standard are considered Wi-Fi Certified. Improved security enhancements. Fourteen channels available in 2.4 GHz band (only 11 can be used in the U.S. due to FCC regulations). Three non-overlapping channels.

> **Travel Advisory**
>
> Most Wi-Fi devices you can buy right now support WPA2, but what about the millions of older Wi-Fi devices out there working for a living? You can update many devices to support WPA2 with a firmware upgrade or driver update. You'll also need to patch earlier versions of Mac OS X and Windows XP. Windows Vista supports WPA2 out of the box.

Infrared Wireless Networking

Wireless networking using infrared technology is largely overlooked these days, probably due to the explosion of interest in the newer and faster wireless standards. This is a shame, because infrared provides an easy and reasonably fast way to transfer data, often without the need to purchase or install any additional hardware or software on your PC.

Infrared Data Association Standard

Communication through infrared devices is enabled via the *Infrared Data Association (IrDA)* protocol. The IrDA protocol stack is a widely-supported industry standard and has been included in all versions of Windows since Windows 95. Apple computers also support IrDA, as do Linux PCs.

Speed- and range-wise, infrared isn't impressive. Infrared devices are capable of transferring data at speeds ranging from about 115 Kbps up to 4 Mbps. Not too shabby, but hardly stellar. The maximum distance between infrared devices is limited—only 1 meter. Infrared links work on a direct line-of-sight basis and are susceptible to interference. An infrared link can be disrupted by anything that breaks the beam of light—a badly placed can of soda, a co-worker passing between desks, or even bright sunlight hitting the infrared transceiver can cause interference.

Infrared is designed to make a point-to-point connection between two devices in ad hoc mode only. No infrastructure mode is available. You can, however, use an infrared access point device to enable Ethernet network communication using IrDA.

Infrared devices operate at half-duplex, meaning that while one is talking, the other is listening—they can't talk and listen at the same time. IrDA has a mode that emulates full-duplex communication, but it's still just half-duplex.

Security-wise, the IrDA protocol offers exactly nothing in the way of encryption or authentication. Infrared's main security feature is the fact that you have to be literally within arm's reach to establish a link.

Clearly, infrared is not the best solution for a dedicated network connection, but for doing a quick file transfer or print job without getting your hands dirty, it'll do in a pinch. Table 14.2 lists infrared's important specifications.

TABLE 14.2	Infrared Specs
Standard	**Infrared (IrDA)**
Max. throughput	Up to 4 Mbps
Max. range	1 meter (39 inches)
Security	None
Compatibility	IrDA
Communication mode	Point-to-point ad hoc
Description	IrDA is good for short range data transfers between devices.

Bluetooth

When it was first introduced, some confusion existed among PC techs about the uses of Bluetooth technology. Since then, much of the confusion has cleared up. Bluetooth is designed to create small wireless *personal area networks (PANs)* that link PCs to peripheral devices such as PDAs and printers; input devices such as keyboards and mice; and even consumer electronics such as cell phones, home stereos, televisions, and home security systems. Bluetooth is *not* designed to be a full-function networking solution, nor is it meant to compete with Wi-Fi. If anything, Bluetooth is poised to replace infrared as a way to connect PCs to peripherals.

The IEEE organization has made Bluetooth the basis for its forthcoming 802.15 standard for wireless PANs. Bluetooth uses the FHSS spread-spectrum broadcasting method, switching between any of the 79 frequencies available in the 2.45 GHz range. Bluetooth hops frequencies some 1600 times per second, making it highly resistant to interference. Bluetooth transfers data at speeds ranging from 723 Kbps to 1 Mbps, with a maximum range of 10 meters (about 33 feet). Some high-powered Bluetooth devices can reach a whopping 2 Mbps throughput speed with a maximum range of up to 300 feet, but these are uncommon.

Travel Advisory

Bluetooth wireless technology is named for Harald Blåtand (Bluetooth in English), a tenth-century Danish king. Special Interest Group (SIG) representatives used *Bluetooth* as a code name for the budding technology, since the king had been instrumental in uniting warring factions in parts of what are now Norway, Sweden, and Denmark, and the technology promised to allow collaboration among different industries. The name stuck. This information does not appear on the CompTIA A+ certification exams, but it's a pretty common question, so now you can sound knowledgeable when some user asks you.

Cellular

Cellular wireless networks enable you to connect to the Internet through a network-aware personal digital assistant (PDA) or cell phone. Figure 14.9 shows a high-end cell phone with an Internet connection. Using an add-on PC Card, you can connect any laptop to a cellular network as well. Figure 14.10 shows a Sprint cellular network card.

In areas with broad cell phone coverage, such as big cities, cellular wireless networks offer high-speed access (400 to 700 Kbps download speeds) anywhere you go. Just fire up your device or portable and start surfing the Web. In remote areas, the speed drops down to something closer to modem connection speeds.

Cellular networks use various protocols to connect, such as Global System for Mobile Communications (GSM), General Packet Radio Service (GPRS), and Code Division Multiple Access (CDMA). These protocols are handled seamlessly by the software and hardware. What the end user sees is TCP/IP, just as if he or she connected through a wired network.

About the only real downside to cellular wireless networks is the price. The cell phone companies (notably Sprint and Cingular) are quite proud of their network service. As the technology matures, competition among the cellular network providers should bring the price down to something affordable for many people. At this point, though, it's usually much more cost-effective to go to a coffee shop or library and connect via Wi-Fi.

FIGURE 14.9 Sony Ericsson phone

FIGURE 14.10 Cellular network card

 Objective 14.03 # Configuring Wireless Networking

The mechanics of setting up a wireless network don't differ much from those for a wired network. Physically installing a wireless network adapter is the same as installing a wired NIC, whether it's an internal PCI or PCIe card, a PC Card, or an external USB device. Simply install the device and let Plug and Play handle detection and resource allocation. Install the device's supplied driver when prompted, and you're practically done. Unless you're using Windows XP, you also need to install the wireless network configuration utility supplied with your wireless network adapter, so that you can set your communication mode, SSID, and so on.

As mentioned, wireless devices want to talk to each other, so communicating with an available wireless network is usually a no-brainer. The trick is to configure the wireless network so that only specific wireless nodes are able to use it and to secure the data that's being sent through the air.

Wi-Fi

Wi-Fi networks support both ad hoc and infrastructure operation modes. Which mode you choose depends on the number of wireless nodes you need to support, the type of data sharing they'll perform, and your management requirements.

Ad Hoc Mode

As mentioned, ad hoc mode is best used for small offices, home offices, study groups, meetings, or any other type of workgroup environment where you don't need centralized control over the network. Ad hoc wireless networks don't need an access point, so they are also somewhat cheaper to set up than infrastructure mode networks.

The only requirements in an ad hoc mode wireless network are that each wireless node be configured with the same SSID, and that no two nodes use the same IP address. You may also have to select a common channel for all ad hoc nodes and ensure that the File and Printer Sharing service is running. Figure 14.11 shows a wireless network configuration utility with ad hoc mode selected.

Infrastructure Mode

Infrastructure mode is better suited to larger network environments where centralized network control is important. Typically, infrastructure mode wireless networks employ one or more WAPs connected to a wired network segment, a corporate intranet or the Internet, or both.

As with ad hoc mode wireless networks, infrastructure mode networks require that the same SSID be configured on all nodes and access points. Figure 14.12 shows a wireless network access point configuration utility set to infrastructure mode. Depending on the capabilities of your WAP, you may also configure DHCP options, filtering, and so on.

FIGURE 14.11 Selecting ad hoc mode in a wireless configuration utility

FIGURE 14.12 Selecting infrastructure mode in a wireless configuration utility

Access Point SSID Configuration WAPs have an integrated Web server and are configured through a browser-based setup utility. Typically, you fire up your Web browser on one of your network client workstations and enter the WAP's default IP address, such as 192.168.1.1, to bring up the configuration page. You will need to supply an administrative password, included with your WAP's documentation, to log in (see Figure 14.13).

Setup screens vary from vendor to vendor and from model to model. Figure 14.14 shows the initial setup screen for a popular Linksys WAP/router.

FIGURE 14.13 Security login for Linksys WAP

FIGURE 14.14 Linksys WAP setup screen

Configure the SSID option where indicated, and you're in business. Channel selection is usually automatic, but you can reconfigure this option if you have particular needs in your organization (such as if multiple wireless networks are operating in the same area). Remember that it's always more secure to configure a unique SSID than it is to accept the well-known default one.

You should also make sure that the option to allow broadcasting of the SSID is disabled. This ensures that, for the most part, only wireless nodes specifically configured with the correct SSID can join the wireless network. You can find software packages that can sniff out an SSID even through this, so don't make this your only line of security.

MAC Filtering Increase security even more by using MAC filtering. This builds a list of wireless network clients that are permitted access to your wireless network because of their unique MAC address.

Figure 14.15 shows the MAC filtering configuration screen on a Linksys WAP. Simply enter the MAC address of a wireless node that you wish to allow (or deny) access to your wireless network.

Encryption Enabling encryption ensures that data packets are secured against unauthorized access. Set up encryption by turning encryption on at the WAP and then generating a unique security key. Then configure all connected

FIGURE 14.15 MAC filtering configuration screen for a Linksys wireless access point

wireless nodes on the network with the same key information. Figure 14.16 shows the encryption key configuration dialog box for a Linksys WAP.

You have the option of automatically generating a set of encryption keys or doing it manually—save yourself a headache and use the automatic method. Select an encryption level—the usual choices are either 64-bit or 128-bit—and then enter a unique passphrase and click Generate (or whatever the equivalent button is called on your WAP). Then select a default key and save the settings.

The encryption level, key, and passphrase must match on the wireless client node or communication will fail. Many WAPs let you export the encryption key data onto a floppy disk for easy transfer to a client workstation. You can also manually configure encryption using the vendor-supplied configuration utility, as shown in Figure 14.17.

WPA and WPA2 encryption, if supported by your wireless equipment, are configured in much the same way. You may be required to input a valid user name and password to configure encryption using WPA/WPA2.

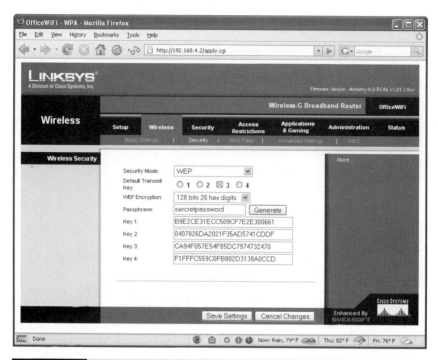

FIGURE 14.16 Encryption key configuration screen on Linksys WAP

FIGURE 14.17 Encryption screen on client wireless network adapter configuration utility

Infrared

IrDA device support is solid in the latest version of Windows—in fact, there's not much for us techs to configure. IrDA links are made between devices dynamically, without user interaction. Typically, there's nothing to configure on an infrared-equipped PC. Check your network settings to ensure that you've got the IrDA protocol installed and enabled, and you should be good to go (see Figure 14.18).

As far as infrared networking goes, your choices are somewhat limited. Infrared is designed to connect only two systems together in ad hoc mode. This can be done simply to transfer files, or with a bit more configuration, you can configure the two PCs to use IrDA in *direct-connection* mode. You can also use a special infrared access point to enable Ethernet LAN access via IrDA.

Transferring Files via Infrared

File transfers via IrDA are as simple as can be. When two IrDA-enabled devices "see" each other, the sending (primary) device negotiates a connection to the receiving (secondary) device, and *voilà*. It's just "point and shoot."

Figure 14.19 shows Windows 2000's Wireless Link applet. Use this to configure file transfer options and the default location for received files.

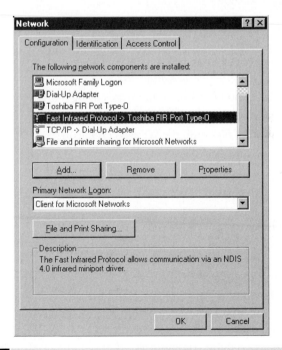

FIGURE 14.18 Confirming the presence of IrDA protocol in Windows Network settings

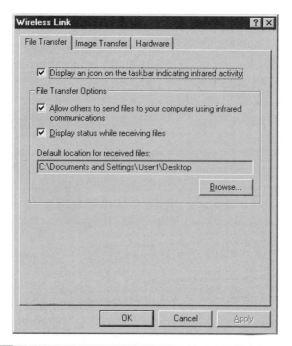

Windows 2000 Wireless Link applet

You can send a file over the infrared connection via any of the following actions:

- Specify a location and one or more files using the Wireless Link dialog box.
- Drag and drop files onto the Wireless Link icon.
- Using Windows Explorer or My Computer, right-click a file (or selection of files), and then select Send To Infrared Recipient.
- Print to a printer configured to use an infrared port.

Networking via Infrared

Direct network connections between two PCs using infrared are similar to using a null-modem cable to connect two PCs together via a serial port. Modern versions of Windows use wizard-driven dialogs to make this type of connection extremely easy. Figure 14.20 shows the Windows 2000 Network Connection wizard. Simply select the *Connect directly to another computer* radio button and follow the prompts, choosing your infrared port as the connection device.

An infrared access point combines an infrared transceiver with an Ethernet NIC and translates the IrDA protocol into an Ethernet signal, enabling you

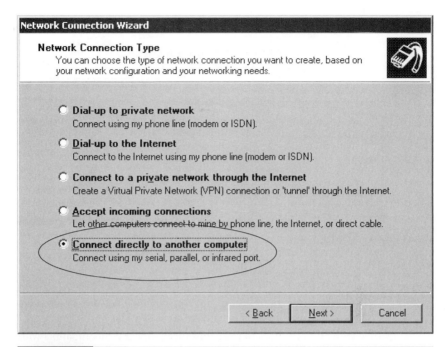

Network Connection Wizard

Network Connection Type
You can choose the type of network connection you want to create, based on your network configuration and your networking needs.

○ **Dial-up to private network**
Connect using my phone line (modem or ISDN).

○ **Dial-up to the Internet**
Connect to the Internet using my phone line (modem or ISDN).

○ **Connect to a private network through the Internet**
Create a Virtual Private Network (VPN) connection or 'tunnel' through the Internet.

○ **Accept incoming connections**
Let other computers connect to mine by phone line, the Internet, or direct cable.

◉ **Connect directly to another computer**
Connect using my serial, parallel, or infrared port.

< <u>B</u>ack <u>N</u>ext > Cancel

FIGURE 14.20 Configuring a direct connection via infrared using the Network Connection wizard

to log on to your network and access resources. Figure 14.21 shows a laptop accessing an Ethernet LAN through an infrared access point.

FIGURE 14.21 Laptop using infrared access point

CHECKPOINT

✔**Objective 14.01: Wireless Networking Basics** Wireless networks operate much like their wired counterparts, except they eliminate the network cabling by using either radio waves or infrared light as a network medium. Wireless NICs usually require configuration software supplied by the manufacturer. Windows XP systems have wireless NIC configuration software built in. Wireless networks operate in ad hoc (decentralized) or infrastructure (centralized) fashion. Security is enabled using SSID identification, MAC filtering, and WEP, WPA, or WPA2 encryption. Speeds range from 2 Mbps to 54 Mbps.

✔**Objective 14.02: Wireless Networking Standards** Wireless networks are based around three standards: IEEE 802.11x, Infrared Data Association (IrDA), and Bluetooth. Of these, 802.11b (11 Mbps throughput) is the most popular. 802.11g (54 Mbps throughput) is becoming more popular and is backward-compatible with 802.11b. 802.11a (54 Mbps throughput) is incompatible with any of the other standards. Infrared is line-of-sight only and tops out at 4 Mbps. Bluetooth is not a true networking standard, due to its limited range (30 feet) and slow speed (1 Mbps). Bluetooth enables you to connect wirelessly a PC to its peripheral devices and synchronize the PC with wireless PDAs.

✔**Objective 14.03: Configuring Wireless Networking** Ad hoc mode is the simplest way to network wireless computers but offers no fine control over shared resources. Infrastructure mode requires more planning and wireless access point (WAP) hardware. Wireless access points are configured using built-in browser-based utilities.

REVIEW QUESTIONS

1. Which wireless networking technology uses the 5 GHz frequency range?

 A. 802.11

 B. 802.11a

 C. 802.11b

 D. 802.11g

2. The 802.11b wireless specification enables what maximum throughput speed?

 A. 2 Mbps

 B. 11 Mbps

 C. 54 Mbps

 D. 4 Mbps

3. The 802.11g wireless specification enables what maximum throughput speed?

 A. 2 Mbps

 B. 11 Mbps

 C. 54 Mbps

 D. 4 Mbps

4. What is the maximum range of current Bluetooth devices?

 A. 1 meter

 B. 3 feet

 C. 10 meters

 D. 300 feet

5. What function does CSMA/CA provide that CSMA/CD does not?

 A. Data packet collision detection

 B. End-to-end data packet encryption

 C. Data packet collision avoidance

 D. Data packet error checking

6. Why should you configure a unique SSID for your wireless network and then not broadcast it?

 A. A unique, non-broadcast SSID enables backward-compatibility between 802.11g and 802.11b.

 B. A unique, non-broadcast SSID boosts wireless network range.

 C. A unique, non-broadcast SSID boosts wireless network data throughput.

 D. A unique, non-broadcast SSID prevents access by any network device that does not have the same SSID configured.

7. What is the maximum speed of IrDA?

 A. 115 Kbps

 B. 2 Mbps

 C. 4 Mbps

 D. 11 Mbps

8. Which of the following advantages does WPA have over WEP? (Select three.)

 A. End-to-end data packet encryption

 B. EAP user authentication

C. Encryption key integrity checking

D. 128-bit data encryption

9. What hardware do you need to enable wireless PCs to connect to resources on a wired network segment in infrastructure mode?

A. A wireless access point

B. A wireless router

C. A wireless hub

D. A wireless bridge

10. What do you call a wireless Ethernet network in infrastructure mode with more than one access point?

A. BSS

B. EBSS

C. PAN

D. PICONET

REVIEW ANSWERS

1. **B** 802.11a operates in the 5 GHz frequency range.

2. **B** The 802.11b wireless networks run at a maximum of 11 Mbps.

3. **C** The 802.11g wireless networks run at a maximum of 54 Mbps.

4. **C** Current Bluetooth devices have a maximum range of 10 meters (~30 feet).

5. **C** CSMA/CA uses the RTS/CTS protocol to provide data packet collision avoidance.

6. **D** A unique, non-broadcast SSID prevents wireless devices that do not have the same SSID from accessing the network.

7. **C** 4 Mbps is the maximum data throughput speed of IrDA.

8. **A B C** WPA upgrades WEP to provide end-to-end data packet encryption, user authentication via EAP, and encryption key integrity checking.

9. **A** A wireless access point enables you to connect wireless PCs to a wired network segment.

10. **B** A wireless network with more than one access point is called EBSS, Extended Basic Service Set.

Operating System Fundamentals

	NEWBIE	SOME EXPERIENCE	EXPERT
ETA	3 hours	2 hours	1 hour

An operating system (OS) brings a PC to life and makes it a useful, even essential, tool for everyone from an actuary to a zoologist. Without an OS, even the most high-end computer is reduced to being nothing more than a slick-looking cup holder.

This chapter examines the general functions of an OS and looks at how an OS manifests. You'll learn how to identify the characteristics of Windows and understand the features and functions common to all available versions of the OS.

Objective 15.01 Characteristics of the Operating System

All OSs share certain common characteristics. First of all, all operating systems have some degree of CPU specificity. Second, all OSs must have their own specifically written applications. Third, all OSs take control of the PC after the POST and keep that control until you shut down the system.

CPU-Specific

The OS must understand important aspects of the CPU, such as the amount of memory the CPU can handle, what modes of operation it is capable of performing, and the commands needed to perform any operation. For that reason, an OS works only with a particular type of processor. The Intel and AMD x86 line of CPUs heavily dominates today's PCs, but other platforms have used different CPUs that were completely incompatible with the Intel and AMD lines. The most obvious example of the latter is the Motorola Power PC, the CPU inside older Macintosh computers.

Application Compatibility

Next, just as an OS has to be matched to a particular CPU, application programs have to be written for particular OSs. Manufacturers always provide a "rule book" that tells programmers how to write programs for their particular OS. These rule books are known as *application programming interfaces (APIs)*. Many applications are able to function on more than one OS through *porting*.

Local Lingo

Porting Porting means to rewrite an application to use another operating system's API. Many of today's development platforms such as Microsoft C# make porting easy to do.

PC Control

An OS takes control of the PC immediately following the POST process (described in Chapter 7) and controls all aspects of the PC operation. The OS continues running until you manually reboot or turn off the PC. You cannot exit from the OS unless you also turn off the PC.

Common Operating System Functions

A ll OSs are not created equal, but every OS provides certain functions:

- First, the OS must communicate, or provide a method for other programs to communicate, with the hardware of the PC.
- Second, the OS must create a user interface—a visual representation of the computer on the monitor that makes sense to the people using the computer.
- Third, the OS, via the user interface, must enable users to determine the available installed programs and run, use, and shut down the program of their choice.
- Fourth, the OS should enable users to add, move, and delete the installed programs and data.

Those four tasks—communicate with hardware, provide a user interface, provide a structure for access to applications, and enable users to manipulate programs and data—are common to any OS. Let's take a look at each of these in more detail.

Communicating with Hardware

It's up to the OS to access the hard drives, respond to the keyboard, and output data to the monitor. The OS works with the system BIOS to deal with these devices. If users want to access the hard drive to retrieve a program, the OS takes the request and passes it to the appropriate hard-drive BIOS instruction that tells the drive to send the program to RAM. If for some compelling reason the BIOS lacks the ability to perform its function, the OS should bypass the system BIOS and "talk" to the piece of hardware directly. Most recent OSs, including Windows, skip the system BIOS and talk directly to almost every piece of hardware.

Installing and configuring hardware devices was discussed in Chapter 10, so you should recall that hardware devices need their own programs to enable them to communicate with the OS—*device drivers*. OS makers provide development tools for hardware makers to create driver software for their products.

Creating a User Interface

Unless you happen to speak the binary language of computers fluently to keep up with the millions of calculation cycles per second that the CPU routinely handles, you need some other way to enter commands. The OS creates a way for you to do this through the *user interface (UI)*.

The UI might be a *command prompt* that enables you to use a keyboard to type simple instructions into the system, or it might be a graphical *desktop* with which you interact using a pointer device such as a mouse, trackball, touchpad, joystick, or even using handwriting or voice commands. Whatever the UI's manifestation, they all do the same thing—enable you to control the computer. The "Operating System Interfaces" section (Objective 15.03) of this chapter covers OS implementations in more detail.

Accessing and Supporting Programs

In addition to creating an environment for a user to interact with the PC, the OS creates the environment that enables users to interact with applications. In the old days, computers ran only one program at a time, but modern PCs are *multitasking* machines and must run two, three, ten, or any number of programs or processes concurrently. As with hardware, the OS must also determine the state of running programs and either correct error states or alert the user when a program has stopped responding.

Additionally, the OS enables you to install new programs and remove old ones with relative ease. Properly written programs should integrate with the OS seamlessly. You see problems when badly written or "buggy" programs are installed.

Organizing and Manipulating Programs and Data

For programs and data to be useful, the OS must organize them into a logical structure. Fortunately, all OSs share the same basic organization method. All programs and data are stored as files. A file is a discrete piece of data organized in such a way that when the CPU loads it, the OS knows what to do with it. All files have two-part names: the first part, the *filename*, is the unique identifier (A+_Passport_Ch15), and the second part, the *extension*, defines the type of

data. (.DOC is the universal extension for Microsoft Word files). You combine these to give the complete filename (A+_Passport_Ch15.DOC).

Files are useless if you can't organize them. All OSs use a directory-tree organization. Each storage device has a name and an icon. You can subdivide each storage device into discrete folders or directories that contain related files. Windows creates a number of folders for the OS itself, but you can create others.

Speaking of creating folders, all these files and folders are useless unless you can manipulate them. The OS enables users to create, manipulate, and arrange files on the storage devices. Common functions of this sort include copying, moving, and deleting data.

One of the greatest challenges to OS designers is making all of these functions comprehensible to users. Over the years, OSs have gone through vast changes trying to use the monitor to show you the system in such a way that you could do these manipulations. The "face" of the OS, the way you see the OS on the screen, is the UI, which has evolved from the dark days of the first PCs to the newest and brightest of today's systems.

Objective 15.03 Operating System Interfaces

A ll OS user interfaces for the PC manifest in two ways: through a *command line interface* and through a *graphical user interface (GUI)*. Undoubtedly, the GUI is more familiar to most users, but the command line has by no means become obsolete.

Command Line Interface

Mainframes and minicomputers of old all used the classic command line interface for many years before the advent of the GUI, and it is still used to this day. Although you won't find modern PCs that use a command line interface exclusively, all modern OSs—Windows, Macintosh, and the many flavors of Linux— enable users to "drop down" to a command prompt to enter instructions. In fact, many high-level functions and utilities can be run *only* from a command line environment; therefore, it's not only relevant but important for techs to understand how to talk to the PC from the command line.

Still considered by many to be an elegant OS, Microsoft's *MS-DOS* is the first OS that most old-school PC techs encountered. Many commands used in DOS, such as COPY, DIR, ATTRIB, and others, are still used today. In fact, it's not

uncommon for folks to (incorrectly) refer to the Windows command line interface as a *DOS window*.

Accessing the Command Line Interface

The command line interface program (also called the *command interpreter*) manifests as a simple text *prompt*—so-called because of the blinking text *cursor* character that prompts you for input. Anytime you've booted the PC using a floppy disk or gone into one of the command line modes from the advanced Windows OS boot menu, you've seen the good old C:\> prompt.

You can also access a command line interface from within Windows. You can find the shortcut to the command line interface program in the Accessories folder accessible from the Start menu (Start | All Programs | Accessories | Command Prompt). Most techs, however, simply start it from the Run menu: Start | Run | *cmd*, as shown in Figure 15.1.

Issuing Instructions Using the Command Line

Working with the command line requires you to use commands recognized by the OS and to type those commands correctly. Each OS has different commands. To see the contents of a folder in Windows, for example, you type the **DIR** command. To see the contents of a folder in Linux, in contrast, you type the **ls** command (in lowercase because Linux is case sensitive).

In both cases, you must type the command properly, using what's called the proper *syntax*. To move the file *beethoven.mp3* from the *c:\temp* folder to the *c:\music* folder, for example, you would type the command followed by the target followed by the destination. Then press ENTER. It looks like this:

> move c:\temp\beethoven.mp3 c:\music

If you reverse the target and destination folders or type something incorrectly, the command simply won't work. You might get an error message or you might not.

FIGURE 15.1 Type **cmd** in the Run dialog box to open a command line interface window in Windows XP.

For a complete list of instructions, simply type **help** at the command prompt and press the ENTER key. For details on the various *switches* and *parameters* that apply to a particular command, type **help** followed by a space and the command name (for example, **help attrib**).

For the moment, concentrate on the handful of commands that you're most likely to use. Table 15.1 lists a few important commands that work in all versions of Windows command lines. Older forms of the commands are provided for reference. You might see these on the exams.

Navigating Using a Command Line Interface

The command prompt is always *focused* on a specific folder. This is important because any commands you issue are performed *on the files in the folder* on which the prompt is focused. If you see a prompt that looks like *C:\>*, for example, you know that the focus is on the root directory of the C: drive.

As noted in Table 15.1, you change the command prompt's focus to another folder by typing **cd** followed by the target folder's name. To see which files are contained in a particular folder, use the **dir** command. Figure 15.2 shows the command prompt focused on the *Documents and Settings\scottj\Desktop* folder of the C: drive.

The **cd** command is *not* used to move between drives. To get the prompt to switch its focus to another hard drive, removable drive, or partition, just type the target drive letter followed by a colon. If, for example, the command prompt

TABLE 15.1 Common Command Line Interface Commands

Command	Description
cd	Changes the focus of the command prompt from one folder (directory) to another. The older form of the command is **chdir**.
copy	Copies files from one folder to another.
del	Permanently deletes files. The command **erase** works as well.
dir	Displays a listing of the files and folders (subdirectories) in a directory.
exit	Closes the command line interface program.
md	Creates a new folder. The older form of the command is **mkdir**.
move	Moves files from one folder to another.
rd	Deletes (removes) a folder. The older form of the command is **rmdir**.
ren	Renames files. You can spell it out as well, using **rename** as the command.
tree	Graphically displays the structure of a path.
ver	Displays the version of Windows.

FIGURE 15.2　Command prompt indicating focus on C:\Documents and Settings\scottj\Desktop

is focused at the *C:\Documents and Settings\scottj\Desktop* directory and you want to switch to the floppy drive (drive A:), just type **a:** and press the ENTER key and the command prompt will point to the floppy drive.

> **Travel Advisory**
>
> Windows navigation commands aren't case-sensitive. Typing **c:** or typing **C:** followed by the ENTER key gets you to the root drive.

Running Applications from the Command Line Prompt

Executing applications from the command line environment is done in the same way as running the built-in Windows command line utilities. Simply navigate to the folder containing the application, type the name of the executable file, and press ENTER. Valid executable files have an extension of *.exe* or *.com*, but typically you don't need to enter the file extension, just the filename.

Graphical User Interface

The GUI implementation of an OS is the most familiar interface for most users. Instead of using a character-based interface to run programs and administer files, you see files, folders, and programs represented as tiny graphics called *icons* arranged in a workspace called the *desktop*. You use a mouse or other pointing device to manipulate icons by selecting them with a *pointer*. Figure 15.3 shows the GUI for Windows Vista.

Modern versions of Windows (Windows 2000/XP/Vista) are pure GUI-based OSs. Accessing vital OS functions and programs is, of course, possible through a command line interface in these OSs, but the command line interface is a

 Windows Vista desktop

function of the GUI, and not the GUI itself. The next section looks at the features of Windows that are common to all versions.

Objective 15.04 Common Microsoft Windows Features

All versions of Windows share certain characteristics, configuration files, and that nebulous quality called *look and feel*. You'll find the same or similar utilities in almost all versions, and once you master one interface—both GUI and command line interface—you've pretty much got them all knocked.

Login Screen

The Windows 2000/XP/Vista login offers a high degree of security. In fact, you can't access Windows without logging in with a valid user account. Figure 15.4 shows a Windows 2000 welcome screen.

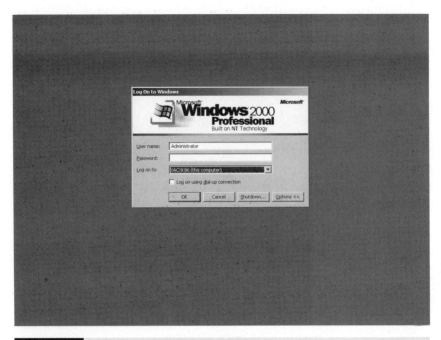

FIGURE 15.4 Windows 2000 welcome screen

Note that you're required to press the CTRL-ALT-DELETE key combination—the infamous *three-fingered salute*—to log into Windows 2000. This is a holdover from Windows NT, designed as a security measure. Windows XP changed the login procedure somewhat in a simple workgroup environment. One version of the Windows XP login screen presents you with a list of user accounts stored on the PC, enabling you to choose one to log in with, as shown in Figure 15.5.

Travel Advisory

Windows XP Professional has two very different login methods. The one shown in Figure 15.5 shows Windows XP configured to log into a workgroup. If you log into a Windows domain, you get a screen almost identical to the one shown for Windows 2000. See Chapter 18 for details on workgroups and domains.

Once you log into the system, you're presented with your user account's desktop, described in the next section.

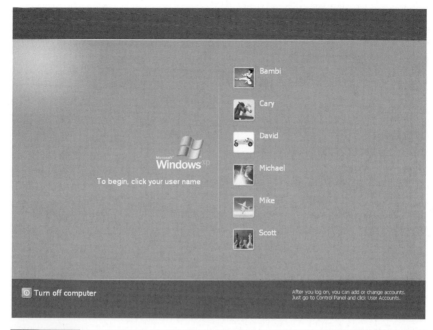

Bambi

Cary

David

Michael

Mike

Scott

To begin, click your user name

Windows XP

Turn off computer

After you log on, you can add or change accounts.
Just go to Control Panel and click User Accounts.

FIGURE 15.5 Windows XP login screen

Desktop

The Windows desktop is your main interface to the OS. The desktop is the workspace where you launch applications, input and manipulate data, configure hardware, and, of course, watch videos and play games. Figure 15.6 shows a typical Windows XP Professional desktop.

The desktop is a highly customizable environment, enabling you to personalize virtually every aspect, including such settings as the background wallpaper and default sound effects, screen resolution and color schemes, and language settings and accessibility options.

Windows systems enable different users to create different desktop environments (usually called *profiles*) that are loaded when a user logs onto the PC. Every Windows desktop, however, still shares a few common features, such as several default folder shortcut icons and the *taskbar*. The paragraphs that follow describe the typical desktop icons you'll find on a Windows PC.

FIGURE 15.6 Windows XP Professional desktop

My Computer

The folder called My Computer enables you to access all drives, folders, and files on the system. Note that Windows XP does not include My Computer on the desktop by default. You can readily access it through the Start menu. To open My Computer, simply double-click the My Computer icon on the desktop, or in XP, choose Start | My Computer. When opened, My Computer shows you all the drives on the system, as shown in Figure 15.7.

The left side provides details of whatever icon you currently have highlighted. Microsoft calls this the Web view. For example, Figure 15.7 has the C: drive highlighted, so the left side provides details about that drive.

Windows assigns different icons to different types of files according to their file type extensions, such as *.EXE* or *.JPG*. As you look at these icons on your own screen, you may notice that you don't see any extensions—that's because current versions of Windows hide them by default.

To reveal the extensions in Windows 2000/XP, choose Tools | Folder Options, and then click the View tab. First, click the *Show hidden files and folders* radio

FIGURE 15.7 My Computer

button; second, uncheck *Hide file extensions for known file types*; and third, uncheck *Hide protected operating system files*. Click the *Apply to All Folders* button. The Windows XP View tab should look like Figure 15.8 when you are done. All file extensions and previously hidden system files (such as BOOT.INI and NTLDR) will be viewable in folders.

In every version of Windows prior to XP, Windows Explorer acted like a separate and distinct tool from My Computer. Windows XP has merged Explorer and My Computer into a single tool, but you can still get the Explorer-like interface by right-clicking a folder and choosing Explore from the pop-up options menu, or by holding down the WINDOWS key on your keyboard and pressing the E key.

My Documents

Windows 2000 provides a special shortcut icon to the logged-on user's My Documents folder on the desktop. Newer Windows programs, such as Microsoft

FIGURE 15.8 Windows XP View tab

Office and Corel Paint Shop Pro, store their user-generated files in My Documents unless you explicitly tell them to use a different folder.

As with My Computer, most Windows XP installations do not show the My Documents folder on the desktop—you can access it readily through the Start menu, or you can add it to your desktop.

Each version of Windows since Windows 98 seems to add more folders like My Documents to cover a whole host of other functions. For example, Windows XP Professional comes with My Documents, My Pictures (that offers filmstrip and thumbnail views of the pictures therein), My Music (that of course is ready to fire up Media Player to play any file), My Videos (again, Media Player), and more.

Recycle Bin

The Recycle Bin shows up on the desktop of all versions of Windows. Windows doesn't completely erase items when you delete them from your drives. Instead, the file, folder, icon, or what-have-you is moved into the Recycle Bin folder. From there, one of three things can occur:

- You manually empty the Recycle Bin.
- You restore the item.

- The Recycle Bin grows larger than a preset amount and the file is permanently deleted to make room for more recently deleted files.

Travel Advisory

Note that these rules only apply when you're dealing with fixed disk drives. Files deleted from removable disks, such as floppy disks or USB thumb drives, don't go to the Recycle Bin when you delete them—once they're deleted, they're gone for good.

Configure Recycle Bin behavior by right-clicking its icon and selecting Properties from the pop-up menu. Figure 15.9 shows the Recycle Bin Properties dialog box.

Travel Advisory

Remember that everything in Windows has a properties setting. You can access these properties by right-clicking and selecting Properties. From here on, when I say "access properties," you know I mean to right-click and then select the word "Properties." You may also access properties by highlighting the object and pressing the ALT-ENTER key combination.

FIGURE 15.9 Recycle Bin Properties dialog box

Important options include these:

- **Configure drives independently** This option enables you to set limits on the amount of disk space reserved for the Recycle Bin for each hard drive or partition. The default setting is to reserve the same percentage of disk space for each drive or partition.
- **Do not move files to the Recycle Bin** This setting effectively disables the Recycle Bin, meaning that any items deleted are unrecoverable. Use this option with caution!
- **Maximum size of Recycle Bin** Displayed in percentage (10% is the default), this is the amount of disk or partition space reserved for deleted items.

Internet Explorer

Most versions of Windows place a shortcut icon to Microsoft's Web browser, Internet Explorer, on the desktop. In keeping with its Spartan look, Windows XP puts an icon for Internet Explorer on the Start menu but not on the desktop.

Taskbar

The *taskbar*, by default, runs along the bottom of all Windows desktops and has up to four sections (depending on the version of Windows and your configuration): the Start button, *Quick Launch*, the *active programs area*, and the *notification area*.

Like the rest of the desktop, the taskbar is fully customizable, enabling you to move it to any edge of your monitor screen (by clicking and dragging it), add and remove icons to the Start button and Quick Launch area, and hide the taskbar altogether when not in use.

Start Menu

The Start button, probably the most clicked button on all Windows systems, is located on the far left-hand side of the taskbar. Clicking the Start button opens the Start menu, as shown in Figure 15.10, as does pressing either the WINDOWS key (if your keyboard has one) or the CTRL-ESC key combination. Different programs may also add their own shortcut icons to the Start menu when you install them, or you can add and remove shortcut icons as you wish.

Quick Launch

If, like most users, you install a lot of applications on your Windows system, you will soon wind up with a crowded Start menu that requires you to navigate

FIGURE 15.10 Windows 2000 Start menu

through several tiers of menu options before you locate the icon you want. The Quick Launch area of the taskbar addresses this by enabling you to place icons for your most frequently used programs where they're always visible and available. As shown in Figure 15.11, the Quick Launch area of the taskbar is located just to the right of the Start button.

Active Programs Area

The bulk of the taskbar is taken up by the active programs area. This is where icons representing currently running applications show up. The active programs area enables you to keep track of and quickly toggle between running programs. Clicking the icon of a running program opens that program on top of other active programs on the desktop if it was running in the background. You can also quickly close a running program by right-clicking its icon in the active programs area and selecting Close from the pop-up menu. Figure 15.12 shows the active programs area of a taskbar with several applications running.

FIGURE 15.11 Taskbar Quick Launch area

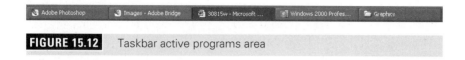

FIGURE 15.12 Taskbar active programs area

Notification Area

Looking all the way to the right end of the taskbar, you'll see the area called the *notification area* by Microsoft, although most techs and users refer to it as the *system tray*. At the least, the notification area displays the current system time. The notification area also shows icons for applications and services that are configured to launch automatically at system startup, or for system controls (such as the volume control) to which you want to have quick access. Figure 15.13 shows a typical Windows XP notification area.

> ### Local Lingo
>
> **System tray** As far as I can discover, Microsoft has always called the notification area just that, but for some reason the industry has always called the area the system tray. You won't find the term in Microsoft documentation, but if you refer to the system tray as the notification area as a tech, most people won't have a clue what you're talking about. For now, use *system tray* in conversation, but *notification area* for exams and for conversing with Microsoft.

Different systems show different icons in the notification area, depending on how they're configured, but you'll usually see icons for such things as PDA synchronizing software utilities, antivirus software, UPS control and configuration software, as well as currently running processes such as print jobs. In fact, many programs aggressively want to launch at startup automatically and install an icon into your notification area to show you they're running and available. You can, of course, control this behavior, as described in the next section.

Configuring the Taskbar

All versions of Windows make it easy to control how your taskbar and Start menu behave. To get to the configuration options, right-click anywhere on the

FIGURE 15.13 Notification area

taskbar and select Properties from the pop-up menu. This opens the Taskbar and Start Menu Properties dialog box (Figure 15.14), where you can configure settings such as the size of the icons displayed on the Start menu, and showing or hiding the system clock, as well as advanced settings that control which program icons are listed on the Start menu, what programs reside in the Startup folder (these are launched automatically at system startup), and so on.

My Network Places

Systems tied to a network, via either a network cable, modem, or wireless connection, have an icon for My Network Places on the desktop or in the Start menu. My Network Places can be thought of as My Computer for the network. Use My Network Places to browse shared resources on the local network or on remote networks such as Web sites or *File Transfer Protocol (FTP)* servers. Figure 15.15 shows a typical Windows XP My Network Places folder.

Hot Keys

Windows has a number of key combinations—called *hot keys*—that enable you to go directly to different programs and places. Here's a list of general-purpose

FIGURE 15.14 Taskbar and Start Menu Properties dialog box

FIGURE 15.15 Windows XP My Network Places folder

commands for Windows. Be aware that some applications may change the use of these commands.

Function Keys

- F1 Help
- F2 Rename
- F3 Search menu
- F4 Open the Address Bar options
- F5 Refresh the current window
- F6 Move among selections in current windows
- F10 Activate menu bar options

Popular Hot Keys

- CTRL-ESC Open Start menu
- ALT-TAB Switch among open programs
- ALT-F4 Quit program
- CTRL-Z Undo the last command
- CTRL-A Select all the items in the current window
- SHIFT-DELETE Delete item permanently

- SHIFT-F10 Open a shortcut menu for the selected item (same as right-clicking an object)
- SHIFT Bypass the automatic-run feature for optical media (by pressing and holding down the SHIFT key while you insert optical media)
- ALT-SPACE Display the main window's System menu (where you can restore, move, resize, minimize, maximize, or close the window)
- ALT-ENTER Open the properties for the selected object

Working with Text

- CTRL-C Copy
- CTRL-X Cut
- CTRL-V Paste
- CTRL-Z Undo
- CTRL-B Bold
- CTRL-U Underline
- CTRL-I Italic

Windows Key Shortcuts These shortcuts use the special Windows key:

- WINDOWS key Start menu
- WINDOWS key-D Show desktop
- WINDOWS key-E Windows Explorer
- WINDOWS key-F Search menu
- WINDOWS key-L Log off Windows
- WINDOWS key-R Run dialog box
- WINDOWS key-CTRL-F Find computer
- WINDOWS key-TAB Cycle through taskbar buttons
- WINDOWS key-BREAK System Properties dialog box

Exam Tip

Only the most basic parts of the Windows desktop are covered in this chapter. The typical Windows desktop will include many other parts, but for techs and for the CompTIA A+ certification exams, what you've learned here about the desktop is more than enough!

OS Files and Folders

As mentioned earlier, one of the characteristics of an OS is that it organizes data stored on the hard drive. This includes organization of the vital OS files themselves. Each modern version of Windows organizes essential files and folders in a similar fashion:

- All have a primary system folder for storing most Windows internal tools and files.
- All use Registry files that keep track of all the hardware loaded and the drivers that enable you to use that hardware.
- Finally, every version has a virtual memory file, enabling more robust access to programs and utilities.

Let's take a more detailed look at these aspects of Microsoft Windows.

System Folder

Evidently, you can't simply go around calling the folder where Windows installs the operating system files "The folder where Windows installs the operating system files." Instead, *SystemRoot* is the tech name given to the folder in which the latest version of Windows is installed. The SystemRoot folder for Windows 2000 is named WINNT by default. Windows XP calls the SystemRoot folder WINDOWS by default. Windows 2000 and Windows XP can be installed onto any primary, active partition, not just the C: drive.

It's handy to know about SystemRoot. You'll find it cropping up in many other tech publications, and it can also be specified when adjusting certain Windows settings to make sure that they work under all circumstances. When used as part of a Windows configuration setting, the term is often written as *%SystemRoot%* (the percent signs indicating that the SystemRoot is a variable parameter).

Travel Advisory

Here's a handy trick. If you don't know where Windows was installed on a particular system, go to a command prompt, type **cd %systemroot%**, and press the ENTER key. The prompt will change focus to the folder in which the Windows OS files are stored.

Registry

The Registry is a database that stores everything about your PC, including information on all the hardware in the PC, network information, user preferences, file types, and virtually anything else you might run into with Windows. Almost any form of configuration done to a Windows system involves editing the Registry. In fact, the Control Panel applets that you know and love are simply user-friendly Registry editing tools.

The Registry in Windows 2000/XP is composed of many files. The numerous Registry files (called *hives*) are stored in the *\%SystemRoot%\System32\config* folder.

Accessing the Registry The main way to access the Registry is through the Control Panel. You can get to the Control Panel in several ways. Double-click the My Computer icon on your desktop, and double-click the Control Panel icon. Alternatively, in XP, choose Start | Control Panel, or in 2000 choose Settings | Control Panel. Figure 15.16 shows the Windows XP Professional Control Panel sporting the Classic View (preferred by four out of five techs worldwide). You

FIGURE 15.16 Windows XP Control Panel

can switch to Category View (the default) by selecting the appropriate option (top left).

Under normal circumstances, everything necessary to configure the system is handled from the Control Panel, and few occasions require direct Registry access. Nevertheless, all good techs should know how to access, navigate, and when necessary edit the system Registry. Microsoft provides tools for doing this—the *Registry Editor.*

Launch the Registry Editor by choosing Start | Run and typing **regedit** or **regedt32**. In Windows 2000, the two commands open 16-bit and 32-bit versions of the Registry Editor, respectively. The commands are interchangeable in Windows XP, opening only the 32-bit version of the Registry Editor. Figure 15.17 shows the 16-bit (top) and 32-bit versions of Registry Editor.

Exam Tip
The Registry files are binary. You cannot edit the Registry with Edit, Notepad, or any other text editor as you could with SYSTEM.INI. You must use the Registry Editor tool.

Registry Components The Registry is a *hierarchical* database, organized in a tree structure similar to the folders in the PC. Open the Registry Editor (16-bit version), and you'll see six main subgroups or root keys:

- HKEY_CLASSES_ROOT
- HKEY_CURRENT_USER
- HKEY_LOCAL_MACHINE
- HKEY_USERS
- HKEY_CURRENT_CONFIG

Try opening one of these root keys, and note that more subkeys are listed underneath them. Many subkeys also have other subkeys or values. The secret to understanding the Registry is to understand the function of the six root keys first. Each of these root keys has a specific function, so let's take a look at them individually:

- **HKEY_CLASSES_ROOT** This root key defines the standard *class objects* used by Windows. A class object is a named group of functions. Pretty much everything that has to do with files on the system is defined by a class object.

FIGURE 15.17 16-bit (top) and 32-bit versions of Registry Editor

- **HKEY_USERS and HKEY_CURRENT_USER** Windows can be configured to support more than one user on the same PC, storing personalized information such as colors, screen savers, and the contents of the desktop. HKEY_USERS stores all of the personalization information for all users on a PC. HKEY_CURRENT_USER stores the current user settings, such as fonts, icons, and colors on systems that are set up to support multiple users.

- **HKEY_LOCAL_MACHINE** This root key contains all the data for a system's non–user-specific configurations. This includes every device in your PC, including devices that you have removed.
- **HKEY_CURRENT_CONFIG** If values in HKEY_LOCAL_MACHINE have more than one option, such as two different monitors, this root key defines which one is currently being used. Because most people have only one type of monitor and similar equipment, this area is almost never touched.

Exam Tip
Make sure you know the default root keys of the Windows Registry.

Virtual Memory

Windows uses *virtual memory* as an extension of system RAM. Virtual memory is a section of hard drive space that's used as a temporary storage box for running programs. When the PC starts running out of real RAM—for instance, when one program needs more resources—the system moves inactive programs from RAM to the virtual memory area on the hard drive, thus opening more space in RAM for programs that are currently active. This process is fully automated, requiring no user intervention. All versions of Windows use virtual memory, although they may call it different things, such as the *swapfile* or *pagefile*.

Local Lingo
Virtual memory, Swapfile, Pagefile All these terms refer to the same thing: space on the hard drive reserved as temporary storage for running programs.

Swapping programs between RAM and virtual memory takes time, because compared to RAM, the hard drive is painfully slow. You may notice a reduction in performance if a lot of "paging" activity is occurring. To counter this performance hit, you can do the following:

- Because virtual memory is brought heavily into play only when there's not enough RAM to accommodate running programs, you can decrease paging by adding more RAM to the system.
- You can change the location of the pagefile. If you have more than one hard drive, you can increase performance by moving the pagefile from

the system disk—the disk that has Windows installed on it—to another hard drive.

We'll talk more about how to increase system performance later in this book.

CHECKPOINT

✔**Objective 15.01: Characteristics of the Operating System** Operating systems are made to work on a particular type of CPU platform. Microsoft Windows runs on the Intel and AMD x86 CPU family. Software applications are likewise made to work on one type of OS (although some are ported to operate on more than one OS). The OS takes over control of the PC after POST and continues to run until you exit the OS or shut down the system. An OS must be flexible enough to enable you to install new hardware and software.

✔**Objective 15.02: Common Operating System Functions** Functions that are common to any OS include communicating with hardware, creating a user interface (a means for the user to issue instructions to the PC and retrieve information from it), enabling users to access application programs, and enabling users to create and manipulate data.

✔**Objective 15.03: Operating System Interfaces** The user interface manifests in two ways: a text-only command line interface, and an icon-driven graphical user interface (GUI). Microsoft DOS is an example of a text-only command line interface OS, and modern versions of Microsoft Windows are GUI-based OSs. GUI versions of Windows also offer command line interface access to the OS.

✔**Objective 15.04: Common Microsoft Windows Features** Different versions of Windows offer different features, but all versions have a common feature set. The Windows user interface is the same or similar in all versions of Windows; it includes the login screen, the desktop, and the taskbar. On networked systems, Windows places the My Network Places icon on the desktop or in the Start menu. All versions of Windows use common OS files and folders, such as the system folder (the folder where the Windows OS files are stored), the Registry, and the virtual memory pagefile.

REVIEW QUESTIONS

1. What is the best way to access the Registry Editor in Windows XP?

 A. Start | All Programs | DOS prompt icon. Type **edit**.

 B. Start | All Programs | Registry Editor.

 C. Start | Run | Type **regeditor** and click OK.

 D. Start | Run | Type **regedt32** and click OK.

2. Which of the following is *not* a Registry root key in Windows 2000/XP?

 A. HKEY_CURRENT_MACHINE

 B. HKEY_CLASSES_ROOT

 C. HKEY_CURRENT_USER

 D. HKEY_DYN_DATA

3. An employee reports that he accidentally deleted a file from his USB thumb drive and cannot find it in the Recycle Bin. What can you do to correct this?

 A. Tell the employee to open My Computer and choose Tools | Folder Options. Then click the View tab and select the *View hidden files and folders* radio button.

 B. Tell the employee to open My Computer, and choose View | Options to open the Options menu. Click the View tab and uncheck the *Hide MS-DOS file extensions for file types that are registered* check box.

 C. Right-click the Recycle Bin icon and select Properties from the pop-up menu. Select the *Do not move files to the Recycle Bin* check box.

 D. You cannot correct this.

4. Which of the following commands entered in the Start | Run dialog box will start the Windows XP 32-bit command interpreter? (Select two.)

 A. CMD

 B. COMMAND

 C. WINNT32

 D. CMD32

5. The mouse on your PC stops responding. The PC is configured to hide the taskbar and Start menu automatically. How can you access the Start button *without* the mouse? (Select two.)

 A. Press the WINDOWS key on the keyboard.

 B. Press the CTRL-ALT-DEL key combination on the keyboard.

 C. Press the CTRL-ESC key combination on the keyboard.

 D. Press the ALT-F4 key combination on the keyboard.

6. What are the major functions of an operating system (OS)?

 A. An OS provides a method for other programs to communicate.

 B. An OS creates a user interface.

 C. An OS enables users to add, move, and delete installed programs and data.

 D. All of the above.

7. Which of the following shows a typical command prompt?

 A. A:\\

 B. D:/>

 C. C:\>

 D. C://

8. Which of the following best describes the operating system's user interface?

 A. It enables the system to communicate with peripheral devices.

 B. It provides a means for the user to enter commands and retrieve data.

 C. It provides a display of the system hardware to the user.

 D. It provides error handling or notification displays when communicating with hardware.

9. To manipulate and organize data and programs, which of the following must the OS do? (Select two.)

 A. Identify all the data and programs on the system and organize them in a binary-code format.

 B. Provide a method to identify data according to the type of program that uses that particular data.

 C. Provide a naming system for each drive.

 D. Give the user an interface to assign drive letters to drives.

10. What type of memory stores running programs in a swapfile on a hard drive?

 A. Extended memory

 B. Flash memory

 C. Virtual memory

 D. Random access memory

REVIEW ANSWERS

1. **D** Start | Run | Type **regedt32** and clicking OK will start the Registry Editor in Windows XP.

2. **D** HKEY_DYN_DATA is not a valid Registry root key in Windows 2000/XP.

3. **D** Files deleted from removable drives are not stored in the Recycle Bin and cannot be retrieved.

4. **A** **B** In Windows XP, typing **cmd** or **command** at the Start | Run dialog box starts the 32-bit command line interface.

5. **A** **C** Pressing the WINDOWS key or the CTRL-ESC key combination brings up the Start menu.

6. **D** All of the above are the major functions of an operating system.

7. **C** C:\> is a typical command prompt.

8. **B** The user interface enables users to input commands and retrieve data.

9. **B** **C** The user must have some method to know which data files are used by particular programs. Further, the OS must provide a naming system for every drive.

10. **C** Virtual memory holds the swapfile (or pagefile).

Windows
in Detail

	NEWBIE	SOME EXPERIENCE	EXPERT
ETA	3 hours	2 hours	1 hour

This chapter picks up where Chapter 15 left off. You've had the overview and user-level tour of Windows. Now it's time to look at tools and the features of Windows techs need to know. You'll learn about tech utilities, the boot process, and the structure of Windows. The chapter wraps with a round-up of the current versions of Windows, from Windows 2000 Professional to Windows Vista Ultimate Edition.

Objective 16.01 Essential Tech Utilities

Windows offers a huge number of utilities that enable techs to configure the OS, optimize and tweak settings, install hardware, and more. The trick is to know where to go to find them. This section shows the five most common locations in Windows where you can go to access utilities: right-click, Control Panel, System Tools, Administrative Tools, and the Microsoft Management Console.

> ### Travel Assistance
>
> You know about one other great location for tech utilities from Chapter 15—the command line. The command line offers all kinds of great tools and quick access to stuff you'll rely on a lot for troubleshooting and maintaining Windows.

Right-Click

Any single thing you see on your desktop is called an *object*. If you want to open any object in Windows, you double-click it. If you want to change something about an object, you right-click it.

Right-clicking on an object brings up a small pop-up, or *context*, menu, and it works on everything in Windows. In fact, try to place your mouse somewhere in Windows where right-clicking does *not* bring up a menu (there are a few places, but they're not easy to find). What you see when you right-click varies dramatically, depending on the item you click. If you right-click a running program in the running program area on the taskbar, you'll see items that relate to a window, such as Move, Size, and Close (Figure 16.1).

One menu item you'll see almost anywhere you right-click is Properties. Every object in Windows has properties. When you right-click an item and can't find what you're looking for, choose Properties to open the Properties window, as shown in Figure 16.2.

Pop-up menu that appears when you right-click a running program

Control Panel

The *Control Panel* handles most of the maintenance, upgrade, and configuration aspects of Windows. As such, the Control Panel is the first set of tools every tech should explore. Choose Start | Settings | Control Panel to open the Control Panel in Windows 2000. In Windows XP, you choose Start | Control Panel.

The Control Panel in Windows 2000 opens in the traditional icon-littered view. In Windows XP and Vista, the Control Panel opens into the Category view, in which all the icons are grouped into broad categories such as "Printers and Other Hardware." This view requires an additional click (and sometimes a guess

System Properties window

about which category includes the icon you need), so most techs use the *Switch to Classic View* link to get back to the icons. Figure 16.3 shows the Windows XP Control Panel in both Category (left) and Classic (right) views.

A large number of programs, called *applets*, populate the Control Panel. The names and selection of applets will vary depending on the version of Windows and whether any installed programs have added applets. But all versions of Windows share many of the same applets, including Display, Add or Remove Programs, and System—what I call the *Big Three* applets for techs. Display enables you to make changes to the look and feel of your Windows desktop and to tweak your video settings. Add or Remove Programs enables you to add or remove programs. The System applet gives you access to essential system information and tools, such as the Device Manager.

Exam Tip

Even common applets vary slightly among Windows versions. The CompTIA A+ certification exams do not test you on every little variance among the same applets in different versions—but you should know what each applet does.

Device Manager

The *Device Manager* enables techs to examine and configure all the hardware and drivers in a Windows PC. As you might suspect from that description, every tech spends a lot of time with this tool. You've seen it at work in several earlier chapters, and you'll work with the Device Manager many more times during the course of your career as a PC tech.

FIGURE 16.3 Windows XP Control Panel—two views

You can access the Device Manager in several ways—make sure you know all of them. The first way is to open the Control Panel and double-click the System applet icon. This brings up the System Properties dialog box. (You can also get to the System Properties dialog box by right-clicking My Computer and selecting Properties.) From here, you access the Device Manager by selecting the Hardware tab and then clicking the Device Manager button. Figure 16.4 shows the Hardware tab of the System Properties dialog box in Windows XP.

Travel Assistance

Holding down the WINDOWS key and pressing the PAUSE key is yet another way to access the System Properties dialog box. Keyboard shortcuts are cool!

The second (and more streamlined) method is to right-click My Computer and choose Manage (Figure 16.5). This opens a window called Computer Management, where you'll see Device Manager listed on the left side of the screen, under System Tools (Figure 16.6). Just click Device Manager and it will open. You can also access Computer Management by opening the Administrative Tools applet in the Control Panel and then choosing Computer Management.

FIGURE 16.4 Windows XP System applet with the Hardware tab selected

Right-click My Computer and choose the Manage option

Why so many ways to open Device Manager? Remember that you're looking only at locations in Windows from which to open utilities, not at the actual utilities themselves. Microsoft wants you to get to the tools you need when you need them; it's better to have multiple paths to a utility rather than just one.

Device Manager in Computer Management

The Device Manager displays every device that Windows recognizes, organized in special groups called *types*. All devices of the same type are grouped under the same type heading. To see the devices of a particular type, you must open that type's group. Figure 16.7 shows a typical Windows XP Device Manager screen with all installed devices in good order—which makes us techs happy. If Windows detects a problem, it shows the device with a red "X," as in the case of the network adapter in Figure 16.8, or a yellow exclamation point (!).

The Device Manager isn't used only for dealing with problems. It also enables you to update drivers with a simple click of the mouse (assuming you have a driver downloaded or on disc). Right-click a device and select Update Driver to get the process started. Figure 16.9 shows the options in Windows XP.

By double-clicking a device (or by selecting the device and clicking the Properties button) and then clicking the Resources tab, you can see the resources used by that device. Figure 16.10 shows the resources for an NVIDIA GeForce 7900 GT video card.

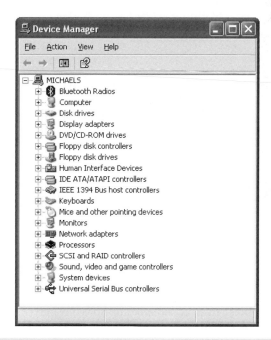

FIGURE 16.7 Happy Device Manager

FIGURE 16.8 Sad Device Manager

Make sure you can get to Device Manager. You will come back to it again and again in subsequent chapters, because it is the first tool you should access when you experience a hardware problem.

System Tools

The Start menu offers a variety of tech utilities in one place: choose Start | Programs | Accessories | System Tools. In the *System Tools* menu, you'll find commonly accessed tools, such as System Information and Disk Defragmenter (Figure 16.11).

FIGURE 16.9 Selecting Update Driver in the Windows XP Device Manager

FIGURE 16.10 Resources revealed in the Windows XP Device Manager

System Tools menu options

Many techs overlook memorizing how to find the appropriate Windows tool to diagnose problems, but nothing hurts your credibility with a client like fumbling around, clicking a variety of menus and applets, mumbling "I know it's around here somewhere." The CompTIA A+ certification exams therefore test you on a variety of paths to appropriate tools. One of those paths is Start | Programs | Accessories | System Tools. Windows XP has all the same tools as Windows 2000, plus a few more, so each tool discussed here shows whether the tool is in Windows 2000 or only in XP.

Backup
The Backup utility enables you to back up selected files and folders to removable media such as tape drives. Backing up is an important function that Chapter19 covers in detail.

Travel Advisory
Neither Windows XP Home nor Windows Media Center automatically includes Backup. You must install the Backup program from the Windows Install CD by running the \Valueadd\MSFT\NTbackup\ NTbackup.msi program.

Character Map

Ever been using a program only to discover you need to enter an uncommon character such as the euro character (€) but your word processor doesn't support it? That's when you need the Character Map. It enables you to copy any Unicode character into the clipboard (Figure 16.12).

Disk Cleanup

Disk Cleanup looks for unneeded files on your computer, which is handy when your hard drive starts to get full and you need space. You must run Disk Cleanup manually in Windows 2000, but Windows XP starts this program whenever your hard drive free disk space gets below 200 MB.

Disk Defragmenter

Disk Defragmenter was discussed back in Chapter 8. You can access this utility in the same way you access the Device Manager; Disk Defragmenter is also found in the Computer Management console. A simpler method is to choose Start | Programs | Accessories | System Tools—you'll find Disk Defragmenter listed there. You can also right-click any drive in My Computer, select Properties, and click the Tools tab, where you'll find a convenient Defragment Now button.

FIGURE 16.12 Character Map

Files and Settings Transfer Wizard (XP Only)

Suppose you have an old computer full of files and settings, and you just got yourself a brand new computer. You want to copy everything from your old computer onto your new computer—what to do? Microsoft touts the *Files and Settings Transfer Wizard* (Figure 16.13) as just the tool you need. This utility copies your desktop files and folders, and most conveniently, your settings from Internet Explorer (IE) and Outlook Express; however, it won't copy over your programs—not even the Microsoft apps—and it won't copy settings for any programs other than IE and Outlook Express. If you need to copy everything from an old computer to a new one, you'll probably want to use a disk imaging tool such as Norton Ghost.

Scheduled Tasks

The Scheduled Tasks utility enables you to schedule any program to start and stop any time you wish. The only trick to this utility is that you must enter the program you want to run as a command on the command line, with all the proper switches. Figure 16.14 shows the configuration line for running the Disk Defragmenter program.

FIGURE 16.13 Files and Settings Transfer Wizard

FIGURE 16.14 Task Scheduler

Security Center (XP Only)

The Security Center is a one-stop location for configuring many security features on your computer. All these security features, and many more, are discussed in detail in their related chapters.

System Information

System Information is one of those tools that everyone (including the CompTIA A+ certification exams) likes to talk about, but it's uncommon to meet techs who say they actually use this tool. System Information shows tons of information about the hardware and software on your PC (Figure 16.15). You can also use it as a launch point for a number of programs by clicking the Tools menu.

System Restore (XP Only)

System Restore is not only handy, it's also arguably the most important single utility you'll ever use in Windows when it comes to fixing a broken system. *System Restore* enables you to take a *snapshot*—a copy of a number of critical files and settings—and return to that state later (Figure 16.16). System Restore holds multiple snapshots, any of which you may restore to in the future.

FIGURE 16.15 System Information

Imagine you're installing some new device in your PC, or maybe a piece of software. Before you actually install, you take a snapshot and call it "Before

FIGURE 16.16 System Restore

Install." You install the device, and then something starts acting weird. You can go back into System Restore and reload the previous snapshot, and the problem goes away. Windows takes some of these snapshots automatically, such as when you install unsigned drivers or apply a major patch to Windows through Windows Update.

System Restore isn't perfect. It backs up only a few critical items, and it's useless if the computer won't boot, but it's usually the first thing to try when something goes wrong—assuming, of course, you made a snapshot.

Microsoft Management Console

One of the biggest complaints about earlier versions of Windows was the wide dispersal of the many utilities needed for administration and troubleshooting. Despite years of research, Microsoft could never find a place for all the utilities that would please even a small minority of support people. In a moment of sheer genius, Microsoft determined that the ultimate utility was one that the support person made for him or herself. This brought on the creation of the amazing Microsoft Management Console (MMC).

> **Exam Tip**
>
> All four CompTIA A+ exams expect you to know about the MMC and other tools discussed in the rest of this chapter, so don't skip it!

The MMC is simply a shell program in Windows 2000 and XP that holds individual utilities called *snap-ins*. You can start the MMC by choosing Start | Run and typing **MMC** to get a blank MMC. Blank MMCs aren't much to look at (Figure 16.17).

You make a blank MMC console useful by adding snap-ins, and most of the utilities you use in Windows are actually snap-ins. Even the good old Device Manager is a snap-in. You can add as many snap-ins as you like, and you have many to choose from. Many companies sell third-party utilities as MMC snap-ins.

For example, to add the Device Manager snap-in, open the blank MMC, select File (Console in Windows 2000) | Add/Remove Snap-in, and then click the Add button to open the Add Standalone Snap-in dialog box. Here you will see a list of available snap-ins (Figure 16.18). Select Device Manager, and click the Add button to open a dialog box that prompts you to choose the local or a remote PC for the snap-in to work with. Choose Local Computer for this exercise, and click the Finish button. Click the Close button to close the Add

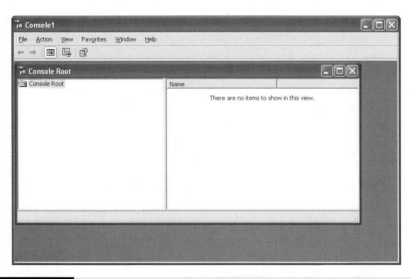

FIGURE 16.17 Blank MMC

Standalone Snap-in dialog box, and then click OK to close the Add/Remove Snap-in dialog box.

You should see Device Manager listed in the console. Click it. Hey, that looks kind of familiar, doesn't it? (See Figure 16.19.)

FIGURE 16.18 Available snap-ins

FIGURE 16.19 Device Manager as a snap-in

Once you've added the snap-ins you want, just save the console under any name, anywhere you want. If you saved this console as Device Manager, for example, and dropped it on your desktop, you'd be just a double-click away from the Device Manager.

Administrative Tools

Windows 2000 and XP have combined almost all of the snap-ins into an applet in the Control Panel called *Administrative Tools*. Open the Control Panel and open Administrative Tools (Figure 16.20).

Administrative Tools is a folder that stores a number of premade consoles. As you poke through these, you'll notice that many of the consoles share some of the same snap-ins. Of the consoles in a standard Administrative Tools collection, those with which you'll spend the most time are Computer Management, Event Viewer, Performance, and Services.

FIGURE 16.20 Administrative Tools

Exam Tip

The CompTIA A+ certification exams have little interest in some of these snap-ins, so this book won't cover them all. If it's not mentioned here, it's almost certainly not on the exams.

Computer Management

The *Computer Management* applet is a tech's best buddy, or at least a place where you'll spend a lot of time when building or maintaining a system (Figure 16.21). You've already spent considerable time with two of its components, System Tools and Storage. System Tools offers System Information, Performance Logs and Alerts, Device Manager, and more. Storage is where you'll find Disk Management. Each of these tools is of particular interest to techs, as you've seen earlier and will see again in Chapter 19.

Event Viewer Event Viewer enables you to tell at a glance what has happened in the last day, week, or more, including when people logged in and when the PC had problems. You'll see more of Event Viewer in Chapter 19.

FIGURE 16.21 Computer Management applet

Performance The Performance console consists of two snap-ins: System Monitor and Performance Logs and Alerts. You can use these for reading *logs*—files that record information over time. The System Monitor can also monitor real-time data (Figure 16.22).

Suppose you got a new cable modem and you want to know how fast you can download data. Click the plus sign (+) on the toolbar to add a counter. Click the *Use local computer counters* radio button, and then choose *Network Interface* from the Performance object pull-down menu. Make sure the *Select counters from list* radio button is selected. Last, select *Bytes Received/sec*. The dialog box should look like Figure 16.23.

Click Add, and then click Close—probably not much is happening. Go to a Web site, preferably one where you can download a huge file. Start downloading and watch the chart jump; that's the real throughput (Figure 16.24).

Travel Assistance

You'll learn more about the Performance console in Chapter 19.

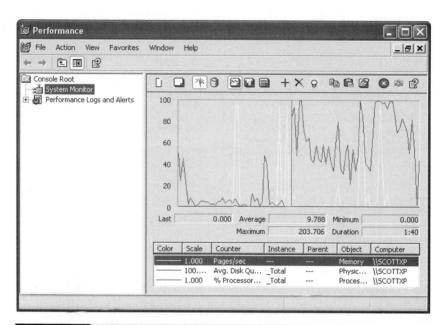

FIGURE 16.22 System Monitor in action

FIGURE 16.23 Setting up a throughput test

FIGURE 16.24 Downloading with blazing speed

Services

Windows runs a large number of separate programs called *services*. The best way to visualize a service is to think of it as something that runs, yet is invisible. Windows comes with about 100 services by default, and they handle a huge number of tasks, from application support to network functions. The Services applet enables you to see the status of all services on the system, including services that are not running (Figure 16.25).

Right-click a service and choose Properties to modify its settings. Figure 16.26 shows the properties for the Alerter service. See the Startup Type pull-down menu? It shows three options: Automatic, Manual, and Disabled. Automatic means it starts when the system starts, Manual means you have to come to this tab to start it, and Disabled prevents anything from starting it. Make sure you know these three settings, and also make sure you understand how to start, stop, pause, and resume services (note the four buttons underneath Startup Type).

FIGURE 16.25 Services applet

FIGURE 16.26 Alerter service properties

> **Exam Tip**
>
> The CompTIA A+ certification exams are not interested in having you memorize all of these services—just make sure you can manipulate them.

Objective 16.02 Windows Structure

Microsoft Windows 2000 and XP are stable, high-performance operating systems (OSs) that offer scalability and, above all else, security. Windows 2000 and Windows XP share the same core structure, files, and features, so the discussion that follows applies to both OSs. Both are covered in detail followed by a discussion of the differences between the two OSs.

OS Organization

Three terms best describe Windows 2000/XP organization: robust, scalable, and cross-platform. Microsoft takes an object-oriented approach to the OS, separating it into three distinct parts: the drivers, the NT Executive, and the subsystems (Figure 16.27).

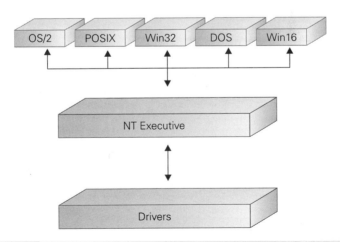

FIGURE 16.27 Windows NT organization

The *NT Executive* is the core power of the Windows 2000/XP OS, handling all of the memory management and multitasking. The NT Executive uses a hardware abstraction layer (HAL) to separate the system-specific device drivers from the rest of the OS (Figure 16.28).

Windows 2000/XP's robustness comes from the separation of running processes into a myriad of subsystems. Each of these subsystems supports different types of applications in separate areas; that way, if one program locks up, it won't cause the entire system to lock up. Windows supports DOS and older programs designed for earlier versions of Windows, as well as current Windows applications, via these numerous subsystems (Figure 16.29).

Windows 2000/XP's scalability makes them the only modern Microsoft OSs to support *symmetric multiprocessing (SMP)*, providing support for systems with up to 32 CPUs. The server versions of Windows go beyond SMP by adding the power of clustering, enabling multiple computers to share redundant data for ultimate protection. If one system goes down, the other systems continue to run.

NT File System (NTFS)

From the beginning, Microsoft designed and optimized every aspect of Windows 2000/XP for multi-user, networked environments. Whereas all previous Microsoft OSs used either FAT16 or FAT32, Windows 2000 and XP use a far more powerful and robust file system, appropriately called *NT File System (NTFS)*.

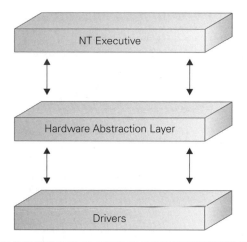

FIGURE 16.28 NT Executive and the HAL

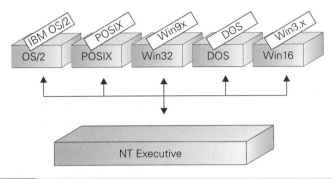

NT Executive can handle a lot of different OSs.

Chapter 8 contains a good basic description of NTFS, but let's go into a bit more detail. NTFS offers the following excellent features:

- Long filenames (LFNs)
- Redundancy
- Backward compatibility
- Recoverability
- Security

Long Filenames
NTFS supported LFNs long before FAT32 even existed. NTFS filenames can be up to 255 characters.

Redundancy
NTFS has an advanced FAT called the *master file table (MFT)*. An NTFS partition keeps a backup copy of the most critical parts of the MFT in the middle of the disk, reducing the chances that a serious drive error can wipe out both the MFT and the MFT copy. Whenever you defrag an NTFS partition, you'll see a small, immovable "chunk" in the middle of the drive; that's the backup MFT.

Backward Compatibility
For all its power, NTFS is amazingly backward compatible. You can copy DOS or Windows 9x/Me programs to an NTFS partition—Windows will even keep the LFNs.

Recoverability
Accidental system shutdowns, reboots, and lockups in the midst of a file save or retrieval wreak havoc on most systems. NTFS avoids this with *transaction*

logging. Transaction logging identifies incomplete file transactions and restores the file to the original format automatically and invisibly.

Security

NTFS truly shines with its powerful security functions. When most people hear the term *security*, they tend to think about networks, and NTFS security works perfectly in a networked environment, but it works equally well on single systems that support multiple users. Let's look at three major features of NTFS security: accounts, groups, and permissions.

Accounts To use a Windows 2000/XP system, you must have a valid account (and, frequently, a password). Without an account, you cannot use the system (Figure 16.30).

Every Windows 2000/XP system has a "super" account called *administrator*. Remember when you saw the installation of Windows and it prompted you for a password for the administrator account? As you might imagine, this account has access to everything—a dangerous thing in the wrong hands!

Groups The administrator creates user accounts with a special program called Users and Passwords in Windows 2000 (Figure 16.31) and User Accounts in Windows XP. Note that the account list has three columns: User Name, Domain, and Group. To understand domains requires an extensive networking discussion, so we'll leave that for Chapter 18. We'll instead focus here on user names and groups. A *user name* defines an account for a person who has access to the PC. A *group* is simply a collection of accounts that share the same access capabilities. A single account can be a member of multiple groups.

FIGURE 16.30 Login failure

FIGURE 16.31 Users and Passwords dialog box in Windows 2000

Groups make Windows administration much easier in two ways. First, you can assign a certain level of access for a file or folder to a group, instead of just to a single user account. For example, you can make a group called Accounting and put all the accounting users' accounts in that group. If a person quits, you don't need to worry about assigning all the proper access levels when you create a new account for her replacement. After you make an account for the new person, you simply add the new account to the appropriate access group.

Second, Windows provides seven built-in groups: Administrators, Power Users, Users, Backup Operators, Replicator, Everyone, and Guests. These built-in groups have a number of preset abilities. You cannot delete these groups, although they can be renamed.

- **Administrators** Any account that is a member of this group has complete administrator privileges. It is common for the primary user of a Windows 2000/XP system to have his or her account in the Administrators group.

- **Power Users** Power users are almost as powerful as administrators, but they cannot install new devices or access other users' files or folders unless the files or folders specifically provide them access.

- **Users** Users cannot edit the Registry or access critical system files. They can create groups but can manage only those groups they create.
- **Backup Operators** Backup operators have the same rights as users, except that they can run backup programs that access any file or folder—for backup purposes only.
- **Replicator** Members of the Replicator group can replicate files and folders in a domain.
- **Everyone** This group applies to any user who can log onto the system. You cannot edit this group.
- **Guests** Someone who does not have an account on the system can log on using a Guest account if the system has been set up to enable that option. This group is useful in certain network situations.

Windows XP diverges a lot from Windows 2000 on user accounts. If you're running XP Professional and you are on a Windows domain, XP offers all the preceding accounts, but it adds four other specialized types, including Help Services Group and Remote Desktop Users. Windows XP Home and XP Professional, when it's installed as a stand-alone PC or connected to a workgroup but not a domain, run in a specialized networking mode called *simple file sharing.* A Windows XP system running simple file sharing has only three account types: Computer Administrator, Limited User, and Guest. Computer Administrators can do anything, as you might suspect. Limited Users can access only certain things and have limits on where they can save files on the PC.

NTFS Permissions In the 2000/XP world, every folder and file on an NTFS partition has a list that contains two sets of data. First, the list details every user and group that has access to that file or folder. Second, the list specifies the level of access that each user or group has to that file or folder. The level of access is defined by a set of restrictions called *NTFS permissions.*

NTFS permissions define exactly what a particular account can or cannot do to the file or folder on an NTFS volume and are thus quite detailed and powerful. You can make it possible, for example, for a person to edit a file but not delete it. You can let someone create a folder and not allow other people to make subfolders. NTFS file and folder permissions are so complicated that entire books have been written about them. Fortunately, the CompTIA A+ certification exams test your understanding of only a few basic concepts of NTFS permissions: Ownership, Take Ownership permission, Change permissions, Folder permissions, and File permissions.

- **Ownership** When you create a new file or folder on an NTFS partition, you become the *owner* of that file or folder. A newly created file or folder by default gives everyone full permission to access, delete, and otherwise manipulate that file or folder. Owners can do anything they want to the files or folders they own, including changing the permissions to prevent anybody, even administrators, from accessing them.

- **Take Ownership permission** This special permission enables anyone with the permission to seize control of a file or folder. Administrator accounts have Take Ownership permission for everything. Note the difference here between *owning* a file and *accessing* a file. If you own a file, you can prevent anyone from accessing that file. An administrator who you have blocked, however, can take that ownership away from you and *then* access that file.

- **Change permissions** Another important permission for all NTFS files and folders is the Change permission. An account with this permission can give or take away permissions for other accounts.

- **Folder permissions** Let's look at a typical folder in my Windows XP system to see how this one works. My E: drive is formatted as NTFS, and on it I created a folder called *E:\MIKE*. In My Computer, it looks like Figure 16.32. I set the permissions for the *E:\MIKE* folder by accessing the folder's properties and clicking the Security tab (see Figure 16.33).

- **File permissions** File permissions are similar to Folder permissions. We'll talk about File permissions right after we cover Folder permissions.

In Windows 2000/XP (except Home edition), just about everything in the computer has a Security tab in its properties, and every Security tab contains two main areas. The top area shows the list of accounts that have permissions for that resource. The lower area shows exactly what permissions have been assigned to the selected account.

Here are the standard permissions for a folder:

- **Full Control** Enables you to do anything you want.
- **Modify** Enables you to do anything except delete files or subfolders.
- **Read & Execute** Enables you to see the contents of the folder and any subfolders.
- **List Folder Contents** Enables you to see the contents of the folder and any subfolders. (This permission seems the same as the Read & Execute permission, but it is inherited only by folders.)

FIGURE 16.32 MIKE folder—isn't it lovely?

FIGURE 16.33 The Security tab lets me set permissions.

- **Read** Enables you to read any file in the folder.
- **Write** Enables you to write to files and create new files and folders.

If you look at the bottom of the Security tab in Windows 2000, you'll see a little check box that says *Allow inheritable permissions from parent to propagate to this object*. In other words, any files or subfolders created in this folder get the same permissions for the same users/groups that the folder has. Unchecking this option enables you to stop a user from getting a specific permission via inheritance. Windows XP has the same feature, except it's accessed through the Advanced button in the Security tab and worded differently. Windows also provides explicit Deny functions for each option (Figure 16.34). Deny overrules inheritance.

FIGURE 16.34 Special permissions

Exam Tip

Don't worry about memorizing special permissions; just appreciate that they exist and that the permissions you see in the Security tab cover the vast majority of your needs.

File permissions are quite similar to folder permissions. Take a look at the Security tab on a typical file (Figure 16.35).

- **Full Control** Enables you to do anything you want.
- **Modify** Enables you to do anything except take ownership or change permissions on the file.
- **Read & Execute** If the file is a program, you can run it.
- **Read** If the file is data, you can read it.
- **Write** Enables you to write to the file.

Take some time to think about these permissions. Why would Microsoft create them? Think of situations where you might want to give a group Modify permission. Also, you can assign more than one permission. In many situations, you'll need to give a user both the Read and Write permissions.

FIGURE 16.35 Security tab

Permissions are cumulative. If you have Full Control on a folder and only Read permission on a file in the folder, you get Full Control permission on the file.

Travel Advisory

Windows XP Home has only a limited set of permissions you can assign. As far as folder permissions go, you can assign only one: *Make this folder private.* To see this in action, right-click a file or folder and select Sharing and Security from the options. Note that you can't just select the properties and see a Security tab as you can in Windows 2000 and XP Professional. Windows XP Home does not have file-level permissions.

Techs and Permissions Techs, as a rule, hate NTFS permissions. You must have administrative privileges to do almost anything on a Windows 2000/XP machine, and most administrators hate giving out administrative permissions (for obvious reasons). If a tech does give you administrative permission for a PC, and something goes wrong with that system while you're working on it, you immediately become the primary suspect.

If you're working on a 2000/XP system administered by someone else, make sure he or she understands what you are doing and how long you think it will take. Have the administrator create a new account for you with administrator privileges. Never ask for the password for a permanent administrator account. That way, you won't be blamed if anything goes wrong on that system: "Well, I told Janet the password when she installed the new hard drive.... Maybe she did it!" When you have fixed the system, make sure that the administrator deletes the account you used.

Travel Advisory

This "protect yourself from passwords" attitude transcends Windows 2000/XP. PC support folks get lots of passwords, scan cards, keys, and ID tags. Most newer techs tend to get an "I can go anywhere and access anything" attitude, and this is dangerous. I've seen many jobs lost and friendships ruined when a tape backup suddenly disappears or a critical file gets erased. Everybody points to the support tech in these situations. In physical security situations, make other people unlock doors for you. In some cases, I've literally made the administrator or system owner sit behind me reading a magazine, jumping up and punching in passwords as needed. What you don't have access to can't hurt you.

Objective 16.03 Booting Windows

Windows 2000 and XP distinguish between the files that start the OS (often called the *system files* or *Windows startup files*) and the rest of the OS files (usually in the \WINDOWS or \WINNT folders). The system files (memorize these!) consist of three required files: NTLDR, BOOT.INI, and NTDETECT.COM. If you're using a SCSI hard drive, there's a fourth file called NTBOOTDD.SYS.NTLDR (pronounced *NT loader*) that begins the boot process.

You know from earlier chapters that to make a drive bootable requires an active, primary partition, right? Let's look at the process in a PC with a hard drive partitioned as C: and D:.

The Boot Process

The CPU wakes up and runs the system BIOS, and then the BIOS sends out a routine looking for a valid OS in the boot sector of the primary, master hard drive. The MFT lives in the boot sector of the C: partition. It points to the location of the Windows 2000/XP system files, also on the C: drive, because that's the bootable drive. Windows calls the primary, active partition the *system partition* or the *system volume* (if it's a dynamic disk).

The Windows 2000/XP *boot files* consist of NTOSKRNL.EXE (the Windows kernel), the \WINNT\SYSTEM32\CONFIG\SYSTEM file (which controls the loading of device drivers), and the device drivers. Even though these files are the core of the Windows 2000/XP OS, they are not capable of booting, or starting, the system. For that feat, they require NTLDR, NTDETECT.COM, and BOOT.INI—the system files.

The system files start the PC and then, at the end of that process, point the CPU to the location of the boot files. The CPU goes over and chats with NTOSKRNL, and the GUI starts to load. The OS is then up and running, and you're able to do work.

The odd part about all this is that Microsoft decided to make the OS files mobile. *The Windows OS files can reside on any partition or volume in the PC.* The \WINDOWS folder, for example, could very well be on drive D:, not drive C:. Whichever drive holds the core OS files is called the *boot partition*. This can lead to a little confusion when you say "the system files are on my C: drive, but Windows is on my D: drive," but that's just the way it is. The vast majority of Windows 2000/XP systems have the system partition and the boot partition both on the same big C: partition.

You've got the process now in general, so let's look more specifically at the makeup and function of the individual files involved in the boot process.

System Partition Files

Windows 2000 and XP require the three system files in the root directory of the system partition:

- NTLDR
- BOOT.INI
- NTDETECT.COM

To see these files, go into My Computer and open the C: drive. Then open Folder Options, as shown in the "My Computer" section of Chapter 15. Click the *Show hidden files and folders* radio button, uncheck the *Hide protected operating system files (Recommended)* option, and click OK. Now when you return to viewing the folder in My Computer, you will see certain critical files that Windows otherwise hides from you, so you don't accidentally move, delete, or change them in some unintended way (Figure 16.36).

FIGURE 16.36 My Computer showing the system files residing in a local disk

NTLDR

When the system boots, the master boot record (MBR) or MFT on the hard drive starts the *NTLDR* program. The NTLDR program then launches Windows 2000/XP or another OS. To find the available OSs, the NTLDR program must read the BOOT.INI configuration file, and to do so it loads its own minimal file system, which enables it to read the BOOT.INI file off the system partition.

BOOT.INI File

The BOOT.INI file is a text file that lists the OSs available to NTLDR and tells NTLDR where to find the boot partition (where the OS is stored) for each of them. The BOOT.INI file has sections defined by headings enclosed in brackets. A basic BOOT.INI in Windows XP looks like this:

```
[boot loader]
timeout=30
default=multi(0)disk(0)rdisk(0)partition(1)\WINDOWS
[operating systems]
multi(0)disk(0)rdisk(0)partition(1)\WINDOWS="Microsoft Windows XP
Professional" /fastdetect
```

A more complex BOOT.INI may look like this:

```
[boot loader]
timeout=30
default=multi(0)disk(0)rdisk(0)partition(1)\WINDOWS
[operating systems]
multi(0)disk(0)rdisk(0)partition(1)\WINDOWS="Microsoft Windows XP
Professional" /fastdetect
multi(0)disk(0)rdisk(0)partition(1)\WINNT="Microsoft Windows 2000
Professional" /fastdetect
```

Such a BOOT.INI would result in the boot menu that appears in Figure 16.37.

This crazy `multi(0)disk(0)rdisk(0)partition(1)` is an example of the *advanced RISC computing (ARC) naming system*. It's a system that's designed to enable your PC to use any hard drive, including removable devices, to boot Windows. Let's take a quick peek at each ARC setting to see how it works.

Local Lingo

ARC ARC stands for *advanced RISC computing*, but because that means very little to techs, most folks simply call it *ARC* as a name rather than an acronym.

`Multi(x)` is the number of the adapter and always starts with 0. The adapter is determined by how you set the boot order in your CMOS setting. For example, if you have a single parallel ATA (PATA) controller and a serial ATA

```
Please select the operating system to start:

  Microsoft Windows 2000 Professional
  Microsoft Windows 2000 Recovery Console
  Previous Operating system on C:

Use ↑ and ↓ to move the highlight to your choice.
Press Enter to choose.
Seconds until highlighted choice will be started automatically: 26

For troubleshooting and advanced startup options for Windows 2000, press F8.
```

FIGURE 16.37 Boot loader in Windows 2000 with System Recovery Console

(SATA) controller, and you set the system to boot first from the PATA, any drive on that controller will get the value `multi(0)` placed in its ARC format. Any SATA drive will get `multi(1)`.

`Disk(x)` is used only for SCSI drives, but the value is required in the ARC format, so with ATA systems it's always set to `disk(0)`.

`Rdisk(x)` specifies the number of the disk on the adapter. On a PATA drive, the master is `rdisk(0)` and the slave is `rdisk(1)`. On SATA drives, the order is usually based on the number of the SATA connection printed on the motherboard, though some systems allow you to change this in CMOS.

`Partition(x)` is the number of the partition or logical drive in an extended partition. The numbering starts at 1, so the first partition is `partition(1)`, the second is `partition(2)`, and so on.

`\WINDOWS` is the name of the folder that holds the boot files. This is important to appreciate. The ARC format looks at the folder, so there's no problem running different versions of Windows on a single partition. You can simply install them in different folders. Of course, you have other limitations, such as file system type, but in general, multibooting in Windows is pretty trivial. Better yet, this is all handled during the install process.

ARC format can get far more complicated. SCSI drives get a slightly different ARC format. For example, if you installed Windows on a SCSI drive, you might see this ARC setting in your BOOT.INI:

```
scsi(0)disk(1)rdisk(0)partition(1)
```

If you want to boot to a SCSI drive, Windows will add a fourth file to your system files called NTBOOTDD.SYS. This file will exist only if you want to boot to a SCSI drive. Most people don't boot to a SCSI, so don't worry if you don't see this file with the other three system files.

On rare occasions, you might find yourself needing to edit the BOOT.INI file. Any text editor handily edits this file, but most of us prefer to edit BOOT.INI via the System Setup dialog box. In Windows 2000/XP, open the System applet from the Control Panel. Click the Advanced tab and then click the Startup and Recovery button. The BOOT.INI options show up at the top (Figure 16.38).

BOOT.INI has some interesting switches at the end of the ARC formats that give special instructions on how the OS should boot. Sometimes Windows puts these in automatically, and sometimes you will add them manually for trouble-shooting. Here are a few of the more common ones:

- **/BOOTLOG** Tells Windows to create a log of the boot process and write it to a file called Ntbtlog.txt.
- **/CMDCONS** Tells Windows to start the Recovery Console.

FIGURE 16.38 BOOT.INI

- **/LASTKNOWNGOOD** Tells Windows to boot the Last Known Good set of files.
- **/NOEXECUTE** Newer CPUs come with Data Execute Protection (DEP) to prevent unruly programs from causing system lockups. The setting for this, /NOEXECUTE=OPTIN, is the default on Windows systems.

NTDETECT.COM

If the NTLDR determines that you have chosen to start Windows 2000/XP, it boots the system into protected mode and then calls on *NTDETECT.COM* to detect the installed hardware on the system. NTLDR then refers to the BOOT.INI file to locate the Windows boot files.

Critical Boot Files

Naming all of the critical boot files for Windows 2000/XP is akin to naming every muscle in the human body—completely possible, but time-consuming and without any real benefit. However, a few of the *most* important files certainly deserve a short mention.

Once NTLDR finishes detections, it loads NTOSKRNL.EXE, HAL.DLL, some of the Registry, and some basic device drivers; then it passes control to the NTOSKRNL.EXE file. NTOSKRNL.EXE completes the Registry loading, initializes all device drivers, and starts the WINLOGON.EXE program, which displays the Windows 2000/XP logon screen (Figure 16.39).

Take the time to memorize the primary boot files and the boot process for Windows 2000/XP. Most boot errors are easily repaired if you know which files are used for booting and in which order they load.

FIGURE 16.39 Where do you want to go today?

Objective 16.04 Windows Versions

Up to this point we've been talking about two different versions of Windows: Windows 2000 Professional and Windows XP Professional. This is a great way to look at the big picture with Windows OSs, but if you want to get detailed—and you need to get detailed—Windows 2000 and Windows XP are really families of Windows OSs. In this section, we'll look at every version of Windows 2000 and XP, as well as a few other versions of Windows, and see the differences in detail.

Before Windows XP came along, Windows was in a bit of a mess. Microsoft had two totally different OSs—each called Windows—that it sold for two different markets. Microsoft sold the old Windows 9x series (Windows 95, Windows 98, and Windows Me) for the home user and small office, and the much more powerful Windows NT was for corporate environments. The Windows 9x OSs were little more than upgrades from the old DOS OS, still tied to old 8088 programs (we call these 16-bit programs), unable to use the powerful NTFS and generally unstable for any serious work. Windows NT had all the power and security we love in Windows 2000 and XP, but it lacked a powerful interface and many other little niceties we expect in our Windows today.

Windows 2000 was the first step toward changing this mess. It was based on the old Windows NT, but for the first time it included a great interface, support for nearly any program, and was generally substantially easier to use than the old Windows NT. Microsoft originally presented Windows 2000 as a replacement for Windows NT, but its stability and ease of use motivated many knowledgeable Windows 9x users to upgrade. Windows 2000 is still popular today, even with Windows XP and Windows Vista now available.

Windows 2000 comes in two versions: Professional and Server. Every description of Windows 2000 thus far in the book has referred to the Professional version, so let's talk about Server. If you were to look at the Windows 2000 Server desktop, you'd be hard-pressed to see any obvious differences from Windows 2000. Windows 2000 Server (Figure 16.40) is the heavy-duty version, loaded with extra software and features that make it superb for running an office server. Windows 2000 Server is also extremely expensive, costing on average around $200 per computer that accesses the server.

Windows XP was designed to be the one-stop OS for everyone. And because Microsoft sees three types of users—professionals, home users, and media junkies—Windows XP comes in three different versions: Windows XP Professional, Windows XP Home; and Windows XP Media Center. There is no official server version of Windows XP.

FIGURE 16.40 Windows 2000 Server

Travel Advisory

Windows Server 2003 is not an official XP version, but it is the server Microsoft likes folks to use with Windows XP.

Windows XP Professional

Microsoft Windows XP Professional offers a complete computing solution, tuned for office environments that support multiple users. It provides full-blown data security, and it is the only version of Windows with the ability to log into a special Windows Server–controlled network called a *domain*. (Windows domains are discussed in detail in Chapter 18.)

Windows XP Home

As its name implies, Windows XP Home is designed for the home and small office user. The best way to describe Windows XP Home is to list the Windows XP

Professional features that Windows XP Home lacks. Windows XP Home does *not* have these features:

- **The ability to log on to a Windows domain** A Windows Home PC may log into any single Windows server, but you must have a user name and password on every single server. With a domain, you can have one user name and password that works on all computers that are members of the domain.

- **Encrypted File System** With Windows XP Professional, you can encrypt a file so that only you can read it.

- **Support for multiple processors** Windows XP Home does not support more than one CPU. Surprisingly, it does support dual-core CPUs.

- **Support for Remote Desktop** A Windows XP Professional PC may be remotely accessed from another computer using the Remote Desktop (Figure 16.41). You cannot access a Windows XP Home system in this fashion.

FIGURE 16.41 Remote Desktop

- **Support for NTFS Access Control** Remember all those neato NTFS permissions like Full Control, Modify, and Read & Execute? Windows XP Home doesn't give you the ability to control these NTFS permissions individually. When you look at the properties of a file or folder in Windows XP Home, you'll notice that there is no Security tab. Instead, Windows XP Home's Sharing tab (Figure 16.42) shows that only one folder, the Shared Documents folder, is open for sharing—very different from XP Professional.

- **Support for group policies** Do you need to keep users from using a certain program? Do you want to prevent them from changing the screensaver? What do you want to do if they try to log in three times unsuccessfully? That's the job of group polices. If you want this level of control on your system, get Windows XP Professional, since XP Home doesn't support them.

Windows XP Professional and XP Home have a few more differences, but these are the ones you're most likely to encounter. Basically, if you want serious control of the folders, files, users, and network, you need XP Professional.

FIGURE 16.42 Windows XP Home Sharing tab

Windows XP Media Center

Microsoft Media Center is a specialized XP version that includes the very handy Windows Media Center program (Figure 16.43). Media Center is a powerful Personal Video Recorder (PVR) program that enables you to watch and record television (you'll need a TV tuner card) and organize all of your media, from photos to music.

On the Microsoft Media Center Web site, Microsoft declares that the Windows XP Microsoft Media Center Edition is based on Windows XP Professional; however, other than the Media Center program, Windows XP Media Center's capabilities are identical to those of Windows XP Home.

Windows 64-Bit Versions

Microsoft has multiple versions of Windows designed to support 64-bit CPUs. Remember from Chapter 5 that two families of 64-bit CPUs exist: those that don't support 32-bit processors (such as the Intel Itanium 2) and those that can run both 64-bit and 32-bit (such as the Intel Core 2). The 64-bit-only version of Windows is called Windows XP 64-bit Edition (apparently Microsoft decided not to get cute when naming that one). Given that it works only on Intel Itanium

FIGURE 16.43 Microsoft Media Center

processors, the chance of you seeing this OS is pretty small unless you decide to work in a place with powerful server needs. The Windows XP Professional x64 Edition is much more common, as it runs on any AMD or Intel processor that supports both 32 and 64 bits (Figure 16.44).

Travel Advisory
Windows Server 2003 also has a 64-bit version.

Windows XP 64-bit versions have had some impact, as they were the first stable Windows versions that truly supported 64-bit processing, but the introduction of Microsoft Vista really started the move into the 64-bit world.

Windows Vista

Even though Windows Vista is not a part of the current CompTIA A+ certification exams, it's important that you at least recognize Vista and know what choices you have when deciding which version of Vista you need for a particular PC. Each of several different versions of Vista is geared toward a particular market segment. Let's look at the different versions.

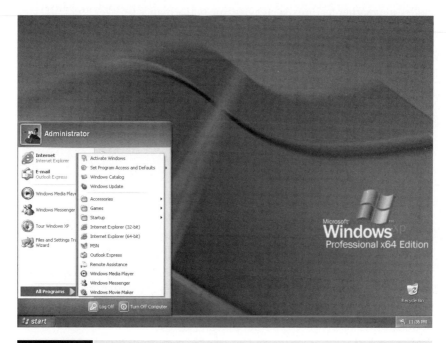

FIGURE 16.44 Windows XP Professional x64 Edition

Windows Vista Home Basic

Vista Home Basic is roughly equivalent to XP Home. Microsoft gears it to home users who don't need advanced multimedia support.

Windows Vista Home Premium

Vista Home Premium is the same as Vista Home Basic, but it adds PVR capabilities similar to those of Windows XP Media Center.

Windows Vista Business

Vista Business is the basic business version and has all the security, file sharing, and access controls available in Windows XP Professional.

Windows Vista Enterprise

Windows Vista Enterprise adds a few features to Vista Business, including more advanced encryption and support for multiple languages from a single install location. This version is available only to enterprise (large corporate) buyers of Windows.

Windows Vista Ultimate

Vista Ultimate combines all of the features of every other Vista version and includes some other features, such as a game performance tweaker and DVD ripping capability.

Windows Mobile

Windows Mobile is a small version of Windows designed for PDAs and phones. Windows Mobile is available only as an Original Equipment Manufacturer (OEM) product, which means you buy the device and it comes with Windows Mobile—you can't buy some PDA or phone and then buy Windows Mobile separately.

Windows XP Tablet PC

A Tablet PC is a laptop with a built-in touch screen (Figure 16.45). The idea behind a Tablet PC is to reduce drastically, if not totally eliminate, the use of a keyboard. Tablet PCs have become popular in several roles, such as teaching and health care. Windows XP Tablet PC edition is Microsoft's operating solution for Tablet PCs. Tablet PC is still Windows XP, but it adds special drivers and applications to support the tablet.

FIGURE 16.45 Tablet PC

CHECKPOINT

✔**Objective 16.01: Essential Tech Utilities** You can access utilities in five common locations in Windows: pop-up menu (right-click), Control Panel, System Tools, Administrative Tools, and the Microsoft Management Console. Throw in the command line, and you've got a sixth.

✔**Objective 16.02: Windows Structure** Windows 2000/XP are robust and scalable. They can handle multiple processors and implement NTFS on hard drives for serious data security. You can enhance security and make user management far more streamlined by using user accounts and groups. These plus NTFS enable you to set permissions of various levels on just about everything in the PC.

✔**Objective 16.03: Booting Windows** The CPU wakes up and runs the system BIOS, and then the BIOS sends out a routine looking for a valid OS in the boot sector of the primary, master hard drive. The MFT lives in the boot sector of the C: partition. It points to the location of the Windows 2000/XP system files, also on the C: drive, because that's the bootable drive.

✔**Objective 16.04: Windows Versions** Windows comes in many versions. Windows 2000 offers Server and Professional. Windows XP has Home, Professional, Media Center, Tablet, and 64-bit versions. Windows Vista comes in Home Basic, Home Premium, Business, Enterprise, and Ultimate.

REVIEW QUESTIONS

1. What's the easiest way to access the properties of an object in Windows?
 A. Right-click and select Properties.
 B. Left-click and select Properties.
 C. Double-click and select Properties.
 D. In the Control Panel, select the Properties applet.

2. Which Control Panel applet enables you to access essential system information and tools, such as Device Manager?
 A. Add or Remove Programs
 B. Display
 C. Program Options
 D. System

3. Which keyboard shortcut opens the System Properties dialog box?
 A. WINDOWS-PAUSE
 B. WINDOWS-ENTER
 C. CTRL-PAUSE
 D. CTRL-ENTER

4. What tool would you use to migrate a co-worker's essential files and folders to a new computer?
 A. Character Map
 B. Disk Cleanup
 C. Files and Settings Transfer Wizard
 D. Migrate Wizard

5. How do you open the Microsoft Management Console?
 A. Start | All Programs | System Tools | MMC
 B. Start | Control Panel | Manage applet
 C. Start | Run | type **MMC**
 D. Start | Run | type **manage**

6. Which tool enables you to view logs and monitor real-time data?

 A. Device Manager

 B. Log console

 C. Performance console

 D. System applet

7. What is the capability of supporting multiple CPUs in a single system called?

 A. HAL

 B. MFT

 C. MMC

 D. SMP

8. Which of the following are advantages of NTFS over FAT32? (Select two.)

 A. Long filenames

 B. Support for Windows 9x files

 C. Security through user accounts

 D. Transaction logging

9. What account type can access anything on a Windows system?

 A. Administrator

 B. Power User

 C. Super User

 D. User

10. Which files are the Windows system files?

 A. NTOSKRNL.EXE, SYSTEM

 B. NTOSKRNL.EXE, NTLDR, BOOT.INI

 C. NTLDR, NTDETECT.COM, BOOT.INI

 D. SYSTEM, NTDETECT.COM, BOOT.INI

REVIEW ANSWERS

1. **A** Right-click any object in Windows and select Properties from the menu to see the properties for that object.

2. **D** The System applet enables you to access essential system information and tools, such as Device Manager.

3. **A** Use the WINDOWS-PAUSE keyboard combination to open the System Properties applet.

4. **C** The Files and Settings Transfer Wizard can assist in migrating from one computer to another.

5. **C** You can open a blank MMC by choosing Start | Run, typing **MMC**, and pressing ENTER.

6. **C** The Performance console offers the System Monitor and Performance Logs and Alerts snap-ins. These enable you to view logs and monitor real-time data.

7. **D** SMP, for symmetric multiprocessing, is the capability of supporting multiple CPUs in a single system.

8. **C D** Among other things, NTFS offers better security through user accounts and recoverability through transaction logging.

9. **A** The Administrator account can access any object in a Windows system.

10. **C** The three system files are NTLDR, NTDETECT.COM, and BOOT.INI.

Installing and Upgrading Windows

	NEWBIE	SOME EXPERIENCE	EXPERT
ETA	4 hours	2 hours	1 hour

This chapter covers installing and upgrading Windows in detail, starting with steps you should take before installing. It also covers both generic installation and the specifics of installing and upgrading Windows 2000 and Windows XP. The chapter wraps with a discussion on troubleshooting installs.

Objective 17.01 Preparing for Installation or Upgrade

Because installing an OS can be a time-consuming task, even when everything goes right, the Windows installation process holds great potential for lost time. Nothing sets the teeth to grinding as much as encountering an indecipherable or ambiguous error message or the infamous Blue Screen of Death 55 minutes into an hour-long system installation.

Preparation tasks help minimize such problems. They go pretty fast and skipping them can cause you gobs of grief later. You need to complete the following nine tasks *before* you insert that CD or DVD:

1. Identify hardware requirements.
2. Verify hardware and software compatibility.
3. Decide whether to perform a clean installation or an upgrade.
4. Determine how to back up and restore existing data, if necessary.
5. Select an installation method.
6. Determine how to partition the hard drive and what file system to use.
7. Determine your computer's network role.
8. Decide on your computer's language and locale settings.
9. Plan for post-installation tasks.

Identify Hardware Requirements

Hardware requirements help you decide whether a computer system is a reasonable host for a particular operating system (OS). Requirements include the CPU model, the amount of RAM, the amount of free hard disk space, and the video adapter, display, and storage devices that may be required to install and run the OS. They are stated as minimums or, more recently, as recommended minimums. Although you could install an OS on a computer with the old minimums that Microsoft published, they were not realistic if you actually wanted to accomplish work. With the last few versions of Windows, Microsoft has published recommended minimums that are much more realistic. You

will find the published minimums on the packaging and at Microsoft's Web site (www.microsoft.com).

Verify Hardware and Software Compatibility

Assuming your system meets the requirements, you next need to find out how well Windows supports the brand and model of hardware and the application software you intend to use under Windows. You have two basic sources for this information: Microsoft and the manufacturer of the device or software. How do you access this information? Use the Web!

If you're installing Windows XP, the Setup Wizard automatically checks your hardware and software and reports any potential conflicts. But please don't wait until you are all ready to install to check this out. With any flavor of Windows, *first do your homework!*

Microsoft goes to great lengths to test any piece of hardware that might be used in a system running Windows through its Windows Marketplace (Figure 17.1). *Windows Marketplace,* formerly known as the *Hardware Compati-*

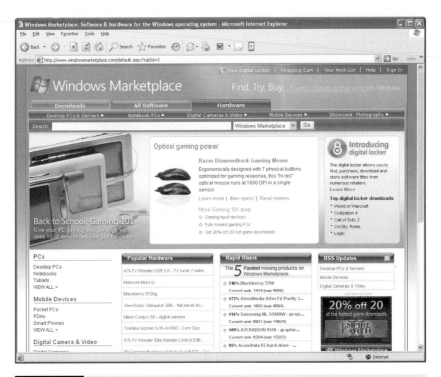

FIGURE 17.1 Windows Marketplace

bility List (HCL), is the definitive authority as to whether your component is compatible with the OS. Every component listed on the Windows Marketplace Web site has been extensively tested to verify it works with Windows 2000 and XP and is guaranteed by Microsoft to work with your installation. The URL for Windows Marketplace is www.windowsmarketplace.com.

> ## Local Lingo
>
> **Windows Catalog** You'll occasionally hear the HCL or Windows Marketplace referred to as the Windows Catalog. The Windows Catalog was a list of supported hardware Microsoft would add to the Windows installation CD. The Windows Marketplace Web site is the modern tech's best source, so use that rather than any printed resources.

When you install a device that's not tested by Microsoft, a rather scary screen appears (Figure 17.2). This doesn't mean the component won't work, only that it's not been tested by Microsoft. Not all component makers go through the process of getting the Microsoft approval so they can list their component in the Windows Marketplace. As a rule of thumb, unless the device is more than five years old, go ahead and install it. If it still doesn't work, you can simply uninstall it later.

When preparing to upgrade, check with the manufacturers of the applications already installed in the previous OS. If software compatibility problems exist with the versions you have, the manufacturer should provide upgrade packs that can be installed during the Windows setup process.

FIGURE 17.2 Untested device

Perform a Clean Installation or an Upgrade

A *clean installation* of an OS involves installing it onto an empty hard drive with no previous OS installed. An *upgrade installation* is an installation of an OS on top of an earlier installed version, thus inheriting all previous hardware and software settings.

You may think the choice between doing a clean installation and an upgrade installation is simple: you do a clean installation on a brand new computer with an empty hard drive, and you do an upgrade of a pre-existing installation. It isn't necessarily so! I'll tell you why as we look at this issue more closely.

Exam Tip

CompTIA A+ certification exams test you on your ability to upgrade a Windows 9x or Windows NT system to Windows 2000 or Windows XP. You do not need to know about Windows 9x or NT for the tests, but you do need to know how to upgrade them.

Clean Installation

A clean installation usually begins with a completely empty hard disk. The advantage to doing a clean installation is that you don't carry problems from the old OS over to the new one, but the disadvantage is that all applications have to be reinstalled and the desktop and each application reconfigured to the user's preferences. You perform a clean install by resetting your CMOS to tell the system to boot from the optical drive before your hard drive. You then boot off a Windows 2000 or XP installation CD-ROM, and Windows will give you the opportunity to partition and format the hard drive and then install Windows.

Upgrade Installation

In an upgrade installation, the new OS installs into the same folders as the old OS, or in tech speak, the new installs *on top of* the old. The new OS replaces the old OS but retains all saved data and inherits all the previous settings (such as font styles, desktop colors and background, and so on), hardware, and applications. You don't have to reinstall your favorite programs!

To begin the upgrade of Windows, you must run the appropriate program from the CD-ROM. This usually means inserting a Windows 2000 or Windows XP installation CD-ROM into your system while your old OS is running, which will start the install program. Then, to do an upgrade, you indicate that

Windows 2000 or XP should install into a directory that already contains an installation of Windows (it will do this by default). You will be asked whether it is an upgrade or a new installation; if you select new installation, it will remove the existing OS before installing.

If for some reason the install program doesn't start automatically, go to My Computer, open the CD-ROM, and locate WINNT32.EXE. This program starts an upgrade to Windows 2000 or XP.

Multiboot

A third option that you need to be aware of is dual boot or *multiboot installation*. Both Windows 2000 and Windows XP can install in a separate folder from your existing copy of Windows. Then every time your computer boots, you'll get a menu asking you which version of Windows you wish to boot. Multiboot sounds great, but it has lots of nasty little problems. For example, let's say you've got a system running Windows Me that you would like to upgrade to Windows XP. Windows Me must use either a FAT or a FAT32 file system; Windows XP can use these old file systems, but you'll miss out on the benefits of using NTFS.

Other Installation Methods

In medium-sized to large organizations, more advanced installation methods are often employed, especially when many computers need to be configured identically. A common method is to place the source files in a shared directory on a network server. Then, whenever a tech needs to install a new OS, it is a simple task of booting up the computer, connecting to the source location on the network, and starting the installation from there. This method alone has many variations, and it can be automated with special scripts that automatically select the options and components needed. The scripts can even install the necessary applications at the end of the OS installation—all without user intervention once the installation has been started.

Another type of installation that is popular for re-creating standard configurations is an *image installation*. An image is a complete copy of a hard disk volume on which an OS and, usually, all required application software has been preinstalled. Images can be on optical discs, in which case the tech runs special software on the computer that copies the image onto the local hard drive. Images can also be stored on special network servers, in which case the tech connects to the image server using special software and copies the image from the server to the local hard drive. A leader in this technology has been Norton Ghost, which is available from Symantec. Other similar programs are PowerQuest's Drive Image and Acronis's True Image.

Beginning with Windows 2000 Server, Microsoft added *Remote Installation Services (RIS)*, which can be used to initiate either a scripted installation or an installation of an image.

Back Up and Restore Existing Data, if Necessary

Whether you are installing or upgrading, you may need to back up existing user data before installing or upgrading because things can go wrong either way, and the data on the hard drive might be damaged. You'll need to find out where the user is currently saving data files. If files are being saved onto the local hard drive, it must be backed up before the installation or replacement takes place, to preserve the data. However, if all data has been saved to a network location, you are in luck because the data is safe from damage during installation.

If the user saves data locally, and the computer is connected to a network, save the data, at least temporarily, to a network location until after the upgrade or installation has taken place. If the computer is not connected to a network, but the computer has a burnable optical drive, copy the data to CDs or DVDs. Wherever you save the data, you will need to copy or restore any lost or damaged data back to the local hard disk after the installation.

Select an Installation Method

Once you've backed up everything important, you need to select an installation method. You have two basic choices: insert the CD-ROM disc into the drive and go, or install over a network. The latter method falls into the realm of CompTIA Network+ technicians or even network administrators, so this book assumes you'll install from disc.

Partition the Hard Drive and Choose a System

If you are performing a clean installation, you need to decide ahead of time how to partition the disk space on your hard disk drive, including the number and size of partitions and the file system you will use. Actually, in the decision process, the file system comes first, and then the space issue follows, as you will see.

If you are not planning a multiboot installation, use NTFS. If you are planning a multiboot configuration, the highest common denominator rule applies, at least for the system volume, and for any volumes you want usable by the oldest OS. Once you know which file system you are using, deciding the size and

number of partitions will follow, because if you decide to use FAT16, you will have the size limitations of FAT16 to deal with.

Your Computer's Network Role

The question of your computer's network role comes up in one form or another during a Windows installation. A Windows computer can have one of several roles relative to a network (in Microsoft terms). One role, called *stand-alone*, is actually a non-network role, and it simply means that the computer does not participate on a network. Any version of Windows can be installed on a stand-alone computer, and this is the only role that a Windows XP Home computer can play on a network. Every other modern version of Windows can be a member of either a workgroup or domain. You will learn more about the workgroup and domain member roles in Chapter 18.

Your Computer's Language and Locale Settings

These settings are especially important for Windows 2000 and Windows XP, because these versions have greatly increased support for various spoken languages and locale conventions. The locale settings determine how date and time information is displayed and which math separators and currency symbols are used for various locations.

Post-Installation Tasks

After installing Windows, you will need to install the latest service pack or update. You may also need to install updated drivers and reconfigure any settings, such as network settings, that were found not to work. You will also need to install any applications (word processor, spreadsheet, database, and so on) required by the user of the computer. Finally, don't forget to restore any data backed up before the installation or upgrade.

 Objective 17.02 # Installing and Upgrading Windows 2000/XP

Installing a modern OS follows pretty standardized steps: insert disc, click at prompts, reboot a few times, and then run through essential post-installation steps. This section looks at generic installation and post-installation, and then examines issues specific to Windows 2000 and Windows XP.

During the Installation

When performing a Windows installation (also called setup) you'll notice that the screen progresses from simple textual information on a plain background to a full graphical interface. During text mode, the computer is inspecting the hardware, and it will then display the *End User License Agreement (EULA)*, which you must accept for setup to continue. It is during the text display portion of an installation that you can partition your hard disk. Also during this time, the computer copies files to the local hard disk, including a base set of files for running the graphical portion of the setup.

When finished with the text part of the setup, the computer reboots, which starts the graphical portion of the installation. You are prompted to enter the *product key*, which is invariably located on the CD/DVD case. Most techs learn the hard way that these covers tend to disappear when you need them most, and they write the product code directly on the CD or DVD itself. (Just don't use a ballpoint pen; it'll scratch the surface of the disc.) See Figure 17.3.

Most of the installation process takes place in the graphical portion. This is where you select configuration options and choose optional Windows components.

FIGURE 17.3 Product key written on the installation CD-ROM

No matter your version of Windows, the installation process always gets to the point where Windows begins to install itself on the system. I call this "The Big Copy" and use this time to catch up on my reading, eat a sandwich, or count ceiling tiles.

Travel Advisory

Windows comes in both upgrade and full versions. Make sure you use the correct CD-ROM (or DVD, in the case of Windows Vista). Some systems, particularly laptops, require a special OEM version made just for that system. Don't bother trying to use an upgrade version to install on a blank drive unless you also possess a CD-ROM with a full earlier version of Windows.

Windows Vista makes this process a little more annoying, requiring you to install a previous version of Windows before you can use a Vista upgrade disc. You can get by this if you don't have a copy of pre-Vista Windows laying around by installing Vista twice, once as an evaluation copy and the second time for real. Either way, though, you're forced to do two complete installations to use the upgrade disc.

Post-Installation Tasks

You might think that's enough work for one day, but a few more tasks remain on your list. They include identifying installation problems (if they occur), updating the OS with patches and service packs, upgrading drivers, and restoring user data files.

Identifying Installation Problems

After you install or upgrade Windows, you need to use your powers of observation to check whether you've had a serious installation problem. The worst problems show up early in the installation process, but others may show up later as you work in Windows. If your installation wasn't successful, check out Objective 17.03 for information and help.

Patches, Service Packs, and Updates

Someone once described an airliner as consisting of millions of parts flying in close formation. I think that's also a good description for an OS. And we can even carry that analogy further by thinking about all the maintenance required to keep an airliner and an OS safely flying. Like an airliner, the parts (programming code) of your OS were created by different people, and some parts may have been manufactured by contractors rather than by the company that makes the OS. Although each component is tested as much as possible, and the

assembled OS is also tested, it's not possible to test for every possible combination of events. Sometimes a piece is simply found to be defective. The fix for such a problem is a corrective program called a *patch*.

In the past, Microsoft would provide patches for individual problems. It would also accumulate patches until they reached some sort of "critical mass" and then bundle them together as a *service pack*. Microsoft still does this, but it also combines appropriate patches and service packs into *updates* to make the process easier for you. These updates are available at Microsoft's Web site or on CD-ROM. Many organizations make the updates available for distribution from network servers. Immediately after installing Windows, install the latest updates on the computer. Chapter 19 covers this process fully.

Upgrading Drivers

Even if you completed all your preinstallation tasks, you may decide to go with the default drivers that come with Windows and then upgrade them to the latest drivers after the fact. This is a good strategy, because installation is a complicated task, and you can simplify it by installing old but adequate drivers. Maybe those newest drivers are just a week old—waiting until after the Windows install to install new drivers will give you a usable driver to go back to if the new driver turns out to be a lemon.

Restoring User Data Files (if Applicable)

Remember when you backed up the user data files before installation? You don't? Well, check again, because now is the time to restore that data. Your method of restoring will depend on how you backed up the files in the first place. If you used a third-party backup program, you will need to install it before you can restore those files, but if you used Windows Backup, you are in luck, because it is installed by default in Windows 2000/XP Professional. If you did something simpler, like copying to an optical disc or a network location, all you have to do is copy the files back to the local hard disk. Good luck!

Installing or Upgrading to Windows 2000 Professional

On the face of it, installing Windows 2000 Professional seems fairly simple. You insert the CD-ROM, access the setup routine, and go. But that conceptualization does not hold up in practice.

Hardware Requirements

The minimum specs represent what Microsoft says you need to install the Windows 2000 Professional OS. However, you need to take these specifica-

tions and at least double them if you want to be happy with your system's performance.

Here are more realistic recommendations for a useful Windows 2000 Professional computer system:

Component	Minimum for a Windows 2000 Professional Computer	Recommended for a Windows 2000 Professional Computer
CPU	Intel Pentium 133 MHz	Intel Pentium II 350 MHz
Memory	64 MB	128 MB
Hard disk	2 GB with 650 MB of free space	6.4 GB with 2 GB of free space
Network	None	Modern network card
Display	Video adapter and monitor with VGA resolution	Video adapter and monitor with SVGA resolution, capable of high-color (16-bit) display
Optical drive	If you don't have an optical drive, you must use a floppy disk drive or install over a network	If you don't have an optical drive, you must use a floppy disk drive or install over a network

If your test system(s) exceeds the recommended configuration, all the better. You can never have too fast a processor or too much hard disk space.

Installing or Upgrading to Windows XP Professional

You prepare for a Windows XP installation just as you would for installing Windows 2000. Windows XP has a few different aspects to it that are worth considering as separate issues.

Upgrade Paths

You can upgrade to Windows XP Professional from all the following versions of Windows:

- Windows 98 (all versions)
- Windows Me
- Windows NT 4.0 Workstation (Service Pack 5 and later)
- Windows 2000 Professional (including service packs)
- Windows XP Home Edition

XP Hardware Requirements

Hardware requirements for Windows XP Professional are higher than for previous versions of Windows but quite in line with even a modestly priced computer today.

Microsoft XP runs on a wide range of computers, but you need to be sure that your computer meets the minimum hardware requirements as shown here. Also shown is a recommended minimum for a system running a typical selection of business productivity software.

Component	Minimum for a Windows XP Computer	Recommended for a Windows XP Computer
CPU	Any Intel or AMD 233 MHz or higher processor	Any Intel or AMD 300 MHz or higher processor
Memory	64 MB of RAM (though Microsoft admits XP will be somewhat crippled with only this amount)	256 MB of RAM or higher
Hard disk	1.5 GB of available hard drive space	4 GB of available hard drive space
Network	None	Modern network card
Display	Video card that supports DirectX 8 with at least 800×600 resolution	Video card that supports DirectX 8 with at least 800×600 resolution
Optical drive	Any CD- or DVD-media drive	Any CD- or DVD-media drive

Hardware and Software Compatibility

You'll need to check hardware and software compatibility before installing Windows XP Professional—either as an upgrade or a new installation. Of course, if you purchase a computer with Windows XP preinstalled, you're spared this task, but you'll still need to verify that the application software you plan to add to the computer will be compatible. Luckily, Microsoft includes the Upgrade Advisor on the Windows XP CD-ROM.

Upgrade Advisor The *Upgrade Advisor* is the first process that runs on the XP installation CD-ROM. It examines your hardware and installed software (in the case of an upgrade) and provides a list of devices and software that are known to have issues with XP. Be sure to follow the suggestions on this list.

The Upgrade Advisor can also be run separately from the Windows XP installation. You can run it from the Windows XP CD-ROM, or, if you want to

find out about compatibility for an upgrade before purchasing Windows XP, you can download the Upgrade Advisor from Microsoft's Web site (www .microsoft.com—search for "Upgrade Advisor"). Follow the instructions in the sidebar to use the online Upgrade Advisor.

Booting into Windows XP Setup

The Windows XP CD-ROMs are bootable, and Microsoft no longer includes a program to create a set of setup boot disks. This should not be an issue, because PCs manufactured in the last several years have the ability to boot from the optical drive. This system BIOS setting, usually described as "boot order," is controlled through a PC's BIOS-based setup program.

In the unlikely event that your lab computer can't be made to boot from an optical disc, you can create a set of six Windows XP setup boot floppy disks using a special program you can download from Microsoft's Web site. Note that Microsoft provides separate boot disk programs for XP Home and XP Pro.

Registration versus Activation

During setup, you will be prompted to register your product and activate it. Many people confuse activation with registration, but these are two separate operations. *Registration* tells Microsoft who the official owner or user of the product is, providing contact information such as name, address, company, phone number, e-mail address, and so on. Registration is still entirely optional. Activation is a way to combat software piracy, meaning that Microsoft wishes to ensure that each license for Windows XP is used solely on a single computer. It's more formally called *Microsoft Product Activation (MPA)*.

Mandatory Activation within 30 Days of Installation Activation is mandatory, but you can skip this step during installation. You will have 30 days in which to activate the product, during which time it will work normally. If you don't activate it within that time frame, it will be disabled. Don't worry about forgetting, though, because once it's installed, Windows XP frequently reminds you to activate it with a balloon message over the tray area of the taskbar. The messages even tell you how many days you have left.

Activation Mechanics Here is how product activation works. When you choose to activate, either during setup or later when XP reminds you to do it, the product ID code that you entered during installation is combined with a 50-digit value that identifies your key hardware components to create an installation ID code. You must send this code to Microsoft, either automatically if you have an Internet connection, or verbally via a phone call to Microsoft. Microsoft then returns a 42-digit product activation code. If you are activating online, you

don't have to enter the activation code; it will happen automatically. If you are activating over the phone, you must read the installation ID to a representative and enter the resulting 42-digit activation code into the Activate Windows by Phone dialog box.

No personal information about you is sent as part of the activation process. Figure 17.4 shows the dialog box that will open when you start activation by clicking the reminder message balloon.

Upgrading Issues for Windows 2000 and Windows XP

Upgrading your computer system from an earlier version of Windows can be a tricky affair, with its own set of pitfalls. It is important to note that you have a somewhat higher risk of running into errors during an upgrade than you do when performing a "clean" installation.

Here are some of the issues that you should be aware of before performing an upgrade:

- You can upgrade directly to Windows 2000 Professional from Windows 95/98 (but not Windows Me) and Windows NT Workstation.

FIGURE 17.4 Activation will take just seconds with an Internet connection.

- Because of differences between Windows 9x and Windows 2000/XP, you might find that some programs that ran well under Windows 9x will not run under Windows 2000/XP. Not only does Windows 2000/XP have new hardware requirements, it also does not like a lot of Windows 9x software!
- Third-party disk compression applications are not supported by Windows 2000/XP.
- Third-party power management applications are also likely to cause problems with a Windows 2000/XP installation.

Obviously, it's worth your time to take a few extra steps before you pop in that installation CD-ROM. If you plan to upgrade rather than perform a clean installation, make sure to do all the preinstallation tasks outlined earlier in this chapter.

The Windows 2000/XP
Clean Install Process

The steps involved in a clean installation of Windows 2000 Professional and Windows XP are virtually identical. The only differences are the order of two steps and some of the art on the screens that appear, so we can comfortably discuss both installations at the same time.

Travel Advisory

Not all screens in the install process are shown here.

A clean install begins with your system set to boot to your optical drive and the Windows install CD-ROM in the drive. You start your PC, and assuming you've got the boot order right, the Setup program starts booting (Figure 17.5). Note at the bottom that it says to press F6 for a third-party SCSI or RAID driver. Pressing F6 is necessary only if you want to install Windows onto a strange drive and Windows does not already have the driver for that drive. Don't worry about this—Windows has a huge assortment of drivers for just about every hard drive ever made, and in the rare situation when you need a third-party driver, the folks who sell you the SCSI or RAID array will tell you ahead of time.

After the system copies a number of files, you'll see the Welcome screen (Figure 17.6). This is an important screen. As you'll see in later chapters, techs often use the Windows install CD-ROM as a repair tool, and this is the screen that lets you choose between installing Windows or repairing an existing installation. Since you're installing anew, press ENTER.

Press F6 if you need to install a third party SCSI or RAID driver...

FIGURE 17.5 Windows Setup text screen

You're next prompted to read and accept the EULA. Nobody reads this, so just press F8 and move to the next screen to start partitioning the drive (Figure 17.7).

If your hard disk is unpartitioned, you will need to create a new partition when prompted. Follow the instructions. In most cases, you can make a single partition, although you can easily make as many partitions as you wish. You can also delete partitions if you're using a hard drive that was partitioned in the past

```
Windows XP Professional Setup

   Welcome to Setup.

   This portion of the Setup program prepares Microsoft(R)
   Windows(R) XP to run on your computer.

       •  To set up Windows XP now, press ENTER.

       •  To repair a Windows XP installation using
          Recovery Console, press R.

       •  To quit Setup without installing Windows XP, press F3.

   ENTER=Continue   R=Repair   F3=Quit
```

FIGURE 17.6 Welcome text screen

```
Windows XP Professional Setup

The following list shows the existing partitions and
unpartitioned space on this computer.

Use the UP and DOWN ARROW keys to select an item in the list.

    •  To set up Windows XP on the selected item, press ENTER.

    •  To create a partition in the unpartitioned space, press C.

    •  To delete the selected partition, press D.

8190 MB Disk 0 at Id 0 on bus 0 on atapi [MBR]

       Unpartitioned space                    8189 MB

 ENTER=Install   C=Create Partition   F3=Quit
```

FIGURE 17.7 Partitioning text screen

(or if you mess up your partitioning). Note that there is no option to make a primary or extended partition; this tool makes the first partition primary and the rest extended.

After you've made the partition(s), you must select the partition on which to install XP (sort of trivial if you have only one partition), and then you need to decide which file system format to use for the new partition. Unless you have some weird need to support FAT or FAT32, format the partition using NTFS (Figure 17.8).

Setup will now format the drive and copy some basic installation files to the newly formatted partition, displaying another progress bar. Go get a book to read while you wait.

After it completes copying the base set of files to the hard drive, your computer reboots, and the graphical mode of Windows setup begins. This is where 2000 and XP begin to vary in appearance, even though they are performing the same steps. The rest of this section shows Windows XP. If you're installing Windows 2000, compare it to the screens you see here—it's interesting to see the different presentation doing the same job.

You will see a generic screen during the install that looks like Figure 17.9. On the left of the screen, white buttons appear next to uncompleted tasks, green buttons appear next to completed tasks, and a red button appears next to the current task. You'll see plenty of advertising to read as you install.

The screens that follow ask questions about a number of things the computer needs to know. They include the desired region and language in which the com-

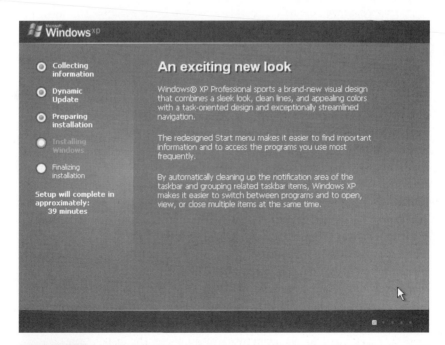

```
Windows XP Professional Setup

The partition you selected is not formatted. Setup will now
format the partition.

Use the UP and DOWN ARROW keys to select the file system
you want, and then press ENTER.

If you want to select a different partition for Windows XP,
press ESC.

    Format the partition using the NTFS file system (Quick)
    Format the partition using the FAT file system (Quick)
    Format the partition using the NTFS file system
    Format the partition using the FAT file system
```

```
ENTER=Continue    ESC=Cancel
```

FIGURE 17.8 Choosing NTFS

puter will operate, your name and organization for personalizing your com-
puter, and a valid product key for Windows XP (Figure 17.10). Be sure to enter
the product key exactly, or you will be unable to continue.

Windows xp

○ Collecting
 information

○ Dynamic
 Update

○ Preparing
 installation

○ Installing
 Windows

○ Finalizing
 installation

**Setup will complete in
approximately:
 39 minutes**

An exciting new look

Windows® XP Professional sports a brand-new visual design
that combines a sleek look, clean lines, and appealing colors
with a task-oriented design and exceptionally streamlined
navigation.

The redesigned Start menu makes it easier to find important
information and to access the programs you use most
frequently.

By automatically cleaning up the notification area of the
taskbar and grouping related taskbar items, Windows XP
makes it easier to switch between programs and to open,
view, or close multiple items at the same time.

FIGURE 17.9 Beginning of graphical mode

Travel Advisory

Losing your product key is a bad thing. Document it—at least write it on the install CD-ROM.

Next, you need to give your computer a name that will identify it on a network. Check with your system administrator for an appropriate name. If you don't have a system administrator, just enter a simple name like *MYPC* for now—you can change this at any time—and read up on networking later in this book. You also need to create a password for the Administrator user account (Figure 17.11). Every Windows system has an Administrator user account that can do anything on the computer. Techs will need this account to modify and fix the computer in the future.

Last, you're asked for the correct date, time, and time zone. Then Windows tries to detect a network card. If a network card is detected, the network components will be installed and you'll have an opportunity to configure the network settings. Unless you know you need special settings for your network, just select the Typical Settings option (Figure 17.12). Relax; XP will do most of the work for you. Plus it's easy to change network settings after the installation.

FIGURE 17.11 Computer name and Administrator password

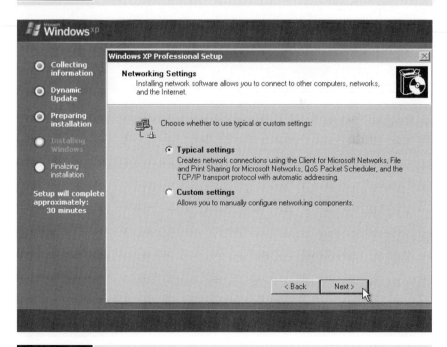

FIGURE 17.12 Selecting typical network settings

Travel Advisory

Even experienced techs usually select the Typical Settings option. Installation is not the time to be messing with network details unless you need to.

Install now begins The Big Copy of files from the CD-ROM to your hard drive. This is a good time to pick up your book, because watching the ads is boring (Figure 17.13).

After the files required for the final configuration are copied, XP will reboot again. During this reboot, XP determines your screen size and applies the appropriate resolution. This reboot can take several minutes to complete, so be patient.

Once the reboot is complete, you can log on as the Administrator. Balloon messages may appear over the tray area of the taskbar—a common message concerns the display resolution. Click the balloon and allow Windows XP to adjust the display settings automatically.

The final message in the installation process reminds you that you have 30 days left for activation. Go ahead and activate now over the Internet or by telephone. It's painless and quick. If you choose not to activate, simply click the Close button on the message balloon. You have successfully installed

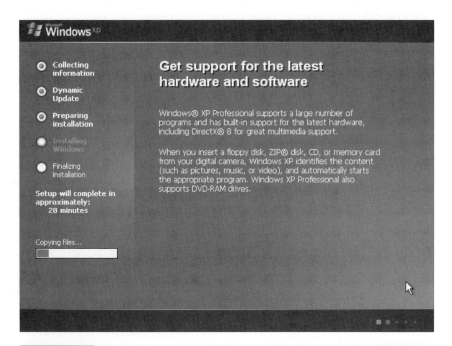

FIGURE 17.13 The Big Copy

Windows XP and should have a desktop with the default Bliss background, as shown in Figure 17.14.

Automating the Install

As you can see, you may have to sit around for quite a while during the install process. Instead of having to sit there answering questions and typing in CD keys, wouldn't it be nice just to boot up the machine and have the install process finish without any intervention on your part? Especially if you have 30 PCs that need to be ready to go tomorrow morning? Fortunately, Windows offers two good options for automating the install process: scripted installations and disk cloning.

Scripting Installations with Setup Manager

Microsoft provides *Setup Manager* to help you create a text file—called an *answer file*—containing all of your answers to the installation questions. Windows doesn't come with Setup Manager, but you can download it from the Microsoft Download Center (www.microsoft.com/downloads) as part of the Windows XP Service Pack 2 Deployment Tools. Setup Manager supports creating answer files for three different types of setups: unattended, sysprep, and Remote Installation

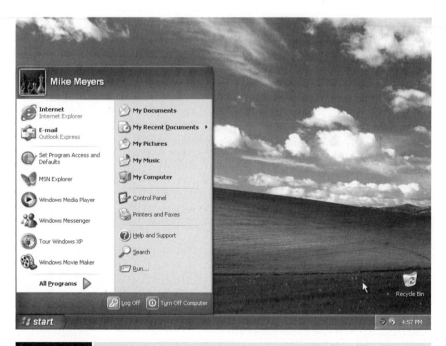

FIGURE 17.14 Windows XP desktop with Bliss background

Services (Figure 17.15). The current version of the tool can create answer files for Windows XP Home Edition, Windows XP Professional, and Windows Server 2003 (Standard, Enterprise, or Web Edition).

Setup Manager can create an answer file to automate the process completely, or it can be used to set default options. You'll almost always want to create an answer file that automates the entire process.

When running a scripted install, you have to decide how to make the installation files themselves available to the PC. While you can always boot your new machine from an install CD, you can save yourself a lot of CD swapping if you just put the install files on a network share and install your OS over the network (Figure 17.16).

When you run Setup Manager, you get to answer all those pesky questions. As always, you will also have to "Accept the Terms of the License Agreement" and specify the product key, but at least by scripting these steps you can do it once and get it over with.

Now it's time to get to the good stuff—customizing your installation. Using the graphical interface, decide what configuration options you want to use—screen resolutions, network options, browser settings, regional settings, and so on. You can even add finishing touches to the installation, installing additional programs such as Microsoft Office and Adobe Reader, by automatically running

FIGURE 17.15 Setup Manager can create three different types of answer files.

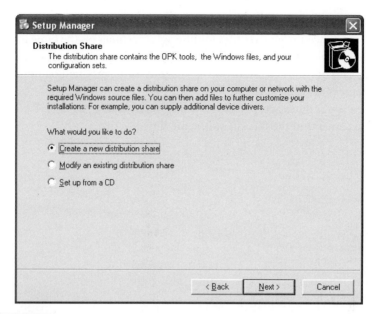

FIGURE 17.16 Choose where to store the install files.

additional commands after the Windows installation finishes (Figure 17.17). You can also set programs to run once.

FIGURE 17.17 Run additional commands.

Remember that computer names have to be unique on the network. If you're going to use the same answer files for multiple machines on the same network, you need to make sure that each one gets its own unique name. You can either provide a list of names to use, or you can have the setup program randomly generate names (Figure 17.18).

When you're done, Setup Manager prompts you to save your answers as a text file. The contents of the file will look something like this:

```
;SetupMgrTag
[Data]
    AutoPartition=1
    MsDosInitiated="0"
    UnattendedInstall="Yes"

[Unattended]
    UnattendMode=FullUnattended
    OemSkipEula=Yes
    OemPreinstall=No
    TargetPath=\WINDOWS

[GuiUnattended]
    AdminPassword=414c1lf760b0064 … [out to 64 characters]
    EncryptedAdminPassword=Yes
    OEMSkipRegional=1
    TimeZone=85
    OemSkipWelcome=1
    AutoLogon=Yes
    AutoLogonCount=1

[UserData]
    ProductKey=FFFFF-FFFFF-FFFFF-FFFFF-FFFFF
    FullName="Scott"
    OrgName="Total Seminars"
    ComputerName=*

[Identification]
    JoinDomain=TOTAL
    DomainAdmin=admin09
    DomainAdminPassword=my-password

[
```

The list goes on for another 100 lines or so, and this is a fairly simply answer file. One thing to note is that if you provide a domain administrator's user name and password for the purpose of automatically adding new PCs to your domain, that user name and password will be in the text file in clear text:

```
[Identification]
    JoinDomain=TOTAL
    DomainAdmin=admin09
    DomainAdminPassword=my-password
```

FIGURE 17.18 Choose your computer names.

In that case, you will want to be very careful about protecting your setup files.

Once you have your answer file created, you can start your installation with this command, and go enjoy a nice cup of coffee while the installation runs:

```
D:\i386\winnt32 /s:%SetupFiles% /unattend:%AnswerFile%
```

For %SetupFiles%, substitute the location of your setup files—either a local path (D:\i386 if you are installing from a CD) or a network path. If you use a network path, don't forget to create a network boot disk so that the install program can access the files. For %AnswerFile%, substitute the name of the text file that you created with Setup Manager (usually unattend.txt).

Of course, you don't have to use Setup Manager to create your answer file. Feel free to pull out your favorite text editor and write one from scratch. Most techs, however, will find it much easier to use the provided tool than to wrestle with the answer file's sometimes arcane syntax.

Scripted installations are a fine option, but they don't necessarily work well in all scenarios. Creating a fully scripted install, including the installation of all additional drivers, software updates, and applications, can be a time-consuming process involving lots of trial-and-error adjustments. Wouldn't it be easier, at least some of the time, to go ahead and take one PC, manually set it up exactly the way you want it, and then automatically create exact copies of that installation on other machines? That's where disk cloning comes into play.

Travel Assistance

You can save time by modifying your installation files to include the latest patches by "slipstreaming" the files. See the following sites for instructions on how to merge (slipstream) Service Pack 2 into your Windows XP installation files:
www.helpwithwindows.com/WindowsXP/winxp-sp2-bootcd.html
www.winsupersite.com/showcase/windowsxp_sp2_slipstream.asp

Disk Cloning

Disk cloning simply takes an existing PC and makes a full copy of the drive, including all data, software, and configuration files. That copy can then be transferred to as many machines as you like, essentially creating "clones" of the original machine. In the old days, making a clone was pretty simple. You just hooked up two hard drives and copied the files from the original to the clone using something like the venerable XCOPY program (as long as the hard drive was formatted with FAT or FAT32). Today, you'll want to use a more sophisticated program, such as Norton Ghost, which enables you to make an image file that contains a copy of an entire hard drive, and then lets you copy that image either locally or over the network.

Local Lingo

Ghosting Norton Ghost is not the only disk imaging software out there, but it is so widely used that techs often refer to disk cloning as "ghosting the drive."

Windows complicates the process of cloning machines because each PC generates a unique security identifier, or *SID*. Each PC must have its own SID, but if you clone a system, each clone will have the same SID, causing a variety of problems whenever two such machines interact over the network. After cloning a PC, you must somehow change the SID of each clone. The easiest way to do this is to use a utility such as Ghostwalker (included with Norton Ghost) or NewSID (available for download at www.microsoft.com/technet/sysinternals/Security/NewSid.mspx).

Sysprep

Cloning a Windows PC and changing its SID works great for some situations, but what if you need to send the same image out to machines that have slightly different hardware? What if you need the customer to go through the final steps of the Windows installation (creating a user account, accepting the license agreement, and so on)? That's when you need to combine a scripted setup and cloning by using the System Preparation Tool, *sysprep*, which can undo portions of the Windows installation process.

After installing Windows and adding any additional software (Microsoft Office, Adobe Acrobat, Yahoo Instant Messenger, and so on), run sysprep (Figure 17.19), and then create your disk image using the cloning application of your choice. The first time a new system cloned from the image boots, an abbreviated version of setup, Mini-Setup, runs and completes the last few steps of the installation process: creating the new SID, installing drivers for hardware, prompting the user to accept the license agreement and create user accounts, and so on. Optionally, you can use Setup Manager to create an answer file to customize Mini-Setup, just as you would with a standard scripted install.

Local Lingo

RIS Microsoft offers an even more advanced way of rolling out new systems: *Remote Installation Services (RIS)*. RIS requires Windows Server and is well beyond the scope of the CompTIA A+ certification exams.

FIGURE 17.19 Sysprep, the System Preparation Tool

Troubleshooting Installations and Upgrades

Objective 17.03

The phrase *installation problem* is rather deceptive. The installation process itself almost never fails. Usually, something else fails during the process that is generally interpreted as an "install failure." Let's look at some typical installation problems and how to correct them.

Text Mode Errors

If you're going to have an install problem, this is the place to get one. It's always better to have the error right off the bat, as opposed to when the installation is nearly complete. Text mode errors most often take place during clean installs and usually point to one of the following problems.

No Boot Device Present when Booting off the Startup Disk

Either the startup disk is bad or the CMOS is not set to look at that disk drive first.

Windows Setup Requires *XXXX* Amount of Available Drive Space

You forgot to format the C: drive, or there's a bunch of stuff on the drive already.

Not Ready Error on Optical Drive

You probably just need to give the optical drive a moment to catch up. Press R for retry a few times. You may also have a damaged installation disc, or the optical drive may be too slow for the system.

A Stop Error (Blue Screen of Death) after the Reboot at the End of Text Mode

This is most common during a Windows 2000/XP installation and may mean that you didn't do your homework in checking hardware compatibility, especially the BIOS. I'll tell you more about stop errors in Chapter 19, but if you encounter one of these errors during installation, check out the Microsoft Knowledge Base at www.microsoft.com, especially article 165863, "Troubleshooting 'Stop 0x0A' Messages in Windows 2000 and Windows NT."

Graphical Mode Errors

Once the install passes the text mode and moves into graphical mode, a whole new crop of problems may arise.

Hardware Detection Errors

You can avoid failure to detect hardware properly by any version of setup by simply researching compatibility beforehand. Or, if you decided to skip that step, you might be lucky and experience a hardware detection error that involves a non-critical hardware device. You can troubleshoot this problem at your leisure. In a sense, you are handing in your homework late, checking out compatibility, and finding a proper driver after Windows is installed. Windows 2000 and Windows XP inherited the underpinnings of Windows NT. They all depend on the Setup program properly detecting the computer type (motherboard and BIOS stuff, in particular) and installing the correct hardware abstraction layer (HAL). (See Chapter 16 for discussion about the HAL.)

Can't Read CAB Files

This is probably the most common of all installation errors. *CAB (as in cabinet) files* are special compressed files, recognizable by their .cab file extension, that Microsoft uses to distribute copies of Windows. If your system can't read them, first check the CD-ROM for scratches. Then try copying all the files from the source directory on the CD (\i386) into a directory on your local hard drive. Then run setup from there, remembering to use the correct program (WINNT32.EXE). If you can't read any of the files on the CD-ROM, you may have a defective drive.

Lockups During Install

Lockups are one of the most challenging problems that can take place during install, as they don't give you a clue as to what's causing the problem. Here are a few things to check if you get a lockup during install.

Smart Recovery, Repair Install

Most system lockups occur when Windows Setup queries the hardware. If a system locks up once during setup, turn off the computer—literally. *Unplug the system.* Do *not* press CTRL-ALT-DEL. Do *not* click Reset. *Unplug it.* Then plug it back in, turn the system on, boot into setup, and rerun the setup program. Windows will see the partial installation and either restart the install process automatically (Smart Recovery) or prompt you for a "Repair Install." Both of these look at the installation progress and complete the installation.

Optical Drive, Hard Drive

Bad optical discs, optical drives, or hard drives may cause lockups. Check the CD or DVD for scratches or dirt, and clean it up or replace it. Try a known good disc in the drive. If you get the same error, you may need to replace the drive.

Log Files

Windows generates a number of special text files called *log files* that track the progress of certain processes. While Windows creates a number of different log files for different purposes, two files most interest us:

- *SETUPLOG.TXT* tracks the complete installation process, logging the success or failure of file copying, Registry updates, reboots, and so on.
- *SETUPAPI.LOG* tracks each piece of hardware as it is installed. This is not an easy log file to read, as it uses Plug and Play code, but it will show you the last device installed before Windows locked up.

Windows 2000 and Windows XP store these log files in the WINNT or Windows directory (the location in which the OS is installed). These OSs have powerful recovery options, so, honestly, the chances of your ever actually having to read a log file, understand it, and then get something fixed as a result of that understanding are pretty small. What makes log files handy is when you call Microsoft or a hardware manufacturer. They *love* to read these files, and they have people on staff who understand them. Don't worry about trying to understand log files for the CompTIA A+ certification exams; just make sure you know the names of the log files and their locations. Leave the details to the übergeeks.

No Installation Is Perfect

Even when the installation seems smooth, issues may slowly surface, especially in the case of upgrades. Be prepared to reinstall applications or deal with new functions that were absent in the previous OS. If things really fall apart, you can always go back to the previous OS.

The procedures laid out in this chapter may seem like a lot of work—how bad could it be to grab an installation CD-ROM, fling a copy of Windows onto a system, and, as the saying goes, let the chips fall where they may? Plenty bad, is how bad. Not only is it important that you understand these procedures for the CompTIA A+ certification exams, they can save your hide once you're a working PC tech and you're tasked to install the latest version of Windows on the boss's new computer!

CHECKPOINT

✔**Objective 17.01: Preparing for Installation or Upgrade** Identify hardware requirements, making sure that your computer meets the recommended minimums for CPU, RAM, free hard disk space, video adapter, display, and other components. Check the Windows Marketplace or the Windows Catalog at the Microsoft Web site to verify that the Windows version you're installing supports the hardware and application software you will run. Use the most advanced file system your version of Windows supports unless you are planning a multiboot configuration.

✔**Objective 17.02: Installing and Upgrading Windows 2000/XP** Installing a modern OS follows pretty standardized steps: insert disc, click at prompts, reboot a few times, and then run through essential post-installation steps, such as patching Windows and upgrading drivers. The Upgrade Advisor can help with Windows XP, though not with Windows 2000. Go with NTFS!

✔**Objective 17.03: Troubleshooting Installations and Upgrades** While the installation process itself rarely fails, you may encounter an installation failure caused by something else. Text mode errors during a clean install may range from "No Boot Device Present" to "Drive C: does not contain a Valid FAT Partition." Graphical mode errors indicate a different set of problems, such as a hardware detection error. If the system locks up during installation, do *not* press CTRL-ALT-DEL or the Reset button to restart the installation. Instead, unplug the system and then turn it back on; Windows will recover.

REVIEW QUESTIONS

 1. Mary's Windows XP installation has failed. What file should she check to see what files failed to copy?

 A. INSTALL.LOG

 B. SETUP.LOG

 C. SETUP.TXT

 D. SETUPLOG.TXT

2. If you do not complete the activation process for Windows XP, what will happen to your computer?

 A. Nothing. Activation is optional.

 B. The computer will work fine for 30 days and then Windows XP will be disabled.

 C. Microsoft will not know how to contact you to provide upgrade information.

 D. You will have to use a floppy disk set to boot to XP.

3. After you have completed a Windows installation and verified that the system starts and runs okay, what should you do next?

 A. Do nothing. You're through.

 B. Install World of Warcraft and enjoy.

 C. Install productivity applications and restore data.

 D. Install the latest service pack or update along with any updated drivers.

4. If Windows locks up during the installation, what should you do?

 A. Press CTRL-ALT-DEL to restart the installation process.

 B. Push the Reset button to restart the installation process.

 C. Press the ESC key to cancel the installation process.

 D. Unplug the computer and restart the installation process.

5. You can upgrade directly to Windows 2000 from which of these operating systems?

 A. Windows 3.11

 B. Windows 95

 C. Windows Me

 D. Windows XP

6. If you get an error message saying that the Setup program cannot read the CAB files, what should you do?

 A. Copy the CAB files from the Windows installation CD-ROM to your local hard drive and run the Setup program from there.

 B. Skip this step since the CAB files are not necessary to install Windows successfully.

 C. Go to the Microsoft Web site and download the latest version of the CAB file wizard.

 D. Cancel the installation process and keep your old operating system, since your hardware does not meet the minimum requirements.

7. If you are not sure your Windows 98 system can support Windows XP, what should you do?

 A. Consult the Windows Catalog.

 B. Consult the Windows Marketplace.

 C. Run the XP Upgrade Advisor.

 D. Install XP and hope for the best, since it will probably work.

8. What is the minimum amount of RAM needed to run Windows XP?

 A. 64 MB

 B. 128 MB

 C. 256 MB

 D. 512 MB

9. Which of the following processes provides Microsoft with contact information for the owner of a Windows license?

 A. EULA

 B. Microsoft Product Activation

 C. Registration

 D. Upgrade Advisor

10. If you plan a single-boot installation, which file system should you use?

 A. FAT

 B. FAT16

 C. FAT32

 D. NTFS

REVIEW ANSWERS

1. **D** Mary should check SETUPLOG.TXT.

2. **B** If you do not complete the activation process for Windows XP, the computer will work fine for 30 days and then Windows XP will be disabled.

3. **D** After you have completed a Windows installation and verified that the system starts and runs okay, you should install the latest service pack or update along with any updated drivers.

4. **D** If Windows locks up during the installation, you should unplug the computer and restart the installation process.

5. **B** You can upgrade directly to Windows 2000 from Windows 95.

6. **A** If you get an error message that the Setup program cannot read the CAB files, you should copy the CAB files from the Windows installation CD to your local hard drive and run the Setup program from there.

7. **C** If you are not sure your Windows 98 system can support Windows XP, you should run the XP Upgrade Advisor.

8. **A** Although it won't run well, Windows XP can install and run on a computer with only 64 MB of RAM.

9. **C** Registration, rather than activation, provides Microsoft with personal details.

10. **D** NTFS is the logical answer here. None of the others provide any kind of local security.

Networking
in Windows

	NEWBIE	SOME EXPERIENCE	EXPERT
ETA	5 hours	3 hours	2 hours

Every modern Windows operating system assumes it will be part of a network, straight out of the box. Windows XP practically *requires* you to log into the Internet for product activation, just to use the OS beyond 30 days. Arguably, you can't have a stable, well-functioning PC today without connecting to the Internet, the biggest network of all.

Once you finish a successful installation or upgrade of the OS, as you did in Chapter 17, you should install and configure networking even before you install drivers for any component except the motherboard. No matter how well intentioned, Microsoft engineers simply cannot produce a bug-free OS on the first try. It's just too huge a project with too many variables on hardware and applications. It's almost surprising that they do as good a job as they do. Regardless, you need to patch your OS and update drivers on every PC. You get those patches and drivers from a central server on a local area network (LAN) or directly from Microsoft and other vendors on the Internet.

This chapter implements networks so you can connect to a LAN and to the Internet. The first objective covers network OSs in detail. The chapter then goes into the ins and outs of setting up a LAN. The third objective launches into the techniques and technologies for connecting to the Internet. The chapter wraps up with a discussion of the primary software tools for using the Internet and a section on general network troubleshooting.

Objective 18.01 Network Operating Systems

In a classic sense, a *network operating system (NOS)* communicates with the PC hardware and makes the connections among multiple machines on a network. The NOS enables one or more PCs to act as a server machine and share data and services over a network—to share *resources,* in other words. You then need to run software on client computers to enable those computers to access the shared resources on the server machine.

Every Windows OS is an NOS and enables the PC to share resources and access shared resources. But it doesn't come out of the box ready to work on all networks. You need to configure Windows to handle all three tasks to make all this work: install a network protocol to communicate with hardware, enable server software to share resources, and install client software to enable the PC to access shared resources.

All NOSs are not alike, even among Windows versions. Before you can share resources across a network, you must answer a number of questions. How do you make that happen? Can everyone share his or her hard drives with everyone

else? Should you place limits on sharing? If everyone needs access to a particular file, where will it be stored? What about security? Can anyone access the file? What if someone erases it accidentally? How are backups to be handled? Different NOSs answer these questions differently.

Network Organization

All NOSs can be broken into three basic organizational groups: client/server, peer-to-peer, and domain-based. All Windows PCs can function as network clients and servers, so this muddies the waters a bit. Let's take a look at traditional network organization.

Client/Server

The client/server solution to all the resource-sharing questions is to dedicate one machine as a resource to be shared over the network. This machine will have a dedicated NOS optimized for sharing files. This special OS includes powerful caching software that enables high-speed file access. It will have extremely high levels of protection and an organization that permits extensive control of the data. This machine is called a *dedicated* server. All of the other machines that use the data are called *clients* (because it's what they usually are) or *workstations*.

The client/server system dedicates one machine to act as a server. Its only function is to serve up resources to the other machines on the network. These servers do not run Windows XP or Macintosh OS X. They use highly sophisticated and expensive NOSs that are optimized for the sharing and administration of network resources. The most popular NOS that fits within the client/server concept is Novell NetWare.

A NetWare server is not used directly by anyone. It does not run Windows; it runs only Novell NetWare. Novell NetWare just *serves* shared resources; it does not run programs like Excel or Photoshop. Many network administrators will even remove the keyboard and monitor from a Novell NetWare server to keep people from trying to use it. NetWare has its own commands and requires substantial training to use, but in return, you get an amazingly powerful NOS.

Travel Advisory

The terms *client* and *server* are, to say the least, freely used in the Windows world. Keep in mind that a client generally refers to any process (or in this context, computer system) that can request a resource or service, and a server is any process (or system) that can fulfill the request.

Client/server NOSs such as Novell NetWare provide excellent security for shared resources. Do you remember the NTFS permissions used by Windows 2000, XP, and Vista? Novell NetWare has similar levels of permissions, but because it is client/server, only the servers have this file protection.

Peer-to-Peer

Some networks do not require dedicated servers—every computer can perform both server and client functions. A *peer-to-peer network* enables any or all of the machines on the network to act as a server. Peer-to-peer networks are much cheaper than client/server networks, because the software costs less and does not require that you purchase a high-end machine to act as the dedicated server. The most popular peer-to-peer NOSs today are Windows 2000/XP and Macintosh OS X.

The biggest limiting factor to peer-to-peer networking is that it's simply not designed for a large number of computers. Windows has a built-in limit (10) to the number of users who can concurrently access a shared file or folder. Microsoft recommends that peer-to-peer workgroups not exceed 15 PCs. Beyond that, creating a domain-based network makes more sense.

Security is the other big weakness of peer-to-peer networks. Each system on a peer-to-peer network maintains its own security.

Windows 2000 Professional and Windows XP Professional enable you to tighten security by setting NTFS permissions locally, but you are still required to place a local account on every system for any user who's going to access resources. So, even though you get decent security in a Windows 2000 Professional or Windows XP Professional peer-to-peer network, system administration entails a lot of running around to individual systems to create and delete local users every time someone joins or leaves the network.

Peer-to-peer workgroups are little more than a pretty way to organize systems to make navigating through My Network Places a little easier (Figure 18.1). In reality, workgroups have no security value. Still, if your networking needs are limited—such as a small home network—peer-to-peer networking is an easy and cheap solution.

Exam Tip	
Know the difference between client/server and peer-to-peer.	

FIGURE 18.1 Multiple workgroups in a network

Domain-Based

One of the similarities between the client/server network model and peer-to-peer networks is that each PC in the network maintains its own list of user accounts. If you want to access a server, you must log on. When only one server exists, the logon process takes only a second and works very well. The trouble comes when your network contains multiple servers. In that case, every time you access a different server, you must repeat the logon process (Figure 18.2). In larger networks containing many servers, this becomes a time-consuming nightmare not only for the user, but also for the network administrator.

A domain-based network provides an excellent solution for the problem of multiple logins. In a domain-based environment, one or more servers hold the security database for all systems. This one database holds a single list of all users and passwords. When you log on to your computer or to any computer, the logon request goes to this single system, called the *domain controller,* to verify the account and password.

No version of Windows covered by the CompTIA A+ certification exams can run as a domain controller. You need a copy of one of Microsoft's server NOSs to

FIGURE 18.2 Multiple logins

do that, such as Windows 2000 Server or Windows Server 2003. The server versions of Windows look and act similar to the workstation versions but come with extra programs to enable them to take on the role of domain controller, among other things. A quick glance at the options in Administrative Tools shows you how much more complicated the server versions are than the workstation versions of Windows. Figure 18.3 shows the Administrative Tools options on a typical Windows XP workstation. These should be familiar to you. Figure 18.4 shows the many extra tools you need to work with Windows 2000 Server.

Every Windows system contains a special account called the *administrator account*. This one account has complete and absolute power over the entire system. When you install Windows 2000 or XP, you must create a password for the

FIGURE 18.3 Administrative Tools in Windows XP Professional

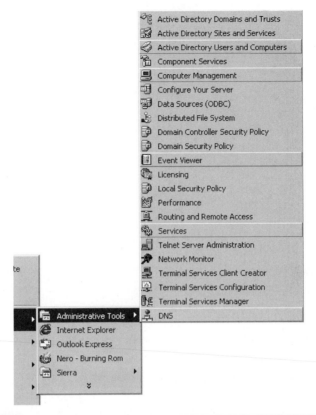

FIGURE 18.4 Administrative Tools in Windows 2000 Server

administrator account. Anyone who knows the administrator password has the ability to install/delete any program, read/change/delete any file, run any program, and change any system setting. As you might imagine, you should protect the administrator password carefully. Without it, you cannot create additional accounts (including additional accounts with administrative privileges) or change system settings. If you lose the administrator password (and no other account with administrative privileges exists), you have to reinstall Windows completely to create a new administrator account—so don't lose it!

In Windows 2000, open the Properties window for My Computer, and select the Network Identification tab, as shown in Figure 18.5. This shows your current selection. Windows XP calls the tab Computer Name and renames a few of the buttons (Figure 18.6). Clicking the Network ID button opens the Network Identification Wizard, but most techs just use the Change button (Figure 18.7). Clicking the Change button does the same thing as clicking the Network ID

FIGURE 18.5 Network Identification tab in Windows 2000

FIGURE 18.6 Computer Name tab in Windows XP

button, but the wizard does a lot of explaining that you don't need if you know what you want to do. Make sure you have a valid domain account or you won't be able to log into a domain.

Objective 18.02 Installing and Configuring a LAN

You've got the basics, now let's install a network. You need to install a network interface card (NIC), including proper drivers. You must install client software so that the PC can see and be seen on the network. The NIC needs to run a properly configured network protocol that matches that of other machines. And finally, you must enable File and Printer Sharing to turn the PC into a server and make its resources available for other users across the network.

Of course, you also need to connect the PC to the network hub or switch via some sort of cable (preferably CAT 6 with Gigabit Ethernet cranking through the wires, but that's just me) or through a wireless standard. When you install a NIC, by default, Windows 2000, XP, and Vista install TCP/IP (configured for Dynamic Host Configuration Protocol, DHCP), the Client for Microsoft Networks, and File and Printer Sharing.

Installing a NIC

The NIC is your computer system's link to the network, and installing one is the first step required to connect to a network. This was covered in Chapter 13, so there's no need to run through the steps here. NICs are manufactured to operate on specific media and network types, such as 100BaseT Ethernet, 802.11g, or Token Ring. Follow the manufacturer's instructions for installation procedures. If your NIC is of recent vintage, Windows will detect, install, and configure it automatically. You might need a driver disc or a driver download from the manufacturer's Web site if you install the latest and greatest Gigabit Ethernet card.

> **Travel Advisory**
>
> If you have the option, you should save yourself potential headaches and troubleshooting woes by acquiring new, name-brand NICs for your Windows installation. This is especially true with Windows XP.

Configuring a Network Client

To establish network connectivity, you need a network client installed and configured properly. You need a client for every type of server NOS to which you plan to connect on the network. Let's look at the two most used for Microsoft and Novell networks.

Client for Microsoft Networks

Installed as part of the OS installation, the Client for Microsoft Networks rarely needs configuration, and, in fact, few configuration options are available. To start it in Windows XP, click Start, and then right-click My Network Places and select Properties. In Windows 2000, click Start | Settings | Network and Dial-up Connections.

In all versions of Windows, your next step is to double-click the Local Area Connection icon, click the Properties button, highlight Client for Microsoft Networks, and click the Properties button. Note that there's not much to do here. Unless told to do something by a network administrator, just leave this alone.

Client Service for NetWare

Microsoft's Client Service for NetWare provides access to file and print resources on NetWare 3.x and 4.x servers. Client Service for NetWare supports some NetWare utilities and NetWare-aware applications. To connect Microsoft client workstations to NetWare servers running NetWare Directory Services (NDS) also requires the Microsoft Service for NDS. Once installed, Client Service for NetWare offers no configuration options.

Travel Advisory

Client Service for NetWare does not support the Internet Protocol (IP), which is used in NetWare 5.*x* and more recent versions of NetWare; you would need the actual Novell Client software for this.

Configuring Simple Protocols

Protocols come in many different flavors and perform different functions on the network. Some, such as NetBEUI, lack elements that allow their signals to travel through routers, making them non-routable (essentially, this protocol is un-suitable for a large network that uses routers to re-transmit data). The network protocols supported by Windows include NetBEUI, NWLink (IPX/SPX), and TCP/IP, although Windows XP drops support for NetBEUI.

NetBEUI

NetBEUI is easy to configure, since no network addresses are needed. Generally, all you need to establish a connection between computer systems using NetBEUI is a NetBIOS computer name. NetBIOS names must be unique and contain 15 or fewer characters, but other than that there isn't much to it.

NWLink (IPX/SPX)

As mentioned, NWLink is Microsoft's implementation of the IPX/SPX protocol. The Microsoft version of NWLink provides the same level of functionality as the Novell protocol and also includes an element for resolving NetBIOS names. NWLink packages data to be compatible with client/server services on NetWare networks, but it does not provide access to NetWare File and Print Services. For this, you also need to install the Client Service for NetWare, as noted earlier.

Follow the same steps used to install NetBEUI to install NWLink, except choose NWLink rather than NetBEUI when you make your final selection. You'll be prompted to reboot after adding the protocol.

NWLink is a relatively easy protocol to configure. Normally, the only settings you may need to specify are the internal network number and frame type (usu-ally, however, the default values are sufficient). The internal network number (Figure 18.8) is used by the network for routing purposes. The frame type speci-fies how the data is packaged for transport over the network. For computers to communicate by NWLink, they must have the same frame types. By default, the frame type is set to Auto Detect, which is usually fine.

I need the actual content.

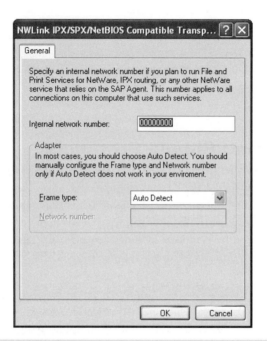

FIGURE 18.8 Configuring NWLink

Configuring TCP/IP

For a PC to access the Internet, it must have TCP/IP loaded. TCP/IP has become so predominant that most network folks use it even on networks that do not connect to the Internet. Although TCP/IP is powerful, it is also a bit of a challenge to set up. So whether you are installing a modem for a dial-up connection to the Internet or setting up 500 computers on their own private *intranet,* you must understand some TCP/IP basics. Let's go through the basic sections of the protocol and then look at specific steps to install and configure TCP/IP.

Network Addressing

Any network address must provide two pieces of information. It must uniquely identify the machine, and it must locate that machine within the larger network. In a TCP/IP network, the *IP address* identifies the PC and the *subnet mask* helps determine in which subnet within the network the machine resides.

IP Addresses In a TCP/IP network, every system has a unique IP address. An *IP address* consists of four sets of eight binary numbers (octets) separated by periods. This is called *dotted-octet notation.* Here's a typical IP address:

 202.34.16.11

Written in binary form, you'd get an address like this:

```
11001010.00100010.00001000.00001011
```

But the TCP/IP folks decided to write the decimal equivalents:

```
00000000 = 0
00000001 = 1
00000010 = 2
...
11111111 = 255
```

The IP address is the unique identification number for your system on the network. Part of the address (the network ID) identifies the network, and another part (the host ID) identifies the local computer (host) address on the network. For example, my computer's IP address is 192.168.4.23. On my network (these are usually different on all networks), my network ID is 192.168.4 and my host ID is 23. A traditional TCP/IP network divides IP addresses into classes, which correspond to the potential size of the network: Class A, Class B, and Class C. Class A addresses were intended for huge organizations, such as major multinational corporations. Class C networks were targeted for LANs. The crushing need for more IP addresses for the Internet pretty much blew the class structure out of the water, but here it is to satisfy your curiosity:

- Class A networks use the first octet to identify the network address and the remaining three octets to identify the host.
- Class B networks use the first two octets to identify the network address and the remaining two octets to identify the host.
- Class C networks use the first three octets to identify the network address and the last octet to identify the host.

Table 18.1 lists range (class) assignments.

Travel Advisory

The 127 address range (i.e., 127.0.0.1) is reserved for network testing (loopback) operations.

TABLE 18.1 Class A, B, and C Addresses

Network Class	Address Range of First Octet	Number of Network Addresses Available	Number of Host Nodes (computers) Supported
A	1–126	126	16,777,214
B	128–191	16,384	65,534
C	192–223	2,097,152	254

Subnet Mask The *subnet mask* is a value that distinguishes which part of the IP address is the network address and which part of the address is the host address. The subnet mask blocks out (or masks) the network portions (octets) of an IP address. Certain subnet masks are applied by default, as shown in Table 18.2.

For example, the Class B IP address 131.190.4.121 with a subnet mask of 255.255.0.0 is distinguished as follows:

- The first two octets (131.190) make up the network address.
- The last two (4.121) make up the host address.

> ### Exam Tip
>
> The CompTIA A+ certification exams do not require you to configure IP addresses and subnet masks, but you should know what they are and how to find them on a PC.

TCP/IP Services

TCP/IP is a different type of protocol. Although it supports File and Printer Sharing, it adds a number of special sharing functions unique to it. These are lumped together under the umbrella term of *TCP/IP services*. The most famous TCP/IP service is called the Hypertext Transfer Protocol (HTTP), the language of the World Wide Web. If you want to surf the Web, you must have TCP/IP. But TCP/IP supplies many other services beyond just HTTP. Using a service called Telnet, you can access a remote system as though you were actually in front of that machine.

TCP/IP can link together multiple LANs to make a *wide area network (WAN)*. LANs are usually linked together via some type of telephone service, ranging from basic dial-ups to dedicated, high-speed (and expensive) data lines. The goal is to make a WAN that uses the expensive links for as little traffic as possible. The machines that connect the phone lines to each LAN are specialized computers called *routers*. To reduce traffic, each router decides which packets on the LAN should go out to the WAN. The router makes these decisions on the basis of the packets' IP addresses.

TABLE 18.2	Subnet Masks for Class A, B, and C Networks

Class	Subnet Mask
Class A	255.0.0.0
Class B	255.255.0.0
Class C	255.255.255.0

TCP/IP Settings

TCP/IP has a number of unique settings that you must set up correctly to ensure proper network functionality. Windows 2000/XP/Vista makes this fairly easy by letting you configure both dial-up and network connections using the Network Connections dialog box (Figure 18.9). To get there, right-click My Network Places and select Properties. Simply select the connection you wish to configure, and then set its TCP/IP properties.

The CompTIA A+ certification exams assume that someone else, such as a tech support person or some network guru, will tell you the correct TCP/IP settings for the network. Your only job is to understand roughly what they do and to know where to enter them so the system works. Following are some of the most common TCP/IP settings.

Exam Tip

The CompTIA A+ certification exams have a rather strange view of what you should know about networking. Take a lot of time practicing how to get to certain network configuration screens. Be ready for questions that ask, "Which of the following steps will enable you to change a particular value?"

FIGURE 18.9 Network Connections dialog box showing dial-up and LAN connections

Default Gateway A computer that wants to send data to another machine outside its LAN is not expected to know all the IP addresses of all the computers on the Internet. Instead, all IP machines know the IP address of one computer, to which they pass all the data they need to send outside the LAN. This machine is called the *default gateway,* and it is usually the local router (Figure 18.10).

Domain Name Service (DNS) Knowing that users were not going to be able to remember lots of IP addresses, early Internet pioneers came up with a way to correlate those numbers with more human-friendly computer designations. Special computers, called *domain name service (DNS) servers,* keep databases of IP addresses and their corresponding names. For example, a machine called TOTAL.SEMINAR1 will be listed in a DNS directory with a corresponding IP address, such as 209.34.45.163. So instead of accessing the \\209.34.45.163\FREDC share to copy a file, you can ask to see \\TOTAL.SEMINAR1\FREDC. Your system will then query the DNS server to get TOTAL.SEMINAR1's IP address and use that to find the right machine. Unless you want to type in IP addresses all the time, a TCP/IP network will need at least one DNS server (Figure 18.11).

The Internet has regulated domain names. If you want a domain name that others can access on the Internet, you must register your domain name and pay a small yearly fee. In most cases, your ISP can handle this for you. Originally,

FIGURE 18.10 Setting a default gateway

FIGURE 18.11 Adding two DNS servers in Windows 2000

DNS names all ended with one of the following seven domain name qualifiers, called *top level domains (TLDs)*:

.com	General business	.org	Nonprofit organizations
.edu	Educational organizations	.gov	Government organizations
.mil	Military organizations	.net	Internet organizations
.int	International		

As more and more countries joined the Internet, an entire new level of domains was added to the original seven to indicate a DNS name in a particular country, such as *.uk* for the United Kingdom. It's common to see DNS names such as *www.bbc.co.uk* or *www.louvre.fr*. The Internet Corporation for Assigned Names and Numbers (ICANN) has announced the creation of several more new domains, including *.name* and *.info*. Given the explosive growth of the Internet, these are unlikely to be the last ones!

WINS The *Windows Internet Name Service (WINS)* enables Windows NetBIOS network names such as SERVER1 to be correlated to IP addresses. All you have to do to set up WINS is either type in the IP address for the WINS server or let

DHCP handle it for you (Figure 18.12). Windows 2000 and XP don't use NetBIOS by default; they use DNS, making WINS obsolete. Even though Windows 2000 and XP no longer need WINS, they support it for communication with older systems.

DHCP Every machine in a TCP/IP network must have an IP address. This can be added manually using the TCP/IP Properties dialog box. A permanent IP address assigned to a machine is known as a *static* IP address.

Dynamic Host Configuration Protocol (DHCP) enables you to create a pool of IP addresses that are given to machines when they need them and are taken away when they are no longer needed. DHCP is especially handy for networks in which many of the client systems dial in. Why give a machine that is on for only a few minutes a day a static IP address? If you add a NIC to a Windows system, the default TCP/IP settings are set to use DHCP. When you accept those automatic settings, you're really telling the machine to use DHCP (Figure 18.13).

TCP/IP Tools

All versions of Windows come with handy tools to test TCP/IP networks. Those that you're most likely to use in the field are Ping, IPCONFIG, NSLOOKUP, and TRACERT. All of these programs are command prompt utilities. You must open a command prompt to run them.

FIGURE 18.12 Setting up WINS to use DHCP

FIGURE 18.13 Obtain an IP address automatically

Ping *Ping* is a great way to determine whether your system can talk to another system. Here's how it works. Get to a command prompt and type **ping** followed by an IP address or by a DNS name, such as **ping "http://www.chivalry.com"**. Press the ENTER key on your keyboard and away it goes. Figure 18.14 shows the common syntax for Ping.

```
C:\WINDOWS\System32\cmd.exe                                      _ □ ×

C:\Documents and Settings\scottj>ping /?

Usage: ping [-t] [-a] [-n count] [-l size] [-f] [-i TTL] [-v TOS]
            [-r count] [-s count] [[-j host-list] ! [-k host-list]]
            [-w timeout] target_name

Options:
    -t             Ping the specified host until stopped.
                   To see statistics and continue - type Control-Break;
                   To stop - type Control-C.
    -a             Resolve addresses to hostnames.
    -n count       Number of echo requests to send.
    -l size        Send buffer size.
    -f             Set Don't Fragment flag in packet.
    -i TTL         Time To Live.
    -v TOS         Type Of Service.
    -r count       Record route for count hops.
    -s count       Timestamp for count hops.
    -j host-list   Loose source route along host-list.
    -k host-list   Strict source route along host-list.
    -w timeout     Timeout in milliseconds to wait for each reply.

C:\Documents and Settings\scottj>
```

FIGURE 18.14 Ping syntax

IPCONFIG Windows 2000/XP offer the command line tool *IPCONFIG* for a quick glance at your network settings. Click Start | Run and type **cmd** to get a command prompt. From the prompt, type **ipconfig /all** to see all of your TCP/IP settings (Figure 18.15).

When you have a static IP address, IPCONFIG does little beyond reporting your current IP settings, including your IP address, subnet mask, default gateway, DNS servers, and WINS servers. When using DHCP, however, IPCONFIG is also the primary tool for releasing and renewing your IP address. Just type **ipconfig /renew** to get a new IP address or **ipconfig /release** to give up the IP address you currently have.

NSLOOKUP *NSLOOKUP* is a powerful command line program that enables you to determine exactly what information the DNS server is giving you about a specific host name. Every version of Windows makes NSLOOKUP available when you install TCP/IP. To run the program, type **nslookup** from the command line and press the ENTER key (Figure 18.16). Note that this gives you a little information, but that the prompt has changed. That's because you're running the application. Type **exit** and press the ENTER key to return to the command prompt.

```
C:\WINNT\System32\cmd.exe                                    _ □ ×

C:\>ipconfig /all

Windows 2000 IP Configuration

        Host Name . . . . . . . . . . . . : mike
        Primary DNS Suffix  . . . . . . . :
        Node Type . . . . . . . . . . . . : Broadcast
        IP Routing Enabled. . . . . . . . : No
        WINS Proxy Enabled. . . . . . . . : No

Ethernet adapter Local Area Connection:

        Connection-specific DNS Suffix  . :
        Description . . . . . . . . . . . : Intel(R) PRO/100+ PCI Adapter
        Physical Address. . . . . . . . . : 00-A0-C9-98-9A-40
        DHCP Enabled. . . . . . . . . . . : Yes
        Autoconfiguration Enabled . . . . : Yes
        IP Address. . . . . . . . . . . . : 192.168.4.12
        Subnet Mask . . . . . . . . . . . : 255.255.255.0
        Default Gateway . . . . . . . . . : 192.168.4.253
        DHCP Server . . . . . . . . . . . : 192.168.4.253
        DNS Servers . . . . . . . . . . . : 204.238.120.5
                                            204.238.120.5
        Lease Obtained. . . . . . . . . . : Tuesday, December 12, 2000 1:45:14 A
M
        Lease Expires . . . . . . . . . . : Wednesday, December 20, 2000 1:45:14
 AM

Ethernet adapter Local Area Connection 2:

        Media State . . . . . . . . . . . : Cable Disconnected
        Description . . . . . . . . . . . : Intel(R) PRO/100+ PCI Adapter #2
        Physical Address. . . . . . . . . : 00-A0-C9-98-12-F4

C:\>_
```

FIGURE 18.15 IPCONFIG /ALL on Windows 2000

FIGURE 18.16 NSLOOKUP in action

Travel Advisory

You can do some cool stuff with NSLOOKUP, and consequently some techs love the tool. It's way outside the scope of CompTIA A+ certification, but if you want to play with it, type **help** at the NSLOOKUP prompt and press ENTER to see a list of common commands and syntax.

TRACERT The *TRACERT* utility shows the route that a packet takes to get to its destination. From a command line, type **tracert** followed by a space and an IP address or DNS name. The output describes the route from your machine to the destination machine, including all devices it passes through and how long each hop takes (Figure 18.17). TRACERT can come in handy when you have to troubleshoot bottlenecks. When users complain that it's difficult to reach a particular destination using TCP/IP, you can run this utility to determine whether

FIGURE 18.17 TRACERT in action

the problem exists on a machine or connection over which you have control, or if it is a problem on another machine or router.

Steps for Configuring TCP/IP

By default, TCP/IP is configured to receive an IP address automatically from a DHCP server on the network (and automatically assign a corresponding subnet mask). As far as the CompTIA A+ certification exams are concerned, Network+ techs and administrators give you the IP address, subnet mask, and default gateway information and you plug them into the PC. That's about it, so here's how to do it manually:

1. In Windows XP, open the Control Panel and double-click the Network Connections applet. Double-click the Local Area Connection icon. In Windows 2000, click Start | Settings | Network and Dial-up Connections, and double-click the Local Area Connection icon.

2. Click the Properties button, highlight Internet Protocol (TCP/IP), and click the Properties button.

3. In the dialog box, click the *Use the following IP address* radio button.

4. Enter the IP address in the appropriate field.

5. Press the TAB key to skip down to the Subnet mask field. Note that the subnet mask is entered automatically (you can type over this if you want to enter a different subnet mask). See Figure 18.18.

FIGURE 18.18 Setting up IP

6. Optionally, enter the IP address for a default gateway (router, or another computer system that will forward transmissions beyond your network).

7. Optionally, enter the IP address of a primary and secondary DNS server.

8. Click the OK button to close the dialog box.

9. Click the Close button to exit the Local Area Connection Status dialog box.

Automatic Private IP Addressing

Windows 2000 and XP support a feature called Automatic Private IP Addressing (APIPA) that automatically assigns an IP address to the system when the client cannot obtain an IP address automatically. The Internet Assigned Numbers Authority (IANA), the non-profit corporation responsible for assigning IP addresses and managing root servers, has set aside the range of addresses from 169.254.0.1 to 169.254.255.254 for this purpose.

If the computer system cannot contact a DHCP server, the computer randomly chooses an address in the form of 169.254.*x.y* (where *x.y* is the computer's identifier) and a 16-bit subnet mask (255.255.0.0) and broadcasts it on the network segment (subnet). If no other computer responds to the address, the system assigns this address to itself. When using APIPA, the system can communicate only with other computers on the same subnet that also use the 169.254.*x.y* range with a 16-bit mask. APIPA is enabled by default if your system is configured to obtain an IP address automatically.

Exam Tip

Know that a computer system on a network with an active DHCP server that has an IP address in the APIPA range usually indicates that there is a problem connecting to the DHCP server.

Sharing and Security

Windows systems can share all kinds of resources: files, folders, entire drives, printers, faxes, Internet connections, and much more. Conveniently for you, the CompTIA A+ certification exams limit their interests to folders, printers, and Internet connections. Let's see how to share folders and printers now; we'll save Internet connection sharing for the Internet section.

Sharing Drives and Folders

All versions of Windows share drives and folders in basically the same manner. Simply right-click any drive or folder and choose Properties. Select the Sharing tab (Figure 18.19). Select *Share this folder*, add something in the *Comment* or

FIGURE 18.19 Windows Sharing tab on NTFS volume

User limit fields if you wish (they're not required), and click Permissions (Figure 18.20).

Hey! Doesn't NTFS have all those wild permissions like Read, Execute, Take Ownership, and all that? Yes, it does, but NTFS permissions and network permissions are totally separate beasties. Microsoft wanted Windows 2000 and XP to support many different types of partitions (NTFS, FAT16, FAT32), old and new. Network permissions are Microsoft's way of enabling you to administer file sharing on any type of partition supported by Windows, no matter how ancient. Sure, your options will be pretty limited if you are working with an older partition type, but you *can* do it.

The beauty of Windows 2000/XP is that both provide another tool—NTFS permissions—that can do much more. NTFS is where the power lies, but power always comes with a price: You have to configure two separate sets of permissions. If you share a folder on an NTFS drive, you must set *both* the network permissions and the NTFS permissions to enable others to access your shared resources. Just set the network permissions to give everyone full control, and then use the NTFS permissions to exercise more precise control over *who* accesses the shared resources and *how* they access them. Open the Security tab to set the NTFS permissions.

FIGURE 18.20 Network permissions

Travel Advisory

Windows 2000 and XP both have two places for setting security on files and folders: share permissions, which apply security to the folder that is designated to be a connection point to the files and folders within that folder, and NTFS security on files and folders. Share permissions affect only network users, accessing the files and folders from across a network, while NTFS security affects both network and local users.

Accessing Shared Drives/Directories

Once you have set up a drive or directory to be shared, the final step is to access that shared drive or directory from another machine. Windows 2000 and XP use My Network Places, although you'll need to do a little clicking to get to the shared resources (Figure 18.21).

Network resources can also be "mapped" to a local resource name. For example, the FREDC share can be mapped to be a local hard drive letter such as E: or F:. From within any My Computer/Explorer window (such as My Documents or My Network Places), choose Tools | Map Network Drive to open the Map

FIGURE 18.21 Shared resources in My Network Places

Network Drive dialog box (Figure 18.22). Click the Browse button to check out the neighborhood and find a shared folder (Figure 18.23).

In Windows 2000, you can also use the handy Add Network Place icon in My Network Places to add network locations you frequently access without using up

FIGURE 18.22 Map Network Drive dialog box

FIGURE 18.23 Browsing for shared folders

drive letters. Windows XP removed the icon but added the menu option in its context bar on the left. Here's how it looks on a Windows 2000 system (Figure 18.24).

All shared resources should show up in My Network Places. If a shared resource fails to show up, make sure to check the basics first: Is File and Printer Sharing activated on the sharing system? Is the device actually shared? Don't let silly errors fool you.

UNC

All computers that share must have a network name, and all of the resources they share must also have network names. Any resource on a network can be described by combining the names of the resource being shared and the system that's sharing it. So, for example, if a machine called SERVER1 is sharing its C: drive as FREDC, the complete name would be described like this:

```
\\SERVER1\FREDC
```

This is called the *universal naming convention (UNC)*. The UNC is distinguished by its use of double backslashes in front of the sharing system's name, and a single backslash in front of the shared resource's name.

FIGURE 18.24 My Network Places

Sharing Printers

Sharing printers in Windows is just as easy as sharing drives and directories. Assuming that the system has printer sharing services loaded, just go to the Printers folder in the Control Panel and right-click the printer you want to share. Select Properties, go to the Sharing tab, click *Shared as*, and give it a name (see Figure 18.25).

To access a shared printer in any version of Windows, simply click the Add Printer icon in the Printers folder. When asked if the printer is Local or Network, select Network; browse the network for the printer you want to access, and Windows takes care of the rest. In almost all cases, Windows will copy the printer driver from the sharing machine. In the rare case where it doesn't, it will prompt you for drivers.

One of the most pleasant aspects of configuring a system for networking under all versions of Microsoft Windows is the amazing amount of the process that is automated. For example, if Windows detects a NIC in a system, it will automatically install the NIC driver, a network protocol (TCP/IP), and Client for Microsoft Networks (the NetBIOS part of the Microsoft networking software). So if you want to share a resource, everything you need is automatically installed.

FIGURE 18.25 Naming a shared printer in Windows 2000

Objective 18.03 # Connecting to the Internet

To use the Internet successfully, you need to connect properly and then run special applications that work with TCP/IP, such as HTTP for Web browsing. Let's start with connections and then hit Internet software.

PCs commonly connect to an Internet service provider (ISP) using one of seven technologies: dial-up, both analog and ISDN; dedicated, such as DSL, cable, and LAN; wireless; and satellite. Analog dial-up is the slowest of the bunch and requires a telephone line and a special networking device called a modem. ISDN uses digital dial-up and has much greater speed. All the others use a regular Ethernet NIC like you played with in Chapter 13, so they require no special extra details here. Satellite requires you to connect via modem, but then it handles downloads and sometimes uploads through a NIC.

Dial-up Networking

A dial-up connection to the Internet requires two pieces to work: hardware to dial up the ISP, such as a modem or ISDN terminal adapter (TA); and software to govern the connection, such as Microsoft's *Dial-up Networking (DUN)*. Modems and TAs install like any other expansion card or device, into a PCI or PCIe slot on the motherboard or to an external expansion connection such as USB. Install the drivers and you're pretty much done with the hardware side of things.

The software side of dial-up networks requires configuration within Windows to include information provided by your ISP. The ISP provides a dial-up telephone number or numbers, as well as your user name and initial password. In addition, the ISP will tell you about any special configuration options you need to specify in the software setup. The full configuration of dial-up networking is beyond the scope of this book, but you should at least know where to go to follow instructions from your ISP. Let's take a look at the Network and Internet Connections applet in Windows XP.

Modems

Modems enable computers to talk to each other via standard commercial telephone lines by converting analog signals to digital signals, and vice versa (Figure 18.26). The individual serial bits of data are converted into 8-bit parallel data that the PC can understand through the *universal asynchronous receiver/transmitter (UART)* chip (Figure 18.27).

The fastest data transfer speed a modem can handle is based on its implementation of one of the *V standards*. Set by the International Telecommunication Union (ITU-T), the current top standards are V.90 and V.92. Both standards offer download speeds of just a hair under 56 Kbps, but they differ in upload speeds: up to 33.6 Kbps for V.90, and up to 48 Kbps for V. 92 modems.

FIGURE 18.26 Modem converting digital signal to analog signal

The UART converts serial data to parallel data that the CPU can read.

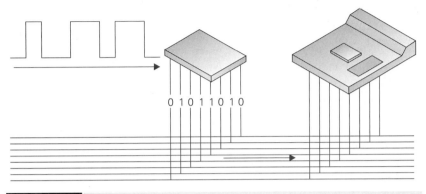

0 1 0 1 1 0 1 0

FIGURE 18.27 UART chip converts serial data to parallel data

Network and Internet Connections

To start configuring a dial-up connection in Windows XP, open the Control Panel. Select Network and Internet Connections from the *Pick a category* menu (Figure 18.28), and then select *Set up or change your Internet connection* from the

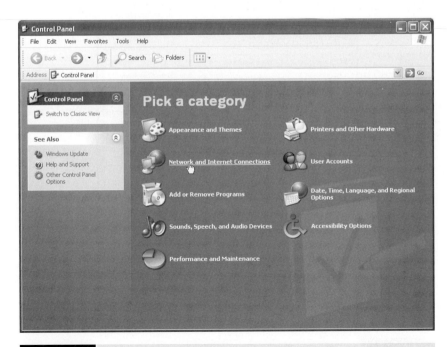

FIGURE 18.28 Selecting the Network and Internet Connections applet

Pick a task menu. (If you're in Classic view in the Control Panel, by the way, simply open the Internet Options applet.) Select the Connections tab on the Internet Properties dialog box if it's not already selected. All your work will proceed from here (Figure 18.29).

Click the Setup button to run the New Connection Wizard and then work through the screens (Figure 18.30). At this point, you're going to need information provided by your ISP to configure your connection properly.

When you finish the configuration, you'll see a new Connect To option on the Start menu. Select Start | Connect To | Show All Connections to see something like Figure 18.31, which shows the option to connect to a fictitious ISP, Cool-Rides.com.

PPP Dial-up links to the Internet have their own special hardware protocol called the *Point-to-Point Protocol (PPP)*. PPP is a streaming protocol developed especially for dial-up Internet access. To Windows, a modem is nothing more than a special type of network adapter. Modems will have their own configuration entry in the Network Connections applet.

Most dial-up "I can't connect to the Internet"–type problems are user errors. Your first line of defense is the modem itself. Use the modem's properties to make sure the volume is turned up. Have the users listen to the connection.

FIGURE 18.29 The Connections tab in the Internet Properties dialog box

FIGURE 18.30 The New Connection Wizard

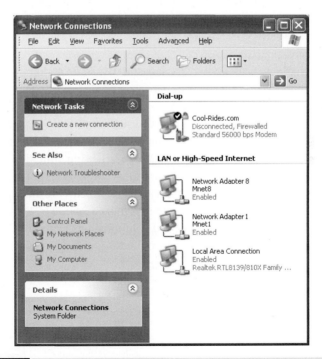

FIGURE 18.31 Connections in Windows XP

Do they hear a dial tone? If they don't, make sure the modem's line is plugged into a good phone jack.

Do they hear the modem dial and then hear someone saying, "Hello? Hello?" If so, they probably dialed the wrong number. Wrong password error messages are fairly straightforward—remember that the password may be correct, but the user name may be wrong. If they still fail to connect, it's time to call the network folks to see what is not properly configured in the Dial-up Networking settings.

ISDN

A standard telephone connection comprises many pieces. First, the phone line runs from your phone out to a network interface box (the little box on the side of your house), and into a central switch belonging to the telephone company. Standard metropolitan areas have a large number of central offices, each with a central switch. These central switches connect to each other through high-capacity *trunk lines.* Before 1970, the entire phone system was analog. Today, the entire telephone system, with the exception of the line from your phone to the central office, is digital.

By adding special equipment at the central office and the user's location, phone companies can now achieve a throughput of up to 64 K per line over the same copper wires already used by telephone lines. This process of sending telephone transmission across fully digital lines end-to-end is called *integrated services digital network (ISDN)* service.

ISDN service consists of two types of channels: Bearer, or B, channels and Delta, or D, channels. B channels carry data and voice information at 64 Kbps. D channels carry setup and configuration information and carry data at 16 Kbps. Most providers of ISDN allow the user to choose either one or two B channels. The more common setup is two B/one D, usually called a *basic rate interface (BRI)* setup. A BRI setup uses only one physical line, but each B channel sends 64 Kbps, doubling the throughput total to 128 Kbps. The big limitation is that you usually need to be within about 18,000 feet of a central office to use ISDN.

The physical connections for ISDN bear some similarity to analog modems. An ISDN wall socket usually looks something like a standard RJ-45 network jack. The most common interface for your computer is a device called a *terminal adapter (TA).* TAs look much like regular modems, and like modems, they come in external and internal variants.

Travel Advisory

Another type of ISDN, called a primary rate interface (PRI), is composed of 23 64-Kbps B channels and one 64-Kbps D channel, giving it a total throughput of 1.5 Mbps. PRI ISDN lines are rarely used as dial-up connections—they are far more common on dedicated lines.

Dedicated Connections

Increasingly, consumers and businesses are using dedicated high-speed connections such as DSL and cable to link their LANs to the Internet. Almost all of these dedicated connections use 10ˣBaseT Ethernet to connect a single PC or a switch to a special receiver called a DSL modem or cable modem.

DSL

Digital subscriber line (DSL) connections to ISPs use a standard telephone line but special equipment on each end to create always-on Internet connections at blindingly fast speeds, especially when compared with analog dial-up connections. Service levels vary around the U.S., but the typical upload speed is ~384 Kbps, while download speed comes in at a very sweet ~2+ Mbps.

> ### Local Lingo
>
> **ADSL and SDSL** The two most common forms of DSL you'll find are *asynchronous (ADSL)* and synchronous *(SDSL)*. ADSL lines differ between slow upload speed (such as 128, 256, or 384 Kbps) and faster download speed (usually 2 Mbps). SDSL has the same upload and download speeds, but telecom companies charge a lot more for the privilege. DSL encompasses many such variations, so you'll often see it referred to as *x* DSL.

DSL requires little setup from a user standpoint. A tech comes to the house to install a NIC in the Internet-bound PC and drop off a DSL receiver (often called a DSL modem; see Figure 18.32). The receiver connects to the telephone line and the PC (Figure 18.33). The tech (or the user, if knowledgeable) then

FIGURE 18.32 A DSL receiver

FIGURE 18.33 DSL connections

configures the TCP/IP options for the NIC to match the settings demanded by the DSL provider, and that's about it. Within moments, you're surfing at blazing speeds. You don't need a second telephone line. You don't need to wear a special propeller hat or anything. The only kicker is that your house has to be within a fairly short distance from a main phone service switching center, something like 18,000 feet. This pretty much stops everybody but inner-city dwellers from having access to DSL service.

Cable

Cable offers a different approach to high-speed Internet access, using regular cable TV cables to serve up lightning-fast speeds. It offers comparable service to DSL with a 384 Kbps upload and 2+ Mbps download. Cable Internet connections are theoretically available anywhere you can get cable TV.

Cable Internet connections start with an RG-6 or RG-59 cable coming into your house. The cable connects to a cable modem that then connects to a NIC in your PC via UTP Ethernet cable. Figure 18.34 shows a typical cable setup. One nice advantage of cable over DSL is that if you have a TV tuner card in your PC,

FIGURE 18.34 Cable connections

you can use the same cable connection (with a splitter) to watch TV on your PC. Both DSL and cable modem Internet connections can be used by two or more computers if they are part of a LAN, including those in a home.

LAN

Most businesses connect their internal LAN to an ISP via some hardware solution that Network+ techs deal with. Figure 18.35 shows a typical small-business wiring closet with routers that connect the LAN to the ISP. You learned all about wiring up a LAN in Chapter 13, so there's no need to go through any basics here. To complete a LAN connection to the Internet, you need to add a second NIC or a modem to one of the PCs and then configure that PC as the default connection. We'll revisit this idea in a moment with Internet Connection Sharing.

Wireless

Every once in a while a technology comes along that, once the kinks are smoothed out, works flawlessly, creating a magical computing experience. Unfortunately, the various wireless networking technologies out there today don't fulfill that dream yet. When they work, it's like magic. You walk into a coffee shop, sit down, and flip open your laptop computer. After firing up your Internet browser, suddenly you're quaffing lattes and surfing Web sites—with no wires or setup at all.

FIGURE 18.35 A wiring closet

You spent a good deal of Chapter 14 working thorough wireless connectivity to a LAN, so none of that is rehashed here. Suffice it to say that connecting to the Internet via wireless means that you must connect to a LAN that's wired to an ISP or connect to a cellular network. The local Internet café purchases high-speed Internet service from the cable or telecom company, for example, and then connects a wireless access point (WAP) to its network. When you walk in with your portable PC with wireless NIC and open a Web browser, the wireless NIC communicates with the *fully wired* DHCP server via the WAP and you're surfing on the Internet. It appears magically wireless, but the LAN to ISP connection still uses wires.

Cellular networking is even more seamless. Anywhere you can connect with your cell phone, you can connect with your cellular network–aware portable or laptop computer.

Travel Advisory

One form of wireless communication does not require local wires. *Wireless Broadband* relies on the ISP putting up a tower, and then any building within the line of sight (perhaps up to 10 miles) can get a high-speed connection.

Satellite

Satellite connections to the Internet get the data beamed to a satellite dish on your house or office; a receiver handles the flow of data, eventually sending it through an Ethernet cable to the NIC in your PC. I can already sense people's eyebrows raising. "Yeah, that's the download connection. But what about the upload connection?" The early days of satellite required you to connect via a modem. You would upload at the slow 26- to 48-Kbps modem speed, but then get super fast downloads from the dish. It worked, so why complain? Newer technology still requires that the initial setup be done via modem, but the download and the upload go through the dish. You can relax on a farm in Africa to write the great Kenyan novel, and still have DSL- or cable-speed Internet connectivity.

Satellite might be the most intriguing of all the technologies used to connect to the Internet today. As with satellite television, though, you need to have the satellite dish point at the satellites (toward the south if you live in the U.S.). The only significant issue to satellite is that the distance the signal must travel creates a small delay called the *satellite latency*. This latency is usually unnoticeable unless the signal degrades in foul weather such as rain and snow.

Internet Connection Sharing

Internet Connection Sharing (ICS) enables one system to share its Internet connection with other systems on the network, providing a quick and easy method for multiple systems to use one Internet connection. Figure 18.36 shows a typical setup for ICS. Note the terminology used here. The PC that connects to the Internet and then shares via ICS that connection with machines on a LAN is called the *ICS host* computer. PCs that connect via LAN to the ICS host computer are simply called *client* computers.

To connect multiple computers to a single ICS host computer requires several things in place. First, the ICS host computer has to have a NIC dedicated to the internal connections. If you connect via dial-up, for example, the ICS host computer uses a modem to connect to the Internet. It will also have a NIC that plugs into a hub. Other PCs on the LAN likewise connect to the hub. If you connect via some faster service, such as DSL that uses a NIC cabled to the DSL receiver, you'll need a second NIC in the ICS host machine to connect to the LAN and the client computers.

Setting up ICS in Windows 2000/XP is simple. Open the Properties dialog for My Network Places, and then access the properties of the connection you wish to share. Click the Sharing tab (Windows 2000) or the Advanced tab (Windows XP), and select *Enable Internet connection sharing for this connection* (Windows 2000) or *Allow other network users to connect through this computer's Internet connection* (Windows XP, Figure 18.37). Clients don't need any special configuration but should simply be set to DHCP for their IP address and other configurations.

FIGURE 18.36 Typical ICS setup

FIGURE 18.37 Enabling Internet Connection Sharing in Windows XP

The Windows XP Internet Connection Firewall

Once you've established a connection to the Internet, you should start thinking about security. Windows 2000 requires you to use some third-party tool, such as a hardware firewall, but Windows XP offers the *Internet Connection Firewall (ICF)* built into the system. ICF basically stops all uninvited access from the Internet. ICF keeps track of when you initiate communication with a particular machine over your Internet connection and then allows communication back from that same machine. This works whether your connection is a single machine directly dialed into an ISP or a group of networked PCs connecting through an ICS host computer. ICF tracks the communication and blocks anything uninvited. You can implement ICF on the same screen as you would ICS (Figure 18.38).

Travel Advisory
ICF enables you to open up specific computers inside a LAN for specific tasks, such as running an FTP server.

FIGURE 18.38 Implementing ICF

When you're running a LAN, implement ICF only on the machine that directly connects to the Internet. If you enable ICF on other machines on the LAN, you can possibly create problems.

Objective 18.04 Internet Software Tools

Once you've established a connection between the PC and the ISP, you still can do nothing on the Internet without applications designed to use one or more TCP/IP services, such as Web browsing and e-mail. TCP/IP has the following commonly used services:

- The World Wide Web
- E-mail

- Newsgroups
- FTP
- Telnet

Each of these services (sometimes referred to by the overused term *TCP/IP protocols*) requires a special application, and each of those applications has special settings. Let's look at all five services and see how to configure them.

The World Wide Web

The Web provides a graphical face for the Internet. All over the Internet are special servers called *Web servers*. These Web servers, in their simplest sense, provide Web sites and Web pages that you can access and thus get more or less useful information. Using Web browser software, such as Internet Explorer or Netscape Navigator, you can click a link on a Web page and be instantly transported, not just to some Web server in your home town, but to a server located anywhere in the world. Figure 18.39 shows Internet Explorer at the home page of my company's Web site, www.totalsem.com. Where is the server located? Does it matter? It could be in a closet in my office or on a huge clustered server in

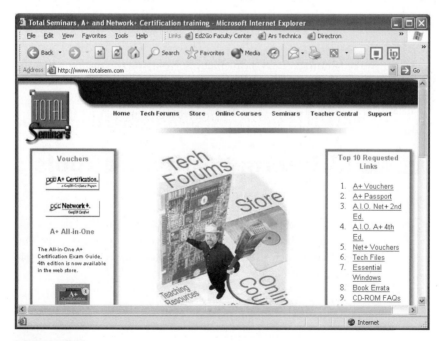

FIGURE 18.39 Internet Explorer showing a Web page

Canada. The great part about the Web is that you can get from here to there and access the information you need with a click or two of the mouse.

Setting up a Web browser takes almost no effort. As long as the Internet connection is working, Web browsers work automatically. This is not to say that there aren't plenty of settings, but the default browser settings work almost every time. If you type in a Web address, such as the best search engine on the planet—www.google.com—and it doesn't work, check the line and your network settings and you'll figure out where the problem is.

Configuring the Browser

Web browsers are highly configurable. On most Web browsers, you can set the default font size, whether it will display graphics or not, and several other settings. Although all Web browsers support these settings, where you go to make these changes varies dramatically. If you are using the popular Internet Explorer that comes with Windows, configuration tools are found in the Internet Options Control Panel applet or under the Tools menu in Internet Explorer.

Proxy Server If your Internet connection runs through a proxy server, you need to set your proxy settings within your browser (and any other Internet software you want to use). A *proxy server* is software that enables multiple connections to the Internet to go through one protected PC, much as ICS does at the LAN level. It's older technology, but it's still very much in use around the world. To configure proxy settings, go to the Tools menu and choose Internet Options; then select the Connections tab. Then click the LAN Settings button to open the Local Area Network (LAN) Settings dialog box (Figure 18.40).

FIGURE 18.40 The LAN Settings dialog box

Note that you have three options here, with automatic detection of the proxy server being the default. You can specify an IP address for a proxy server by clicking the third check box and simply typing it in (Figure 18.41). Your network administrator or a CompTIA Network+ tech will give you information on proxy servers if you need it to configure a machine. Otherwise, you can safely leave the browser configured to search automatically for a proxy server.

Security and Scripts While we're on the subject of configuration, make sure you know how to adjust the security settings in your Web browser. Many Web sites come with programs that download to your system and run automatically. These programs are written in specialized languages and file formats with names like Java or Active Server Pages. These programs make modern Web sites powerful and dynamic, but they can also act as a portal to malicious programs. To help with security, all better Web browsers let you determine whether you want these potentially risky programs to run. What you decide depends on personal factors. If your Web browser refuses to run a Java program (you'll know because you'll get an error, as in Figure 18.42), check your security settings because your browser may simply be following orders. To get to the security configuration screen in Internet Explorer, go to Tools | Internet Options | Security tab (Figure 18.43).

Internet Explorer gives you the option of selecting preset security levels by clicking the Custom Level button on the Security tab and then opening the pull-down menu (Figure 18.44). Changing from Medium to High security, for

FIGURE 18.41 Specifying the proxy server address

FIGURE 18.42 Error notice about running ActiveX

example, makes changes across the board, disabling everything from ActiveX to Java. You can also manually select which features to enable or disable in the scrolling menu, also visible in Figure 18.44.

Security doesn't stop with programs. Another big security concern relates to Internet commerce. People don't like to enter credit card information, home phone numbers, or other personal information for fear this information might be intercepted by hackers. Fortunately, there are methods of encrypting this information, the most common being HTTP over SSL (HTTPS) Web sites. It's easy to tell if your Web site is using HTTPS because the Web address will start with HTTPS instead of just HTTP, and you'll usually see a tiny lock in the lower right-hand corner of the browser window.

FIGURE 18.43 The Security tab in the Internet Options dialog

FIGURE 18.44 Changing security settings

There's one security risk that no computer can completely defend against: you. In particular, be careful when downloading programs from the Internet. The Internet makes it easy to download programs that you can then install and run on your system. There's nothing intrinsically wrong with this unless the program you download has a virus, is corrupted, or is incompatible with your OS. The watchword here is *common sense*. Download programs only from reliable sources. Take time to read the online documentation so that you're sure you're downloading a version of the program that works on your OS. Finally, always run a good antivirus program, preferably one that checks incoming programs for viruses before you install them. Failure to do this can lead to lockups, file corruption, and boot problems that you simply should not have to deal with.

E-Mail

You need an e-mail program to access e-mail. The two most popular are Microsoft's Outlook Express and Netscape's Messenger. E-mail clients need a little more setup. First, you must provide your e-mail address and password. All e-mail addresses come in the now-famous accountname@Internet domain format.

Travel Advisory

To create, access, or edit an account in Outlook Express, open
Outlook Express and go to Tools | Accounts. Select the Mail tab
and then click Add for a new account or select an existing account
and click Properties.

The second thing you must add are the names of the Post Office Protocol version 3 (POP3) or Internet Message Access Protocol (IMAP) server and the Simple Mail Transfer Protocol (SMTP) server. The POP3 or IMAP server is the computer that handles incoming (to you) e-mail. POP3 is by far the most widely used standard, although the latest version of IMAP, *IMAP4,* supports some features POP3 doesn't. For example, IMAP4 enables you to search through messages on the mail server to find specific keywords and select the messages you want to download onto your machine. Even with the advantages of IMAP4 over POP3, the vast majority of incoming mail servers use POP3.

The SMTP server handles your outgoing e-mail. These two systems may often have the same name, or close to the same name, as shown in Figure 18.45. All

FIGURE 18.45 POP3 and SMTP information in Outlook Express

these settings should be provided to you by your ISP. If they are not, you should be comfortable knowing what to ask for. If one of these names is incorrect, either you will not get your e-mail or you will not be able to send e-mail. If an e-mail setup that has been working well for a while suddenly encounters errors, it is likely that either the POP3 or SMTP server is down, or the DNS server has quit working.

Newsgroups

Newsgroups are one of the oldest services on the Internet. To access a newsgroup, you must use a newsreader program. A number of third-party newsreaders exist, such as the popular Forté Free Agent, but Microsoft's Outlook Express is the most common of all newsreaders (not surprising, since it comes free with most versions of Windows). To access a newsgroup, you must know the name of a news server. *News servers* run the *Network News Transfer Protocol (NNTP)*. There are public news servers, but these are extremely slow. Your ISP will tell you the name of the news server and provide you with a user name and password if necessary (Figure 18.46).

FIGURE 18.46 Configuring Outlook Express for a news server

File Transfer Protocol

The *File Transfer Protocol (FTP)* can be used to access systems that you would otherwise not be able to access. FTP is also a great way to share files, but you need an FTP server. To access an FTP site, you must use an FTP client such as WS_FTP, although later versions of Internet Explorer and other Web browsers provide support for FTP. Just type in the name of the FTP site. Figure 18.47 shows Internet Explorer accessing ftp.microsoft.com.

Even though you can use a Web browser, all FTP sites require you to log on. Web browsers know only the most common method, using the user name "anonymous" and then your e-mail address for a password. Called an anonymous logon, this works fine for most public FTP sites. However, if you need to access a site that requires a special user name and password, third-party programs are preferable, because they store these settings. This enables you to access the FTP site more easily later. Figure 18.48 shows my personal favorite FTP application, WS_FTP.

Telnet

Telnet is a terminal emulation program for TCP/IP networks that enables you to connect to a server and run commands on that server as if you were sitting right in front of it. This way, you can remotely administer a server and communicate

FIGURE 18.47 Accessing an FTP site in Internet Explorer

WS_FTP

with other servers on your network. As you can imagine, this is rather risky. If *you* can remotely control a computer, what's to stop others from doing the same? Of course, Telnet does not allow just *anyone* to log on and wreak havoc with your network. You must enter a special user name and password to run Telnet.

Exam Tip

The CompTIA A+ certification exams test your knowledge of a few networking tools, such as Telnet, but only enough to let you support a Network+ tech or network administrator. If you need to run Telnet, you will get the details from a network administrator. Implementation of Telnet falls well beyond CompTIA A+ certification exams.

Troubleshooting Networks

Objective 18.05

O nce you go beyond a single PC and enter the realm of networked computers, your troubleshooting skills need to take a giant leap up in quality. Think of the complexity added with networks. Suddenly you have multiple PCs with multiple users who could, at the drop of a hat, do all kinds of inadvertent damage to a fully functional PC. Networked PCs have a layer of networked hardware and resource sharing that adds a completely new dimension to a user's cry for help, "I can't print!" This section looks at two models for network troubleshooting: the Open System Interconnection (OSI) seven-layer model and my four-layer model.

OSI Seven-Layer Model

A lot of people think about networks and troubleshoot networking issues using the OSI seven-layer model. Using this model helps you isolate problems and then implement solutions. Here are the seven layers of the OSI model:

- **Layer 1** Physical
- **Layer 2** Data Link
- **Layer 3** Network
- **Layer 4** Transport
- **Layer 5** Session
- **Layer 6** Presentation
- **Layer 7** Application

The *Physical layer* defines the physical form taken by data when it travels across a cable. Devices that work at the physical layer include NICs, hubs, and switches. Figure 18.49 shows a sending NIC turning a string of ones and zeros into an electrical signal, and a receiving NIC turning it back into the same ones and zeros.

The *Data Link layer* defines the rules for accessing and using the Physical layer. MAC addresses and Ethernet's CSMA/CD operate at the Data Link layer.

The *Network layer* defines the rules for adding information to the data packet that controls how routers move it from its source on one network to its destination on a different network. The IP protocol that handles IP addressing works on Layer 3.

FIGURE 18.49 The Physical layer turns binary code into a physical signal and back into ones and zeros.

The *Transport layer*, Layer 4, breaks up data it receives from the upper layers (that is, Layers 5–7) into smaller pieces for transport within the data packets created at the lower layers. In TCP/IP networks, the protocols that typically handle this transition between upper and lower layers are TCP and UDP.

The *Session layer* manages the connections between machines on the network. Protocols such as NetBIOS and sockets enable a computer to connect to a server, for example, and send and receive e-mail or download a file. Each different task you can perform on a server would require a different kind of session.

The *Presentation layer* presents data from the sending system in a form that a receiving system can understand. Most Layer 6 functions are handled by the same software that handles Layer 7 functions.

The *Application layer* is where you (or a user) get to interact with the computers. These are programs that make networking happen, such as Web browsers and e-mail applications.

The key to using the OSI seven-layer model is to ask the traditional troubleshooting question: What can the problem be? If Jill can't browse a Web site, for example, could this be a Layer 7 issue? Sure: If her browser software was messed up, this could stop her from browsing. It could also be a lower level problem, though, and you need to run through the questions. Can she do anything over the network? If her NIC doesn't show flashing link lights, that could point all the way down to the Physical layer and a bad NIC, cable, hub, or switch.

If she has good connectivity to the overall network but can't ping the Web server, that could point to a different problem altogether. Figure 18.50 shows the OSI seven-layer model graphically.

The only drawback to the OSI seven-layer model, in my view, is that it's too complex. I like to conceptualize network issues into fewer layers—four to be precise. Let's take a look.

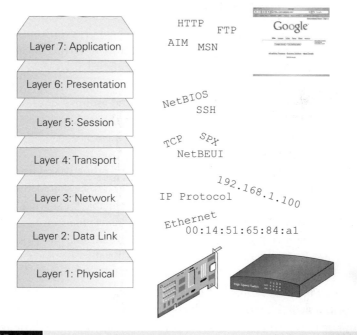

FIGURE 18.50 OSI seven-layer model

Mike's Four-Layer Model

Network problems, by the very nature of the complexity of a network, usually make for more complex problems. Given that, I have created a four-step process that I modestly call "Mike's Four-Layer Model." These four things go through my mind every time I have a problem. I think about four distinct "categories" to help me isolate the symptoms and make the right fix.

Hardware

Hardware is probably the most self-explanatory of the four categories. This covers the many different ways data can be moved from one PC to another. Does the system have a good connection—how's the cabling? This also covers network cards—are they installed properly and tested? Plus, the Hardware category hits on all of those interesting boxes, such as hubs, switches, and repeaters, among which all of the wires in the network run. If you can see it, it's under this category.

Protocols

This category covers the protocols, such as TCP/IP or NetBEUI. Is the protocol installed? Is it configured properly? Does any particular system's configuration prevent it from working with another system?

Network

The network category has two parts: servers and clients. Network operating systems must differentiate systems that act as server from those that do not. If a system is a server, some process must take place to tell it to share resources. Additionally, if a system is intended to share, it must be given a name. This category also includes defining and verifying users and groups—does your system need them? Do the right accounts exist, and are they working properly?

Shared Resources

Once all the systems, users, and groups are working properly, you need to identify the resources they will share. If a drive or folder is to be shared, the OS must provide a way to identify that drive or folder as available for sharing. The rules for naming shared resources are called *naming conventions*. A great example would be a system that offers its D:\FRED directory for sharing. This D:\FRED directory needs a network name, such as FRED_FILES. This network name is displayed to all of the devices on the network.

Sharing a resource is only half the battle. Individual systems need to be able to access the shared resources. The network needs a process whereby a PC can look out on the network and see what is available. Having found those available resources, the PC then needs to make them look and act as though they were local resources. A network also needs to control access to resources. A laser printer, for example, might be available for sharing, but only for the accounting department, excluding other departments.

CHECKPOINT

✔**Objective 18.01: Network Operating Systems** Network OSs enable PCs to share resources and access shared resources across a network. They provide a network organization, such as client/server or peer-to-peer. You can make a PC a member of a workgroup or, in high-end settings, a member of a domain.

✔**Objective 18.02: Installing and Configuring a LAN** It takes at least four components to have a functional network: NIC, client software, protocol, and server software. First, you need to install a NIC, including proper drivers. Second, you must install client software so that the PC can see and be seen on the network. Windows installs the Client for Microsoft Networks by

default when you install a NIC. Third, the NIC needs to run a properly configured network protocol that matches that of other machines. The most common protocol in use is TCP/IP, the protocol of the Internet. DHCP sets up your IP address, subnet mask, default gateway, and more, automatically. Any manual settings you'll get from a network administrator. And finally, you must enable File and Printer Sharing to turn the PC into a server and make its resources available for other users across the network. Sharing resources is a matter of selecting the properties for a folder or device and coming up with a share name. You use My Network Places to access shared resources on a LAN.

✔**Objective 18.03: Connecting to the Internet** To use the Internet successfully, you need to connect properly and then run special applications that work with TCP/IP services. Many users connect to an ISP using a modem and Dial-up Networking. DUN uses PPP to enable access to remote resources. Other users connect via a dedicated solution, such as cable or DSL. Windows offers Internet Connection Sharing to enable computers on a LAN to connect to the Internet through a single machine. Windows XP offers the Internet Connection Firewall to protect the exposed computer.

✔**Objective 18.04: Internet Software Tools** The TCP/IP services used commonly on the Internet are HTTP for Web browsing, POP3 and SMTP for e-mail, NNTP for newsgroups, FTP for transferring files, and Telnet for controlling remote computers.

✔**Objective 18.05: Troubleshooting Networks** Two models help break networks down into component parts so you can troubleshoot problems more easily. Most of the industry uses the OSI seven-layer model, and that's what you're likely to see on the CompTIA A+ certification exams. I use a four-layer model that categorizes networks in terms of hardware, protocols, network, and shared resources. Either model will get you where you need to go as a tech.

REVIEW QUESTIONS

1. Richard sets up a small LAN composed of five Windows XP computers connected to a router that connects to a DSL connection. What kind of network has he set up?

 A. Client/server

 B. Domain-based

C. Peer-to-peer

D. Not enough information

2. Simon's Windows 2000 system can't contact a DHCP server to obtain an IP address automatically, but he can still communicate with other systems on his subnet. What feature of Windows 2000 makes this possible?

 A. Subnet masking

 B. Windows Internet Name Service

 C. Automatic Private IP Addressing

 D. Client for Microsoft Networks

3. Which of the following are true of NetBEUI? (Select two.)

 A. No logical addresses are required.

 B. It is supported only on Microsoft network systems.

 C. It supports routing.

 D. It is supported by all versions of Windows through XP.

4. In a TCP/IP network, the two parts of an IP address are the _____ and the _____.

 A. Network ID, host ID

 B. IP address, subnet mask

 C. Client, server

 D. TCP address, IP address

5. You need to check the status of the local area connection of a Windows XP machine on your Microsoft network. How do you get to the screen where you can perform this task? (Select two.)

 A. Start | right-click My Network Places | Properties | Local Area Connection

 B. Start | Settings | Network and Dial-up Connections | Local Area Connection

 C. Start | Control Panel | Network Connections | Local Area Connection

 D. Right-click My Computer | Properties | Network Connections | Local Area Connection

6. The router that your PC uses to connect to your ISP is referred to as the _____.

 A. Loopback address

 B. Backbone

C. IP address

D. Default gateway

7. To configure dial-up networks with Windows XP, use the
_____ applet.

A. Network and Internet Connections

B. Network Neighborhood

C. Internet Connection Sharing

D. Remote Assistance

8. To check to see if the Web server you are trying to reach is available or
is down, you can use the command line utility called _____.

A. Ping

B. ICS

C. TELNET

D. NNTP

9. A _____ is either hardware or software that protects your
computer or network from probing or malicious users.

A. Router

B. Firewall

C. Protocol

D. Spyware

10. Liz can receive her e-mail, but she cannot send e-mail. Which of
the following is most likely causing her problem?

A. POP3

B. SMTP

C. IMAP

D. UART

REVIEW ANSWERS

1. **C** Because no server is involved, Richard must have set up a
peer-to-peer network.

2. **C** Automatic Private IP Addressing is the Windows 2000 feature
that makes it possible for Simon's system to communicate with other
systems on his subnet even though he can't obtain an IP address.

3. **A** **B** NetBEUI doesn't require logical addresses and is supported only on Microsoft network systems. It is non-routable, however, and is not available to install in Windows XP.

4. **A** The two parts of an IP address are the network ID and the host ID.

5. **A** **C** To check the status of the local area connection of a Windows XP machine on your Microsoft network, you can select either Start | right-click My Network Places | Properties | Local Area Connection, or Start | Control Panel | Network Connections | Local Area Connection.

6. **D** The router that your PC uses to connect to your Internet service provider is referred to as the default gateway.

7. **A** To configure dial-up networks with Windows XP, use the Network and Internet Connections applet.

8. **A** To check to see if the Web server you are trying to reach is available or is down, you can use the command line utility called Ping.

9. **B** A firewall is either hardware or software that protects your computer or network from probing or malicious users.

10. **B** Liz can receive her e-mail, but she cannot send e-mail. SMTP is the most likely cause of her problem. Remember, SMTP is used to send, while POP3 and IMAP are used to receive e-mail.

Maintaining, Optimizing, and Troubleshooting Windows 2000/XP

	NEWBIE	SOME EXPERIENCE	EXPERT
ETA	5 hours	3 hours	1.5 hours

An installed Windows operating system (OS) needs occasional optimization, ongoing maintenance, and troubleshooting when it doesn't work correctly. Microsoft has done such a good job with the latest versions of Windows that, out of the box, they are easy to optimize and maintain, although troubleshooting—and all OSs share this—is still a bit of a challenge.

Objective 19.01 Maintaining Windows

To maintain Windows properly, you need to run various utilities periodically. This includes patching, managing users, cleaning up hard drives and the Registry, and keeping your security settings up to date.

Patches, Updates, and Service Packs

You must keep Windows patched and polished. All OSs have flaws and Windows is no exception. The Internet has enabled Microsoft to make updates available, and the *Windows Update* program can grab those updates and patch user systems easily and automatically. Microsoft provides the Windows Update utility in Windows 2000 and Windows XP.

You can also start Windows Update manually. When your computer is connected to the Internet, start the utility in Windows 2000 by selecting Start | Windows Update. In Windows XP you will find it at Start | All Programs | Windows Update. When you run Windows Update manually, the software connects to the Microsoft Web site and scans your computer to determine what updates may be needed. Within a few seconds or minutes, depending on your connection speed, you'll get a straightforward screen, like the one shown in Figure 19.1.

You have several choices here, although two are most obvious. If you click the Express button, Windows Update will grab any high-priority updates—these are security patches—and install them on your computer. If you click the Custom button, you can select from a list of optional updates (Figure 19.2).

Automatic Update

Updates are so important that Microsoft gives you the option of updating Windows automatically through the *Automatic Updates* feature. Actually, it nags you about it! Soon after installing XP (a day or two, in my experience), a message

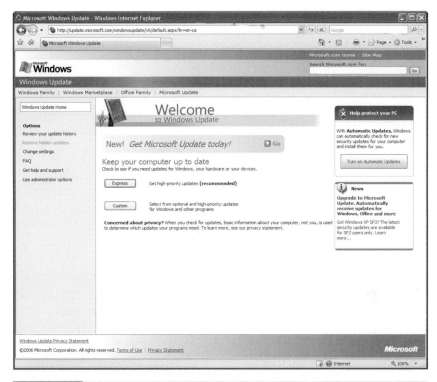

FIGURE 19.1 Microsoft Windows Update page

balloon will pop up from the taskbar suggesting that you automate updates. If you click this balloon, the Automatic Updates Setup Wizard will run, enabling you to configure the update program. You can also right-click My Computer, select Properties, click the Automatic Updates tab, and select Automatic Update options. Or, open the Control Panel and double-click the Automatic Updates icon. Then, whenever your computer connects to the Web, it checks the Windows Update page. What happens next depends on the setting you choose. You have four choices:

- **Automatic (recommended)** Windows Update will keep your computer patched up and ready to go. This is the best option for most users, although not necessarily good for users of portable computers. Nobody wants to log into a slow hotel dial-up connection and have

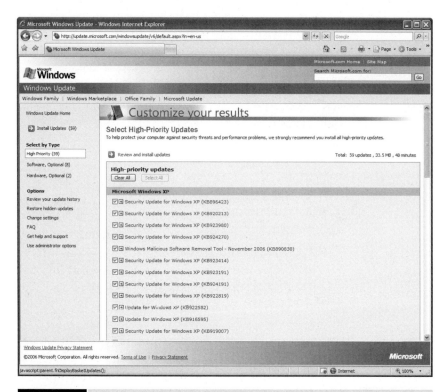

FIGURE 19.2 Choose updates to be installed

most of your bandwidth sucked away by Automatic Update downloading hot fixes!

- **Download updates for me** Windows Update downloads all patches in the background and then, when they're complete, tells you about them. You have the option at that point to install or not install.

- **Notify me** Windows Update simply flashes you a dialog box that tells you updates are available but does not download anything until you say go. This is the best option for users of portable computers. You can download files when it's convenient for you, such as when you're home rather than traveling on business.

- **Turn off Automatic Updates** This does precisely what is advertised. You get neither automatic patches nor notification that patches are available. Use this option only on a system that does not or cannot

connect to the Internet. If you're online, your computer needs to be patched!

When Windows Update works the way Microsoft wants it to work, it scans the Microsoft Web site periodically, downloads patches as they appear, and then installs them on your computer. If you opted for the download but don't install option, Windows Update simply notifies you when updates are downloaded and ready to install (Figure 19.3).

Managing User Accounts and Groups

The most basic element of Windows security is the *user account*. Each user must present a valid user name and password of a user account to log into to a Windows computer. There are ways to make this logon highly simplified, even invisible in some cases, but there is no exception to this rule. Each user is also a member of one or more *groups* of users. Groups enable the system administrator to assign the same rights and permissions to all members of the group without the need to set those rights and permissions individually.

Windows 2000/XP have several built-in groups and two user accounts created during installation—Administrator and Guest—with only the Administrator account enabled by default. When you install Windows, you supply the password for the Administrator account. This is the only usable account you have to log into the computer, unless you joined the computer to a domain or until you create a new user account.

You can manage users and groups using the Local Users and Groups node in the Computer Management console, accessed by right-clicking My Computer and selecting Manage. Local Users and Groups can also be used on stand-alone computers, but Microsoft includes simpler GUI tools for that purpose in Windows 2000/XP. In Windows XP, Microsoft made significant changes in the GUI tools for managing users and groups, so I'll break up this discussion between these two OSs.

FIGURE 19.3 Windows Update balloon message

Using the Users and Passwords Applet in Windows 2000

When you install Windows 2000 Professional, assuming your computer is not made a member of a domain, you may choose to let the OS assume that you are the only user of the computer and do not want to see the logon dialog box. You can check this setting after installation by opening the Users and Passwords applet in Control Panel to see the setting for *Users must enter a user name and password to use this computer*. Figure 19.4 shows this choice selected, which means that you will see a logon box every time you restart your computer. Also notice that the Administrator is selected. That's the account you're using to log on.

Using the Administrator account is just fine when you're performing administrative tasks such as installing updates, adding printers, adding and removing programs and Windows components, and creating users and groups. Best prac-

FIGURE 19.4 Security begins with turning on *Users must enter a user name and password to use this computer*

tice for the workplace is to create one or more user accounts and log in only with the user accounts, not the Administrator account. This gives you a lot more control over who or what happens to the computer.

Travel Advisory

If the user name and password requirement is turned off or you have user accounts that aren't password protected in Windows 2000 (or XP, for that matter), anyone with physical access to your computer can turn it on and use it by pressing the power button. This is potentially a very bad thing!

Creating a New User in Windows 2000

Creating a new user account enables that user to log on with a user name and password. This lets an administrator set the rights and permissions for the user as well as audit access to certain network resources. For that reason, it is good practice to create users on a desktop computer. You are working with the same concepts on a small scale that an administrator must work with in a domain. Let's review the steps in this procedure for Windows 2000.

Exam Tip

Remember that to create and manage users, you must be logged on as the Administrator, be a member of the Administrators group, or have an Administrator account (in Windows XP). Assign a password to the Administrator account so that only authorized users can access this all-powerful account.

If you're logged on in Windows 2000 as the Administrator or a member of the local Administrators group, open the Users and Passwords applet from Control Panel and click the Add button. This opens the Add New User Wizard (Figure 19.5). Enter the user name that the user will use to log on. Enter the user's first and last names in the Full Name field, and if you wish, enter some text that describes this person in the Description field. If you're at work, enter a job description in this field. The Full Name and Description fields are optional.

After entering the user information, click the Next button to continue. This opens a password dialog box (Figure 19.6), where you can enter and confirm the initial password for this new user. Click the Next button to continue.

FIGURE 19.5 Adding a new user

Now you decide to which groups the new user should belong. Select one of the two suggested options—Standard User or Restricted User—or select the Other option button and choose a group from the drop-down list. Select *Standard user*, which on a Windows 2000 Professional desktop makes this person a member of the local Power Users group as well as the local Users group. Click the Finish button to close the dialog box. You should see your new user listed in the Users and Passwords dialog box. While you're there, note how easy it is for an administrator to change a user's password. Simply select a user from the list and

FIGURE 19.6 Create user password

then click the Set Password button. Enter and confirm the new password in the Set Password dialog box. Figure 19.7 shows the Set Password dialog box with the Users and Passwords dialog box in the background.

To change a password, select the new user in the *Users for this computer* list on the Users page. Then click the Set Password button on the Users page. Enter and confirm the new password and then click the OK button to apply the changes.

Managing Users in Windows XP

Although Windows XP has essentially the same type of accounts database as Windows 2000, the User Accounts applet in the Control Panel replaces the Users and Passwords applet and further simplifies user management tasks.

Windows XP gives you two different ways to deal with user accounts and how you log into a system: the blank user name and password text boxes, reminiscent of Windows 2000, and the Windows XP Welcome screen (Figure 19.8). If your Windows XP computer is a member of a Windows domain, your system automatically uses the Windows Classic style, including the requirement to press CTRL-ALT-DEL to get to the user name and password text boxes, just as in Windows 2000. If your Windows XP computer is not a member of a domain, you may use either method, although the Welcome screen is the default. Win-

FIGURE 19.7 Set Password dialog box

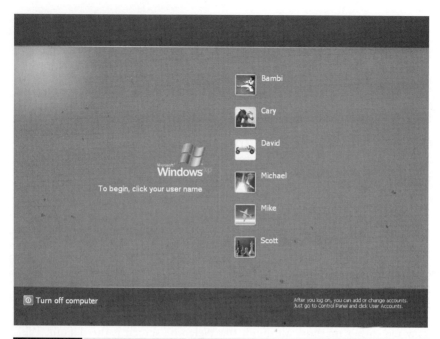

FIGURE 19.8 Windows XP Welcome screen

dows XP Home and Windows XP Media Center cannot join a domain, so these versions of Windows use only the Welcome screen. Windows Tablet PC Edition functions just like Windows XP Professional.

Assuming that your Windows XP system is *not* a member of a domain, I'll concentrate on the XP Welcome screen and some of the options you'll see in the User Accounts Control Panel applet.

The User Accounts applet is very different from the Users and Passwords applet in Windows 2000. User Accounts hides the complete list of users, using a simplistic reference to account types that is actually a reference to its group membership. An account that is a member of the local Administrators group is said to be a Computer Administrator; an account that belongs only to the Local Users group is said to be a Limited account. Which users the applet displays depends on which type of user is currently logged on (see Figure 19.9). When an Administrator is logged on, he or she will see both types of accounts and the Guest account. A Limited user will see only his or her own account in User Accounts.

Windows XP requires you to create a second account that is a member of the Administrator's group during the initial Windows installation. This is for simple redundancy—if one administrator is not available or is unable to log into the computer, another one can.

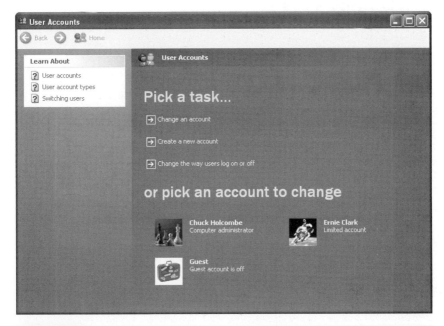

FIGURE 19.9 User Accounts dialog box showing a Computer Administrator, a Limited account, and the Guest account (disabled)

Travel Advisory

If you upgrade from Windows NT, Windows 2000, or a Windows 9*x installation in which user accounts were enabled, Setup will migrate the existing accounts to Windows XP.*

Creating users is a straightforward process. You need to provide a user name (a password can be added later), and you need to know which type of account to create: Computer Administrator or Limited. To create a new user in Windows XP, open the User Accounts applet from the Control Panel and click *Create a new account.* On the *Pick an account type* page (Figure 19.10) you can create either type of account. Simply follow the prompts on the screen. After you have created your local accounts, you'll see them listed when you open the User Accounts applet. It will look something like Figure 19.11.

Head back to the User Accounts applet and look at the *Change the way users log on and off* option. Select it; you will see two check boxes (Figure 19.12). If you select the *Use the Welcome screen* check box, Windows will bring up the friendly Welcome screen shown in Figure 19.13 each time users log in. If this box is unchecked, you'll have to enter a user name and password, just like in Windows 2000.

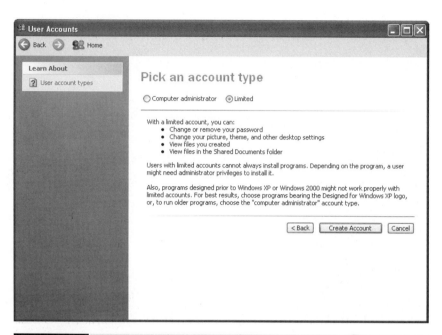

FIGURE 19.10 The *Pick an account type* page showing both options available

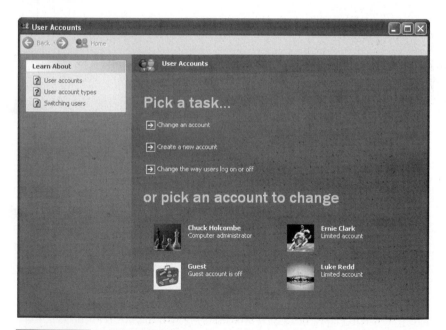

FIGURE 19.11 New Limited account listed in User Accounts

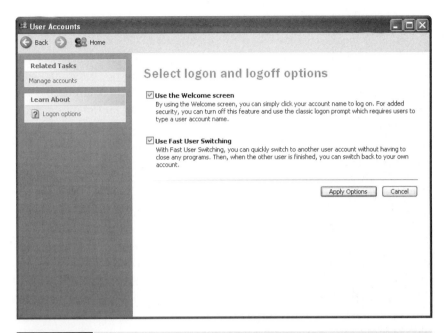

FIGURE 19.12 Select logon and logoff options

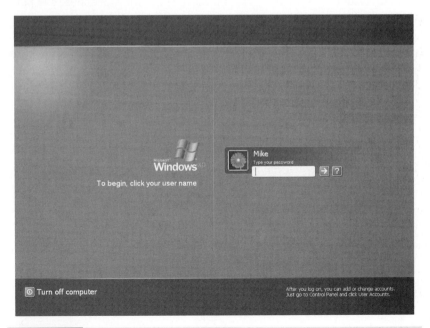

FIGURE 19.13 Single account logon screen

The second option, *Use Fast User Switching*, enables you to switch to another user without logging off the currently running user. This is a handy option when two people actively share a system, or when someone wants to borrow your system for a moment but you don't want to close all your programs. This option is active only if you have the *Use the Welcome screen* check box enabled. If *Fast User Switching* is enabled, when you click the Log Off button on the Start menu, you get the option to switch users, shown in Figure 19.14.

Passwords

Passwords are the ultimate key to protecting your computers. A user account with a valid password will get you into any system. Even if the user account has only limited permissions, you still have a security breach. Remember that for a hacker, just getting into the network is half the battle.

Protect your passwords. Never give out passwords over the phone. If a user loses a password, an administrator should reset the password to a complex combination of letters and numbers, and then allow the user to change the password to something else. All of the stronger OSs have this capability.

Make your users choose good passwords. I once attended a security seminar, and the speaker had everyone stand up. She then began to ask questions about our passwords—if we responded yes to the question we were to sit down. She began to ask questions such as "Do you use the name of your spouse as a password?" and "Do you use your pet's name?" By the time she was done asking about 15 questions, only 6 people out of some 300 were still standing! The reality is that most of us choose passwords that are amazingly easy to hack. Make sure you use strong passwords: at least six to eight characters in length, including letters, numbers, and punctuation symbols.

FIGURE 19.14 Switch User option

Exam Tip

Keep in mind that using non-alphanumeric characters makes any password much more difficult to crack for two reasons. First, adding non-alphanumeric characters forces the hacker to consider many more possible characters than just letters and numbers. Second, most password crackers use combinations of common words and numbers to try to hack a password. Because non-alphanumeric characters don't fit into common words or numbers, including a character such as an exclamation point will defeat these common-word hacks. Not all serving systems allow you to use characters such as @, $, %, or \, however, so you need to experiment to see if a particular server will accept them.

Resetting Forgotten Passwords in Windows XP Windows XP allows the currently logged-on user to create a *password reset disk* that can be used in case of a forgotten password. This is important to have, because if you forget your password, and an administrator resets the password using User Accounts or Local Users and Groups, then when you log on using the new password, you will discover that you cannot access some items, including files that you encrypted when logged on with the forgotten password. When you reset a password with a password reset disk, you can log on using the new password and still have access to previously encrypted files.

Best of all, with the password reset disk, users have the power to fix their own passwords. Encourage your users to create this disk; you have this power only if you remember to create a password reset disk *before* you forget the password! If you need to create a password reset disk for a computer on a network (domain), search the Help system for "password reset disk" and follow the instructions.

Hard Drive Tools and Tasks

Keeping drives healthy and happy is a key task for every tech. Three tools enable you to accomplish this task: Error-checking, Disk Defragmenter, and Disk Cleanup. You learned about all three tools back in Chapter 8, "Hard Drives," so there's no need to recap here how to run them. Just run them regularly!

Registry Maintenance

Your Registry is a huge database that Windows constantly updates. As a result, the Registry tends to get clogged with entries that are no longer valid. These usually don't cause any problems directly, but they can slow down your system.

Interestingly, Microsoft does not provide a utility to clean up the Registry. (Back in the old Windows 9x days, you could use a Microsoft tool called REGCLEAN, but it was never updated for Windows 2000/XP.) To clean your Registry, you need to turn to a third-party utility. Quite a few Registry cleaner programs are available, but my favorite is the freeware EasyCleaner by ToniArts (Figure 19.15). You can download the latest copy at http://personal.inet.fi/business/toniarts/ecleane.htm.

Travel Advisory

The www.toniarts.com Web site is a scam—do *not* use anything from that Web site!

Before you start cleaning your Registry with wild abandon, keep in mind that all Registry cleaners are risky in that there is a chance that it may delete something you want in the Registry. I've used EasyCleaner for a while and it has worked well for me—your experience may differ! You can use EasyCleaner's handy undo feature so that you can restore what you deleted.

EasyCleaner is a powerful optimization tool that does far more than just clean your Registry. Check out the file duplicate finder, space usage, and other

FIGURE 19.15 EasyCleaner

tools that come with this package. If you like this program, go to the Web site and donate some money to Toni.

Security: Spyware/Antivirus/Firewall

You simply cannot run a computer today without a large number of security programs to protect you from malicious attacks from spyware, malware, viruses, and hacking. In fact, the installation, monitoring, and updating of these programs (and possibly even hardware) is so important that they get their own chapter. Head to Chapter 20 for a complete discussion of how to keep your computer safe.

Objective 19.02 Optimizing Windows

Maintenance is about keeping Windows' performance from degrading with time and use. Of course, we don't just want to keep trouble at bay—we want to make our systems better, stronger, faster! Anything you do that makes Windows better than it was before, such as adding a piece of software or hardware to make something run better, is an optimization.

Installing and Removing Software

The most common optimization performed on any PC is probably adding and removing applications. Installing and removing software is part of the normal life of any PC. Each time you add or remove software, you make changes and decisions that can affect the system beyond whatever the program does, so it pays to know how to do it right.

Installing Software

Most application programs are distributed on CD-ROMs. Luckily, Windows supports *Autorun*, a feature that enables it to look for and read a special file called—wait for it—*Autorun* immediately after a CD-ROM is inserted, and then run whatever program is listed in AUTORUN.INF. Most application programs distributed on CD-ROM have an Autorun file that calls up the installation program.

Travel Advisory

Programs keep getting bigger and bigger, and distributors have started using DVDs for applications. Expect that trend to continue in a big way. Apple switched over to DVD for OS X some time ago, and Microsoft has followed suit with Windows Vista. Autorun works with DVDs just fine.

Sometimes, however, it is necessary to institute the installation sequence yourself. Perhaps the install CD lacks an Autorun installation program, or perhaps Windows is configured so that programs on a CD-ROM must be started manually. In some cases, a CD-ROM may contain more than one program, and you must choose which of them to install. Regardless of the reason, beginning the installation manually is a simple and straightforward process using the *Add or Remove Programs* applet in the Control Panel. (Windows 2000 calls the applet Add/Remove Programs.) Click the Add New Programs button (Figure 19.16), follow the prompts, and provide the disk or location of the files.

As long as you have sufficient permissions to install an application—your account is a member of the Administrators group in Windows 2000, for example, or is an Administrator account in Windows XP—the application will begin its install routine. If you don't have sufficient permissions to install an application, Windows will stop the installation.

Removing Software

Each installed application program takes up space on your computer's hard drive, and programs that you no longer need simply waste space that could be used for other purposes. Removing unnecessary programs can be an important piece of optimization.

FIGURE 19.16 Add New Programs

You remove a program from a Windows PC in much the same way that you install it. That is, you use the application's own uninstall program, when possible. You normally find the uninstall program listed under the application's icon on the Start menu, as shown in Figure 19.17.

If an uninstall program is not available, then use Windows' Add or Remove Programs applet from Control Panel. Figure 19.18 shows this applet. You select the program you want to remove and click the Change/Remove button. You should not be surprised by now to hear that it does not disappear in a flash. First you'll see a message warning you that the program will be permanently removed from your PC. If you're certain you want to continue, click Yes.

You may then see a message telling you that a shared file that appears to no longer be in use is about to be deleted, and asking your approval. Generally speaking, it's safe to delete such files. If you do not delete them, they will likely be orphaned and remain unused on your hard disk forever. In some cases, clicking the Change/Remove button will start the application's install program (the one you couldn't find before) so that you can modify the installed features. This is a function of the program you're attempting to remove. The end result should be the removal of the application and all of its pieces and parts, including files and Registry entries.

Adding or Removing Windows Components

When you installed Windows, it tried to guess which optional Windows components you would need. It installed Notepad, modem support, and games on your computer. These Windows components can be removed from your system if you like, and other components can be added as well. If you're adding components, you'll need a copy of your Windows CD or another location where the

FIGURE 19.17 Uninstall me

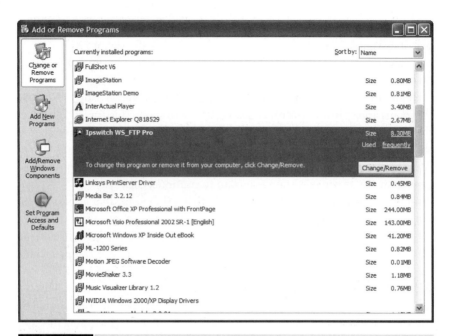

FIGURE 19.18	Add or Remove Programs applet

Windows source files are stored. This task really hasn't changed from previous versions of Windows.

To add or remove a Windows component, open the Add or Remove Programs applet in the Control Panel (Add/Remove Programs in Windows 2000). From here, select Add/Remove Windows Components, which opens the Windows Components Wizard (Figure 19.19). You can select an installed program; see how frequently it is used, how much disk space it uses, and (sometimes) the last time it was used.

Installing/Optimizing a Device

The processes for optimizing hardware in Windows 2000/XP are absolutely identical, even down to the troubleshooting and backup utilities, and are similar to the steps for installing a new device. The install process is covered in every chapter of this book that deals with one type of device or another, so this section concentrates on the issues that fit best under optimization.

FIGURE 19.19 Windows Components Wizard

Exam Tip
All four CompTIA A+ certification exams test you on installing and optimizing devices.

Driver Updates

Device manufacturers occasionally update their device drivers. Most of these updates are intended to fix problems, but many updates incorporate new features. Whatever the case, when one of your devices gets an updated driver, it's your job to install it. Windows / Microsoft Update provides an easy method to update drivers from manufacturers that take advantage of the service. The only trick to this is that you usually need to select the Custom option to see these updates because Windows installs only high-priority updates using the Express option. When you click the Custom option, look under Hardware, Optional (on the left) to see if Windows has any driver updates (Figure 19.20). Take some time and read what these updates do—sometimes you may choose not to install a driver update because it's not necessary or useful to your system.

If Windows does not put a driver update in the Windows Update tool, how do you know a device needs updating? The trick is to know your devices. Video card manufacturers update drivers quite often. Get in the habit of registering

FIGURE 19.20 Hardware, Optional

your video card with the manufacturer to stay up to date. Any new device is also a good candidate for an update. When you buy that new cool toy for your system, make a point to head over to the manufacturer's Web site and see if any updates have come out since it was packaged for sale. That happens more often than you might think!

Driver Signing

Device drivers become part of the OS and thus have the potential to cause lots of problems if they're written poorly. To protect Windows systems from bad device drivers, Microsoft uses *driver signing,* which means that each driver has a digital signature. Any drivers included on the Windows CD-ROM or at the Windows Update Web site are digitally signed. Once you have installed a driver, you can look at its Properties to confirm that it was digitally signed. Figure 19.21 shows a digitally signed network card driver.

A digitally signed driver

When an unsigned driver is detected during hardware installation, you'll see the message in Figure 19.22 offering you the choice to stop or continue the installation. Signed drivers are more or less a sure thing, but that doesn't mean unsigned ones are a problem—just consider the source of the driver and ensure your device works properly after installation.

Stop or continue installation of an unsigned driver

You can control how Windows behaves when drivers are being installed. Click the Driver Signing button on the Hardware tab of the System Properties dialog box to display the Driver Signing Options dialog box shown in Figure 19.23. If you select Ignore, Windows will install an unsigned driver without warning you. If you select Warn, you will be prompted when Windows detects an unsigned driver during driver installation, and you will be given the opportunity either to stop or continue the installation. Choosing Block will prevent the installation of unsigned drivers.

The default Driver Signing setting is Warn. This is also the default setting during installation, so you will always be warned when Windows detects an unsigned driver. This is no problem for a standard installation, when you are sitting at the computer, responding to all prompts—but it is a problem for automated, unattended installations. This is a good reason to check out all your device drivers before installing Windows.

Device Manager

You've worked with the Device Manager in other chapters when installing and troubleshooting devices; it's also the tool to use when you're optimizing device drivers. Right-click a device in Device Manager to display the context menu. From here you can update or uninstall the driver, disable the device, scan for hardware changes, or display the Properties dialog box. When you open the Properties dialog box, you'll see several tabs that vary according to the specific

FIGURE 19.23 Driver Signing Options dialog box

device. Most have General, Driver, Details, and Resources. The tab that matters most for optimization is the Driver tab.

The Driver tab has buttons labeled Driver Details, Update Driver, Roll Back Driver, and Uninstall. Driver Details lists the driver files and their locations on disk. Update Driver opens the Hardware Update Wizard—not very useful given that the install programs for almost all drivers do this automatically. The Roll Back Driver option is a different story. It enables you to remove an updated driver, thus rolling back to the previous driver version. Rollback (Figure 19.24) is a lifesaver when you install a new driver and suddenly discover it's worse than the driver it replaced! Uninstall removes the driver.

Adding a New Device

Windows should automatically detect any new device you install in your system. If Windows does not detect a newly connected device, use the Add Hardware Wizard (Figure 19.25) to get the device recognized and drivers installed. In Windows 2000, you'll find it on the Hardware tab of the System Properties dialog box. Windows XP has an Add Hardware applet in the Control Panel.

Click Next on the Welcome screen, and the wizard will search for hardware that has been connected but does not yet have a driver installed. If it detects the device, select the device, and the wizard will install the driver. You may have to point to the source location for the driver files. If it does not detect the device, which is likely, it will ask you if the hardware is connected. When you answer yes and click Next, it will give you a list of installed hardware, similar to Figure 19.26.

If the device is in the list, select it and click Next. If not, scroll to the bottom and select Add a New Hardware Device, and then click Next. If the device is a printer, network card, or modem, select *Search for and install the hardware automatically* and click Next. In that case, once it detects the device and installs the driver, you're done. If you do see your device on the list, your best hope is to select *Install the hardware that I manually select from a list*. In the subsequent screens, select the appropriate device category, select the device manufacturer and the correct model, and respond to the prompts from the Add Hardware Wizard to complete the installation.

FIGURE 19.24 Rollback

FIGURE 19.25 Add Hardware Wizard

Performance Options

One optimization you can perform on both Windows 2000 and Windows XP is setting Performance Options. *Performance Options* are used to configure CPU, RAM, and virtual memory (page file) settings. To access these options, right-

FIGURE 19.26 List of installed hardware

click My Computer and select Properties, click the Advanced tab, and click the Options button (Windows 2000) or Settings button (Windows XP) in the Performance section of that tab. The Performance Options dialog box differs between the two families of OSs.

In Windows 2000, the Performance Options dialog box shows a pair of radio buttons called Applications and Background Services. These radio buttons set how processor time is divided between the foreground application and all other background tasks. Set this to Applications if you run applications that need more processor time. Set it to Background Services to give all running programs the same processor usage. You can also adjust the size of the page file in this dialog box, but in most cases I don't mess with these settings and instead leave control of the page file to Windows.

The Windows XP Performance Options dialog box has three tabs: Visual Effects, Advanced, and Data Execution Prevention (Figure 19.27). The Visual Effects tab enables you to adjust visual effects that impact performance. Try clicking the top three choices in turn and watch the list of settings. Notice the

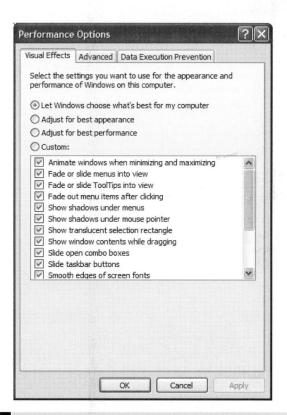

FIGURE 19.27 Windows XP Performance Options dialog box

tiny difference between the first two choices. The third choice, *Adjust for best performance*, turns off all visual effects, and the fourth option is an invitation to make your own adjustments. If you're on a computer that barely supports Windows XP, turning off visual effects can make a huge difference in the responsiveness of the computer. For the most part, though, just leave these settings alone.

The Advanced tab, shown in Figure 19.28, has three sections: *Processor scheduling*, *Memory usage*, and *Virtual memory*. Under the *Processor scheduling* section, you can choose to adjust for best performance of either Programs or Background services. The *Memory usage* settings enable you to allocate a greater share of memory to programs or to the system cache. Finally, the *Virtual memory* section of this page enables you to modify the size and location of the page file.

Microsoft introduced *Data Execution Prevention (DEP)* with Windows XP Service Pack 2. DEP works in the background to stop viruses and other malware from taking over programs loaded in system memory. It doesn't prevent viruses

FIGURE 19.28 Advanced tab of Performance Options dialog box

from being installed on your computer, but it does make them less effective. By default, DEP monitors only critical OS files in RAM, but the Data Execution Prevention tab enables you to have DEP monitor all running programs. It works, but you'll take a performance hit. Like other options in the Performance Options dialog box, leaving the DEP settings as default is the best option most of the time.

Resource Tracking

One big issue with optimization is knowing when something needs optimization. Let's say your Windows computer seems to be running more slowly. Resource tracking is important for identifying the performance problem. Task Manager and the Performance console are tools you can use to figure out what (if anything) has become a bottleneck.

Task Manager

The *Task Manager* has many uses. Most users are aware of only the Applications tab, used to shut down a troublesome program. For optimization purposes, Task Manager is a great tool for investigating how hard your RAM and CPU are working at any given moment and why. The quick way to open the Task Manager is to press CTRL-SHIFT-ESC. Click the Performance tab to reveal a handy screen with the most commonly used information: CPU usage, available physical memory, the size of the disk cache, commit charge (memory for programs), and kernel memory (memory used by Windows). Figure 19.29 shows a system with a dual-core processor, which is why you see two screens under CPU Usage History. A system with a single-core processor would have a single screen.

Not only does Task Manager tell you how much CPU and RAM usage is occurring, but it also tells you what program is using those resources. Let's say your system is running slowly. You open Task Manager and see that your CPU usage is at 100 percent. You then click the Processes tab to see all the processes running on your system. Click the CPU column to sort all processes by CPU usage to see who's hogging the CPU (Figure 19.30). To shut off a process, just right-click the process and select End Process. Many times a single process will open many other processes. If you want to be thorough, click End Process Tree to turn off not only the one process, but also any other processes it started.

Local Lingo	
Processes Every program that runs on your system is composed of one or more processes.	

FIGURE 19.29 Task Manager

FIGURE 19.30 CPU Usage

Performance Console

Task Manager is good for identifying current problems, but what about problems that happen when you're not around? What if your system is always running at a CPU utilization of 20 percent—is that good or bad? Windows provides a tool called the *Performance console* that is used to log resource usage so that you can track items such as CPU and RAM usage over time. Performance is an MMC console file, PERFMON.MSC, so you call it from Start | Run or through the Performance icon in Administrative Tools. Use either method to open the Performance console (Figure 19.31). You can see two nodes in this figure: System Monitor and Performance Logs and Alerts.

Objects and Counters To begin working with the Performance console, you need to understand two terms: *object* and *counter*. An *object* is a system

Performance console

component that is given a set of characteristics and can be managed by the OS as a single entity. A *counter* tracks specific information about an object. For example, the Processor object has a counter, %Processor Time, which tracks the percentage of elapsed time the processor uses to execute a non-idle thread. Many counters can be associated with an object.

System Monitor *System Monitor* gathers real-time data on objects such as memory, physical disk, processor, and network and displays this data as a graph (line graph), histogram (bar graph), or a simple report. Think of System Monitor as a more detailed, customizable Task Manager. When you first open the Performance console, the System Monitor shows data in graph form. The data displayed is from the set of three counters listed below the chart. If you want to add counters, click the Add button (the one that looks like a plus sign) or press CTRL-I in Windows XP to open the Add Counters dialog box. Click the Performance object drop-down list and select one of the many different objects you can monitor. The Add Counters dialog box includes a helpful feature: you can select a counter and click the Explain button to learn about the counter, just like Figure 19.32. Try that now.

FIGURE 19.32 Add Counters dialog box

Even with just three counters selected, the graph can get a little busy. That's where one of my favorite System Monitor features shines. If you want the line of charted data from just one counter to stand out, select the counter in the list below the graph and then press CTRL-H. See how this trick makes the %Processor Time line stand out in Figure 19.33? Imagine how useful that would be when you are monitoring a dozen counters.

Performance Logs and Alerts The *Performance Logs and Alerts* snap-in enables Windows 2000/XP to create a written record of just about anything that happens on your system. Do you want to know if someone is trying to log into your system when you're not around? The following procedure is specific to Windows XP, but the steps are nearly identical in Windows 2000.

To create the new event log, right-click Counter Logs and select New Log Settings. Give the new log a name—in this example, "Unauthorized Accesses." Click OK, and a properties box for the new log will open, similar to that shown in Figure 19.34.

To select counters for the log, click Add Counters and then select the *Use local computer counters* radio button. Select Server from the Performance object pull-down menu, and then select Errors Logon from the list of counters; click Add and then Close.

FIGURE 19.33 Pressing CTRL-H makes one set of data stand out

Creating a new performance log

Back in the properties box for your new log, click the Schedule tab and set up when you want this thing to start running—probably at the end of the workday today. Then select when it should stop logging—probably tomorrow morning when you start work. Click the Log Files tab to see where the log file will be saved—probably C:\PerfLogs—and make a note of the filename. The filename will consist of the name you gave the log and a number. In this example I named the new performance log "Unauthorized Accesses," so the filename is *Unauthorized Accesses_000001.blg*.

When you come back in the morning, open the Performance console, select Performance Logs and Alerts, and then select Counter Logs. Your log should be listed on the right. The icon by the log name will be green if the log is still running or red if it has stopped. If it has not stopped, select it and click the stop button (the one with the black square). See Figure 19.35.

To view the log, open the Performance console, select System Monitor, change to Report view, and load the file as a new source using the properties box.

FIGURE 19.35 Stopping the performance log

Preparing for Problems

The secret to troubleshooting Windows is preparation. You must have critical system files and data backed up and tools in place for the inevitable glitches. The various versions of Windows offer five different tools for the job, although none offer them all: System Restore, the Backup or Restore Wizard (called NTBackup if you want to run it from the command prompt), the Emergency Repair Disk (ERD), Automated System Recovery (ASR), and the Recovery Console. Table 19.1 shows which OS gets which tool.

System Restore

Every technician has war stories about the user who likes to add the latest gadget and cool software to his or her computer. Then the user is amazed when things

TABLE 19.1 Backup and Recovery Tools in Windows

	System Restore	Backup or Restore Wizard	Automated System Recovery	Emergency Repair Disk	Recovery Console
Windows 2000 Professional	No	Yes, but called "Backup"	No	Yes	Yes
Windows XP Home[1]	Yes	No	No	No	No
Windows XP Professional[2]	Yes	Yes	Yes	No	Yes

[1] Also applies to Windows XP Media Center Edition
[2] Also applies to Windows XP Tablet PC Edition

go very, very wrong: the system locks up, refuses to boot, or simply acts "weird." This user also can't remember what he or she added or when. All the user knows is that you should be able to fix it—fast.

This is not news to the folks at Microsoft, and they have a solution to this problem. It's called *System Restore*, and they first introduced it in Windows Me, with further refinements in Windows XP. The System Restore tool enables you to create a *restore point*, a copy of your computer's configuration at a specific point in time. If you later crash or have a corrupted OS, you can restore the system to its previous state.

To create a restore point, go to Start | All Programs | Accessories | System Tools | System Restore. When the tool opens, select *Create a restore point* and then click Next (Figure 19.36). Type in a description on the next screen. There's no need to include the date and time because System Restore adds them automatically. Click Create and you're done.

The System Restore tool creates some of the restore points in time automatically. For instance, by default, every time you install new software, XP creates a restore point. Thus, if installation of a program causes your computer to malfunction, simply restore the system to a time point prior to that installation, and the computer should work again.

During the restore process, only settings and programs are changed. No data is lost. Your computer will include all programs and settings as of the restore

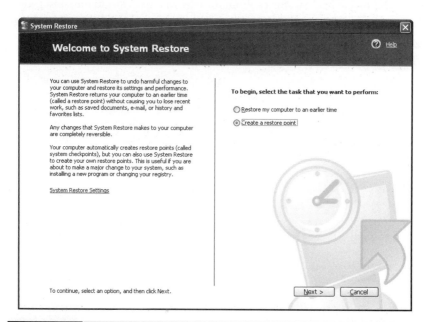

FIGURE 19.36 Create a restore point

date. This feature is absolutely invaluable for overworked techs. A simple restore will fix many user-generated problems.

To restore to a previous time point, start the System Restore Wizard by choosing Start | All Programs | Accessories | System Tools | System Restore. Then select the first radio button, *Restore my computer to an earlier time*, and click Next. Figure 19.37 shows a calendar with restore points. Any day with a boldface date has at least one restore point. These points are created after you add or remove software or install Windows updates and during normal shutdown of your computer. Select a date on the calendar; then select a restore point from the list on the right and click Next.

The last screen before the system is restored shows a warning. It advises you to close all open programs and reminds you that Windows will shut down during the restore process. It also states that the restore operation is completely reversible. Thus, if you go too far back in time, you can restore to a more recent date.

You don't have to count on the automatic creation of restore points. You can open System Restore at any time and simply select *Create a restore point*. Consider doing this before making changes that might not trigger an automatic restore point, such as directly editing the Registry.

System Restore is turned on by default and uses some of your hard disk space to save information on restore points. To turn off System Restore or change the disk space usage, open the System Properties applet in Control Panel and select the System Restore tab (Figure 19.38).

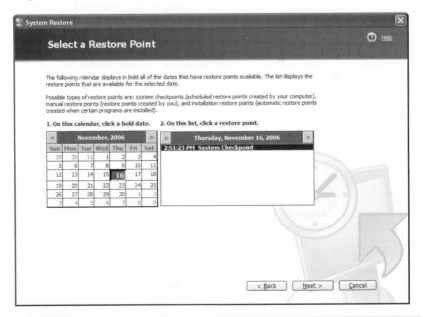

FIGURE 19.37 Calendar of restore points

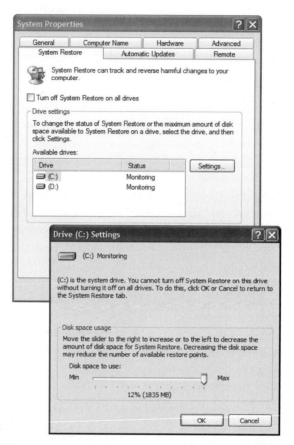

FIGURE 19.38 System Restore tab in System Properties applet

Backup Utility (NTBackup)

Windows 2000 Backup and Windows XP Backup utility provide almost all the tools you need to back up files and folders. It has come a long way from its origins in Windows NT. It supports a greater variety of devices, enabling you to back up to network drives, logical drives, tape, and removable disks (but not optical discs). Most folks, however, still turn to third-party utilities to create system, e-mail, browser, and personal data backups.

Travel Advisory

The Backup utility is not included in the default installation of Windows XP Home. You must install it manually from the Windows CD-ROM.

You can start Backup by choosing Start | All Programs | Accessories | System Tools, or by clicking the Backup Now button on the Tools page of the local disk properties box. I prefer to start it from Start | Run by typing the command **NTBACKUP**. Click the Backup Wizard button to run the Backup Wizard. This technique works in both Windows 2000 and Windows XP. To use the Windows XP version in Advanced Mode (Figure 19.39), click Advanced Mode on the opening screen. To have it always open in Advanced Mode, uncheck the *Always start in wizard mode* check box. If the program is in Advanced Mode and you want to run it as a wizard, click the Wizard Mode link to open the Backup or Restore Wizard.

To create a backup, start the Backup utility, click Advanced Mode, and choose the Backup tab. Check the boxes next to the drives and files you want to include in the backup. To include your system state information, such as Registry and boot files (which you should do), click the System State check box. To specify where to put the backup file you're creating, either type the path and file name in the *Backup media or file name* box or click Browse, select a location, type the file name, and click Save. Click Start Backup. Choose whether you want to append this backup to a previous one or overwrite it. Click Advanced to open the Advanced Backup Options dialog box, select *Verify data after backup*, and click OK. Click Start Backup again. A dialog box will show you the utility's progress. When it's done, click Close and then close the Backup utility.

Both versions of Backup give you three choices after you click Advanced Mode: Backup Wizard (Advanced), Restore Wizard (Advanced), and a third choice that is very important. The third option in Windows 2000 is the Emergency Repair Disk. As you can see in Figure 19.40, the third option in Windows XP is the Automated System Recovery Wizard.

Windows 2000 Emergency Repair Disk (ERD) Let's first consider the Windows 2000 *Emergency Repair Disk (ERD)*. This disk saves critical boot files and partition information and is your main tool for fixing boot problems in Windows 2000. It is not a bootable disk, nor does it store much information; the ERD does not replace a good system backup! It works with a special folder called *\WINNT\REPAIR* to store a copy of your Registry. It's not perfect, but it gets you out of most startup problems. It's good practice to make a new ERD before you install a new device or program. Then the ERD is ready if you need it.

So, you have this great ERD that will take care of all of your system repair problems—you just pop it in the floppy drive and go, right? Not just yet. As I mentioned, the ERD itself is not a bootable disk. To use the ERD, you must first boot the system using the Windows installation CD-ROM. Follow these steps to repair a system using the ERD:

1. Boot the system using either your set of boot diskettes or installation CD-ROM.

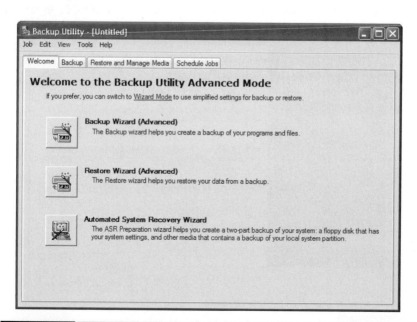

FIGURE 19.40 Windows XP Backup utility options

2. In the Welcome to Setup dialog box, press the R key to select the option to repair a Windows 2000 installation.

3. The Windows 2000 Repair Options menu appears. You have the option of either entering the Recovery Console or using the ERD.

4. Press the R key to select the option to repair Windows 2000 using the emergency repair process.

5. The next screen offers the choice of Manual or Fast repair:

 • Manual repair lets you select the following repair options: inspect the startup environment, verify the system files, and inspect the boot sector.

 • Fast repair doesn't ask for any further input.

6. Follow the on-screen instructions and insert the ERD when prompted.

7. Your system will be inspected and, if possible, restored. When finished, the system will restart.

Windows XP Automated System Recovery (ASR) The Windows XP *Automated System Recovery (ASR)* looks and acts similar to the Windows 2000 ERD. The ASR Wizard lets you create a backup of your system. This backup includes a floppy disk and backup media (tape or CD-R) containing the system partition and disks containing OS components (Figure 19.41).

The restore side of ASR involves a complete reinstall of the OS, preferably on a new partition. This is something you do when all is lost. Run Setup and

FIGURE 19.41 Creating an ASR backup

press F2 when prompted during the text-mode portion of Setup. Follow the prompts on the screen, which will first ask for the floppy disk and then for the backup media.

Backup Wizard Data files are not backed up by the ERD or by the ASR. Therefore, you have to back up data files. If you run the Backup Wizard and click the Next button on Welcome screen, you'll open the dialog box shown in Figure 19.42. You have three options here. The first two are fairly self-explanatory: You can back up everything or just selected drives and files.

The third option needs some explanation. The *Only back up the System State data* radio button enables you to save "other" system-critical files, but with Windows 2000/XP, it's not much more than making an ERD with the Registry backup. This option really makes sense for Windows 2000 Server and Windows Server 2003 systems because it saves Active Directory information (which your Windows 2000/XP systems do not store) as well as other critical, server-specific functions. But the CompTIA A+ certification exams may still expect you to know about it!

Tape Backup The odd fact that Microsoft has not updated the Backup or Restore Wizard to enable you to back up to optical media of any sort has kept alive the practice of tape backups. Tape drives connect to the ATA or SCSI bus, just like optical drives, but rather than using a shiny CD-R or DVD+R disc, you have to back up to magnetic tape (Figure 19.43).

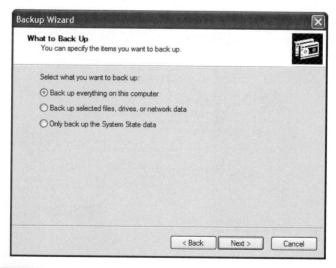

FIGURE 19.42 Backup Wizard options

FIGURE 19.43 Backup tapes

Tape drive manufacturers have done pretty much everything they can do to make tape backups as fast as possible, but the technology suffers from two huge drawbacks. First, it's tape, which means all data must be stored and restored in sequential access. The drive has to go through Files 1 and 2 before reaching File 3, in other words. Second, tape is painfully slow in comparison to hard drives, optical drives, or flash media drives.

The only great benefit to tape is that it's relatively cheap to buy multiple tapes with a lot of storage capacity. With hard drive and recordable DVD prices at rock bottom today, though, tape's days are numbered.

Installing Recovery Console

When things get really bad on a Windows system, you need to turn to the Recovery Console. The *Recovery Console* is a text-based startup of Windows that gets you to a command prompt similar to the Windows command prompt.

If you have the Windows 2000/XP CD-ROM, you can start the Recovery Console by running Setup, choosing Repair, and then choosing Recovery Console. If you like to be proactive, however, you can install the Recovery Console on your hard drive so that it is one of your startup options and does not require the Windows 2000 or XP CD-ROM to run. The steps to do this in Windows 2000 and Windows XP are nearly identical.

First, you need to log into the system with the Administrator account. Grab your Windows 2000 or XP installation CD-ROM and drop it in your system. If the Autorun function kicks in, just click the No button. To install the Recovery Console and make it a part of your startup options, click the Start button, select Run, and type the following:

```
d:\i386\winnt32 /cmdcons
```

If your CD-ROM drive uses a different drive letter, substitute it for the D: drive. Then just follow the instructions on the screen. If you are connected to the Internet, allow the Setup program to download updated files. From now on, every time the system boots, the OS selection menu will show your Windows OS (Windows 2000 Professional or Windows XP) and the Microsoft Windows Recovery Console. It may also show other choices if yours is a multi-boot computer.

Objective 19.03 Troubleshooting Windows

You know about Disk Management, Device Manager, Event Viewer, and more. You've spent countless hours preparing systems for disaster with NTBackup and System Restore. While learning about the tools, you also learned how to use them. This section puts it all together and shows you a plan to deal with potential disasters for a Windows computer.

This section looks at Windows problems from the ground up. It starts with catastrophic failure—a PC that won't boot—and then discusses ways to get past that problem. The next section covers the causes and workarounds when the Windows GUI fails to load. Once you can access the GUI, the world of Windows diagnostic and troubleshooting tools that you've spent so much time learning about comes to your fingertips. First, though, you have to get there.

Failure to Boot

Windows boot errors take place in those short moments between the time the POST ends and the Loading Windows screen begins. For Windows to start loading the main OS, the critical system files NTLDR, NTDETECT.COM, and BOOT.INI must reside in the root directory of the C: drive, and BOOT.INI must point to the Windows boot files. If any of these requirements aren't in place, the system won't get past this step. Here are some of the common errors you see at this point:

- No Boot Device Present
- NTLDR Bad or Missing
- Invalid BOOT.INI

Note that these text errors take place early in the startup process. That's your big clue that you have a boot issue. If you get to the Windows splash screen and then lock up, that's a whole different game, so know the difference.

If you get one of the catastrophic error messages, you have a three-level process to get back up and running:

1. You first should attempt to repair.

2. If that fails, then attempt to restore from a backup copy of Windows.

3. If restore is either not available or fails, then your only recourse is to rebuild. You will lose data at the restore and rebuild phases, so you definitely want to spend a lot of effort on the repair effort first!

Attempt to Repair Using Recovery Console

To begin troubleshooting one of these errors, boot from the installation CD-ROM and have Windows do a repair of an existing installation. Windows will ask you if you want to use the Recovery Console or the emergency repair process (ASR/ERD). Start with the Recovery Console.

If you've been following along, you installed the Recovery Console onto your system and have it as an option when you boot the system. If not, start it as described earlier using the Windows 2000 or XP installation CD-ROM. When you select the Recovery Console, you will see a message about NTDETECT, another one that the Recovery Console is starting up, and then you will be greeted with the following message and command prompt:

```
Microsoft Windows XP<TM> Recovery Console.
The Recovery Console provides system repair and recovery functionality.
Type Exit to quit the Recovery Console and restart the computer.

1: C:\WINDOWS
Which Windows XP installation would you like to log onto
<To cancel, press ENTER>?
```

The cursor is a small, white rectangle sitting to the right of the question mark on the last line. If you are not accustomed to working at the command prompt, this may be disorienting. If only one installation of Windows XP is on your computer, type the number *1* at the prompt and press the ENTER key. If you press ENTER before typing in a valid selection, the Recovery Console will cancel and the computer will reboot. The only choice you can make in this example is 1. Having made that choice, the only change to the screen is a new line:

```
Type the Administrator password:
```

This is also followed by the cursor. Enter the Administrator password for that computer and press ENTER. The password will not display on the screen; you will see asterisks in place of the password. The screen still shows everything that

has happened so far, unless something has happened to cause an error message. It now looks like this:

```
Microsoft Windows XP<TM> Recovery Console.
The Recovery Console provides system repair and recovery functionality.
Type Exit to quit the Recovery Console and restart the computer.

1: C:\WINDOWS
Which Windows XP installation would you like to log onto
<To cancel, press ENTER>? 1
Type the Administrator password: ********
C:\Windows>
```

By now, you've caught on and know that a rectangular prompt is located immediately after the last line. Now what do you do? Use the Recovery Console commands, of course. The Recovery Console uses many of the commands that work in the Windows command line interface, as well as some uniquely its own. Table 19.2 lists the common Recovery Console commands.

The Recovery Console shines in the business of manually restoring registries, stopping problem services, rebuilding partitions (other than the system partition), and using the EXPAND program to extract copies of corrupted files from a CD-ROM or floppy disk.

Using the Recovery Console, you can reconfigure a service so that it starts with different settings, format drives on the hard disk, read and write on local FAT or NTFS volumes, and copy replacement files from a floppy or CD-ROM. The Recovery Console enables you to access the file system and is still constrained by the file and folder security of NTFS, which makes it a more secure tool to use than some third-party solutions.

The Recovery Console is best at fixing three items: repairing the MBR, reinstalling the boot files, and rebuilding BOOT.INI. Let's look at each of these.

A bad boot sector usually shows up as a No Boot Device error. If it turns out that this isn't the problem, the Recovery Console command to fix it won't hurt anything. At the Recovery Console prompt, type **fixmbr**. This fixes the MBR.

The second problem the Recovery Console is best at fixing is missing system files, usually indicated by the error NTLDR Bad or Missing. Odds are good that if NTLDR is missing, so are the rest of the system files. To fix this, get to the root directory and type the following line:

```
copy d:\i386\ntldr
```

Then type this line:

```
copy d:\i386\ntdetect.com
```

TABLE 19.2	Common Recovery Console Commands

Command	Description
attrib	Changes attributes of selected file or folder
cd (or chdir)	Displays current directory or changes directories
chkdsk	Runs CheckDisk utility
cls	Clears screen
copy	Copies from removable media to system folders on hard disk; no wildcards
del (or delete)	Deletes service or folder
dir	Lists contents of selected directory on system partition only
disable	Disables service or driver
diskpart	Replaces FDISK—creates/deletes partitions
enable	Enables service or driver
extract	Extracts components from CAB files
fixboot	Writes new partition boot sector on system partition
fixmbr	Writes new master boot record for partition boot sector
format	Formats selected disk
listsvc	Lists all services on system
logon	Lets you choose which Windows installation to log into if more than one
map	Displays current drive letter mappings
md (or mkdir)	Creates a directory
more (or type)	Displays contents of text file
rd (or rmdir)	Removes a directory
ren (or rename)	Renames a single file
systemroot	Makes current directory system root of drive into which you're logged
type	Displays a text file

This takes care of two of the big three and leads us to the last issue, rebuilding BOOT.INI. If the BOOT.INI file is gone or corrupted, run this command from the Recovery Console:

```
bootcfg /rebuild
```

The Recovery Console will then try to locate all installed copies of Windows and ask you if you want to add them to the new BOOT.INI file it's about to create. Say yes to the ones you want.

If all goes well with the Recovery Console, do a thorough backup as soon as possible (just in case something else goes wrong). If the Recovery Console does not do the trick, the next step is to restore Windows XP.

Attempt to Restore

If you've been diligent about backing up, you can attempt to restore to an earlier, working copy of Windows. You have two basic choices depending on your OS. In Windows 2000, you can try the ERD. Windows XP limits you to the ASR.

Local Lingo
Restore To use the Windows XP System Restore, you need to be able to get into Windows. *Restore* in the context used here means to give you an option to get into Windows.

If you elected to create an ERD in Windows 2000, you can attempt to restore your system with it. Boot your system to the Windows 2000 installation CD-ROM and select Repair Installation, but in this case opt for the ERD. Follow the steps outlined earlier in the chapter and you might have some success.

ASR can restore your system to a previously installed state, but you should use it only as a last resort. You lose everything on the system that was installed or added after you created the ASR disk. If that's the best option, though, follow the steps outlined earlier in the chapter.

Rebuild

If faced with a full system rebuild, you have several options depending on the particular system. You could simply reboot to the Windows CD-ROM and install right on top of the existing system, but that's usually not the optimal solution. To avoid losing anything important, you'd be better off swapping the C: drive for a blank hard drive and installing a clean version of Windows.

Most OEM systems come with a misleadingly named *Recover CD* or *recovery partition*. The Recover CD is a CD-ROM that you boot to and run. The recovery partition is a hidden partition on the hard drive that you activate at boot by holding down a key combination specific to the manufacturer of that system. (See the motherboard manual or users' guide for the key combination and other details.) Both "recover" options do the same thing—restore your computer to the factory-installed state. If you run one of these tools, you will wipe everything off your system—all personal files, folders, and programs will go away! Before running either tool, make sure all important files and folders are backed up on an optical disc or spare hard drive.

Failure to Load the GUI

Assuming that Windows gets past the boot part of the startup, it will then begin to load the real Windows OS. You will see the Windows startup image on the screen (Figure 19.44), hiding everything until Windows loads the desktop.

Several issues can cause Windows to hang during the GUI-loading phase, such as buggy device drivers or Registry problems. Even autoloading programs can cause the GUI to hang on load. The first step in troubleshooting these issues is to use one of the Advanced Startup options (covered later in the chapter) to try to get past the hang spot and into Windows.

Device Drivers

Device driver problems that stop Windows GUI from loading look pretty scary. Figure 19.45 shows the infamous Windows *Stop error,* better known as the *Blue Screen of Death (BSoD).* The BSoD appears only when something causes an error from which Windows cannot recover. The BSoD is not limited to device driver problems, but bad device drivers can cause you to see the BSoD.

Whenever you get a BSoD, take a moment and read what it says. Windows BSoDs tell you the name of the file that caused the problem and usually suggest a recommended action. Once in a while these are helpful—but not often.

BSoD problems due to device drivers almost always take place immediately after you've installed a new device and rebooted. Take out the device and

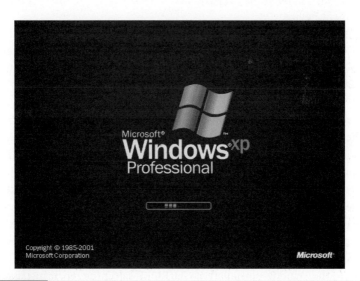

| **FIGURE 19.44** | GUI time |

```
A problem has been detected and windows has been shut down to prevent damage
to your computer.

NO_MORE_IRP_STACK_LOCATIONS

If this is the first time you've seen this stop error screen,
restart your computer. If this screen appears again, follow
these steps:

Check to make sure that any new hardware or software is properly installed.
If this is a new installation, ask your hardware or software manufacturer
for any windows updates you might need.

If problems continue, disable or remove any newly installed hardware
or software. Disable BIOS memory options such as caching or shadowing.
If you need to use Safe Mode to remove or disable components, restart
your computer, press F8 to select Advanced Startup Options, and then
select Safe Mode.

Technical information:

*** STOP: 0x00000035 (0x00000000,0xF7E562B2,0x00000008,0xC00000000)

***     wdmaud.sys - Address F7E562B2 base at F7E56000, DateStamp 36B047A5
```

FIGURE 19.45 The Blue Screen of Death (BSoD)

reboot. If Windows loads properly, head over to the manufacturer's Web site. A new device producing this type of problem is a serious issue that should have been caught before the device was released. In many cases, the manufacturer will have updated drivers available for download or will recommend a replacement device.

The second indication of a device problem that shows up during the GUI part of startup is a freeze-up: the Windows startup screen just stays there and you never get a chance to log on. If this happens, try one of the Advanced Startup Options, covered shortly.

Registry

Your Registry files load every time the computer boots. Windows does a pretty good job of protecting your Registry files from corruption, but from time to time something may slip by Windows and it will attempt to load a bad Registry. These errors may show up as BSoDs that say "Registry File Failure" or text errors that say "Windows could not start." Whatever the case, you need to restore a good Registry copy. The best way to do this is the Last Known Good Configuration boot option (see the upcoming section). If that fails, you can restore an earlier version of the Registry through the Recovery Console.

Boot to the Windows installation CD-ROM, select the repair installation to get to the Recovery Console, and type these commands to restore a Registry. (Notice I didn't say "your" Registry in the previous sentence. Your Registry is corrupted and gone, so you need to rebuild.)

```
delete c:\windows\system32\config\system
delete c:\windows\system32\config\software
delete c:\windows\system32\config\sam
delete c:\windows\system32\config\security
delete c:\windows\system32\config\default

copy c:\windows\repair\system c:\windows\system32\config\system
copy c:\windows\repair\software c:\windows\system32\config\software
copy c:\windows\repair\sam c:\windows\system32\config\sam
copy c:\windows\repair\security c:\windows\system32\config\security
copy c:\windows\repair\default c:\windows\system32\config\default
```

Advanced Startup Options

If Windows fails to start up, use the Windows *Advanced Startup Options* menu to discover the cause. To get to this menu, restart the computer and press F8 after the POST messages, but before the Windows logo screen appears. Windows 2000 and Windows XP have similar menus. Central to these advanced options are Safe Mode and Last Known Good Configuration.

There are several differences between the two OSs in this menu. First, the Windows 2000 option called Boot Normally is called Start Windows Normally in Windows XP. In addition, Windows XP has options not available in Windows 2000: *Disable automatic restart on system failure* and *Reboot*. A Windows system with multiple OSs might also have the *Return to OS Choices Menu*. Here's a rundown of the menu options.

Exam Tip
Windows 9*x* had an option for *Step-by-step confirmation*, but that is not a choice in Windows 2000/XP. Look for it as a wrong answer on the exams!

Safe Mode *Safe Mode* (Figure 19.46) starts up Windows but loads only very basic, non–vendor-specific drivers for mouse, VGA monitor, keyboard, mass storage, and system services. Some devices, such as your USB mouse, may not work in Safe Mode.

Once in Safe Mode, you can use tools such as Device Manager to locate and correct the source of the problem. When you use Device Manager in Safe Mode, you can access the properties for all the devices, even those that are not working in Safe Mode. The status displayed for the device is the status for a normal startup. Even the network card will show as enabled. You can disable any suspect device or perform other tasks, such as removing or updating drivers. If a problem with a device driver is preventing the OS from starting normally, check the Device Manager for yellow question mark warning icons that indicate an unknown device.

FIGURE 19.46 Safe Mode

Safe Mode with Networking This mode is identical to plain Safe Mode except that you get network support. I use this mode to test for a problem with network drivers. If Windows won't start up normally, but it does start up in Safe Mode, I then reboot into Safe Mode with Networking. If it fails to start up with Networking, then the problem is a network driver. I reboot back to Safe Mode, open Device Manager, and start disabling network components, beginning with the network adapter.

Safe Mode with Command Prompt When you start Windows in this mode, after you log on, rather than loading the GUI desktop, it loads the command prompt (CMD.EXE) as the shell to the OS, as shown in Figure 19.47. This is a handy option to remember if the desktop does not display at all, which, after you have eliminated video drivers, can be caused by the corruption of the EXPLORER.EXE program. From the command prompt you can delete the corrupted version of EXPLORER.EXE and copy in an undamaged version. This requires knowing the command line commands for navigating the directory structure, as well as knowing the location of the file that you are replacing. Although Explorer is not loaded, you can load other GUI tools that don't depend on Explorer. All you have to do is enter the correct command. For instance, to load Event Viewer, type **eventvwr.msc** at the command line and press ENTER. (See the "Event Viewer" section a bit later for more details.)

FIGURE 19.47 Safe Mode with command prompt

Enable Boot Logging This option starts Windows normally and creates a log file of the drivers as they load into memory. The file is named *Ntbtlog.txt* and is saved in the *%SystemRoot%* folder. If the startup failed because of a bad driver, the last entry in this file may be the driver the OS was initializing when it failed.

Reboot and go into the Recovery Console. Use the Recovery Console tools to read the boot log (type **ntbtlog.txt**) and disable or enable problematic devices or services.

Enable VGA Mode Enable VGA Mode starts Windows normally but loads only a default VGA driver. If this mode works, it may mean that you have a bad driver, or it may mean that you are using the correct video driver, but it is configured incorrectly (perhaps with the wrong refresh rate and/or resolution). Whereas Safe Mode loads a generic VGA driver, this mode loads the driver Windows is configured to use, but starts it up in standard VGA mode rather than using the settings for which it is configured. After successfully starting in this mode, open the Display Properties and change the settings.

Last Known Good Configuration When Windows' startup fails immediately after installing a new driver, but before you have logged on again, you may want to try the *Last Known Good Configuration* option. This can be a rather fickle and limited tool, but it never hurts to try it.

Directory Services Restore Mode (Does Not Apply to Professional) The title says it all here—this option only applies to Active Directory domain controllers, and Windows 2000 Professional and Windows XP can never be domain controllers. I have no idea why Microsoft includes this option. If you choose it, you simply boot into Safe Mode.

Debugging Mode If you select this choice, Windows 2000/XP starts in kernel debug mode. It's a super-techie thing to do, and I doubt that even über-techs do debug mode anymore. To do this, you have to connect the computer you are debugging to another computer via a serial connection, and as Windows starts up, a debug of the kernel is sent to the second computer, which must also be running a debugger program.

Disable Automatic Restart on System Failure Sometimes a BSoD will appear at startup, causing your computer to reboot spontaneously. That's all well and good, but if it happens too quickly, you might not be able to read the BSoD to see what caused the problem. Selecting *Disable automatic restart on system failure* from the Advanced Startup Options menu stops the computer from rebooting on Stop errors. This gives you the opportunity to write down the error and hopefully find a fix.

Start Windows Normally This choice will simply start Windows normally, without rebooting. You already rebooted to get to this menu. Select this if you changed your mind about using any of the other exotic choices.

Reboot This choice will actually do a soft reboot of the computer.

Return to OS Choices Menu On computers with multiple OSs, you get an OS Choices menu to select which OS to load. If you load Windows XP and press F8 to get the Advanced Startup Options menu, you'll see this option. This choice will return you to the OS Choices menu, from which you can select the OS to load.

Troubleshooting Tools in the GUI

Once you're able to load Windows, whether through Safe Mode or one of the other options, the whole gamut of Windows tools are available for you. If a bad device driver caused the startup problems, for example, you can open Device Manager and begin troubleshooting, just as you've learned in previous chapters. If you suspect some service or Registry issue caused the problem, head on over to Event Viewer and see what sort of logon events have happened recently.

Event Viewer

Event Viewer enables you to examine logs kept by Windows about important events, such as application failures and OS errors. If you've just had to recover from a catastrophic error, fire up Event Viewer as soon as you can access the GUI.

You can start Event Viewer from Administrative Tools. In Windows 2000, open the Control Panel, double-click the Administrative Tools icon, and double-click the Event Viewer icon. In Windows XP, open the Control Panel, double-click the Performance and Maintenance icon, then Administrative Tools, and then Event Viewer. The Event Viewer will display events from three or four log files, Application, Security, System, and Internet Explorer (with Internet Explorer 7 or later installed). Figure 19.48 shows the contents of a System event log in Event Viewer.

Types of Events Event Viewer displays five types of events. The System and Applications logs have Error, Warning, and Information events, while the Security log displays Success Audit and Failure Audit events. Figure 19.49 shows an Application log with two types of events displayed.

FIGURE 19.48 System event log in Event Viewer

FIGURE 19.49 Application log showing two types of events

An Error event is bad news—something's broken or data has been lost. In the Application log, this can mean an entire application hung up or an operation failed. In the System log, this can mean that a service failed. A *service* is a special program that provides specific functionality to the OS. A warning is something that isn't critical but may mean there is trouble to come. For instance, if disk space is low, a Warning event is logged. An Information event is the only good news, because it means an application, driver, or service successfully completed an operation.

Travel Advisory

Real techs don't waste time slogging through the menus for tools they use frequently. A quicker way is to start up the console by typing its name in the Run dialog box. For example, start Event Viewer by selecting Start | Run and typing the filename of the console: **eventvwr** (the .msc extension isn't necessary).

Event Viewer Settings In Event Viewer, right-click System and select Properties. In Properties, look at the Log Size box, which defines the maximum size to which a log file may grow, and what action should be taken when the log file

reaches the maximum. The defaults are *512KB* and *Overwrite Events Older Than 7 Days.* You can easily reconfigure these settings, but be aware that large log files take up a lot of space on the hard disk drive.

If scrolling through large log files makes you dizzy, you can use Filter settings to make the viewer show only specific selections. In Windows XP, simply select the Filter tab to see Figure 19.50.

Change the filter settings so that when you are viewing a large log file, you can filter out events by type, source, category, ID, user, computer, and date. Keep in mind that this controls only what Event Viewer displays; all events will still be logged to the file, so you can change your filter settings without worrying about losing logged data.

Clearing, Archiving, and Opening a Log File Clear the System log by right-clicking System Log and selecting Clear All Events. You'll be prompted to save the System log. To do so, click the Yes button. You can archive a log file that you want to be able to view later by saving it with a unique filename. To open the file you just saved, click the Action menu, select Open Log File, select the file, then the log type (System, Application, or Security), and then click Open.

FIGURE 19.50 Event Viewer Filter settings

Event Viewer might reveal problems with applications failing to load, a big cause of Windows loading problems. It might also reveal problems with services failing to start. Finally, Windows might run into problems loading DLLs. You can troubleshoot these issues individually or you can use System Restore in Windows XP to load a restore point that predates the bugginess.

Autoloading Programs

Windows loves to autoload programs so they start at boot. Most of the time this is an incredibly handy option, used by every Windows PC in existence. The problem with Autoloading programs is when one of them starts behaving badly—you need to shut off that program!

At least five different locations in folders, files, and the Registry are accessed by Windows to autoload programs. To help you, Windows XP includes the handy *System Configuration Utility (MSCONFIG.EXE)*, a one-stop spot to see and maintain every program (and service) that autoloads at startup (Figure 19.51).

Exam Tip
Know that Windows 2000 Professional does *not* have the System Configuration Utility.

The System Configuration Utility enables you to keep individual programs and services from autoloading, but it does not actually remove the programs/ services. If you want to delete a program completely, you'll need to find the uninstall or Add/Remove Program option. If the program doesn't have either of these, you'll need a third-party tool like EasyCleaner to delete the program.

FIGURE 19.51 System Configuration Utility

Services

Windows loads a number of services as it starts. If any critical service fails to load, Windows will tell you at this point with an error message. The important word here is *critical*. Windows will not report *all* service failures at this point. If a service that is less than critical in Windows' eyes doesn't start, Windows usually waits until you actually try to use a program that needs that service before it prompts you with an error message (Figure 19.52).

To work with your system's services, go to the Control Panel | Administrative Tools | Services and verify that the service you need is running. If not, turn it on. Also notice that each service has a Startup Type—Automatic, Manual, or Disabled—that defines when it starts. It's common to find that a service has been set to Manual when it needs to be set to Automatic so that it starts when Windows boots (Figure 19.53).

System Files

Windows lives on dynamic link library (DLL) files. Almost every program used by Windows—and certainly all of the important ones—call to DLL files to do most of the heavy lifting that makes Windows work. Windows protects all of the critical DLL files carefully, but once in a while you may get an error saying Windows can't load a particular DLL.

Although rare, the core system files that make up Windows itself may become corrupted, preventing Windows from starting properly. You usually see something like "Error loading XXXX.DLL," or sometimes a program you need simply won't start when you double-click its icon. In these cases, the tool you need is the System File Checker.

The System File Checker is a command prompt program (SFC.EXE) that is used to check a number of critical files, including the ever-important DLL cache. SFC takes a number of switches, but by far the most important is /scannow. Go to a command prompt and type **sfc /scannow** to start the program. SFC will automatically check all critical files and replace any it sees as corrupted. During this process, it may ask for the Windows installation CD-ROM, so keep it handy.

FIGURE 19.52 Service error

FIGURE 19.53 Autostarting a service

System Restore

Windows XP systems enable you to recover from a bad device or application installation by using System Restore to load a restore point. Follow the process explained earlier in the chapter. System Restore is the final step in recovering from a major Windows meltdown.

CHECKPOINT

✔ **Objective 19.01: Maintaining Windows** It is important that you keep Windows updated with the latest security patches from Microsoft. Automatic Updates of Windows are configurable in Windows XP through the My Computer Properties window's Automatic Updates tab or the Automatic Updates Control Panel applet. Each Windows computer user must log on with a valid user name and password. User accounts enable a system administrator to set permissions for the user and to audit their access to files and network resources. Keep the hard drive running properly by regularly running Error-checking, Disk Defragmenter, and Disk Cleanup.

✔**Objective 19.02: Optimizing Windows** Removing applications that are no longer needed is an important piece of housekeeping. When possible, use the uninstall program that came with the application. You can add or remove Windows components as needed. From the Add or Remove Program applet, simply select Add/Remove Windows Components. Installing the proper driver for a hardware device is essential. You can find the driver on the discs that come with the device, at Microsoft's Web site, or at the Web site of the device manufacturer. To protect Windows systems from bad device drivers, Microsoft uses *driver signing*. The Device Manager is one of the most important tools for checking hardware, drivers, and resources. Resource tracking can help solve performance problems. The Task Manager and Performance tools help identify bottlenecks. Finally, preparation is the key to troubleshooting Windows 2000 and XP. Five different tools prepare for possible problems: System Restore, the Backup Utility, Emergency Repair Disk, Automated System Recovery, and Recovery Console.

✔**Objective 19.03: Troubleshooting Windows** The Recovery Console is excellent for restoring registries, stopping problem services, or using EXPAND to extract copies of files from the CD-ROM. You can restore the Registry by choosing the Last Known Good Configuration boot option or use the ASR to point to a restore point you made. If Windows will not start, use the Advanced Startup Options menu. Safe Mode starts with only basic, non–vendor-specific drivers. You can then use the Device Manager to locate the source of the problem. The System Configuration Utility is useful in managing programs and services that are set to run at startup. You can disable items you suspect are troublesome, reboot, and see if the problem has gone away.

REVIEW QUESTIONS

1. Your Windows XP Professional system fails to boot up. You suspect that the boot sector has become corrupted. You start the system using the set of boot disks and then launch the Recovery Console. Which command should you use to write a new boot sector into the system partition?

 A. chkdsk

 B. fdisk

 C. fixmbr

 D. fixboot

2. Which of the following commands would you use to install the Recovery Console?

 A. Start | Run; then type **d:\i386\winnt32 /cmdcons**

 B. Start | Run; then type **d:\i386\winnt32 /rc**

 C. Start | Run; then type **d:\i386\winnt32 /cmd:command_line**

 D. Start | Run; then type **d:\i386\winnt32 /copydir:recovery_console**

3. Which tool in Windows XP Home would you use to back up your essential system files?

 A. System Restore

 B. Backup and Recovery Wizard

 C. Emergency Repair Disk

 D. Recovery Console

4. Phil tried to install a printer on his Windows XP Professional machine but found he didn't have permission. What could be the problem? (Select two.)

 A. Phil is logged on with a Limited account.

 B. Phil is logged on as a Local User.

 C. Phil is logged on as a Local Administrator.

 D. Phil is logged on as Guest.

5. Mary wants to get a quick snapshot of her System Resources on a Windows XP Home machine. How does she get to the appropriate tool?

 A. Start | Run | Perfmon

 B. Start | Control Panel | Administrative Tools | Performance

 C. Start | All Programs | Accessories | System Resources

 D. Press CTRL-ALT-DEL once and click the Performance tab

6. What tool should Bill use to track who logs on and off of the busy library terminal for which he is responsible?

 A. Event Viewer

 B. Performance console

 C. System Resource Meter

 D. Task Manager

7. Sven loaded a new video card on his system, but now everything looks very bad. What should he do first?

 A. Go to Event Viewer and check the log.

 B. Go to Device Manager.

 C. Go to the printed manual.

 D. Call tech support.

8. Which of the following is a command line utility?

 A. Event Viewer

 B. Microsoft Management Console

 C. Task Manager

 D. Recovery Console

9. Which of the following passwords will probably be the most secure one?

 A. MaryEllen

 B. MEO2144

 C. M-21e44

 D. MikeM

10. What's another name for a Windows Stop error?

 A. ASR

 B. BSoD

 C. ERD

 D. Virus

REVIEW ANSWERS

1. **D** The Recovery Console command **fixboot** writes a new partition boot sector to the system partition. The Recovery Console command **chkdsk** runs the CheckDisk utility; **fdisk** is not a valid command for the Recovery Console; and **fixmbr** writes a new master boot record for the partition boot sector.

2. **A** Start | Run; then type **d:\i386\winnt32 /cmdcons** is the correct command to install the Recovery Console.

3. **A** System Restore is the only tool in Windows XP Home for backing up essential system files.

4. **A** **D** Phil needs to be logged on as an Administrator, not a Limited account or Guest.

5. **D** Mary should press CTRL-ALT-DEL once and click the Performance tab.

6. **A** Event Viewer is the tool Bill needs.

7. **B** Always go to Device Manager first when hardware goes awry.

8. **D** The Recovery Console is a command line utility.

9. **C** The combination of letters, numbers, and non-alphanumeric characters makes M-21e44 the strongest password.

10. **B** A Windows Stop error is better known as a Blue Screen of Death (BSoD).

Computer
Security

	NEWBIE	SOME EXPERIENCE	EXPERT
ETA	4 hours	3 hours	1.5 hours

Your PC is under siege. Through your PC, a malicious person can gain valuable information about you and your habits. He can steal your files. He can run programs that log your keystrokes and thus gain account names and passwords, credit card information, and more. He can run software that takes over much of your computer processing time and use it to send spam or steal from others. The threat is real and right now. Worse, he's doing one or more of these things to your clients as I write these words. You need to secure your computer and your users from these attacks.

This chapter begins by analyzing the threat to your computers; it then looks at methods for securing both local and networked systems.

 Analyzing Security Threats

Threats to your data and PC come from two directions: accidents and malicious people. All sorts of things can go wrong with your computer, from a user getting access to a folder he or she shouldn't see to a virus striking and deleting folders. Files can get deleted, renamed, or simply lost. Hard drives can die, and optical discs get scratched and rendered unreadable. Accidents happen and even well-meaning people can make mistakes.

Unfortunately, a lot of people out there intend to do you harm. That intent, along with a talent for computer programming, is a deadly combination. Let's look at the following issues:

- Unauthorized access
- Data destruction—accidental or deliberate
- Administrative access
- Catastrophic hardware failures
- Viruses/spyware

Unauthorized Access

Unauthorized access occurs when a user accesses resources in an unauthorized way. Resources in this case refer to data, applications, and hardware. A user can alter or delete data; access sensitive information, such as financial data, personnel files, or e-mail messages; or use a computer for purposes for which the owner did not intend.

Not all unauthorized access is malicious—often a problem arises when users who are randomly poking around in a computer discover that they can

access resources that they should not be accessing. Unauthorized access can sometimes be very malicious when outsiders knowingly and intentionally take advantage of weaknesses in security to gain information, use resources, or destroy data.

Data Destruction

Often an extension of unauthorized access, *data destruction* means more than just intentionally or accidentally erasing or corrupting data. It's easy to imagine some evil hacker accessing your network and deleting all your important files, but consider the case in which authorized users access certain data, but what they do to that data goes beyond what they are authorized to do. A good example is the person who legitimately accesses a Microsoft Access product database to modify product descriptions, only to discover he or she can change the prices of the products, too.

This type of threat is particularly dangerous when users are not clearly informed about the extent to which they are authorized to make changes. A fellow tech once told me about a user who managed to mangle an important database due to someone giving him incorrect access. When confronted, the user said, "If I wasn't allowed to change it, the system wouldn't let me do it!" Many users believe that systems are configured in a paternalistic way that wouldn't allow them to do anything inappropriate. As a result, users will often assume they're authorized to make any changes they believe are necessary when working on a piece of data they know they're authorized to access.

Administrative Access

Every operating system (OS) enables you to create user accounts and grant those accounts a certain level of access to files and folders in that computer. As an administrator, supervisor, or root user, you have full control over just about every aspect of the computer. Windows XP, in particular, makes it entirely too easy to give users administrative access to the computer; Windows XP Home is especially susceptible, because it allows only two kinds of users: administrators and limited users. Because you can't do much as a limited user, most home and small office systems use multiple administrator accounts. If you need to control access, you need to use Windows 2000 or XP Professional.

System Crash/Hardware Failure

Like any technology, computers can and will fail—usually when you can least afford for it to happen. Hard drives crash, the power fails—it's all part of the joy of working in the computing business. You need to create redundancy in areas

prone to failure (such as installing backup power in case of electrical failure) and perform those all-important data backups. Chapter 19, "Maintaining, Optimizing, and Troubleshooting Windows," goes into detail about using Microsoft Backup and other issues involved in creating a stable and reliable system.

Virus/Spyware

Networks are without a doubt the fastest and most efficient vehicles for transferring computer viruses among systems. News reports focus attention on the many virus attacks from the Internet, but a huge number of viruses still come from users who bring in programs on floppy disks, writeable optical discs, and USB drives. The "Protecting Networked Computers" section of this chapter describes the various methods of virus infection and what you need to do to prevent infection of your networked systems.

 # Protecting Local Computers

To create a secure computing environment, you need to establish control over local resources. You need to back up data and make sure that retired hard drives and optical discs have no sensitive data stored on them. You should recognize security issues and be able to respond properly. You need to implement good access control policies, such as having all computers in your care locked down with proper passwords or other devices that recognize who should have access. Finally, and this is particularly important for the CompTIA A+ 602 exam (IT Technician), you need to be able to implement methods for tracking computer usage. If someone is doing something wrong, you and the network or computer administrator should be able to catch him or her.

What to Back Up

Systems in your care should have regular backups performed of essential OS files and, most importantly, data files. Chapter 19 covered the process of backing up data, such as running the Backup or Restore Wizard in Windows 2000 and Windows XP, so the mechanics aren't covered in this chapter. Instead, it looks more critically at what files to back up and how to protect those files.

Essential Data

By default, the Backup or Restore Wizard in Windows XP (Figure 20.1) offers to back up your Documents and Settings folder. You also have options of backing up everyone's documents and settings. That takes care of most, but not all, of your critical data. You have other issues to consider.

First, if you use Microsoft Outlook for your e-mail, the saved e-mail messages—both received and sent—will not be backed up. Neither will your Address Book. If you care about these things—if, for example, you share a computer with multiple users who use these features—you need to make certain that you or the users back up both their e-mail and Address Book manually and then put the backup files in the Documents and Settings folder. That way, the Backup or Restore Wizard will grab those files during the backup process.

Second, if you or others on the computer use any folders outside the Documents and Settings environment, you need to select the *Let me choose what to back up* option from the Backup or Restore Wizard when prompted. This opens the Items to Back Up dialog, where you can select individual files and folders for backup (Figure 20.2).

Server Environments

If you work in an environment that requires you to back up Windows 2000 Server or Windows Server 2003 computers, you need to back up some extra

FIGURE 20.1 Backup or Restore Wizard

FIGURE 20.2 Selecting items to back up

data. This is especially true if you are running a Windows network. Windows networking features *Active Directory*, a system that enables you to share files easily within the network, yet still maintain rock-solid security. A user has to log in only once to an Active Directory server to have access to resources throughout the Active Directory network (assuming, of course, that the user has permission to access those resources).

To back up the extra data, you need to run the Backup Wizard and select the *Only back up the System State data* (Figure 20.3) radio button. The System State data takes care of most of the Registry, security settings, the desktop files and folders, and the default user.

If you want to back up more than that, close the wizard and select the Backup tab in the Backup dialog box. Check the box next to System State and then add a check mark next to any other file or folder that you want backed up (Figure 20.4). From this same dialog box, you can select where to back up the data, such as to a tape drive or external hard drive.

Off-Site Storage

Backing up your data and other important information enables you to restore easily in case of a system crash or malicious data destruction, but to ensure proper security, you need to store your backups somewhere other than your

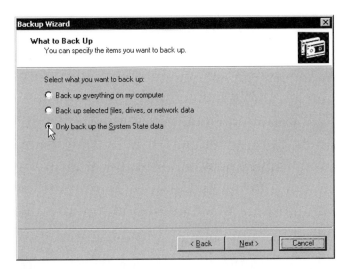

FIGURE 20.3 Back up extra data in the Backup Wizard

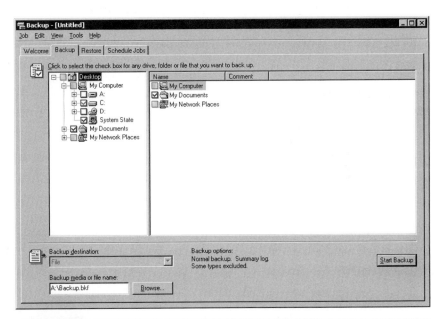

FIGURE 20.4 Backup tab in the Backup dialog box with System State and My Documents selected

office. *Off-site storage* can mean that you take the tape or portable hard drive that contains your backup and lock it in a briefcase. Take it home and put it in your home safe, if you have one. This way, if the office building burns down or some major flood renders your office inaccessible, your company can be up and running very quickly from a secondary location.

Exam Tip
The CompTIA A+ certification exams most likely *won't* ask you about off-site storage, but in today's world, anything less would be illogical.

Migrating and Retiring

Seasons change and so does state of the art computing. At a certain point in a computer's life, you'll need to retire an old system. This means you must move the data and users to a new system or at least a new hard drive—a process called *migration*—and then safely dispose of the old system. Chapter 16 went through the details of the Files and Settings Transfer Wizard, so I won't bore you by repeating that here. When talking about migration or retirement in terms of security, you need to answer one question: what do you do with the old system or drive?

All but the most vanilla of installations have sensitive data stored on them, even if the data is simply e-mail messages or notes-to-self that would cause embarrassment if discovered. Most PCs, especially in a work environment, contain a lot of sensitive data. You can't just format the C: drive and hand it over.

Follow these three principles when migrating or retiring a computer.

- Migrate your users and data information in a secure environment.
- Remove data remnants from hard drives that you store or give to charity.
- Recycle the older equipment; don't throw it in the trash. PC recyclers go through a process of deconstructing hardware, breaking system units, keyboards, printers, and even monitors into their basic plastics, metals, and glass for reuse.

Migration Practices

Migrate your users and data information in a secure environment. Until you get passwords properly in place and test the security of the new system, you can't consider that system secure. Don't set a copy to run while you go out to lunch, but rather stick around to supervise and remove any remnant data that might still reside on any mass storage devices, especially hard drives.

You might think that, as easy as it seems to be to lose data, you could readily get rid of data if you tried. That's not the case with magnetic media, though, such as hard drives and flash memory. It's difficult to clean a drive completely. Repeated formatting won't do the trick. Partitioning and formatting won't work. Data doesn't necessarily get written over in the same place every time, which means that a solid wipe of a hard drive by writing zeroes to all the clusters still potentially leaves a lot of sensitive and recoverable data, called *remnants,* on the drive.

Although you can't make data 100 percent unrecoverable short of physically shredding or pulverizing a drive, you can do well enough for donation purposes by using one of the better drive-wiping utilities, such as Webroot's Window Washer (Figure 20.5). Window Washer gives you the ability to erase your Web browsing history, your recent activity in Windows (such as what programs you ran), and even your e-mail messages permanently. As an added bonus, you can create a bootable disk that enables you to wipe a drive completely.

Recycle

An important and relatively easy way to be an environmentally conscious computer user is to *recycle*. Recycling products such as paper and printer cartridges not only keeps them out of overcrowded landfills, but also ensures that the more toxic products are disposed of in the right way. Safely disposing of hardware

FIGURE 20.5 Webroot Window Washer security software

containing hazardous materials, such as computer monitors, protects both people and the environment.

Anyone who's ever tried to sell a computer more than three or four years old learns a hard lesson—they're not worth much, if anything at all. It's a real temptation to take that old computer and just toss it in the garbage, but never do that!

First of all, many parts of your computer—such as your computer monitor—contain hazardous materials that pollute the environment. Luckily, thousands of companies now specialize in computer recycling and will gladly accept your old computer. If you have enough computers, they might even pick them up. If you can't find a recycler, call your local municipality's waste authority to see where to drop off your system.

An even better alternative for your old computer is donation. Many organizations actively look for old computers to refurbish and to donate to schools and other organizations. Just keep in mind that the computer can't be too old—not even a school wants a computer more than five or six years old.

Exam Tip

CompTIA certification exams consider security to be an extremely important topic, whether you're at the Essentials level or any of the Technician levels. So you need to know everything in this chapter to pass any of the four CompTIA A+ certification exams.

Social Engineering

Although you're more likely to lose data through accident, the acts of malicious users get the vast majority of headlines. Most of these attacks come under the heading of *social engineering*—the process of using or manipulating people inside the networking environment to gain access to that network from the outside. The term *social engineering* covers the many ways humans can use other humans to gain unauthorized information. This unauthorized information may be a network login, a credit card number, company customer data—almost anything you might imagine that one person or organization may not want a person outside of that organization to access.

Social engineering attacks aren't hacking—at least in the classic sense of the word—although the goals are the same. Social engineering occurs when people attack an organization through the people within the organization or physically access the organization to get the information they need. Following are a few of the more classic types of social engineering attacks.

Travel Advisory

It's common for attack types to be used together, so if you discover one of them being used against your organization, it's a good idea to look for others.

Infiltration

Hackers can physically enter your building under the guise of someone who might have a legitimate reason for being there, such as cleaning personnel, repair technicians, or messengers. They then snoop around desks, looking for whatever they can find. They might talk with people inside the organization, gathering names, office numbers, department names—little things in and of themselves, but powerful tools when combined later with other social engineering attacks.

Telephone Scams

Telephone scams are probably the most common social engineering attack. The attacker makes a phone call to someone in the organization, misrepresenting himself or herself as someone inside the organization in an attempt to gain information. Probably the most famous of these scams is the "I forgot my user name and password" scam. In this gambit, the attacker first learns the account name of a legitimate person in the organization, usually using the infiltration method. The attacker then calls someone in the organization, usually the help desk, in an attempt to gather information, in this case a password.

Dumpster Diving

Dumpster diving is the generic term for when a hacker goes through your refuse, looking for information. The amount of sensitive information that makes it into any organization's trash bin boggles the mind! Years ago, I worked with an IT security guru who gave me and a few other IT people a tour of our office's trash. In one, 20-minute tour of the personal wastebaskets of one office area, we had enough information to access the network easily, as well as to embarrass seriously more than a few people. When it comes to getting information, the trash is the place to look!

Physical Theft

Thieves use social engineering to gain access to sensitive areas and physically steal data and equipment. Not very elegant, perhaps, but you can certainly lose a lot that way. Never forget that the best software security measures can be rendered useless if you fail to protect your systems physically.

Access Control

Access is the key. If you can control access to the data, programs, and other computing resources, you've secured your system. *Access control* is composed of five interlinked areas that a good, security-minded tech should think about: physical security, authentication, the file system, users and groups, and security policies. Much of this you know from previous chapters, but this section should help tie it all together as a security topic.

Secure Physical Area and Lock Down Your System

The first order of security is to block access to the physical hardware from people who shouldn't have access. This isn't rocket science. Lock the door. Don't leave a PC unattended when logged in. In fact, don't ever leave a system logged in, even as a limited user. You tempt fate if you walk away from a server still logged in as an Administrator.

For that matter, when you see a user's computer logged in and unattended, do the user and your company a huge favor and lock the computer. Just walk up and press CTRL-L on the keyboard to lock the system. It works in Windows 2000 and all versions of Windows XP and Windows Vista.

Authentication

Security starts with properly implemented *authentication,* which means, in essence, how the computer determines who can or should access it. And, once accessed, what that user can do. A computer can authenticate users through software or hardware, or via a combination of both.

Software Authentication: Proper Passwords

It's still rather shocking to me if I power up a friend's computer and go straight to his or her desktop; or with my married-with-kids friends, to click one of the parent's user account icons and not get prompted for a password. This is just wrong! I'm always tempted to assign passwords right then and there—and not tell them the passwords, of course—so they'll see the error of their ways when they try to log in next. I don't do it, but always try to explain gently the importance of good passwords.

You know about passwords from Chapter 19, so I won't belabor the point here. Suffice it to say that you need to make certain that all your users have proper passwords. Don't let them write passwords down or tape them to the underside of their mouse pads either.

It's not just access to Windows that you need to think about. If you have computers running in a public location, there's always the temptation for people to

hack the system and do mean things, like change CMOS settings to render the computer inoperable to the casual user until a tech can undo the damage. All modern CMOS setup utilities come with an access password protection scheme (Figure 20.6).

Hardware Authentication Smart cards and biometric devices enable modern systems to authenticate users with more authority than mere passwords, as you'll recall from Chapter 10. *Smart cards* are credit-card–sized and contain circuitry that can be used to identify the bearer of the card. Smart cards are relatively common for tasks such as authenticating users for mass transit systems, for example, but fairly uncommon in computers. Figure 20.7 shows a smart card and keyboard combination.

Clever manufacturers have developed key fobs and smart cards that use radio frequency identification (RFID) to transmit authentication information, so users don't have to insert something into a computer or card reader. The Privaris plusID combines, for example, a biometric fingerprint fob with an RFID tag that makes security as easy as opening a garage door remotely. Figure 20.8 shows a plusID device.

NTFS, not FAT32

The file system on a hard drive matters a lot when it comes to security. On a Windows machine with multiple users, you simply must use NTFS or you have no security at all. Not just primary drives, but any secondary drives in computers in your care should be formatted as NTFS.

When you run into a multiple-drive system that has a second or third drive formatted as FAT32, you can use the CONVERT command line utility to go from FAT to NTFS. The syntax is pretty straightforward. To convert a D: drive from FAT or FAT32 to NTFS, for example, you'd type the following:

```
CONVERT D: /FS:NTFS
```

FIGURE 20.6 CMOS access password request

FIGURE 20.7 Smart card and keyboard reader (photo courtesy of Cherry Corp.)

You can substitute a mount name in place of the drive letter in case you have a mounted volume. The command has a few extra switches as well, so at the command prompt, type **a /?** after the **CONVERT** command to see all your options.

Users and Groups

In Windows, user accounts and groups are the bedrock of access control. A user account gets assigned to a group, such as Users, Power Users, or Administrators, and by association gets certain permissions on the computer. Using NTFS enables the highest level of control over data resources.

FIGURE 20.8 The plusID (photo courtesy of Privaris, Inc.)

Assigning users to groups is a great first step in controlling a local machine, but this feature really shines once you go to a networked environment. Let's go there now.

Objective 20.03 ## Protecting Networked Computers

The vast majority of protective strategies related to internal threats are based on policies rather than technology. Even the smallest network will have a number of user accounts and groups scattered about with different levels of rights/permissions. Every time you give a user access to a resource, you create potential loopholes that can leave your network vulnerable to unauthorized access, data destruction, and other administrative nightmares. To protect your network from internal threats, you need to implement the correct controls over user accounts, permissions, and policies.

Networks are under threat from the outside as well, so this section looks at issues involving Internet-borne attacks, firewalls, and wireless networking. The section finishes with discussion of the tools you need to track computer and network activity and, if necessary, lock down your systems.

User Account Control Through Groups

Access to user accounts should be restricted to the assigned individuals, and those accounts should have permission to access only the resources they need, and no more. Tight control of user accounts is critical to preventing unauthorized access. Disabling unused accounts is an important part of this strategy, but good user account control goes far deeper than that. One of your best tools for user account control is groups. Instead of giving permissions/rights to individual user accounts, give them to groups; this makes keeping track of the permissions assigned to individual user accounts much easier. Figure 20.9 shows me giving permissions to a group for a folder in Windows 2000. Once a group is created and its permissions set, you can then add user accounts to that group as needed. Any user account that becomes a member of a group automatically gets the permissions assigned to that group. Figure 20.10 shows me adding a user to a newly created group in the same Windows 2000 system.

Giving a group permissions for a folder in Windows 2000

Adding a user to a newly created group in Windows 2000

Groups are a great way to get increased complexity without increasing the administrative burden on network administrators, because all network OSs combine permissions. When a user is a member of more than one group, which permissions does he or she have with respect to any particular resource? In all network OSs, the permissions of the groups are *combined,* and the result is what you call the *effective permissions* the user has to access the resource. Let's use an example from Windows 2000. If Rita is a member of the Sales group, which has List Folder Contents permission to a folder, and she is also a member of the Managers group, which has Read and Execute permissions to the same folder, Rita will have both List Folder Contents *and* Read and Execute permissions to that folder.

Watch out for *default* user accounts and groups—they can become secret back doors to your network! All network OSs have a default Everyone group, and it can be used to sneak into shared resources easily. This Everyone group, as its name implies, literally includes anyone who connects to that resource. Windows 2000 gives full control to the Everyone group by default, for example, so make sure you know to lock this down.

Travel Advisory

All of the default groups—Everyone, Guest, Users—define broad groups of users. Never use them unless you intend to permit all those folks to access a resource. If you use one of the default groups, remember to configure them with the proper permissions to prevent users from doing things you don't want them to do with a shared resource.

All these groups do only one thing for you: They let you keep track of your user accounts, so you know they are available only for those who need them, and they access only the resources you want them to use.

Security Policies

While permissions control how users access shared resources, you should control other functions that are outside the scope of resources. For example, do you want users to be able to access a command prompt on their Windows system? Do you want users to be able to install software? Would you like to control what systems or what time of day a user can log in? All network OSs provide you with some ability to control these and literally hundreds of other security parameters, under what Windows calls *policies*. I like to think of policies as permissions for activities as opposed to true permissions, which control access to resources.

A policy is usually applied to a user account, a computer, or a group. Let's use the example of a network composed of Windows XP Professional systems with a Windows Server 2003 system. Every Windows XP system has its own local policies program, which enables policies to be placed on that system only. Figure 20.11 shows the tool you use to set local policies on an individual system, called *Local Security Settings,* being used to deny the user account Danar the ability to log on locally.

Local policies work well for individual systems, but they can be a pain to configure if you want to apply the same settings to more than one PC on your network. If you want to apply policy settings *en masse,* you need to step up to Windows Active Directory domain-based *Group Policy.* Using Group Policy, you can exercise deity-like—Microsoft prefers to use the term *granular*—control over your network clients.

Want to set default wallpaper for every PC in your domain? Group Policy can do that. Want to make certain tools inaccessible to everyone except authorized users? Group Policy can do that, too. Want to control access to the Internet, redirect home folders, run scripts, deploy software, or just remind folks that unauthorized access to the network will get them nowhere fast? Group Policy is the answer. Figure 20.12 shows Group Policy; I'm about to change the default title on every instance of Internet Explorer on every computer in my domain.

That's just one simple example of the types of settings you can configure using Group Policy. You can apply literally hundreds of "tweaks" through Group Policy, from the great to the small, but don't worry too much about familiarizing yourself with each and every one. Group Policy settings are a big topic in the Microsoft Certified Systems Administrator (MCSA) and Microsoft Certified

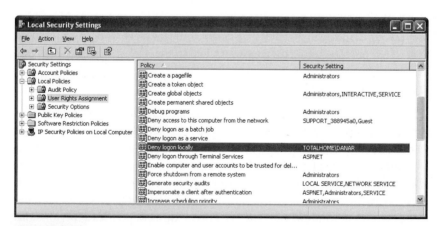

FIGURE 20.11 Local Security Settings

FIGURE 20.12 Using Group Policy to make the IE title say "provided by Mike!"

Systems Engineer (MCSE) certification tracks, but for the purposes of the CompTIA A+ certification exams, you simply need to be comfortable with the concept behind Group Policy.

Although I could never list every possible policy you can enable on a Windows system, here's a list of some of those more commonly used:

- **Prevent Registry Edits** If you try to edit the Registry, you get a failure message.
- **Prevent Access to the Command Prompt** This policy keeps users from getting to the command prompt by turning off the **Run** command and the MS-DOS Prompt shortcut.
- **Log on Locally** This policy defines who may log on to the system locally.
- **Shut Down System** This policy defines who may shut down the system.
- **Minimum Password Length** This policy forces a minimum password length.
- **Account Lockout Threshold** This policy sets the maximum number of logon attempts a person can make before he or she is locked out of the account.

- **Disable Windows Installer** This policy prevents users from installing software.
- **Printer Browsing** This policy enables users to browse for printers on the network, as opposed to using only assigned printers.

While the CompTIA A+ certification exams don't expect you to know how to implement policies on any type of network, you are expected to understand that policies exist, especially on Windows networks, and that they can do amazing things in terms of controlling what users can do on their systems. If you ever try to get to a command prompt on a Windows system, only to discover the Run command is grayed out, blame it on a policy, not the computer.

Malicious Software

The beauty of the Internet is the ease of accessing resources just about anywhere on the globe, all from the comfort of your favorite chair. This connection, however, runs both ways, and people from all over the world can potentially access your computer from the comfort of their evil lairs. The Internet is awash with malicious software—*malware*—that is—even at this moment—trying to infect your systems. Malware consists of computer programs designed to break into or cause havoc on computers. The most common types of malware are viruses, worms, spyware, Trojan horses, adware, and grayware. You need to understand the different types of malware so you can combat them for you and your users successfully.

Viruses

Just as a biological virus gets passed from person to person, a computer *virus* is a piece of malicious software that gets passed from computer to computer (Figure 20.13). A computer virus is designed to attach itself to a program on your computer. It could be your e-mail program, your word processor, or even a game. Whenever you use the infected program, the virus goes into action and does whatever it was designed to do. It can wipe out your e-mail or even erase your entire hard drive! Viruses are also sometimes used to steal information or send spam e-mails to everyone in your Address Book.

Trojans

Trojans are true, freestanding programs that do something other than what the person who runs the program thinks they will do. An example of a *Trojan virus* is a program that a person thinks is a game but is actually a CMOS eraser. Some Trojans are quite sophisticated. It might be a game that works perfectly well, but when the user quits the game, it causes some type of damage.

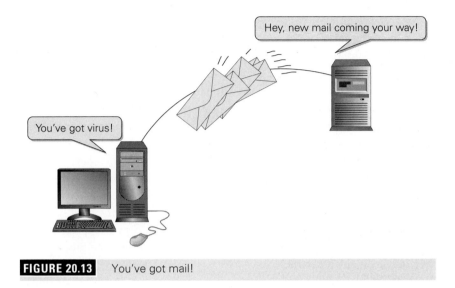

Worms

Similar to a Trojan, a *worm* is a complete program that travels from machine to machine, usually through computer networks. Most worms are designed to take advantage of security problems in OSs and install themselves on vulnerable machines. They can copy themselves over and over again on infected networks and can create so much activity that they overload the network, in worst cases even bringing chunks of the entire Internet to a halt.

You can do several things to protect yourself and your data against these threats. First, make sure you are running up-to-date virus software—especially if you connect to the Internet via an always-on broadband connection. You should also be protected by a firewall, either as part of your network hardware or by means of a software program. (See the sections "Viruses and Antivirus Programs" and "Firewalls," later in this chapter.)

Since worms most commonly infect systems because of security flaws in OSs, the next defense against them is to make sure you have the most current version possible of your OS and to check regularly for security patches. In other words, run Windows Update!

Viruses and Antivirus Programs

The only way to protect your PC permanently from getting a virus is to disconnect from the Internet and never permit any potentially infected software to touch your precious computer. Because neither scenario is likely these days, you need to use a specialized antivirus program to help stave off the inevitable virus assaults.

An *antivirus program* protects your PC in two ways. It can be both sword and shield, working in an active seek-and-destroy mode and in a passive sentry mode. When ordered to seek and destroy, the program will scan the computer's boot sector and files for viruses, and if it finds any, it will present you with the available options for removing or disabling them. Antivirus programs can also operate as *virus shields* that passively monitor your computer's activity, checking for viruses only when certain events occur, such as a program executing or a file being downloaded.

Antivirus programs use different techniques to combat different types of viruses. They detect boot sector viruses simply by comparing the drive's boot sector to a standard boot sector. This works because most boot sectors are basically the same. Some antivirus programs make a backup copy of the boot sector. If they detect a virus, the programs will use that backup copy to replace the infected boot sector. Executable viruses are a little more difficult to find because they can be on any file in the drive.

To detect executable viruses, the antivirus program uses a library of signatures. A *signature* is the code pattern of a known virus. The antivirus program compares an executable file to its library of signatures. Sometimes, a perfectly clean program can coincidentally hold a virus signature. Usually the antivirus program's creator will provide a patch to prevent further alarms. Antivirus programs detect macro viruses through the presence of virus signatures or certain macro commands that indicate a known macro virus.

Now that you understand the types of viruses and how antivirus programs try to protect against them, let's review a few terms that are often used when describing certain traits of viruses.

Polymorphics/Polymorphs A *polymorph virus* attempts to change its signature to prevent detection by antivirus programs, usually by continually scrambling a bit of useless code. Fortunately, the scrambling code itself can be identified and used as the signature—once the antivirus makers become aware of the virus. One technique used to combat unknown polymorphs is to have the antivirus program create a checksum on every file in the drive. A *checksum* in this context is a number generated by the software based on the contents of the file rather than the name, date, or size of that file. The algorithms for creating these checksums vary among different antivirus programs (they are also usually kept secret to help prevent virus makers from coming up with ways to beat them). Every time a program is run, the antivirus program calculates a new checksum and compares it with the earlier calculation. If the checksums are different, it is a sure sign of a virus.

Stealth The term *stealth* is more of a concept than an actual virus function. Most *stealth virus* programs are boot sector viruses that use various methods to hide from antivirus software. The AntiEXE stealth virus will hook on to a little-known but often-used software interrupt, for example, running only when that interrupt runs. Others make copies of innocent-looking files.

Virus Prevention Tips The secret to preventing damage from a malicious software attack is to keep from getting a virus in the first place. As discussed earlier, all good antivirus programs include a virus shield that will scan e-mail, downloads, running programs, and so on automatically (see Figure 20.14).

Use your antivirus shield. It is also a good idea to scan PCs daily for possible virus attacks. All antivirus programs include terminate-and-stay resident programs (TSRs) that will run every time the PC is booted. Last but not least, know the source of any software before you load it. While the chance of commercial, shrink-wrapped software having a virus is virtually nil (there have been a couple of well-publicized exceptions), don't install that illegal copy of Unreal Tournament you borrowed from a local hacker!

Keep your antivirus program updated. New viruses appear daily, and your program needs to know about them. The list of viruses your antivirus program can recognize is called the *definition file,* and you must keep that definition file

FIGURE 20.14 A virus shield in action

up to date. Fortunately, most antivirus programs will update themselves automatically.

E-mail is still a common source of viruses, and opening infected e-mails is a common way to get infected. If you view an e-mail in a preview window, that opens the e-mail message and exposes your computer to some viruses. Download files only from sites you know to be safe, and of course the less reputable corners of the Internet are the most likely places to pick up computer infections.

Viruses are not, however, the only malicious software lurking in e-mail. Sometimes the e-mail itself is the problem.

Spam

E-mail that comes into your Inbox from a source that's not a friend, family member, or colleague, and that you didn't ask for, can create huge problems for your computer and you. This unsolicited e-mail, called *spam*, accounts for a huge percentage of traffic on the Internet. Spam comes in many flavors, from legitimate businesses trying to sell you products to scammers who just want to take your money. Hoaxes, pornography, and get-rich-quick schemes pour into the Inboxes of most e-mail users. They waste your time and can easily offend.

You can use several options to cope with the flood of spam. The first option is defense. Never post your e-mail address on the Internet. One study tested this theory and found that *over 97 percent* of the spam received during the study went to e-mail addresses they had posted on the public Internet.

Travel Assistance

The Center for Democracy and Technology conducted the study in 2003, entitled "Why Am I Getting All This Spam? Unsolicited Commercial E-mail Research Six Month Report." Here's the Web link if you're curious: www.cdt.org/speech/spam/030319spamreport.shtml.

Filters and filtering software can block spam at your mail server and at your computer. AOL implemented blocking schemes in 2004, for example, that dropped the average spam received by its subscribers by a large percentage, perhaps as much as 50 percent. You can set most e-mail programs to block e-mail from specific people—good to use if someone is harassing you—or to specific people. You can block by subject line or keywords. Most people use a third-party antispam program instead of using the filters in their e-mail program.

Travel Assistance

Spam-filtering software that you purchase and put on your computer can help, but you have to do some research to see which software offers the best performance. You want to avoid software that causes *false positives*— mislabeling acceptable e-mail as spam—because then you miss legitimate e-mail messages from family, co-workers, and friends. So, time to fire up your trusty Web browser and do some searching.

Start by going to Google and searching for *antispam software reviews*. One of the first sites that should come up takes you to *PC Magazine's* review list that they keep up to date. What's the current Editor's Choice? What other options do you have?

Pop-ups, Spyware, and Adware

On most systems, the Internet Web browser client is the most often used piece of software. Over the years, Web sites have come up with more and more ways to try to get you to see what they want you to see: their advertising. When the Web first got underway, we were forced to look at an occasional banner ad. In the last few years, Web site designers have become much more sophisticated, creating a number of intrusive and irritating ways to get you to part with your money in one form or another.

Three basic Web browser problems can irritate users: pop-ups, spyware, and adware. *Pop-ups* are those surprise browser windows that appear automatically when you visit a Web site, proving themselves unwanted and nothing else. *Spyware,* meanwhile, defines a family of programs that run in the background on your PC, sending information about your browsing habits to the company that installed it on your system. *Adware* is not generally as malicious as spyware, but it works similarly to display ads on your system. As such, these programs download new ads and generate undesirable network traffic. Of the three, spyware is much less noticeable but far more nefarious. At its worst, spyware can fire up pop-up windows of competing products on the Web site you're currently viewing. For example, you might be perusing a bookseller's Web site only to have a pop-up from a competitor's site appear.

Most Web browsers have features to prevent pop-up ads in the first place, but I've found that these types of applications are sometimes *too* thorough. That is, they tend to prevent *all* new browser windows from opening, even those you want to view. Still, they're free to try, so have a look to see if they suit your needs.

Dealing with Spyware Some types of spyware go considerably beyond this level of intrusion. They can use your computer's resources to run *distributed computing* applications, capture your keystrokes to steal passwords, and more.

Windows comes with Windows Defender, a fine tool for catching most spyware, but it's not perfect. The better solution is to back up Windows Defender with a second spyware removal program. Several are on the market, but two that I highly recommend are Lavasoft's Ad-Aware (Figure 20.15) and PepiMK's Spybot Search & Destroy.

Local Lingo

Grayware Some programs, called *grayware*, are not destructive in and of themselves, but they leach bandwidth in networks and can turn a speedy machine into a doddering shell of a modern computer. These programs are called grayware because some people consider them beneficial (their effects are not black and white, in other words). They might even be beneficial in the right setting. The primary example of grayware is the highly popular peer-to-peer file sharing programs, such as BitTorrent. Peer-to-peer file sharing programs enable a lot of users to upload portions of files on demand so that other users can download them. By splitting the load to many computers, the overall demand on a single computer is light.

| FIGURE 20.15 | Lavasoft's Ad-Aware |

Firewalls

Firewalls are essential tools in the fight against malicious programs on the Internet. *Firewalls* are devices or software that protect an internal network from unauthorized access to and from the Internet at large. Hardware firewalls protect networks using a number of methods, such as hiding IP addresses and blocking TCP/IP ports. Most small office/home office (SOHO) networks use a hardware firewall, such as the Linksys router shown in Figure 20.16. These devices do a great job.

Windows XP comes with an excellent software firewall, called the Windows Firewall (Figure 20.17), as you'll recall from Chapter 18. It can also handle the heavy lifting of port blocking, security logging, and more.

Encryption

Firewalls do a great job controlling traffic coming into or out of a network from the Internet, but they do nothing to stop interceptor hackers who monitor traffic on the public Internet looking for vulnerabilities. Once a packet is on the Internet itself, anyone with the right equipment can intercept and inspect it. Inspected packets are a cornucopia of passwords, account names, and other tidbits that hackers can use to intrude into your network. Because hackers can't be

FIGURE 20.16 Linksys router as a firewall

FIGURE 20.17 Windows Firewall

stopped from inspecting these packets, the industry turns to *encryption* to make the packets unreadable.

Network encryption occurs at many different levels and is in no way limited to Internet-based activities. Not only does network encryption come in many levels, but each encryption level provides multiple standards and options, making encryption one of the most complicated of all networking issues. You need to understand where encryption comes into play, what options are available, and what you can use to protect your network.

Network Authentication

Modern network OSs such as Windows NT/2000/XP/2003/Vista and NetWare 4.*x*/5.*x*/6.*x* use standard authentication encryptions such as MIT's *Kerberos*, which enable multiple brands of servers to authenticate multiple brands of clients. These LAN encryptions are usually transparent and work quite nicely even in mixed networks.

Unfortunately, this uniformity falls away as you begin to add remote access authentications. With so many different remote access tools, based on UNIX/Linux,

Novell NetWare, and Windows serving programs, most remote access systems have to support a variety of different authentication methods.

PAP *Password Authentication Protocol (PAP)* is the oldest and most basic form of authentication. It's also the least safe, because it sends all passwords in clear text. No network OS uses PAP for a client system's login, but almost all network OSs that provide remote access service will support PAP for backward compatibility with a host of older programs (such as Telnet) that use only PAP.

CHAP *Challenge Handshake Authentication Protocol (CHAP)* is the most common remote access protocol. CHAP has the serving system challenge the remote client. A *challenge* occurs when the host system asks the remote client some secret—usually a password—that the remote client must then respond with for the host to allow the connection.

MS-CHAP *MS-CHAP* is Microsoft's variation of CHAP. It uses a slightly more advanced encryption protocol.

Configuring Dial-up Encryption

The server, not the client, controls the choice of dial-up encryption. Microsoft clients can handle a broad selection of authentication encryption methods, including no authentication at all. On the rare occasion that you have to change your client's default encryption settings for a dial-up connection, you'll need to journey deep into the bowels of its properties. Figure 20.18 shows the Windows 2000 security options in a dial-up connection's dialog box, where you configure encryption. The person who controls the server's configuration will tell you which encryption method to select here.

Data Encryption

Encryption methods don't stop at the authentication level. A number of ways can be used to encrypt network *data* as well. The choice of encryption method is dictated to a large degree by the method used by the communicating systems to connect. Many networks consist of multiple networks linked together by some sort of private connection, usually some kind of telephone line such as ISDN or T1. Microsoft's encryption method of choice for this type of network is called *IPSec* (derived from *IP security*). IPSec provides transparent encryption between the server and the client. IPSec will also work in virtual private networks (VPNs), but other encryption methods are more commonly used in those situations.

FIGURE 20.18 Setting dial-up encryption in Windows 2000

Application Encryption

Netscape's *Secure Sockets Layer (SSL)* security protocol is an *application encryption* you use to create secure Web sites. Microsoft incorporates SSL into its more far-reaching *HTTPS* (HTTP over SSL) protocol. These protocols make it possible to create the secure Web sites we use to make purchases over the Internet. HTTPS Web sites can be identified by the *HTTPS://* included in the URL (see Figure 20.19).

To make a secure connection, your Web browser and the Web server must encrypt their data. That means both the Web server and your browser must have a way to encrypt and decrypt each other's data. This is done by the server sending a public key to your Web browser so the browser knows how to encrypt a message to the server to start a session. These public keys are sent in the form of a *digital certificate*. This certificate not only provides the public key but also is

FIGURE 20.19 A secure Web site

signed by a trusted authority that guarantees the public key you are about to get is actually from the Web server and not from some evil person trying to pretend to be the Web server. A number of companies issue digital certificates to Web sites, and probably the most famous is VeriSign, Inc.

Your Web browser has a built-in list of trusted authorities. If a certificate comes in from a Web site that uses one of these highly respected companies, you won't see anything happen in your browser; you'll just go to the secure Web page and a small lock will appear in the lower right-hand corner of your browser. Figure 20.20 shows the Certificate Manager, with a list of trusted authorities built in to the Firefox Web browser.

If you receive a certificate from someone *not* listed in your browser, however, the browser will warn you and ask you whether you want to accept the certificate, as shown in Figure 20.21.

Trusted authorities

What you do here is up to you. Do you want to trust this certificate? In most cases, you simply click OK, and this certificate is added to your SSL cache of certificates. However, on some occasions, an accepted certificate becomes invalid, usually due to something boring—for instance, it expires or the public

Incoming certificate

key changes. This never happens with the "big name" certificates built in to your browser—you'll see this more often when a certificate is used, for example, in-house on a company intranet and the administrator forgets to update their certificates. If a certificate goes bad, your browser issues a warning the next time you visit that site. To clear invalid certificates, you need to clear the SSL cache. The process varies on every browser, but on Internet Explorer, go to the Content tab under Internet Options and click the Clear SSL State button (Figure 20.22).

Wireless Issues

Wireless networks add a level of additional security headaches for techs to face, as you know from Chapter 14. Following are some of the points to remember or to go back and look up:

- Set up wireless encryption—at least WEP but preferably WPA or the more secure WPA2—and configure clients to use them.
- If you use DHCP, only allot enough DHCP addresses to meet the needs of your network to avoid unused wireless connections.
- Change the WAP's SSID from default and disable SSID broadcasting.

FIGURE 20.22 Clearing an SSL state on the Content tab

- Filter by MAC address to allow only known clients on the network.
- Change the default user name and password. Every hacker has memorized the default user names and passwords.
- Update the firmware as needed.
- If available, make sure the WAP's firewall settings are turned on.

Reporting

As a final weapon in your security arsenal, you need to report any security issues so a network administrator or technician can take steps to make them go away. You can set up two tools within Windows so that the OS reports problems to you: Event Viewer and Auditing. You can then do your work and report those problems.

Event Viewer

Chapter 19 explored Event Viewer in the context of troubleshooting OS and application errors, but Event Viewer offers security features as well. The Security section of Event Viewer doesn't show you anything by default, though. To unlock the full potential of Event Viewer, you need to set up auditing. *Auditing* in the security sense means to tell Windows to create an entry in the Security Log when certain events happen—for example, a user logs on, called *event auditing*, or tries to access a certain file or folder, called *object access auditing*. Figure 20.23 Shows Event Viewer tracking logon and logoff events.

FIGURE 20.23　Event Viewer displaying security alerts

> ### Exam Tip
>
> The CompTIA A+ certification exams don't test you on creating a brilliant auditing policy for your office—that's what network administrators do. You simply need to know what auditing does and how to turn it on or off so that you can provide support for the network administrators in the field.

To turn on auditing at a local level, go to Local Security Settings in Administrative Tools. Select Local Policies and then click Audit Policies. Double-click one of the policy options and select one or both of the check boxes. Figure 20.24 shows the Audit Object Access dialog box.

Incidence Reporting

Once you've gathered data about a particular system or you've dealt with a computer or network problem, you need to complete the mission by telling your supervisor what you found. This is called *incidence reporting*. Many companies have pre-made forms that you simply fill out and submit. Other places are less formal.

Incidence reporting does a couple of things for you. First, it provides a record of work you've accomplished. Second, it provides a piece of information that, when combined with other information that you might or might not know,

FIGURE 20.24 The Audit Object Access dialog box

reveals a pattern or bigger problem to someone higher up the chain. A seemingly innocuous security audit report, for example, might match other such events in numerous places in the building at the same time and thus show conscious, coordinated action rather than a glitch was at work.

CHECKPOINT

✔ **Objective 20.1: Analyzing Security Threats** Threats to your data come from two sources: malicious people and accidents. Unauthorized access occurs when a user accesses resources in an unauthorized way. Authorized access can lead to data destruction by users who do not intend to be malicious. When users have access to a file or database, they typically believe the system won't let them make any changes they are not authorized to make. Computers, hard drives, and power all fail. As a tech, you need to plan for redundancy in these areas.

✔ **Objective 20.2: Protecting Local Computers** Backups should be stored off-site. Migrate user and data information in a secure environment, remove data from hard drives, and recycle old equipment. Most computer attacks are accomplished through social engineering rather than hacking. Controlling access to programs, data, and other computing resources is the key to securing your system. All hard drives should be formatted with NTFS, not FAT32. Windows uses user accounts and groups to control access.

✔ **Objective 20.3: Protecting Networked Computers** Use the Local Security Settings tool to manage policies for an individual computer. Group Policy enables you to control such things as setting each computer in a domain to use the same wallpaper or deploy software. Malware includes viruses, worms, Trojan horses, adware, and grayware. To help protect a computer from malware, make sure you run up-to-date antivirus software, use a firewall, and apply all security patches for your software and OS. Use MS-CHAP if possible for encryption over a network. Incidence reporting means telling your supervisor about the data you've gathered regarding a computer or network problem.

REVIEW QUESTIONS

1. Which of the following would you select if you need to back up an Active Directory server?

 A. Registry

 B. System State data

 C. My Computer

 D. My Server

2. Peter migrated his server data to a bigger, faster hard drive. At the end of the process, he partitioned and formatted the older hard drive before removing it to donate to charity. How secure is his company's data?

 A. Completely secured. The drive is blank after partitioning and formatting.

 B. Mostly secured. Only super-skilled professionals have the tools to recover data after partitioning and formatting.

 C. Very unsecured. Simple software tools can recover a lot of data, even after partitioning and formatting.

 D. Completely unsecured. The data on the drive will show up in the Recycle Bin as soon as someone installs it into a system.

3. What is the process of using or manipulating people to gain access to network resources?

 A. Cracking

 B. Hacking

 C. Network engineering

 D. Social engineering

4. Which of the following might offer good hardware authentication?

 A. Strong password

 B. Encrypted password

 C. NTFS

 D. Smart card

5. Randall needs to change the file system on his second hard drive (currently the D: drive) from FAT32 to NTFS. Which of the following commands would do the trick?

 A. CONVERT D: /FS:NTFS

 B. CONVERT D: NTFS

 C. NTFS D:

 D. NTFS D: /FAT32

6. Which of the following tools would enable you to stop a user from logging into a local machine, but still enable him to log onto the domain?

 A. AD Policy

 B. Group Policy

 C. Local Security Settings

 D. User Settings

7. Which type of encryption offers the most security?

 A. MS-CHAP

 B. PAP

 C. POP3

 D. SMTP

8. Which of the following should Mary set up on her Wi-Fi router to make it the most secure?

 A. NTFS

 B. WEP

 C. WPA

 D. WPA2

9. What single folder on a stand-alone PC can be backed up to secure all users' My Documents folders?

 A. All Users folder

 B. Documents and Settings folder

 C. System32 folder

 D. Windows folder

10. A user account is a member of several groups, and the groups have conflicting rights and permissions to several network resources. The culminating permissions that ultimately affect the user's access is referred to as what?

 A. Effective permissions

 B. Culminating rights

 C. Last rights

 D. Persistent permissions

11. What is true about virus shields?

 A. They automatically scan e-mails, downloads, and running programs.

 B. They protect against spyware and adware.

 C. They are effective in stopping pop-ups.

 D. They can reduce the amount of spam by 97 percent.

12. What does Windows use to encrypt the user authentication process over a LAN?

 A. PAP

 B. MS-CHAP

 C. HTTPS

 D. Kerberos

13. Which threats are categorized as social engineering? (Select two.)

 A. Telephone scams

 B. Dumpster diving

 C. Trojans

 D. Spyware

REVIEW ANSWERS

1. **B** Select System State data to back up an Active Directory server.

2. **C** Peter's data is very unsecured. Simple software tools can recover a lot of data, even after partitioning and formatting.

3. **D** Social engineering is the process of using or manipulating people to gain access to network resources.

4. **D** A smart card might offer good hardware authentication.

5. **A** CONVERT D: /FS:NTFS will change the file system on the D: drive from FAT32 to NTFS.

6. **C** Local Security Settings would enable you to stop a user from logging into a local machine, but still enable him to log onto the domain.

7. **A** MS-CHAP offers more security than PAP; POP3 and SMTP are not types of encryption.

8. **D** Mary should set up WPA2 on her WAP.

9. **B** The Documents and Settings folder contains the My Documents folder for every user.

10. **A** Effective permissions are the result of combined permissions and determine access to resources.

11. **A** Virus shields automatically scan e-mails, downloads, and running programs.

12. **D** Windows uses Kerberos to encrypt the user authentication process over a LAN.

13. **A** **B** Telephone scams and dumpster diving are forms of social engineering.

About the CD-ROM

The CD-ROM included with this book comes with tools you can use to get CompTIA A+ certified and enhance your tech skills. For studying, you get a sample version of the Total Tester practice exam software with eight full practice exams, an extensive glossary, an electronic copy of the book, a document from CompTIA with a list of acronyms that you should know for the CompTIA A+ exams, and a sample of LearnKey's online training featuring Mike Meyers. All the software—exams, applications, and video—are easy to install on any Windows 98/NT/2000/XP/Vista computer and must be installed to access the Total Tester practice exams and LearnKey video sample. The glossary, eBook, and CompTIA A+ acronyms list are Adobe Acrobat files. If you don't have Adobe Acrobat Reader, it is available for installation on the CD-ROM.

The CD-ROM also includes a copy of several freeware and shareware programs that the authors use and recommend. Shareware programs enable you to try before you buy. Freeware programs are just that—free for you to use.

System Requirements

The testing and studying software on the CD-ROM requires Windows 98 or higher, Internet Explorer 5.0 or above, and 50 MB of hard disk space for full installation. To access the online training from LearnKey, you must have Windows Media Player 9, which will be automatically installed when you launch the online training.

Installing and Running Total Tester

If your computer's CD-ROM drive is configured to autorun, the CD-ROM will automatically start upon inserting the disc. If the autorun feature does not launch the CD's splash screen, browse to the CD-ROM and double-click the Launch.exe icon.

From the splash screen, you may install Total Tester by clicking the *Install A+ Practice Exams* button. This will begin the installation process, create a program

group named Total Seminars, and put an icon on your desktop. To run Total Tester, go to Start | Programs |Total Seminars or just double-click the icon on your desktop.

To uninstall the Total Tester software, go to Start | Settings | Control Panel | Add/Remove Programs and select the A+ Total Tester program. Select Remove, and Windows will completely uninstall the software.

About Total Tester

Total Tester provides you with a simulation of the actual exam with four suites: Essentials, 220-602, 220-603, and 220-604. Each suite contains two exams that can be taken in either practice or final mode. Practice mode provides an assistance window with hints, references to the book, an explanation of the answer, and the ability to check your answer as you take the test. Both practice and final modes provide an overall grade and a grade broken down by certification objective. To launch a test, select Suites from the menu at the top, select an exam, and choose from the list of available practice exams. Additional practice exams are available for all four of the CompTIA A+ exams. Visit our Web site at www.totalsem.com or call 800-446-6004 for more information.

Accessing the Glossary, eBook, and CompTIA A+ Acronyms List

To access these PDF documents, first be sure you have a copy of Adobe Acrobat Reader installed. If not, you can install it from the CD-ROM by clicking the *Install Adobe Acrobat Reader* button. Once you have installed Acrobat Reader, simply select the document you want to view from the CD-ROM's splash screen to open and view the document.

LearnKey Online Training

The *Install LearnKey demo* button will launch a wizard to install the software on your computer. Follow the instructions for installation. To run the LearnKey demo, choose Start | Programs | LearnKey or just double-click the icon on your desktop. Enter a user name and password to begin your video training.

Technical Support

For questions regarding the Total Tester software, visit www.totalsem.com or e-mail support@totalsem.com, or e-mail customer.service@mcgraw-hill.com. For customers outside the United States, e-mail international_cs@mcgraw-hill.com.

For technical problems with the software (installation, operation, or uninstalling the software) and for questions regarding LearnKey Video Training, e-mail techsupport@learnkey.com.

Career Flight Path

CompTIA A+ certification generally serves as the base of origin for any number of career flight paths. Most IT companies big and small see CompTIA A+ certification as the entry point to IT. From CompTIA A+, you have a number of certification options, depending on whether you want to focus more on hardware or move toward network administration (although these are not mutually exclusive goals). Take a look at these five in particular:

- CompTIA Network+ certification
- CompTIA Server+ certification
- Microsoft networking certification
- Novell NetWare certification
- Cisco certification

CompTIA Network+ Certification

If haven't already taken the CompTIA Network+, make it your next certification. Just as CompTIA A+ shows you have solid competency as a PC technician, CompTIA Network+ demonstrates your skill as a network technician, including understanding of network hardware, installation, and troubleshooting. CompTIA's Network+ is a natural fit for continuing toward your Microsoft, Novell, or Cisco certifications. Take the CompTIA Network+, it's your obvious next certification!

CompTIA Server+ Certification

Like CompTIA Network+, CompTIA Server+ certification fits very nicely as a more in-depth testing of your knowledge of PC and server-specific hardware and operating systems. If you plan to go the path of the high-end hardware tech, CompTIA Server+ is the next step. Plus, CompTIA Server+ is a natural lead-in to Cisco certifications.

Microsoft Networking Certification

Microsoft's ever popular Microsoft Certified Systems Engineer (MCSE) holds a lot of clout for those looking to work in the networking field. Microsoft Windows 2000/2003 and Windows XP operating systems control a huge portion of all the installed networks out there, and those networks need qualified support people to make them run. The MCSE consists of seven exams: four core and three electives. Check out Microsoft's training Web site at www.microsoft.com/learning for details. Most techs will find the Windows XP/2003 track the most obvious choice, and almost everyone takes the Microsoft 70-270–Installing, Configuring, and Administering Microsoft Windows XP Professional followed by the 70-290–Installing, Configuring, and Administering Microsoft Windows Server 2003 as the first two exams toward their MCSE.

Novell NetWare and Linux Certifications

Novell's NetWare may not be the powerhouse it once was, but a huge installed base of NetWare networks are still out there! The surge of techs toward Microsoft certifications had actually created a bit of a shortage of good NetWare-certified techs. The Certified NetWare Engineer (CNE) is the certification to go for if you want to get into Novell NetWare networks. Novell has a number of tracks, but most techs start with the 50-686–Foundations of Novell Networking: NetWare 6.5, and the 50-690–Novell Network Administration: NetWare 6.5 exams.

Additionally, Novell offers several certifications for Linux administrators, such as the Novell Certified Linux Professional certification. If you're planning to go into Linux environments after getting CompTIA A+ and Network+ certified, going the Novell way is an excellent step. Check out Novell's certification Web site at www.novell.com/training/certinfo/cne/ for more details.

Cisco Certification

Cisco routers pretty much run the Internet and most intranets in the world, and Cisco provides three levels of certification for folks who want to show their skills at handling Cisco products. Most everyone interested in Cisco certification starts with the Certified Cisco Network Associate (CCNA). The CCNA is only one exam (640-801) and a darn easy way to slap the word *Cisco* on your resume! After your CCNA you should consider the CCNP (Certified Cisco Networking Professional) certification. See the Cisco certification Web site at www.cisco.com/en/US/learning/le3/learning_career_certifications_and_learning_paths_home.html for more details.

Index